Happy Investing!

Shannon Pratt

Investing In The Great Northwest

A Layman's Guide
To Northwest Stocks and Bonds

Shannon P. Pratt

Lawrence R. Ross

Library of Congress Catalog Number: 75-36334

Printed in the United States of America

Cover: Depicts three of the Northwest's most important resources —
hydroelectric power, timberlands, and scenic beauty. Artist Robert
Mircovich's conception is based on Pacific Power and Light
photograph of Merwin Dam on the Lewis River in Southwest
Washington.

Preface

This book has been written with the hope that readers of all ages and walks of life will find the subject entertaining and informative, whether they are investors or not.

The stock and bond markets affect the lives of all of us, much more than most people realize. Investor-owned companies are all around us, and we are involved with many of them every day. They provide us our electricity and gas, products we use daily, stores to shop in, and a large variety of essential and desired services. What is going on with these companies is fascinating and exciting to know.

The book has two purposes: (1) to provide an easy-to-use guide to the stocks and bonds available from over 200 Northwest companies, and (2) to give the public as a whole better insight into how investor-owned companies and the markets for their securities contribute to our economy and standard of living.

The subjects are organized into short sections, so that a person can read as much or as little as he pleases at one sitting and can pick it up any time at almost any place in the book without losing continuity. There is also an extensive table of contents and a thorough index, to enable a person to pick up the book at any time as a reference source and readily find what he is looking for.

Most of the statistics have been put into tabular form apart from the text, to make the company and topical discussions easily readable, and many pictures and illustrations have been included.

The book is the culmination of five years' research on Northwest companies by Shannon Pratt and the staffs of the *Northwest Investment Review* and *Northwest Stock Guide,* and it also reflects three years of experience by Larry Ross as director of research for a Northwest-headquartered stock brokerage firm. Its scope is fully comprehensive to the extent of including some discussion of every company headquartered in Washington, Oregon, Idaho, Alaska, Montana, and Wyoming whose stock is listed on the New York, American, or Pacific stock exchanges or the *NASDAQ* OTC quotation system, as well as many smaller companies in those six states. It also includes over 20 Utah companies of interest to investors, plus a few companies headquartered elsewhere with major Northwest operations.

A subject of this magnitude condensed into 320 pages cannot be as completely comprehensive as one might like, but it is a first step in bringing together information on the publicly-traded securities of the region. Material for the book was based on the latest available information at press time, and great care was taken in editing. Obviously, however, we can not guarantee against the possibility of some error in this huge quantity of data.

The authors believe that the free enterprise system is the best system for our economy, and that it will endure in spite of its problems. There are things that all of us can do to make it work better, some of which are discussed in portions of the book.

The authors also believe that buyers of stocks and bonds of sound corporations will be well rewarded, and especially that virtually everyone should have some stocks in their investment program as a part of their protection against inflation. In this regard, many Northwest stocks are very attractive because of natural resource assets, well-maintained productive capacity, sound managements, and other attributes. It is hoped that the book will make a contribution to the already growing awareness of the Northwest as an attractive and rewarding area for investment.

Substantial editorial assistance was provided by J. Stanley Deakin and Linda C. Sorenson, both Associate Editors of the *Northwest Investment Review*. Assistance in compiling data was provided by Laurence D. Kirsch, Research Assistant on the *Northwest Investment Review* staff.

All companies discussed in the book assisted by providing company data; and many offered additional material on their industries, as well as a great deal of other information and assistance. To try to single out a few that were most helpful would be unfair to the many others.

We dedicate the book to a healthy economy, through better understanding and more informed action, and to prosperous investing in the Great Northwest.

Shannon P. Pratt

Lawrence R. Ross

November, 1975

Contents

Part I

Fundamentals of Northwest Investing

5

PART II

The Industries and the Companies

Appendixes

Special Sections and Reprints

Part I

Fundamentals of

Northwest Investing

AN OVERVIEW OF

204 PUBLICLY-TRADED
NORTHWEST COMPANIES

AS OF SEPTEMBER 30, 1975

Number Shareholders:	**About 1.3 Million***
Shares Outstanding:	**Over 2.3 Billion**
Market Value of Stocks:	**Over $17 Billion**
Face Value of Marketable Bonds:	**Over $5 Billion**
Total Assets:	**Over $48 Billion**
Annual Revenue:	**Over $30 Billion**
Annual Net Profit:	**About $1.5 Billion**
Annual Dividend Payments:	**Over $600 Million**
Annual Bond Interest:	**About $400 Million**

*Number shareholders shown is total shareholders of record for the 204 companies. There is some double-counting, because there is no way to determine how many shareholders own more than one of the stocks. On the other hand, a single holder of record such as a brokerage street name account or a bank trust department "nominee name" account actually represents many beneficial owners.

1

Introduction

In these days of rapidly increasing prices for natural resources of all kinds, the resource-rich Pacific Northwest is gaining well-deserved national attention as a geographical area in which to invest.

The Northwest's vast resource base covers the gamut of energy sources, precious metals, minerals and timber. The development of these resources is also stimulating population growth, retail and wholesale trade, banking and finance, and huge increases in transportation activity.

The Northwest-Intermountain area is the nation's primary repository for low-sulphur coal, one of the most important resources in meeting the energy needs of this generation. Underlying other developing energy resources is the Northwest's established hydro-electric power base, supplying electricity to the region at half the national average cost per KWH. Also, from Alaska through the Wyoming Rockies, the area is rich in uranium, oil, and natural gas.

The Northern Idaho Coeur d'Alene district is by far the nation's largest silver-producing region. The Coeur d'Alene and other areas of the Northwest also yield large amounts of zinc, copper, antimony, molybdenum, potash and even some gold.

The Northwest is also the country's most important timber resource region, and is experiencing rapid advances in the technologies of accelerated tree growth and more efficient wood fiber utilization.

Over 200 Companies in 14 Industry Groups

Over 200 actively traded publicly held companies thrive in this environment. The market value of their publicly traded stocks and bonds is well over $20 billion, even at today's depressed market prices.

The Northwest has always been a net importer of capital from the rest of the country, and the new capital formation that will be required to develop the region's resources assures that this will continue to be true for many years to come. Stimulating investment interest to attract funds to Northwest companies and industries is essential to the economic welfare of both the region and the nation. At the same time, the Northwest's demand for both equity and debt capital provides an outstanding array of attractive stocks and bonds for investors.

NORTHWEST STOCK GUIDE'S "TOP 20"

Rank By Market Value of Stock
(September 30, 1975)

1. Weyerhaeuser Co.	NYS	$4,487,000,000
2. Georgia-Pacific Corp.	NYS	2,247,840,000
3. Crown Zellerbach	NYS	865,388,000
4. Pacific Northwest Bell	ASE	677,476,000
5. Boise Cascade Corp.	NYS	656,086,000
6. The Boeing Co.	NYS	564,371,000
7. Pacific Power & Light Co.	NYS	538,965,000
8. Safeco Corp.	OTC	380,799,000
9. Potlatch Corp.	NYS	334,350,000
10. Tektronix, Inc.	NYS	330,047,000
11. Louisiana-Pacific Corp.	NYS	278,481,000
12. Farmers New World Life Ins.	OTC	247,500,000
13. Portland General Electric Co.	NYS	244,125,000
14. Seafirst Corp.	OTC	243,000,000
15. Willamette Industries	OTC	234,087,000
16. Utah Power & Light Co.	NYS	214,148,000
17. Paccar, Inc.	OTC	208,313,000
18. Idaho Power Co.	NYS	202,125,000
19. Montana Power Co.	NYS	200,088,000
20. Consolidated Freightways	NYS	192,500,000

Rank By Total Assets
(Year-End 1974)

1. Seafirst Corp.	OTC	$4,624,890,000
2. U.S. Bancorp	OTC	2,902,990,000
3. Weyerhaeuser Co.	NYS	2,878,510,000
4. Rainier Bancorporation	OTC	2,623,698,000
5. Georgia-Pacific Corp.	NYS	2,230,670,000
6. First Security Corp.	OTC	1,825,265,000
7. Pacific Northwest Bell	ASE	1,712,956,000
8. The Boeing Co.	NYS	1,683,059,000
9. Pacific Power & Light Co.	NYS	1,588,430,000
10. Boise Cascade Corp.	NYS	1,575,697,000
11. Crown Zellerbach	NYS	1,526,875,000
12. Safeco Corp.	OTC	1,241,162,000
13. Idaho First National Bank	OTC	984,180,000
14. Portland General Electric Co.	NYS	850,952,000
15. Peoples National Bank of Wash.	OTC	815,825,000
16. Utah Power & Light Co.	NYS	798,954,000
17. Amfac	NYS	749,824,000
18. Evans Products Co.	NYS	709,105,000
19. Idaho Power Co.	NYS	708,401,000
20. Equitable Savings and Loan	OTC	698,673,000

Source: *Northwest Stock Guide,* Fall 1975.

NORTHWEST STOCK GUIDE'S "TOP 20"

Rank By Total Revenues
(Fiscal 1974)

1. The Boeing Co.	NYS	$3,750,000,000
2. Weyerhaeuser Co.	NYS	2,529,013,000
3. Georgia-Pacific Corp.	NYS	2,432,350,000
4. Crown Zellerbach	NYS	1,766,190,000
5. Boise Cascade Corp.	NYS	1,453,550,000
6. Amfac	NYS	1,145,362,000
7. Evans Products Co.	NYS	1,132,892,000
8. Albertson's Inc.	NYS	1,046,105,000
9. Paccar, Inc.	OTC	907,987,000
10. Consolidated Freightways	NYS	798,579,000
11. Morrison-Knudsen Co.	NYS	677,947,000
12. Pacific Northwest Bell	ASE	672,528,000
13. Safeco Corp.	OTC	615,161,000
14. Fred Meyer	OTC	536,760,000
15. Univar Corp.	NYS	522,050,000
16. Skaggs Cos., Inc.	NYS	500,696,000
17. Potlatch Corp.	NYS	487,868,000
18. Pacific Gamble Robinson	OTC	481,518,000
19. Louisiana-Pacific Corp.	NYS	460,100,000
20. Willamette Industries	OTC	388,712,000

Rank By Number of Shareholders
(Year-end 1974)

1. Northwest Energy Co.	NYS	111,000
2. Georgia-Pacific Corp.	NYS	93,683
3. Louisiana-Pacific Corp.	NYS	83,621
4. The Boeing Co.	NYS	81,800
5. Boise Cascade Corp.	NYS	78,686
6. Pacific Power & Light Co.	NYS	77,935
7. Portland General Electric Co.	NYS	53,000
8. Montana Power Co.	NYS	36,710
9. Pacific Northwest Bell	ASE	35,622
10. Crown Zellerbach	NYS	32,980
11. Utah Power & Light	NYS	31,556
12. The Washington Water Power Co.	NYS	31,074
13. Weyerhaeuser Co.	NYS	29,751
14. Puget Sound Power & Light	NYS	25,370
15. Sunshine Mining Co.	NYS	22,000
16. Idaho Power Co.	NYS	18,761
17. Northwest Natural Gas Co.	OTC	18,020
18. Alaska Airlines	ASE	16,000
19. Hecla Mining Co.	NYS	16,000
20. Consolidated Freightways	NYS	13,000

Source: *Northwest Stock Guide,* Fall 1975.

The 200-plus Northwest companies with publicly-traded stocks and bonds are the subject matter of this book. We are interested in the companies that issue stocks and bonds to the public through which the individual investor and the investment institutions can profit by investing funds in this great region.

Geographically, the heart of this vast territory is the Pacific Northwest. The "Pacific Northwest," by some definitions, includes the states of Oregon, Washington, Idaho, and the eleven counties of Montana situated west of the Continental Divide. This region includes a total of 270,563 square miles of land plus 3,315 square miles of water.

From an economic and investment point of view, we have elected to include several areas contiguous to the Pacific Northwest, inasmuch as they relate directly to the business and commerce of the Northwest region. For example, we view certain business enterprises in Wyoming and Northern Utah as having an affinity with the Northwest rather than some other region.

Then, there is the question of Alaska. For decades there was little activity in Alaska for investors to get excited about. However, world political and economic events of the past 10 years have brought the Alaskan economy to everyone's attention. We can safely say that Alaskan activity impinges on many aspects of the Northwest economy and that she is now a full member in good standing.

Everything about Alaska is remarkable. Originally purchased from Russia for the sum of $7.2 million, Alaska has the highest mountain in North America. The largest of all states in land area, Alaska borders on two oceans, two seas, and one gulf. Alaska is the most Northern of all the states, the most Western of all states, and, because the Aleutian Islands cross the 180th meridian, it is at the same time the most Eastern of all states. Of the 7,093 miles of coastline in the Pacific Northwest, Alaska accounts for 6,640 miles. In fact, Alaska's coastline comprises more than one-half of the 12,383 miles surrounding the entire United States.

As with statisticians defining "greater metropolitan areas," we have taken the authors' license to define this expanded version of the Pacific Northwest as the *"Great Northwest."*

We have arbitrarily classified fourteen major areas of commercial activity which offer attractive opportunities for investment in publicly traded shares. These industries are the following:

Forest Products	Transportation
Building Materials, Construction, and Real Estate	Retailing and Wholesaling
	Services
Manufacturing	Commercial Banking
Food and Beverage Processing	Non-Bank Financial Companies
Silver and Metals Mining	Insurance
Energy Resources	Multi-Line Companies
Utilities	

In all, our study includes more than 200 publicly traded companies in the above industry categories. All of these companies are either headquartered in the Northwest or derive a significant portion of their revenue in the region.

A full discussion of the fourteen basic industries and selected companies occupies the bulk of our study.

The Performance Record for Northwest Stocks

By linking the studies conducted at the *Portland State University Investment Analysis. Center* with later studies carried on by the *Northwest Investment Review,* we have almost a 15-year history of performance of Northwest stocks that can be compared with the national averages. The statistics show that the Northwest stocks have substantially outperformed the national averages during the past 15 years.

The 1961-1970 study at Portland State University included an unweighted average of all over-the-counter stocks quoted in the N.A.S.D. daily quotation lists in Seattle, Portland, and Boise, a total of 95 stocks at the end of the time period. That was most of the Pacific Northwest publicly-traded stocks at the time. It included, for example, companies like *Albertson's, Pay Less Drug Stores Northwest, Morrison-Knudsen, Cascade Natural Gas,* and *Pope & Talbot* that have since listed on the *New York Stock Exchange.* The Northwest results are shown in the accompanying graph, and the strong superiority of Northwest results over national averages is shown in the accompanying table. The full

---

NORTHWEST STOCK PERFORMANCE
COMPARED TO NATIONAL AVERAGES
December 31, 1960-December 31, 1970

(Study conducted by the *Portland State University Investment Analysis Center)*

Pacific Northwest OTC Composite	**+104%**
Standard & Poor's 500-Stock Composite	**+ 59%**
Pacific Northwest OTC Industrials	**+179%**
Standard & Poor's 425 Industrials	**+ 64%**
Dow Jones Industrial Average	**+ 36%**

December 31, 1970-September 30, 1975

(Study conducted by Willamette Management Associates, publishers of *Northwest Investment Review* and *Northwest Stock Guide)*

Northwest Listed and OTC Composite	**—2%**
Standard & Poor's 500-Stock Composite	**—9%**
Dow Jones Industrial Average	**—5%**

PACIFIC NORTHWEST INDEX

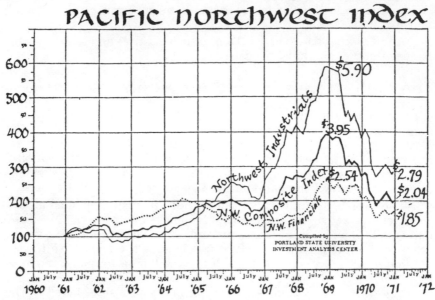

The ten-year record of Pacific Northwest OTC stock performance, compiled at Portland State University. In an article on January 10, 1971, the Portland *Oregonian* described the study as "the most comprehensive regional overview of OTC stock performance presented in the United States." Northwest listed stocks also did very well during the same time period (see accompanying text).

Northwest OTC Composite group did almost twice as well as the national averages, and the Northwest Industrials did even better!

A similar study was also conducted on the Washington, Oregon, and Idaho stocks listed on the New York and American Stock Exchanges during the same ten-year period (1961-1970), a total of 23 stocks at the end of the period. It was not directly comparable, because it included dividends, but the results were outstanding. If one held equal amounts of each listed Northwest stock and reinvested the dividends, he *gained 174% for the 10-year period!* Even after adjusting for dividends, which averaged about 4% per year, this record far exceeded the 59% gain on the *Standard & Poors Composite Index* and the 36% for the *Dow Jones Industrial Average.*

When the *Northest Investment Review* started publishing in 1971, it picked up the continuity of the Northwest performance statistics where the Portland State University studies left off, combining the Northwest listed and OTC stocks into a single index. For the four years and nine months from the beginning of 1971 to September 30, 1975 (the latest date available for use in this book), the stock market went up and down a lot, but ended the period just slightly below where it started. As the accompanying chart and table show, the Northwest stocks again weathered the vicissitudes better than the national averages, closing the period with only a 2% loss compared with a 9% drop for the Standard & Poor's 500-Stock Composite.

RELATIVE PERFORMANCE OF
NORTHWEST COMPOSITE INDEX VS.
S & P 500-STOCK COMPOSITE
DECEMBER 31, 1970—SEPTEMBER 30, 1975
(December 1970 = 100)

As the above graph shows, the market closed at September 30, 1975 just below its level of almost 5 years earlier, December 30, 1970. Northwest stocks had a better upthrust in the rising market periods, leaving them in better position than the national averages as of the latest figures. Will Northwest stocks again outperform national averages in the next upswing?

So whither from here? Company earnings and net asset values for the entire stock market, including Northwest companies, have increased substantially in the last five years, even though stock prices have not. This means that, relative to book values and on a price/earnings ratio basis, stocks are better values at the end of 1975 than they were at the end of 1970 and certainly far better than at the end of 1968 or 1966! We think it is a good time to buy common stocks.

The natural resource orientation of the Northwest region is an even more positive force in the national economic scene today than it was in past years. The companies are every bit as well managed today as in the past, if not better. For the first time, the rest of the nation is beginning to discover the Northwest as an important geographical region for investment. Some institutions are making it a point to include it specifically in their investment planning. We see many reasons why the Northwest should continue to be a sound and growing region for investment funds.

PACIFIC NORTHWEST DEMOGRAPHIC FORECAST
(Actual Figures 1950-1970, Projected 1975-1990)

Year	Population	Employment	Housing Units
1950	4,674,671	1,797,100	1,578,845
1960	5,489,729	2,014,000	1,929,287
1970	6,435,283	2,522,700	2,288,394
Projected			
1975	6,695,700	2,784,500	2,501,300
1980	7,194,800	3,054,500	2,787,100
1985	7,806,900	3,330,500	3,100,700
1990	8,441,200	3,611,000	3,399,600

Source: Bonneville Power Administration, Branch of Power Requirements, U.S. Department of the Interior.

PACIFIC NORTHWEST EMPLOYMENT PROJECTIONS, 1968-1990

	1968	1970	1980	1990
TOTAL EMPLOYMENT	2,497,300	2,522,700	3,054,500	3,611,000
Agriculture	174,900	170,500	146,500	127,000
Non-agricultural Self-employed	297,500	292,600	325,600	355,800
Mining	8,500	10,500	13,200	14,600
Construction	102,900	96,700	115,800	131,000
Manufacturing	509,800	464,000	510,300	565,800
Transportation and Public Utilities	140,000	141,000	151,000	157,700
Wholesale and Retail Trade	444,000	465,200	588,200	712,200
Finance, Insurance, and Real Estate	97,600	104,000	136,700	170,100
Services	298,200	325,000	459,400	605,100
Government	423,900	453,200	607,700	771,700
MANUFACTURING EMPLOYMENT	509,800	464,000	510,300	565,800
Food and Kindred Products	67,000	68,900	75,900	82,100
Textile Mill Products	3,300	3,500	3,800	4,200
Apparel	8,300	8,600	11,000	13,400
Lumber and Wood Products	139,100	129,100	112,400	97,500
Furniture	7,100	7,300	9,200	11,300
Paper and Allied Products	30,100	30,500	33,800	38,000
Printing and Publishing	19,000	19,700	25,100	31,200
Chemicals and Allied Products	10,700	10,000	12,100	14,100
Petroleum Refining	1,600	1,700	2,200	2,700
Stone, Clay, and Glass Products	9,900	10,200	12,900	15,800
Primary Metals	23,800	25,300	33,800	40,500
Fabricated Metal Products	16,100	16,400	21,100	25,800
Machinery	18,700	20,900	29,100	37,800
Electrical Equipoment	14,400	15,400	22,700	30,100
Transportation Equipment (excluding aerospace)	24,100	24,600	33,600	41,500
Aerospace	104,500	61,500	59,000	64,500
Other Manufacturing	11,500	10,400	12,600	15,300

Source: U.S. Dept. of the Interior, **Population, Employment, and Housing Units, Projections to 1990 for the Pacific Northwest**, February, 1973, pp. 38-39.

2

The Northwest Economy

Abundant Resources Support Strong Economy

The industries of the Northwest rely on an abundance of natural resources. Forest products, agriculture, energy resources, and metals all are important to the economy of the region. In this period of rapidly rising values of these resources and increasing national recognition of their importance, this natural resource orientation is a very attractive economic base for investment in the region.

Another economic asset of the Northwest region is the quality of its people. The *Battelle Memorial Institute* made the following statement in a report entitled *"The Pacific Northwest . . . a Study of Economic Growth in a Quality Environment"* (see bibliography):

> "One of the factors which enhance growth prospects of the region is the high level of education of its residents. Every adult age group in the Northwest, on the average, is better educated than the corresponding group in the nation. This educational factor is a dynamic asset in view of the growing technological sophistication of the economy and the increasing demand for high quality human resources, ranging from skilled craftsmen to highly-trained professionals.

> "The tempo of economic growth in the Pacific Northwest has increased in recent years. This rapid regional economic expansion has generated momentum which, with proper leadership, can stimulate further strong growth in the future.

> ". . .This projected growth is more than a simple extrapolation of the favorable experiences during the most recent time period; it represents strong economic factors in relation to national and international developments."

As shown in the accompanying table of employment figures, retail and wholesale trade, manufacturing and government rank about equally as the three largest broad segments of employment. Projections show the relative amount of employment going down in manufacturing and agriculture, while employment in the services, retail-wholesale and government sectors are on the increase. This is *not* because of decreasing over-all economic importance of manufacturing and agriculture, but because of increasing production efficiency. Implementation of the increased efficiency, however, requires capital for the necessary equipment and facilities.

By far the largest single manufacturing industry in the Northwest

PERSONAL INCOME IN THE NORTHWEST, BY STATE
(Millions of Dollars)

	1950	1960	1970	1973
Alaska	300	700	1,400	1,900
Idaho	800	1,200	2,400	3,300
Montana	1,000	1,400	2,400	3,200
Oregon	2,500	3,900	7,800	10,500
Utah	900	1,800	3,500	4,600
Washington	4,000	6,700	13,700	17,100
Wyoming	500	700	1,300	1,700
TOTAL NORTHWEST	10,000	16,400	32,500	42,300
Total United States	226,200	398,700	803,500	1,032,000
The Northwest as Percent of U.S.	4.4%	4.1%	4.0%	4.1%

Source: U.S. Dept. of Commerce, **Statistical Abstract of the U.S.,** 1974, p. 380.

is lumber and wood products, which employed over 150,000 in 1973. When one adds paper and other related items, the dominant importance of the forest products industry as a whole is even more apparent. The center of the forest products industry is Oregon, where total forest products employment is greater than in any other state.

The next two largest manufacturing industries are food and beverage processing and aerospace. Food and beverage processing has been relatively stable, with aerospace quite volatile. Food production is the number one manufacturing employer in Idaho and Alaska, and would be the number two manufacturing employer regionwide but for the size of aircraft manufacturing in Washington, dominated by *Boeing.* Aerospace reached a peak in 1968, employing over 100,000 before dropping almost in half at one point in 1970. Aerospace employment in 1973 was about 75,000.

More than 50 million acres of land are devoted to farming in the Northwest. Although farming provides employment for relatively few workers, it continues to be of prime importance to the area by providing raw materials to the food processing industry and generating jobs in other industries such as trade, transportation, finance and services. Commercial fishing, although no longer among the largest industries in the Northwest, continues to make an important contribution to the region's economy.

The retail industry is the largest single employer in the Northwest, and when combined with wholesale trade the total employment surpasses that for all manufacturing industries and for all levels of government.

Construction is also an important industry. Employment in the Northwest's contract construction industry averaged 115,000 in 1973.

Alaska and Wyoming rank tops in the region in mineral production (including oil), and, of course, both states are rapidly increasing production. Idaho is the leader in mining, with silver, zinc, lead, antimony, potash, and many other metals and minerals. The economic importance of the extractive industries is, of course, far greater than their relative employment figures would indicate.

One of the great natural resources of the Northwest region is its vast waterways. They provide fresh water for irrigation, a low-cost and reliable hydroelectric power base, thousands of miles of low-cost water transportation routes, and a scenic and sporting mecca for recreation and tourism.

The Pacific Northwest area enjoys the good fortune of having near-ly 30% of the nation's water resources — 29.7 to be exact. In addition to coastal waters and bays, the Columbia, Willamette, Snake and Salmon river systems are an important economic factor, supporting much industrial activity. Once again, Alaska dominates the area, possessing 85.8% of the water resources. This includes the 1,875 mile long Yukon River, the longest in any one state.

Examination of the accompanying table and projections gives us a good view of the economic health of the Pacific Northwest region. Forecasts for 1980 and 1990 show clearly that the area's population will be up, housing units will be up, and employment will be up. In short, the region is ripe for capital investment with meaningful appreciation potential of the funds so employed.

Alaska—The New Economic Dimension

In discussing the Northwest, one cannot deny the impact of the booming Alaskan economy. However, it is virtually impossible to gather statistics or consider future prospects in a grouping with other states in the region. If done, the resulting figures become bizarre.

For example, the total area of Alaska is greater than that of Texas, California and Montana (second, third, and fourth largest states) combined. In size, Alaska represents 70% of the entire Northwest territory, and yet it contains just 4.6% of the region's population. In fact, the entire population of the state of Alaska is less than that of the Tacoma, Washington metropolitan area.

Whereas the state of Washington has a population density of 51.2 people per square mile (1970 census figures), Alaska has a scant density of 0.5 people per square mile.

In most respects Alaska's economy is quite similar to other areas of the Northwest. It is a natural resource state. The state is rich in minerals and forest products, and active in both fishing and tourism. The one undeniable, overwhelming difference is the presence of huge quantities of oil.

The discovery of massive oil reserves in 1968 on Alaska's North Slope is no longer news. However, the implications of this single event for the state's economy (and the entire Northwest region) become greater and greater each year.

The Prudhoe Bay field on the North Slope is estimated to contain one-fourth of the nation's proved crude oil reserves as well as one-tenth of the nation's proved natural gas reserves. Current projections show that, by 1985, Prudhoe Bay oil will account for 15% of total U.S. production and about 10% of the total U.S. consumption of crude oil.

A very interesting point in considering all of this oil is that the North Slope is just one of 12 major sedimentary basins where oil might be expected to be found. To date, only one of these other eleven basins has been thoroughly explored. That is the Cook Inlet/Kenai Peninsula area, near Anchorage. Oil from this field is already being produced and shipped to the West Coast and Japan.

Prudhoe Bay alone holds 9.6 billion barrels of oil reserves (an estimated 16-year supply). Altogether, industry sources estimate that other discoveries may lead to the production of more than 100 billion barrels of crude oil.

The magnitude of the construction of this historic pipeline ranks as one of the top construction projects of all time. Nearly 800 miles long, this endeavor carries an estimated price tag of $4 billion. The pipeline story has been thoroughly documented many times. However, many people assume that after the peak construction period (1975-1976) passes, activity will soon subside. This is not the case.

In a speech before the *Portland Society of Financial Analysts*, Robert R. Richards, vice-president and economist for the **National Bank of Alaska** said:

> **"For at least four years after the major portion of construction is completed and oil is flowing at the rate of 600,000 barrels per day, a substantial amount of construction will continue, raising the pipeline capacity to two million barrels per day."**

Mr. Roberts then pointed out that the North Slope field is estimated to hold nine per cent of the total U.S. natural gas reserves. A second major pipeline will be necessary to transport this natural gas either to southern Alaska or through Canada to the U.S. Midwest. This construction project should begin in the late 1970's. Therefore. related construction activities will be an economic factor in the Northwest for much longer than originally anticipated.

Since new sources of energy are a cause of national and, indeed, international concern today, it is exciting to contemplate Alaska's huge coal reserves.

On the western side of Cook Inlet, near Anchorage, lies the Beluga coal basin. Estimated recoverable coal reserves within the Beluga basin are estimated to be 2.4 billion tons. This compares with 1.8 billion tons held by *Pacific Power & Light,* the largest reserve of any Northwest utility. By comparison, the nation's largest presently active coal mine now produces about 7 million tons of coal annually. At this rate, it would take about 350 years to exhaust this deposit.

Beluga coal is a low-sulphur steam-grade coal. As such, it could easily be converted to an oil equivalent. One ton of coal would equal about five barrels of oil. In other words, the total Beluga deposit would equate to about twelve billion barrels of oil. This is about 25% greater than the proved reserves of the Prudhoe Bay field.

Although presently smaller in scope than forestry in other

Northwest states, Alaska's timber production is still an important economic factor.

The annual timber harvest is about 687 million board feet, approximately one-third of the annual allowable cut. Some 90% of this production is sold to Japan. By 1980, annual production should exceed one billion board feet annually.

Other industries indigenous to Alaska are tourism and fisheries. Major fishery species are salmon, king crab, snow crab, shrimp and halibut. The total activity, of course, has created booming business for all the supportive industries, such as housing, transportation, communications, retail and wholesale trade, and all aspects of finance.

In a recent business meeting, Miner H. Baker, vice-president and economist of the Seattle-First National Bank (major subsidiary of parent *Seafirst Corp.*) attempted to evaluate the economic impact of Alaskan activity on Seattle and the Northwest:

"The waterborne shipments of material through the Port of Seattle still today run something over three tons per year for every man, woman, and child in Alaska. That is a key fact for all of the subsequent discussion of potential impact. This is the supply point for Alaska."

There is no doubt that Seattle is the major proximate Alaskan supply point, but Oregonians would take issue with describing it as **the** supply point, as the Alaska-bound tonnage over Oregon ports is also on the increase.

Responsibility in the Free Enterprise System

The following remarks were delivered by James H. Wiborg, Chief Executive Officer of Univar Corp., at the close of their 1975 annual stockholders' meeting. We feel that his points are so important and well articulated that his remarks should be shared with as many people as possible.

Before closing, I would like to make a few comments on social responsibility. Much has been said in regard to the social responsibilities of business, and businessmen have oftentimes risen to the defense of their businesses and the free enterprise system. I am not here today to defend the free enterprise system or what is done by responsible businessmen. Instead, I am here today to praise it. Too often we have been on the defensive where we should stand back in awe and admiration of the only economic system ever to function in the world to provide freedom and the right of free choice to each individual who will make an effort within that system.

Throughout all of the written history of the western world, men have strived to obtain individual freedom and a right of each person to ownership of his own property and to the enjoyment thereof. In the middle ages the world suffered from feudalism and serfdom but with the dawning of the industrial revolution and the concepts of individual freedom introduced in England and reaching their culmination in America, each man had the right to his own property and the rewards of his own effort. Freedom meant that no other man had a right to those rewards or to the sweat of another's brow. Slavery was abolished but with the insidiousness of a plague, slavery began to reappear in the form of Marxism so that today we are told each of us is obligated, not through enlightened self-interest and not through our own sense of consciousness but through Government mandate and taxation to give of our effort and our production and our capabilities to others who will not make this effort. In the Communist countries the pendulum has swung fullfold to slavery. Freedom has been so instilled in the western nations that those who would bring slavery back have not dared to use force, but we are permitting them to achieve the same result.

I think all of us must be conscious of our obligations to help those who are truly infirm, aged or incapable of providing for themselves. Beyond that, increasing taxation eventually becomes slavery through depriving one man who is willing to work and produce through his own effort of the rewards of the effort by transferring a portion of these rewards to another who is not willing to apply himself.

Freedom of the individual requires the right of self-initiative and of private ownership and the rewards that flow therefrom. It is incumbent upon all of us at every possible opportunity to speak of the glories and benefits of our free enterprise system rather than defend its weaknesses. There will always be those who abuse as there have been in business, labor and government but no other system has given so many people such a wonderful and prosperous way of life.

Our company last year fully carried its social responsibilities and beyond, as did the people who worked so productively in it. We contributed sizeable amounts to charity. We paid enormous amounts of taxes. We built fine plants and maintained them well. We created jobs through employment of capital and through ingenuity of management. We provided employee benefits and improved them. Our people individually gave of their time in their communities as well as through their own taxes earned by their productivity effort. What I am saying to you is that responsible businesses are not only carrying their load of social responsibility but beyond, and it is time to point the finger accusingly at those who want and expect to receive something in exchange for nothing, those who will not produce, although capable of doing so, and at governments who continue to burden the productive elements of our system with heavier and heavier loads until the golden wagon will surely break.

3

The Capital Formation Process

Often we hear of an individual investor being accused of "playing the market." This statement is made as if investing were some kind of game or mindless roulette wheel eternally spinning.

To many individuals, this description may be an accurate one. However, the "game," if that be the name, is a deadly serious one for the participants, for the health of our economy, and for all individual citizens, whether they are active investors or not.

American business needs fresh capital to survive. Investment is an eternal process. New plants, new equipment, new discoveries, research . . . all require massive infusions of new money, year after year.

Capital provides jobs. According to the *National Association of Manufacturers,* it presently requires more than $25,000 of investment capital to support one full-time job. This figure has increased substantially in recent years.

Raising New Capital

The modern corporation has only three ways in which to obtain investment capital: (1) initial startup capital, subscribed by the founders; (2) retained earnings, generated by operating profits; and (3) subsequent sales of securities, that is, stocks or bonds.

To generate pools of capital beyond the resources of the entrepreneurs operating the business, securities are sold in offerings made available to the general public. The raising of new capital funds is a kind of partnership between the corporation and the investing public, with the securities industry acting as a marriage broker.

Whether it is the first time that shares are sold to the public ("going public") or many times later, more than likely the services of an *underwriter* will be used. While an underwriter is also a stockbroker, he performs many additional duties for the company issuing the securities.

Many of these chores are to protect the new investor, as well as to insure that the issuer complies with applicable state and federal securities laws. Some of the tasks performed include inspecting the company's facilities, obtaining audited financial statements, discussing sales and earnings forecasts with management, and negotiating terms of the sale.

NEW ISSUE   August 22, 1975

2,000,000 SHARES

PORTLAND GENERAL ELECTRIC COMPANY

COMMON STOCK

(PAR VALUE $3.75 PER SHARE)

PRICE $15.625 PER SHARE

Copies of the Prospectus may be obtained from such of the under-
writers as are qualified to act as dealers in securities in this State.

Blyth Eastman Dillon & Co.	**Dean Witter & Co.**
Incorporated	Incorporated

Drexel Burnham & Co.	**The First Boston Corporation**	**Goldman, Sachs & Co.**
Incorporated		
Halsey, Stuart & Co. Inc.		**Hornblower & Weeks-Hemphill, Noyes**
Affiliate of Bache & Co. Incorporated		Incorporated
E. F. Hutton & Company Inc.	**Kidder, Peabody & Co.**	**Lehman Brothers**
	Incorporated	Incorporated
Loeb, Rhoades & Co.		**Merrill Lynch, Pierce, Fenner & Smith**
		Incorporated
Paine, Webber, Jackson & Curtis		**Reynolds Securities Inc.**
Incorporated		
Salomon Brothers	**Smith, Barney & Co.**	**White, Weld & Co.**
	Incorporated	Incorporated
Foster & Marshall Inc.		**Shearson Hayden Stone Inc.**
Bateman Eichler, Hill Richards	**Birr, Wilson & Co., Inc.**	**Boettcher & Company**
Incorporated		
Bosworth, Sullivan & Company	**Crowell, Weedon & Co.**	**Davis, Skaggs & Co., Inc.**
Incorporated		
Shuman, Agnew & Co., Inc.	**Sutro & Co.**	**Black & Company, Inc.**
	Incorporated	
Edelstein, Campbell & Co.	**Hambrecht & Quist**	**Hinkle Northwest, Inc.**
Stern, Frank, Meyer & Fox	**Stone & Youngberg**	**Wagenseller & Durst, Inc.**
Incorporated		
Young, Smith & Peacock, Inc.	**Belford, Hammerbeck, Inc.**	**Blakely, Strand & Williams, Inc.**
Gallagher & Jensen Inc.	**Paul Kendrick & Co., Inc.**	**Mitchum, Jones & Templeton**
		Incorporated
Morgan, Olmstead, Kennedy & Gardner	**Somers, Grove & Co., Inc.**	**Henry F. Swift & Co.**
Incorporated		
Wedbush, Noble, Cooke, Inc.	**L. J. Werschkul & Sons**	**Wulff, Hansen & Co.**

As the details of the securities to be offered are being worked out, the underwriter forms an *underwriting group,* a loose federation of numerous other stock brokerage firms who will assist in selling the particular offering in question. In order to make a true distribution of the new issue, care is taken to include a wide assortment of brokerage firms in all parts of the country if a sizeable issue is involved. When appropriate, the underwriter also seeks to interest financial institutions in purchasing the new issue. We should make the point, however, that local stockholders are the most loyal shareholders in periods of market adversity. It is in the issuer's best interests, therefore, that underwriting support be strong in their own region.

The accompanying advertisement describes an underwiting done in 1975 for the *Portland General Electric Company.* .The offering was co-managed by *Dean Witter & Co.* and *Blyth Eastman Dillon & Co.,* whose names appear at the top of the underwriting group. It is normal for the underwriter to place this type of ad (termed a *"tombstone"* in the industry) the day after an underwriting is completed. The names of the underwriters' selling group that participated in distributing the PGE bonds included seven brokerage houses headquartered in the Northwest and 13 houses headquartered elsewhere but with offices in one or more of the Northwest cities.

This is the heart of the capital formation process. Portland General Electric Company received a total of $31,250,000, less related underwriting expenses, to be used for its construction and expansion program. In turn, investors received new shares in a quality utility company offering a current dividend yield of 10% based on the stock's offering price of $15.625 and the annual dividend rate of $1.58 per share in effect at the time of the offering, plus the prospect of increased dividends to maintain the purchasing power of the return on their investment in the face of inflation.

In order to keep the capital formation process viable, a good enough rate of return has to be in prospect to induce people and companies to save their money and to invest it to build manufacturing and service facilities that provide jobs and produce goods and services. Without profit, there would be no incentive to invest. The prospect of good profits is a requisite to raising the billions of dollars of new capital urgently needed in the next few years. We feel that the accompanying reprint entitled "Lemonade stand-type economics" is an easily readable contribution to understanding the essential role of corporate profits.

The Secondary Markets—Listed and OTC

While the need to raise fresh capital for industry is clear, the need for subsequent stock trading on a stock exchange or in the over-the-counter (OTC) market is less clear to some people. We often get the question, "How does a corporation benefit from its stock trading back and forth in the market place?"

At first glance, it might seem that a corporation would have no interest in the aftermarket trading in its stock. The corporation is not a party to subsequent trading in any way, and does not receive any of the proceeds thereof. However a growing, thriving corporation will undoubtedly have the need to come to the capital markets again in the future. Also, a corporation is owned by and ultimately responsible to its shareholders. Who would invest in a stock which he could not readily sell, or which he thought he could sell only at a substantial discount from its reasonable intrinsic value? The question answers itself. It is only because of the existence of an active, vital secondary market that most

Lemonade stand-type economics don't work in real business world

By DAVID W. EWING

Special to the Oregonian Forum

The author is executive editor — planning, Harvard Business Review.

BOSTON — Reports from Washington and corporate boardrooms show that many companies' profits are going up again. Yet millions of wage-earners are unable to get pay raises and consumers are harder pressed than ever to make their checkbooks balance. "How come?" many Americans are asking. "Why should large companies get rewarded with higher profits when all we get is higher costs?"

The fact that the question makes sense to so many people may have more to do with the economic malaise of this country than do most other problems on which our predicament is blamed, such as the money supply and energy shortages. Public thinking about profits has been dominated for years by the Lemonade Stand School of Economics, and the country is choking as a result.

When you were a kid and your mother helped you put up a table and sell lemonade to passers-by on hot summer days, you counted the nickels and dimes afterward and proudly announced how much money you had made. This was your profit, your reward for being enterprising.

However, in the grown-up world of auto makers, oil companies, chain stores, and other big businesses, profit is a different thing. Out of habit, people may call it a "reward," because of course much of it does go to stockholders as a payback on their investment, and many stockholders get back more than they invested. But in reality, profit

is not a reward. Calling it a reward makes about as much sense as calling a driver's license a "reward" for paying the fee.

In all our major industries where there is competition, profit is a cost. It is just as much a cost as employe salaries and the water bill are. Salaries are a cost because if a company doesn't pay them, no one will come to work for it. The water bill is a cost because unless it is paid the water will be shut off. Similarly, profits are a cost because if not earned, or if not large enough, the company will be unable to raise needed funds on the stock market or borrow from banks. Who wants to invest in a company that can't pay dividends, or lend to a firm that can't pay the loan back on time?

Profits are also a cost of "going it alone" into a new business. If an engineer at Chrysler comes up with a promising new idea for a high-mileage engine, or if a scientist at General Foods develops a new cereal product, the financial backing often must come from the company's own treasury — from "retained earnings," as they are usually called. The fact that corporations' retained earnings last year were less than a fourth of their 1965 level (5 per cent as against 23 per cent, after removing phantom inventory profits from the accounting) is going to mean fewer new businesses — and "Help Wanted" ads — in the future.

According to studies by General Electric's top economists, reported by Reginald H. Jones in the September-October Harvard Business Review, nonfinancial corporations will have to raise $60 billion a year on the stock market from 1977 to 1980. That prodigious sum is more than five times the record amount obtained in any past year (the record was $11.4 billion, raised in 1971). Even with the current upswing in profits, corporations are not close to being able to tempt investors to part with that much money.

Nevertheless, because of the hold the Lemonade Stand School of Economics has on the public mind, a majority of Americans believe corporate profits are too high and should be limited by the government, according to surveys by Opinion Research Corporation. Ironically, this new high in hostility toward profits comes when corporations are more deeply in debt than ever before. In 1974, Jones reports, nonfinancial corporations owed two dollars for every dollar of net worth — twice as much as they did in 1954.

In the business community it is pop- ular to blame radical economists, union officials, and teachers for public misunderstanding about the size of profits. This is nonsense.

One culprit is inflation, which swells a company's profit figure artificially and makes it seem yeastier than it really is. Another culprit is business' own success. When a company grows and obtains more stockholders, it needs more profit just to stay in proportion. As they say in the tire business, the longer the spoke, the larger the tire.

Still another culprit is business publicity. For instance, the Lemonade Stand School of Economics popped up in a recent issue of Ralston Purina Magazine, which advertised company profits as "the rewards of a job well done."

Peter Drucker once said that if archangels, instead of businessmen, sat in company boardrooms, they would still have to be concerned with profitability. If archangels ever worry over finances, this would be the time.

Reprinted by permission of David W. Ewing

investors can be persuaded to invest their original capital in our capital formation process.

Even if a corporation does not plan to raise new capital, it still has the responsibility to encourage a liquid market in its stock at a reasonable price because of its responsibility to its shareholders. Most corporate managements recognize that an effective program of communications between the security issuer and the investment community is necessary and desirable to maintain a healthy market for their companies' shares.

Presently much work is being done in the securities industry to set up and implement a "central market," accessible to all brokers on equal terms. Some form of this undoubtedly will develop over a period of time. At present, however, there are two distinct types of markets for securities trading. These are (1) organized securities exchanges and (2) the over-the-counter (OTC) market.

The two primary stock exchanges, of course, are the *New York Stock Exchange* and the *American Stock Exchange*. In addition, there are a number of regional exchanges, such as the *Pacific Stock Exchange* (headquartered in San Francisco), the *Spokane Stock Exchange,* and the *Intermountain Stock Exchange* (Salt Lake City). Many Northwest stocks that are listed on the New York Stock Exchange are also "dually listed" on the Pacific Stock Exchange, and a few also on the Spokane and Intermountain exchanges, in which cases competitive markets exist and there is a choice of more than one place that an order can be executed. Also, the PSE stays open later in the afternoon than the NYSE.

The two New York exchanges (primarily the NYSE) do the bulk of the listed trading volume, by far. Listing requirements for the NYSE are more stringent than those of the ASE. Broadly speaking, listing requirements cover such matters as number of shares traded, number of stockholders, the company's net worth, record of past profitability, and other measures of size and liquidity.

The primary difference between the listed and OTC markets is that exchanges conduct *"auction markets"* for investors through their brokers, while the OTC market is run by dealers who *negotiate prices* on every trade.

This leads us to another distinction. A *broker* is one who acts as an agent for his client, and is not a party to the trade in question. A *dealer* is one who trades for his own account and may "make a market" in certain stocks. Thus, in the OTC market you may buy from or sell to a dealer as the other party to your trade.

The market-making function is little understood by the public, although it is relatively simple. Essentially, a broker who makes a market in a stock takes a "position," in the form of inventory, just like a dealer inventorying merchandise for sale in a store. This is what gives rise to the name, "over-the-counter market." He may quote his market as "15 bid, 16 asked." This means that he will buy stock at 15 or sell at 16, whichever is desired. His profit comes from the "spread," the difference between his purchase and sale prices. He takes the risk that the market for a stock may go down while he is holding an inventory of its shares.

Many companies with active OTC market makers find that the liquidity in their stocks is very good in the OTC market, and they choose not to list on exchanges, even long after they would be eligible for exchange listing. One should not draw any conclusions that OTC stocks are "worse" than listed stocks, or, conversely, that listed stocks are somehow "better." For example, major corporations such as *American Express, Anhaeuser-Busch,* and *Bank of America* have always traded in the OTC market. Similarly, many outstanding Northwest companies are traded OTC.

About 50 of the 200 plus Northwest companies discussed in this book are listed on the New York, American and Pacific Stock Exchanges, and the balance are traded over-the-counter. Northwest companies have been slower than those in other parts of the country to list on major exchanges, with the result that Northwest companies constitute an unusually strong segment of the OTC market.

For example, all of the Northwest's largest banking, finance and insurance institutions are traded OTC. These include *Seafirst Corp., U.S. Bancorp, Rainier Bancorp, First Security Corp., Idaho First National Bank, Washington Bancshares, Equitable Savings & Loan, Safeco,* and many others, even though many smaller financial organizations

elsewhere have listed on exchanges. The OTC market also includes the area's two largest natural gas distributors, *Northwest Natural Gas* and *Washington Natural Gas*; retailers such as *Fred Meyer, Pacific Gamble Robinson* and *Pay 'n Save*; and many other well-known companies such as *Paccar, Hyster, Olympia Brewing,* and *Willamette Industries.*

The commission a broker charges to execute an order as your agent generally is about the same for a listed stock as for an OTC stock. Members of the New York Stock Exchange used to have a fixed commission schedule, but that was abolished on May 1, 1975, and commission policy now varies somewhat from one brokerage house to another. Prior to May of 1975 many non-member firms already had started discounting commissions. The first brokerage house in the Northwest to offer discounted commissions that we are aware of was *Omega Securities* of Portland, which has been offering reductions of up to 50% of what used to be the standard minimum commissions for more than two years to customers who want minimal services. Such discounted commissions generally are available to those who just want their orders executed and little, if any, other service. Each customer should decide what kind of services he wants from his broker, and the amount of commission he should expect to pay should be determined primarily by the level of service he desires, and not by the market in which his stocks trade.

Public Enemy Number One—Inflation

Everyone who has placed his faith in fixed dollar investments over the years has had a substantial portion of his assets confiscated through inflation. This includes bond purchasers, purchasers of life insurance, savings account depositors, and those on fixed incomes such as pensions and social security.

Interest is defined conceptually as the "rental of money." Most lenders, if there were no inflation, would be satisfied to receive a 3%-4% interest return on their investments. One reason that interest costs on prime risks have ranged from 6% to 12% in recent years is to offset the effect of inflation.

The investor who purchased long-term bonds in recent years at par may have substantial unrealized losses, based on recent market values. Several examples will illustrate the point: U.S. Treasury Bonds are the highest "quality" available, involving no credit risk whatever. Consider these prices (October, 1975):

U.S. Treasury Bonds $6\frac{3}{8}$% of 1984—91.10
$6\frac{1}{8}$% of 1986—85.16
$6\frac{3}{4}$% of 1993—86.80
$3\frac{1}{2}$% of 1998—76.16

"91.10" means the current market price is 91.1% of face value, or $911 for a $1,000 bond. In each of the above cases, investors who must sell at these prices would suffer a loss. This loss is not because of any U.S. Government credit risk, but simply because interest rates have risen since the bonds were issued, so the bonds have to sell at a discounted price in order to make the effective yield competitive with new bonds being issued today. In order to get interest rates back down, it will be necessary to reduce the rate of inflation.

Inflation is a seemingly endless process dating back thousands of years. There never has been a sustained period in history when currency has not eventually been debased. Gold, and, to some extent, silver have always been regarded as a measure and storehouse of value. It is no accident that the price of both silver and gold have increased several-fold in the past decade. Ancients were noted for "coin clipping," a practice of shaving metal from the edge, a crude but effective form of inflation. Even today our coins have milled edges to prevent this abuse. Now our government debases coins to begin with, saving us the trouble.

Who is the culprit? Not individuals, whose cash income and outflow must eventually match. Not corporations, whose budgets must balance, including a return on their capital acceptable to the market. The party capable of causing inflation is the one which continues to exist without balancing its budget, the Federal government. The problem is caused by those politicians whose appetites are continually bigger than their stomachs.

Politicians, as a group, are responsive to public demands, and they should be. But there is a fierce temptation to create monstrous new projects, necessary or not. When it comes to votes, one is anxious to outdo the other in terms of new "benefits" to bestow upon the public. Our quarrel with them is that the adverse consequences of their actions are never clearly explained to the public.

Government officials are continually "giving" us something: welfare, school aid, revenue sharing, medicare, subsidies, old-age benefits, etc. This book is in no way big enough to list all of the related disbursements sponsored by the Federal government.

We would, however, like to articulate a natural law which we will call the *"Ross-Pratt Rule:"*

"The government cannot give anything to anyone which it does not either sooner or later take from someone else."

We hope you will keep this principle in mind when the next wonderful government program is proposed.

PACCAR President Charles M. Piggott stated the case succinctly in his President's message in PACCAR's 1974 Annual Report:

"through our congressional representatives, we should point out that unnecessary and extravagant government programs only add to governmental deficits that continue to erode savings, pensions, current income, and lead to still more taxes. We must strive to achieve a society wherein those who want to work can and do not have their wages confiscated by taxes. Until we effectively communicate this thought to the government, we can expect high inflation with a consequent lower standard of living."

In short, the free enterprise system is threatened by inflation, the primary cause of which is government deficits. The accompanying table shows how business would fare under deficits such as the Federal government has incurred.

($70,000,000,000)

For the current fiscal year the U. S. Government is projecting $300,000,000,000 in revenues with a $70,000,000,000 deficit. In the language of business this means a 23% loss on each dollar of sales! If some prominent Northwest companies were to experience equivalent losses the results would be disastrous:

	Actual 1974/5 Sales (000)	Equiv. 23% Loss (000)	Loss per Share	Loss as a % of Net Worth
Boeing	$3,750,000	$(863,000)	$(40.50)	(90)%
Georgia-Pacific	2,432,000	(559,000)	(9.05)	(62)
Tektronix	337,000	(78,000)	(8.88)	(39)

No private corporation could survive losses of this magnitude for very long. Expenditures would have to be brought in line with revenues to avoid bankruptcy.

The U. S. Government supports its deficits with the dollar printing press and passes the burden to the American public in the form of inflation. How many dollars will the U. S. Government have to print to meet this and subsequent years' deficits and what will they be worth when the presses are finally turned off?

Reprinted from the *Northwest Investment Review* September 22, 1975.

The only way we know of to protect yourselves from the "inflators" is through the ownership of equity investments. By this we mean that common shares of sound corporations must be acquired in addition to whatever fixed income securities you may own.

Many Northwest companies offer excellent anti-inflation vehicles, in that many of them relate directly to natural resource assets. If inflation continues, as it gives every indication of doing, natural resources will also increase in value. Stocks of companies that own such resources as precious and other metals, coal, oil and gas, uranium, and timber can be expected to increase in market value along with the price appreciation of their underlying assets.

Another class of common stocks that should provide good protection against inflation are those that own productive capacity and have kept it up in top modern and efficient working condition. Instead of the burden of having to replace outmoded facilities with much higher cost new plants, these companies will benefit by being able to receive higher market prices for the goods produced in their existing plant facilities.

While interest payments from fixed income investments will never increase, periodic dividend increases on common stock holdings can at least alleviate some of the burdens of inflation. Except for very short periods of time, dividends on common stocks have increased faster than inflation over the entire recorded history of the U.S. stock market.

WHAT I BELIEVE

In recent years, the gloom merchants have been having a field day. Looking about themselves and perceiving that the market is doing poorly, they proceed to make a common, fundamental mistake. They insist on projecting their experience of the immediate past into the future indefinitely. This is contrary to all logic since the one certain thing that we know about the future is that it is unpredictable and will therefore be different from the immediate past. They have about succeeded in scaring the wits out of most people.

Some advisors and prophets (?) are scurrying about the country advising the public to withdraw all investments, send money out of the country, and to bury money, gold, silver, or what have you in the back yard. In short, they are preparing for the ultimate disaster.

I have news for them. If world conditions are that bad, they will not be saved either! They will go down with the ship, just like everyone else. When you analyze their arguments, it is clear that they are planning for failure. What kind of sense is that? Speaking philosophically, if an individual plans to fail, he very often achieves his goal.

I prefer to plan for success.

People sometimes say to me "This isn't a good time to invest". My reply is that there never was a good time to invest! What people give as a reason often turns out to be an excuse.

There is always a crisis somewhere. If our country can handle the Civil War, World War I, the Great Depression of the 1930's, World War II, and the Atomic Bomb, I am not going to panic over current problems.

Just in the last 20 years, there have been a multitude of disasters: President Eisenhower's heart attack; Egypt's seizure of the Suez Canal; the Cuban Bay of Pigs invasion; President Kennedy's assassination; the Watts riots; LSD and other drugs; two Arab-Israeli wars; and so on.

In spite of all this, our country grows and prospers. Take a period 100 years ago; fifty years ago; or 25 years ago and compare. Our health care is better, civil rights problems are gradually being solved, schools are better, Social Security benefits are better, information and news is more available, and science and industry are more efficient. New products and services (radio, television, air transportation, and others) which were not even available formerly, are now commonplace. Does anyone doubt that new services and opportunities lie ahead?

Karl Marx got a lot of mileage out of a small paper he once wrote titled *"The Communist Manifesto"*. I would like to offer my own views, as follows:

THE CAPITALIST MANIFESTO

1. I believe in the United States of America.

2. I believe in the Capitalist System.

3. I believe that profits generated by private enterprise can solve any problem better than any solution imposed by politicians and political agencies.

4. I believe that American businessmen and workers are capable of overcoming any temporary problems, domestic or international.

5. I believe that the overwhelming bulk of opportunities for business, labor, and investors lie ahead of us, not behind us.

6. I believe that the creativeness and inventiveness of our present society is far superior to anything in the past.

7. I believe that adversity breeds opportunity and that human resources represent our country's greatest wealth.

8. In the stock market, I believe that bulls can run faster than bears.

9. I believe that funds carefully invested today will return several-fold in the next 10 or 20 years.

10. I believe that we will see new beneficial technologies and products in this lifetime which will far exceed the contributions of science and industry in the past.

Reprinted from **Investing in Low-Risk Growth Companies** by Lawrence R. Ross, published by Willamette Management Associates, Portland, Oregon, 1975, pp. 28-30.

4

Investor Protection and Information

Investors are better protected today than at any time in the history of the securities markets. This is the result of the combined effects of the Securities and Exchange Commission, state securities regulators, the National Association of Securities Dealers, the Securities Investor Protection Corporation, and substantially improved investor communications by the companies that issue publicly-traded stocks and bonds.

While there obviously is no protection against bad judgment in reaching an investment decision, investors are aided in practically every other conceivable way. Particularly, investors are better protected than ever before against losses arising from brokers' financial failures and also against fraud and deceptive practices. There is also much better information available today on which to base investment decisions, both from the companies themselves and also from independent information and analytical sources.

Federal Securities Regulation

Cornerstones of Federal regulation are two major pieces of legislation: (1) *The Securities Act of 1933* and (2) *The Securities Exchange Act of 1934.*

To oversee and supervise enforcement of these Acts, the *Securities and Exchange Commission* (SEC) was created. Today, the SEC is responsible for supervising virtually all Federal securities regulations. In chronological sequence, the major legislative acts monitored by the SEC are these:

The Securities Act of 1933
The Securities Exchange Act of 1934
The Public Utility Holding Company Act of 1935
The Trust Indenture Act of 1939
The Investment Company Act of 1940
The Investment Advisors Act of 1940
The Securities Acts Amendments of 1964

The 1933 Act is primarily concerned with regulating the issuance and sale of new securities. Primary emphasis is placed upon disclosure as a means of protecting the public. The Act itself describes its purpose as follows: "To provide full and fair disclosure of the character of securities sold in interstate and foreign commerce and through the mails."

Enforcement of the Securities Act of 1933 is accomplished through the registration process. With some exceptions (such as U.S. Treasury issues and municipal bonds) all new securities offered for sale on an interstate basis must first be registered. The financial condition and business affairs of the corporation must be disclosed in excruciating detail according to a complex maze of registration procedures. A summary of the registration statement, called the "prospectus," is then delivered to all buyers of the security. Most securities are subject to the full registration requirements, but offerings of $500,000 or less may be registered with a less detailed form under "Regulation A."

Note that SEC jurisdiction, like other Federal commissions, is limited to "securities offered for sale on an interstate basis." If a securities offering is confined to residents of a single state, it may escape Federal registration and be registered only with the securities authorities in the state in which it is being sold, usually a less costly procedure in terms of legal, accounting, printing and other costs. This is why investors frequently see an ad or prospectus with a legend such as "Offered only to bona fide residents of the State of Oregon."

The more comprehensive Securities Exchange Act of 1934 established a number of conditions which are taken for granted today.

The Act called for the registration and regulation of securities exchanges. In addition, it requires the registration of securities traded on those exchanges, plus periodic reports. Also required to be registered are all securities broker-dealer firms.

While commercial banks do a substantial amount of trading for their own accounts and for clients, they are not required to register as broker-dealers. Since banks are supervised and regulated by other state and federal agencies, they do not come within the scope of the Securities and Exchange Commission's administration.

Other matters covered for the first time in the 1934 Act involve restrictions on "insider" trading, proxy solicitations, personnel records of employees, and provisions against fraudulent and deceptive trading in securities.

An "insider" is defined as any officer, director or beneficial owner of 10% or more of the shares of a publicly-traded company. Insiders are required to report their own purchases or sales of the stock of their companies to the SEC by the 10th day of the month following the month in which the transaction took place. These transactions for all registered stocks are reported monthly in the SEC's *Official Summary of Security Transactions and Holdings.* Insider transactions for all registered Northwest stocks discussed in this book are reported in the *Northwest Investment Review.*

The SEC's Northwest regional office is located at 1411 4th Avenue, Seattle, Washington 98101.

State Securities Regulation

With the exception of the State of Delaware, which has no securities law, every state has some form of Securities Commission or agency to supervise trading in addition to federal regulation.

A large part of state regulation concerns requirements for registration of securities, known as *"blue sky"* laws, which exist in all 50 states, except for Delaware. The term "blue sky" arises from a celebrated court

---

NORTHWEST SECURITIES ADMINISTRATORS

OREGON
Mr. Frank J Healy
Corporation Commissioner
Department of Commerce
Corporation Division
158 - 12th Street N.E.
Salem, Oregon 97310
503-378-4333

ALASKA
Mr. Langhorne A. Motley
Commissioner of Commerce
Dept. of Commerce and
   Economic Development
Pouch "D"
Juneau, Alaska 99811

Mr. Miles S. Schlosberg
Director
Division of Banking, Securities,
   Small Loans & Corporations
Dept. of Commerce and
   Economic Development
Pouch "D"
Juneau, Alaska 99811
907-465-2521

MONTANA
Mr. E. V. "Sonny" Omholt
State Auditor & Ex-Officio
Commissioner of Insurance
Investment Commissioner
Capitol Building
Helena, Montana 59601
406-449-2040

UTAH
Mr. William P. Sargeant
Director, Securities Commission
330 East 4th South
Salt Lake City, Utah 84111
801-533-5661

WASHINGTON
Mr. Eugene G. Olson
Administrator, Securities Section
Division of Professional Licensing
P.O. Box 648
Olympia, Washington 98501

Ruth Ramsaur
Administrative Assistant

Mr. Robert Klein
Camp Clubs/Franchise Officer

Mr. John Maxwell
Assistant Administrator

Mr. Lyman C. Stone
Chief Financial Officer
206-753-6928

IDAHO
Mr. Tom D. McEldowney
Director of Finance
413 W. Idaho
Boise, Idaho 83720

Mr. Melvin Baptie
Deputy Administrator for
   Securities Bureau

Mrs. Dee Tallman
Securities Technician
208-384-3313

WYOMING
Mrs. Thyra Thomson
Secretary of State &
   Securities Administrator
Capitol Building
Cheyenne, Wyoming 82002
307-777-7378

case involving securities. According to Justice McKenna (Hall vs. Geiger-Jones, 242 U.S. 539,550 1917), "The name that is given to the law indicates the evil at which it is aimed; that is, to use the language of a cited case, 'speculative schemes which have no more basis than so many feet of blue sky'."

Some of the states, most notably Oregon, go beyond Federal disclosure requirements in registering new securities issues, requiring also that the terms of the issue be "fair, just, and equitable." As a result of this requirement, administered in Oregon by the staff of the Corporation Commission, there have been many new securities offerings registered in other states that have been rejected in Oregon. The Oregon Commission also has required in many instances of new offerings that promoters' stock be held in escrow until the company has met certain earnings or other requirements for some specified period of time.

Oregon is widely recognized as a national leader in state securities legislation and enforcement. Much of the credit for this is due to Frank Healy, who has been Oregon Corporation Commissioner for over 20 years and is highly respected in all securities enforcement circles.

A regional securities enforcement conference is held in the Northwest at least once a year, generally for three days. It involves SEC people, state securities regulators, the NASD regional staff and officers, attorneys involved in securities work, compliance officers of broker-dealer organizations, and other relevant people. This regular communication among all the related parties undoubtedly has been a positive influence for investor protection in the Northwest.

In addition to state securities commissioners, various other state agencies may have some say in securities regulation from time to time. These could include banking commissions, insurance commissions, real estate commissions, and utility commissions, for example.

The National Association of Securities Dealers

Called the NASD, in short, the Association was founded in August, 1939. The NASD is authorized under the *Maloney Act,* an amendment to the *Securities Exchange Act of 1934.* Although it is under the supervision of the *Securities and Exchange Commission,* the NASD is primarily a self-policing organization. Its influence in the securities industry has grown dramatically in recent years.

The Board of Governors and other officers of the NASD are all industry representatives who serve on a voluntary basis. The NASD also has full-time staff people in Washington, D.C. and New York, as well as in each of its regional offices around the country. NASD District 1, including Washington, Oregon, Idaho, Montana, and Alaska, has its district office in the IBM Building, Seattle, Washington 98101.

The NASD is designed primarily to regulate over-the-counter market trading. However, the scope of their work also includes testing and licensing of salesmen, periodic audits and examinations of NASD member firms, regulation of advertising material, arbitration of disputes, upholding of ethical standards, and much more.

The NASD also operates the *NASDAQ* OTC quotation system, discussed in another chapter. In addition to making markets more efficient, the NASDAQ computerized system has provided input into a "Stock Watch" program that sometimes has triggered an *"Anti-Fraud Squad"* investigation into possible manipulative practices. The "Anti-Fraud Squad" was established in 1973 by the NASD in conjunction with the SEC, to go beyond routine examiner functions in investigating suspicious practices that could involve manipulation or fraud. As a result of these and other efforts, the securities markets are much more free of such practices than at any time in the past.

While we feel that there are many regulatory practices of the SEC and other bodies that should be improved or handled differently, nevertheless the trend is clearly established for better investor protection. In a speech in 1974, the then NASD Senior Regional Examiner, Robert E. Davies, said, "Those segments of the securities industry that cannot adjust to the future for whatever reasons will have to drop out. Those are harsh words, but these are harsh times. There is a great need to regain customer confidence." The steps are being taken.

Davies left the NASD in July of 1975 to help further that effort as Executive Director of a new non-profit corporation, the *American Investment Institute,* at this writing headquartered in Tacoma. The Institute provides consulting services to broker-dealers and other investment industry organizations "to assure and promote compliance with regulatory requirements." More broadly, the Institute's purposes are stated to include "research and analysis to develop effective legislation, management, administration, and supervision of investment practices and activities."

Membership categories in the Institute include broker-dealers, other financial institution members such as banks and investment advisory companies, corporate security issuers, professional members such as securities attorneys and C.P.A.'s, and public investors. We wish this effort well.

The Securities Investor Protection Corporation

One safeguard the investor has now that was not present in the 1960's is the *Securities Investor Protection Corporation (SIPC),* the result of Congressional enactment of the *Securities Investor Protection Act of 1970.* This act, for the first time, affords investors protection similar to that possessed by depositors in banks and savings and loan associations.

The protection offered is not against the investor's trading actions, but rather protects him against possible losses in case of insolvency on the part of the brokerage firm with which he is dealing. In the past, when some brokerage firms closed their doors, investors were simply out of luck. Securities left on deposit as well as cash either disappeared or were hopelessly entangled in endless litigation.

While the SIPC act has many rules and restrictions, the basic proposition is that customer claims for up to $50,000 in securities and cash that may have been left on deposit with a brokerage firm at time of liquidation of the firm will be paid by a court-appointed Trustee.

Members of SIPC include all members of national securities exchanges and all broker-dealers registered with the SEC except those engaged exclusively in the sale of mutual funds, variable annuities, insurance, or advice to investment institutions.

The insurance pool is being built up to a sum of $150 million through assessments made against each member's gross revenue. In addition, SIPC has the right to borrow up to $1 billion from the U.S. Treasury to meet any unforeseen crisis.

For the most part, then, investors can deal with their brokers with complete confidence. This was not the case prior to enactment of SIPC in 1970.

Investor Information from Companies

As we have emphasized, no amount of regulation can protect against bad investment decisions. However, the tools available to make more informed investment decisions are getting better and becoming more easily available to the individual investor all the time.

The average publicly-held corporation is doing a much better job of communicating with the average investor than was the case five years ago. The stockholder (and the capital he controls) is getting higher priority attention by top management. Some of the results are better annual reports, better stockholder meetings, better press communications, and more money being spent more wisely on generally improved investor relations programs.

We are defining "better" in this context to mean "more informative," which is not to be equated with just blowing the same old horn a little louder. During the 1967-68 "hot stock syndrome," people generally invested first, investigated later (if ever), and "investor relations" as practiced by many companies and consultants was unfortunately little more than just touting stocks.

Not so today. Investor relations is becoming more professional, with the focus on acquainting the investor as thoroughly as possible with all facets of the company. They are "letting it all hang out," getting away from the old tendency to try to hide the bad news and just tell the good news.

The annual meeting, for many years a dull and ritualistic affair for most companies, is increasingly becoming recognized as an appropriate and useful forum for informing investors and answering their questions. A typical example of increased effort in this direction is an elaborate 15-minute slide presentation prepared by *Columbia Corp.* for their 1975 annual meeting.

Another area of investor communications that has improved significantly is the annual report. Almost all publicly held companies will be glad to give you a copy of their annual report, even if you are not a stockholder. Furthermore, the average quality of their annual reports

has improved greatly over the last five years, in terms of both information content and also attractive and easily readable presentation.

This year the improvement in that category was accelerated by new
SEC requirements for inclusion of more detailed information, much of
which formerly was required only to be reported to the SEC on Form 10-
K, normally read only by the attorneys and a handful of analysts. More
and more reports are also including general information about their industries as well as their own companies.

Many companies also will provide a variety of other investment information materials such as descriptive brochures, statistical fact
sheets, transcripts of officers' speeches to investment groups, reprints of
articles that have been written about them, or special reports the companies have had prepared for them by financial analysts or public
relations firms.

Boise Cascade, for example, publishes an extremely interesting
"Boise Cascade Quarterly" which it distributes with its interim reports,
and it also did an excellent annual report. *Moduline International* sends
an informative letter to its stockholders about once a month. These are
just two of many examples.

Many Northwest companies have created full-time professional investor relations positions, and the trend toward having such positions is
growing. Many other companies use outside firms to assist in investor
relations.

The end result of all of these efforts is more and better information
readily available to the individual investor to make his investment
decisions. Such better information helps to reduce the risk of error in
securities investment decisions, and should help to increase the investor's confidence.

We believe in the adage "investigate before you invest." Happily,
the information readily available for you to investigate is more comprehensive, more interesting and more readily obtainable than ever. We
suggest that investors take full advantage of these improved communications efforts, and think that many will find the exercise of such
study interesting as well as profitable.

Professional Investment Groups in Northwest

The availability of professionally qualified investment analysts,
managers and advisors in the Northwest has increased markedly in the
last ten years. With more active, serious-minded professional investment
people in the area, members of the investment communities of the
Northwest/Intermountain states have formed several professional clubs
and associations in recent years with the objectives of continuing
members' education and sharing information of common interest.

We hope the following paragraphs, giving summary descriptions of
these groups, will be useful to readers wishing to join or attend meetings,
and that the information will aid in the scheduling of special meetings
and activities by individuals and firms. We especially recommend that

companies sponsoring private meetings for investment people avoid the organizations' regularly scheduled meeting dates, as such conflicts dilute the attendance of both.

The *Portland Society of Financial Analysts* and the *Seattle Society of Financial Analysts* are two of the 46 constituent societies of the national *Financial Analysts Federation*. Their goals are to provide a professional society for financial analysts, to foster interchange of information among members, to add to the knowledge of members, and to foster a high standard of ethics and professional conduct among members. Anyone regularly engaged in the field of financial analysis as it relates to securities investment is eligible for membership, and guests are welcome at both societies' programs.

Most members of the Analysts' Societies are affiliated with bank trust departments, registered investment advisory organizations, or other investment organizations. For example, of the 66 members of the Portland Society of Financial Analysts at this writing, 33 are in banks, 15 with registered investment advisory companies, 6 with insurance companies, 4 university professors, 4 with brokerage houses, 3 with state or private investment funds, and one (formerly with a bank) in charge of investor relations and other activities at *Portland General Electric*. Many of the registered representatives of the brokerage houses regularly attend both the Portland and Seattle Societies' meetings.

Members of the Financial Analysts Federation may also pursue an educational and examination program leading to the professional designation of *Chartered Financial Analyst*. Ten members of the Portland Society, for example, are Chartered Financial Analysts.

The Seattle Society meets irregular Thursdays, once or twice a month at the Rainier Club. The Portland Society meets first and third Thursdays at the Benson Hotel. Both societies have occasional meetings on other dates, depending on the availability of desired speakers. Most of the meetings consist of a presentation by one of the publicly-held companies. About half the company presentations are by companies discussed in this book, and the rest are by companies headquartered elsewhere that come to make their presentation to Northwest analysts. Other meetings feature qualified speakers dealing with special subjects of importance to the investment markets, such as Federal monetary policy.

The *Spokane Stock and Bond Club* was formed as a loose association designed to bring companies and securities programs to Spokane. Members come from brokerage firms and banks in Spokane, and guests are always welcome at the Club's luncheon meetings, usually held once a month on an irregular schedule.

The *Utah Bond Club's* educational goals are met through irregular monthly meetings in Salt Lake City which feature guest speakers on various investment subjects. Anyone involved in the investment industry qualifies for membership, and guests are welcome at presentations.

The purpose of the *Seattle Option Society* is to educate, develop, encourage, and promote option strategies and their use in portfolio management. The Society has meetings each month, with the dates varying depending on the availability of guest speakers. The organization also holds seminars for the general public with various guest speakers to promote the option idea. Anyone who shares the Society's goals is eligible for membership.

There is both an *Oregon Chapter* and a *Sea-Tac Chapter* of the *International Association of Financial Planners*. The goals of the chapters as quoted from the Association's code of ethics, are to "promote conceptual financial planning, combining cash, insurance and investments prudently for the realization of financial objectives in case of life, death, disability, inflation, and deflation in such a manner as to provide the maximum return consistent with the ability of the client to assume risk." Members are people dealing with the public in financial products and services. These include stock brokerage registered representatives, mutual fund and insurance sales people, investment advisors, trust officers, and tax and estate planning attorneys and C.P.A.'s. There is a national educational and examination program available to members leading to the professional designation of *Certified Financial Planner*. The C.F.P. program is only three years old at this writing, and there are about 15 Certified Financial Planners in the Northwest.

Sea-Tac's usual luncheon meetings take place the fourth Thursday of the month at the Royal Fork Restaurant in Seattle, and feature speakers on various aspects of financial planning, as well as discussions of current topics. Guests and non-members are invited to attend regular meetings. The Oregon Chapter holds luncheon meetings the second Tuesday of each month at Portland's Mallory Hotel, which feature panel discussions, workshops, and outside speakers from various industries and vocations from the financial community. Guests are welcome.

5

Investing in Common Stocks

We think that almost all investment portfolios should include some common stocks. The reason for this is the potential for both capital appreciation and increasing dividend payments in a period when these factors are needed to offset the certain erosion in the value of the dollar that we are facing.

The 204 common stocks that are the primary subject matter of this book represent a range all the way from the most speculative untested companies on one end of the spectrum to large, seasoned companies that have been paying cash dividends regularly for *over 75 years*. In other words, the group includes something for everybody.

Natural resource stocks, of which the Northwest has many, represent ownership of assets which are appreciating in value. Manufacturing stocks represent ownership of the productive capacity of the region. Finance, merchandising, transportation, utility, and service stocks represent ownership of the support facilities of the region. It is the ownership of the underlying assets and the earning power that give stocks their present value and the expectations that the group as a whole will grow in value and increase their dividend-paying capacity over time.

With the rewards of common stock investing, there are also risks. However, these risks can be reduced sharply by building a properly diversified portfolio and by selecting individual issues that represent sound values for the dollars invested. These two key elements of common stock investing will be discussed in turn.

Building a Diversified Portfolio

The first thing the investor must decide in planning his portfolio policy is where he wants to be on the risk spectrum. Some investors may want an ultra-conservative portfolio, while some younger people with much earning power ahead of them apart from their investments may want a completely speculative portfolio.

We frequently find people who want a predominantely conservative portfolio with a few speculative situations mixed in to have at least an outside chance of scoring a big profit. It is extremely rare, however, to

A DIVERSIFIED PORTFOLIO OF 25 NORTHWEST STOCKS
(Prices and Dividends as of September 30, 1975)

Mkt.	Company	Industry	No. Shares	Price Per Share	Amount	Annual Dividend
NYS	Albertson's	Retailing	200	20	$4,000	$120
NYS	Boeing	Aerospace	200	26½	5,300	160
NYS	Boise Cascade	Forest Products	200	22¼	4,450	130
NYS	Cascade Natural Gas	Gas Utility	500	8	4,000	460
OTC	Columbia Corporation	Multi-Line	1,000	4	4,000	None
OTC	Equitable Savings & Loan	Savings & Loan	700	7	4,900	252
OTC	First Farwest Corp.	Insurance & Other	5,000	1⅛	5,313	250
OTC	Hyster	Lift Truck Mfg.	400	12¾	5,100	240
OTC	International Kings Table	Restaurant Chain	1,000	3¼	3,250	70
NYS	Jantzen	Sportswear Mfg.	400	13	5,200	280
OTC	Loomis Corp.	Armored Car Service	800	5¾	4,600	80
NYS	Louisiana-Pacific	Forest Products	500	10⅝	5,313	100
OTC	Fred Meyer	Retailing	300	14⅞	4,463	90
NYS	Morrison-Knudsen	Eng. & Construction	200	20⅝	4,125	176
OTC	Olympia Brewing Co.	Brewing	200	21	4,200	160
NYS	Omark Industries	Saw Chain Mfg.	500	11	5,500	250
OTC	Oregon Portland Cement	Cement	500	10¾	5,375	800
NYS	Pacific Power & Light	Elec. Utility	300	18⅛	5,438	510
NYS	Payless Drug Stores N.W.	Retailing	400	13½	5,400	140
OTC	Rainbow Resources	Oil & Gas Exploration	500	6⅞	3,438	None
OTC	Rainier Bancorporation	Banking	200	25½	5,100	200
NYS	Sunshine Mining Co.	Silver Mining	400	12¼	4,900	144
NYS	Tektronix	Oscilloscope Mfg.	100	37⅝	3,763	24
NYS	Univar	Multi-Line	200	28¾	5,750	280
OTC	Willamette Industries	Forest Products	300	19⅝	5,963	216
					$118,841	$5,132

find a situation where it would be appropriate to hold a portfolio of stocks spread all the way across the risk spectrum from one end to the other.

The main factor to consider in building a well-diversified portfolio is to have the risks inherent in each individual stock in the portfolio as little connected with the risks involved in each other stock in the portfolio as possible. A portfolio of 10 utility stocks, for example, has almost no diversification at all, since many of the risk factors that affect one utility stock affect other utility stocks as well.

A properly diversified 10-stock portfolio might include, for example, one utility stock, a forest products company with both timber stands and manufacturing facilities, a consumer goods manufacturer, a heavy industrial goods manufacturer, a silver and metals mining company with significant reserves and production, a retailing chain, a bank, an insurance company, a company involved in some aspect of consumer or commercial services, and a transportation company. The following chapters discuss many stocks in each of these categories as well as other industry groups.

Although the Northwest does not have all of America's industries represented by any means, the degree of investment diversification available within the area is much greater than most people realize. This is amply demonstrated by the sample 25-stock Northwest portfolio shown in the table accompanying this chapter. The heaviest single industry representation is in forest products (the Northwest's largest industry), well under 15% of the total portfolio value. The sample diversified portfolio has a 4.5% dividend yield, even including 2 stocks that pay no dividend at all.

(The sample fixed income portfolio in the following chapter includes 15 bonds and preferred stocks, all issued by different companies than the sample equity portfolio in this chapter.)

There are other ways to diversify besides just by industry group. One can diversify across risk classes (as discussed briefly earlier), by size of company, by age of company, by geographical area (there is a lot of room for this across the vast Northwest-Intermountain area), and by market in which the stock is traded.

In this latter regard, as discussed earlier in the book, the over-the-counter market is far more efficient than it used to be, and includes many excellent companies. Those that would shun a company because it is not listed on an exchange would exclude from their consideration such fine companies as Safeco, Seafirst, U.S. Bancorp, Northwest Natural Gas, Paccar, Hyster and many others. Many of the stocks traded actively in the OTC market have far better liquidity than others listed on the New York Stock Exchange.

Valuing Public and Privately-Owned Stocks

Many of the principles of valuing publicly-traded and privately-owned stocks are the same, and the disciplines used in valuing stocks in many different situations bring perspective to the job of determining value in each individual case.

We have had the responsibility of placing a value on companies for mergers and acquisitions, public and private stock offerings, Employee Stock Ownership Trusts, gift and estate taxes, divorces, and other purposes, as well as for regular stock market buy and sell decisions. The main difference between valuing a privately-owned company and a publicly-traded stock is the relative isolation of the privately-owned situation from short-term market psychology and market fads.

The extremely high stock market prices of late 1968 and the ridiculously low prices of late 1974 are examples of public emotion and other market factors driving practically all stock prices out of perspective for a short time relative to reasonable measures of the companies' intrinsic values. If everyone buying or selling a stock stepped back and asked themselves, "What is the **whole** company worth?" rather than just looking at it as a share of stock, people probably would make much more rational valuations and much more profitable buy and sell decisions.

The primary factors determining the value of a stock, whether it is closely held or publicly traded, are earnings and net worth, both present and what is anticipated for the future. Risk factors must also be considered, as higher degrees of risk reduce the present value of a security. Liquidity (the ability to convert the security to cash at any time) also must be considered, as lack of liquidity reduces present value.

The matter of liquidity, of course, is one factor that differentiates privately held company stocks from public stocks. Other things being equal, a stock with no public trading market would be worth less than one that could be sold on the open market any time the owner desired.

Earnings are most commonly related to stock prices by the "price-earnings multiple," usually defined as the stock's price per share divided by the latest year's earnings per share. A high price-earnings multiple is justified by the expectation of rapid earnings growth in the future, low degrees of risk factors, and good liquidity in the stock.

The "quality" of earnings is also important. Accounting is by no means the exact science that the uninitiated may think it to be. There is a great deal of latitude that is both legally and professionally acceptable within the scope of generally accepted accounting standards. Since valuation of a company on an earnings basis requires some sort of comparison with available investments in other companies, the valuation analyst must somehow take into consideration any differences in accounting practices between the company he is valuing and other companies that may be used for comparative purposes. If the company he is valuing uses any unusual accounting practices, he may adjust their earnings from the way the company reports to the way the earnings would be reported if the company used accounting methods more typical for its industry. The more conservative the basis of reporting earnings, the higher the price-earnings multiple that is justified.

A more sophisticated way to relate earnings to value is to project expected earnings several years into the future and then discount the projected earnings to a present value, using an appropriate capitalization rate. This technique is preferable to the more familiar "price-earnings multiple" approach, providing that good earnings projections can be prepared and expert consideration is given to the appropriate capitalization rate to be used.

The net worth per share, also called the "book value," is also a relevant factor in valuation. It is determined by subtracting the company's total liabilities from its total assets, and dividing the equity thus derived by the number of shares of stock outstanding. These net worth figures are based on what the company actually paid for its assets, less allowances for depreciation. In adjusting such book value to some approximation of fair market value, many factors must be considered, such as liquidating value of the assets and the true value of intangible assets, which may be more or less than the amounts shown on the company's books.

Dividend-paying capacity is also an element to consider, and a factor to which the market seems to accord more weight today than it did five or ten years ago.

Like most other economic variables in the world, values of the stocks of both publicly traded and privately owned companies are more relative than absolute. The fair market value of a company must be determined partially in comparison to prices of other companies in the same industry and with other similar characteristics. Value is also relative to the cost of capital in the market—the higher the general level of interest rates, the lower the present value of any given expected future earnings stream.

These general principles apply, with varying interpretations and degrees of emphasis, to the stocks of any on-going business enterprise, publicly or privately owned. They apply to valuing a company for gift and estate tax litigation or planning, divorce or other civil litigation, establishing an employee stock ownership trust, mergers, acquisitions, divestitures, tender offers, and new public stock offerings, as well as to just buying or selling a stock on the open market.

Individual stock purchase and sale decisions can be improved by consideration of the same fundamental factors used in both legal and business valuations of private companies: earnings, net worth, risk factors, liquidity, and dividend-paying capacity, evaluated for the individual company and in comparison with other companies and economic factors.

A DIVERSIFIED PORTFOLIO
OF 15 NORTHWEST BONDS AND PREFERRED STOCKS

(Prices as of September 30, 1975)

Mkt.	Shares or Face Value	Company, Int. or Div. Rate, Bond Maturity	Industry	Price	Amount	Interest or Dividend
STRAIGHT BONDS						
NYS	$10,000	First Security Corp. Floating Rate, 1999	Banking	100⅛	$10,013	$ 1,050*
OTC	$10,000	Idaho Power 10%, 2004	Elec. Utility	93⅜	9,338	1,000
OTC	$10,000	Montana Power 8.625%, 2004	Elec. & Gas Util.	88⅜	8,838	862
OTC	$10,000	Paccar 8.1%, 1996	Truck Mfg.	83½	8,350	810
NYS	$10,000	Pacific N.W. Bell 8.625%, 2010	Telephone Utility	90½	9,050	862
NYS	$10,000	Safeco 7%, 1978	Insurance	98	9,800	700
NYS	$10,000	Utah Power & Light 10.25%, 1983	Elec. Utility	105	10,500	1,025
OTC	$10,000	Washington Water Power 4.625%, 1994	Elec. & Gas Util.	53⅛	5,313	462
NYS	$10,000	Weyerhaeuser 5.2%, 1991	Forest Products	71¾	7,175	520
STRAIGHT PREFERRED STOCKS						
NYS	100	Crown Zellerbach $4.20 Pfd.	Forest Products	52	5,200	420
OTC	100	Portland General Electric $11.50 Pfd.	Elec. Utility	100⅜	10,038	1,115
CONVERTIBLE BONDS						
ASE	$10,000	Alaska Airlines 6.5%, 1986, cv. to 151.06 com.	Airline	85	8,500	650
NYS	$10,000	Evans Products 6.25% 1994 cv. to 49.26 com.	Bldg. Mats. & Other	50½	5,050	625
OTC	$10,000	U.S. Bancorp 8%, 1985, cv. to 40 com.	Banking	100½	10,050	800
CONVERTIBLE PREFERRED BONDS						
PSE	1,000	Amfac $1 Pfd. cv. to .5897 com.	Multi-Line	11½	11,500	1,000
					$128,715	$11,901

*Based on rate at date of publication

6

Bonds and Preferred Stocks

With interest and dividends on bonds and preferred stocks at record high levels in recent years, there has been renewed interest in these classes of securities on the parts of investors everywhere.

While each company usually has only a single issue of common stock outstanding, they may have several different issues of bonds and preferred stocks. As shown in the accompanying summary tables, there are 22 of the companies discussed in this book that have straight mortgage or debenture bonds outstanding. These 22 companies have a total of 137 different straight bond issues outstanding totaling over $4.5 billion face value and paying over $350 million total annual interest.

In addition, 13 of the companies have convertible bonds outstanding, with a total of 17 different issues. An even dozen of the companies have straight preferred stocks outstanding, and these total 43 different issues. Finally, half a dozen companies have a total of 7 issues of convertible preferred stocks outstanding. This makes a total of 204 bond and preferred stock issues outstanding among the companies discussed in this book, a wide selection for investors interested in high income securities.

The table accompanying this chapter showing a sample portfolio of 15 Northwest bond and preferred issues emphasizes the wide diversification of investment selections that is available among Northwest fixed income securities. The group is widely diversified by industry, by type of issue, by year of maturity in the case of bonds, and by trading market. The portfolio has an over-all yield well over 9%, even including the 4 convertible issues.

It is interesting to note that the trading markets for the bonds and preferred stocks are not necessarily the same as the trading market for the common stock of any given company. For example, the common stocks of *Idaho Power, Montana Power, Pacific Power and Light* and *Washington Water Power* are all listed on the New York Stock Exchange (NYSE) but their bonds are traded in the over-the-counter (OTC) market. Conversely, however, the common stocks of *Safeco* and *U.S. Bancorp* are traded OTC, while the *Safeco* and *U.S. National Bank* bonds are listed on the NYSE. (U.S. National Bank is the bank subsidiary of holding company U.S. Bancorp.)

SUMMARY OF PUBLICLY-TRADED
NORTHWEST BONDS

STRAIGHT MORTGAGE AND DEBENTURE BONDS

Issuer	Face Value
Boeing Co.	$ 7,260,000
Boise Cascade	a) 149,257,000
Cascade Natural Gas	3,300,000
Consolidated Freightways	25,000,000
Crown Zellerbach	200,000,000
First Security Corp.	55,000,000
Idaho Power	349,026,000
Montana Power	206,886,000
Northwest Natural Gas	70,142,000
Paccar, Inc.	15,000,000
Pacific Northwest Bell	590,000,000
Pacific Power & Light Co.	797,570,000
Portland General Electric	271,079,000
Puget Sound Power & Light	342,770,000
Rainier Bancorporation	30,000,000
Safeco Corp.	25,000,000
Tektronix	35,000,000
U.S. Natl'l Bank of Oregon	50,000,000
Utah Power & Light	357,000,000
Washington Natural Gas	34,775,000
Washington Water Power	191,960,000
Weyerhaeuser	903,000,000

a) includes bonds issued by American & Foreign Power and guaranteed by Boise Cascade.

CONVERTIBLE BONDS

Issuer	Face Value
Alaska Airlines	$ 2,978,000
Alaska Interstate	8,334,000
Amfac, Inc.	50,086,000
Baza'r Inc.	1,137,000
Evans Products Co.	50,000,000
Georgia-Pacific Corp.	300,000,000
Golconda Corp.	4,441,000
Intermountain Gas	1,720,000
Fred Meyer	15,000,000
Sunshine Mining	20,000,000
U.S. Bancorp	20,000,000
USBanTrust	4,091,000

SUMMARY OF PUBLICLY-TRADED NORTHWEST PREFERRED STOCKS

STRAIGHT PREFERRED STOCKS

Issuer	Number of Shares
California-Pacific Utilities	250,000
Cascade Natural Gas	471,337
Crown Zellerbach	155,489
Idaho Power	365,000
Intermountain Gas	33,376
Montana Power	219,589
Northwest Natural Gas	213,405
Pacific Power & Light	1,172,360
Portland General Electric	1,100,000
Puget Sound Power & Light	1,002,964
Utah Power & Light	5,000,000
Washington Natural Gas	133,000

CONVERTIBLE PREFERRED STOCKS

Issuer	Number of Shares
Amfac, Inc.	965,398
Boise Cascade	85,284
Baza'r Inc.	25,884
Cascade Natural Gas	220,053
First Security Corp.	166,859
Golconda Corp.	383,212
Puget Sound Power & Light	296,100

Pacific Northwest Bell common stock is listed on the American Stock Exchange, but three issues of their bonds are traded on the NYSE and the rest of their bonds (six other issues) are traded OTC. *Utah Power & Light* and *Puget Sound Power & Light* also have part of their bonds traded on the NYSE and others traded OTC.

With the big needs for new capital, as we have discussed elsewhere in the book, new issues of bonds and preferred stocks are being sold by Northwest companies every month.

With so many different issues of bonds and preferred stocks outstanding, any given issue may not necessarily be available in the market at an attractive price on any given day. Therefore, it usually pays to let your broker shop around to find the issues that are most attractively priced to fit your needs at any given time.

Mortgage and Debenture Bonds

Most bonds are of either the *"mortgage"* or *"debenture"* variety. A mortgage bond is one that has specific real estate pledged behind it as collateral. A debenture bond is one that is not secured by any specific collateral, but is issued solely on the basis of the general credit standing of the company behind it.

Almost all bonds pay interest semi-annually, and different bonds pay their interest in different months of the year. Thus it is possible to structure a portfolio of as few as 6 bonds and have some interest income coming in every month.

Bonds are issued in denomination of $1000 each, but the bond prices are generally quoted in the newspaper as percentages of face value. Thus, if the *Pacific Northwest Bell* 8⅝% bond maturing in the year 2010 is quoted at "90½", this means you would pay $905 per bond (plus commission and accrued interest) to buy that bond in the open market. The 8⅝% *"coupon rate"* applies to the $1000 face value, so you would receive $86.25 interest per year on the bond, plus the $1000 face value when it matures in 2010.

The interest yield on bonds is generally stated in two ways, the *"current yield"* and the *"yield to maturity"*. The current yield is simply the number of dollars of interest you receive each year on each bond divided by the price you pay for each bond. In the case of the *Pacific Northwest Bell* 8⅝% bond, the current yield would be:

$$\frac{\$\ 86.25\ \text{(annual interest)}}{\$905\ \text{(market price of bond)}} = 9.5\%$$

The "yield to maturity" reflects the fact that the bondholder will receive an even $1,000 for the bond when it matures, which may be more or less than what he paid for it. In the above case, he will get $95 per bond more than what he paid, so the yield to maturity is higher than the current yield. However, the $95 discount has to be amortized over 30 years, so the yield to maturity is only slightly higher than the current yield. For the same number of dollars of difference between the price paid and the $1,000 face value, the shorter the time remaining to maturity the greater the difference between the current yield and yield to maturity. If a bond is selling at a premium over its face value, then the yield to maturity is less than the current yield, because the holder at maturity will receive less than the bond's present market price.

Bond prices tend to adjust in the market so that the effective yields on bonds already outstanding are more or less comparable to the yields on new bonds being issued. Thus, as interest rates increase, the prices of outstanding bonds go down; and as interest rates decline, the prices of outstanding bonds go up. The longer the time remaining to maturity, the greater the potential fluctuation in the market price of an outstanding bond for any given amount of change in the general level of interest rates.

Straight Preferred Stocks

Most preferred stocks, like common stocks, pay dividends quarterly, with different issues paying interest in different months of the quarter. This makes it possible to construct a portfolio of as few as 3 preferred stocks to have some income coming in regularly each month.

Since preferred stocks, also like common stocks, have no maturity date, the yield is simple to calculate. The percentage yield is merely the annual dividend amount divided by the market price. For example, if you bought the *Pacific Power & Light* $9.08 preferred and paid $88 per share for it, the yield would be:

$$\frac{\$ \ 9.08 \ \text{(annual dividend)}}{\$88.00 \ \text{(market price of stock)}} = 10.3\%$$

Like bonds, the market prices of preferred stocks fluctuate inversely with the general level of interest rates. When interest rates go up, the prices of preferred stocks must come down so that the effective yield adjusts to a competitive market rate. Similarly, when interest rates go down, the prices of outstanding preferred stocks go up. Since there is no maturity date at which any fixed principal sum will be paid, market prices of preferred stocks tend to fluctuate more than market prices of bonds for any given amount of change in the general level of interest rates.

Preferred stocks have a special (and significant) tax advantage over bonds for corporations that wish to hold income-producing securities. That is, 85% of the dividends received by one corporation from another are exempt from Federal income tax. Because of this tax advantage for corporate holders, many of the preferred stocks outstanding are held in insurance companies' income portfolios.

Convertible Bonds and Preferreds

A *"convertible"* bond or preferred means that it can be exchanged for a specified number of shares of common stock at the option of the holder.

For example, each *Alaska Airlines* 6½% bond maturing in 1986 may be exchanged for 151.06 shares of *Alaska Airlines* common stock at any time prior to maturity if the bond owner so desires. Similarly, each share of the *Puget Sound Power & Light* $3.625 preferred stock may be exchanged for 1.5 shares of *Puget Sound Power & Light* common stock at any time at the discretion of the owner of the convertible preferred.

It is hard to generalize about convertible issues, because of the very wide variety of terms and conditions. In the broadest general terms, they represent a compromise between a fixed income security and a common stock, having some of the benefits of both. As senior securities, their income is more secure than the dividends on the common stock. A company may very well reduce or omit the dividend on their common stock and still pay the bond interest or the preferred dividend. At the same time, the holder of the convertible has the opportunity through conversion to participate in the common stock's market price appreciation, if that occurs, an opportunity the holder of a straight bond or preferred does not enjoy.

Obviously, the investor must make some sacrifice for these advantages. The interest or dividend yield on the convertible bond or preferred normally is less than the yield on a non-convertible bond or preferred (although it is usually higher than the dividends on the common stock into which it is convertible). Also, the buyer of the convertible usually pays some premium over "*conversion value*", that is, he usually pays something more than the current market value of the stock he would receive if he chooses to convert.

The terms of different convertibles vary, but most increase the number of shares of common that will be received, to avoid dilution of the convertible holder's interest, in cases where a stock dividend is paid on the common stock.

With 24 different issues of convertible bonds and preferreds outstanding among the companies discussed in this book, the investor interested in convertibles has a nice variety available to study and choose for his portfolio. When an investor is considering buying a company's stock or bonds, it frequently pays to check as to whether there is a convertible issue available that might be more attractive.

7

Environment and the Economy

It has been fashionable for the past decade and more for certain groups and individuals to protest vigorously almost any commercial or industrial development as pollutant or otherwise harmful to the environment in some way. We do not deny that there are problems, but these environmentalists would have the public believe that industry is doing nothing about the matter.

Such is not the case. According to the *U.S. Department of Commerce,* more than $20 billion annually is being spent for pollution abatement and control. In the Northwest, we can cite hundreds of examples.

In the brewing industry, *Rainier Brewing Company* makes all of its beer containers reusable or recyclable. They are also working on solutions to roadside litter problems (which are caused by the consumer, not the company). The *Olympia Brewing Company,* at a cost of more than $2 million, has built a bottle handling and washing system which has rinsed over 255 million bottles to date.

Cascade Steel has installed new air pollution control equipment at its McMinnville plant costing more than $750,000, a major item for a relatively small company.

MILLIONS SPENT ON POLLUTION CONTROL

Hundreds of millions of dollars have been spent on both air and water pollution control by the paper industry in the Northwest. Tens of millions of dollars are being spent on pollution control equipment for *every* new electric generation plant being built. It is all adding substantially to the costs of goods and services, but the job is being done.

Forest product companies now routinely make useful byproducts from wood shavings, chips, and sawdust which were once a waste problem. What cannot be manufactured is used as fuel, an energy conservation measure. Technological advances such as these are not only environmentally sound, but also are economical.

Environmentalists (which we will use as a collective term for all varieties of the species) can be wonderfully inconsistent folk. Many totally fail to see any relationship between cause and effect. In addition to disclaiming any responsibility for their actions, they fail to spell out to the public the consequences of the actions they demand on the public's behalf.

As a general rule, when someone or some group appoints themselves as your protector, they bear as much watching as a thief in the night.

Protests concerning the construction of the Alaskan pipeline successfully delayed the project for more than six years. Costs of the project due to the delay have more than doubled, exceeding $4 billion. Does anyone doubt that this added cost will ultimately be paid by the consumer? Who has been protected?

Huge amounts of money were lost by Alaskans during the years of delays while equipment and parts brought up for the project and support activities at great expense rusted and rotted in the state's severe climate. Alaskans were understandably bitter about these enormous losses resulting from environmentalist-caused delays, and a popular bumper sticker in Alaska read, "Let the bastards freeze in the dark."

Environment and the Energy Resources

Public utilities are a favorite target of environmental groups. In protesting new plants, they wistfully opine that maybe the new power isn't needed. However, the facts are, as pointed out by *Idaho Power* President Albert Carlsen:

> "The number of children *already born* will dictate, between now and 1985, a 34% increase in the number of new households, a 25% rise in the labor force, and a 61% increase in consumers in the 25-34 age bracket. Unless we legislate that our children may not live as well as we, there is already in existence a wave of demand for electricity."

In Idaho, there are millions of acres of barren land that would be productive farm land if sufficient water were made available. This is eminently feasible with the use of electric pump irrigation. In 1949, 132,259 acres in Idaho were irrigated by 1,903 pumps. In 1975, 1.5 million acres were under irrigation watered by nearly 13,000 electric irrigation pumps. It is disgustingly ironic that some of the same groups which applaud this type of land reclamation at the same time roundly castigate Idaho Power for needing to generate more electricity.

Environmental groups for years have fought *Consolidated Edison's* plans to build nuclear power plants along the Hudson River. As a result, using other fuels, utility bills in New York have doubled and tripled. We are eagerly waiting to see which consumer protection group takes credit for this result.

Wendell J. Satre, President of the *Washington Water Power Company,* in a recent speech, pointed out that a decline in the U.S. gross national product always produces a decline in energy use. He believes that the reverse is also true. A decline in energy use means lower production and fewer jobs. We believe there is no doubt about the truth of this point.

The sign of maturity and wisdom is the capability of changing one's mind when necessary. We would like to refer you to the following statements by Robert Duncan, Congressman from Oregon, in a September, 1975 speech before the Portland, Oregon *Rotary Club,* concerning the construction of a proposed Hells Canyon hydro project:

> ". . . . I served on the Congressional Committee in 1962 and 1964 that produced the Wilderness bill at a time when few thought it possible."
>
> ". . . . Accordingly, I am thoroughly re-appraising my position on Hells Canyon. I still reserve the right to change my mind, but it seems to me at this point we should — at the very least — not lock up for all time the hydroelectric sites above the Salmon and Imnaha River. Two dams — Pleasant Valley and Mountain Sheep — would produce a block of power sufficient to satisfy the needs of a population approximately the size of Oregon's.
>
> "They are estimated to save 12 million barrels of oil or 4 million tons of coal annually. And hydro production is substantially less expensive than alternatives . . . The dams won't solve all of our problems — but because they won't do everything is no reason to do nothing."

Another frantic target of our protectors is strip mining of coal deposits. Unlike earlier mines in the East, new strip mines are now in barren, sparsely populated areas of the West. Any insurance or labor statistics will show that present underground coal mining is dirty, hazardous work. Conditions such as black lung disease, cave-ins, fires, and other disasters are commonplace. None of this is possible by strip mining. In protesting strip mining, how many miners' lives are environmentalists willing to lose?

Hysterical demonstrations concerning off shore oil wells have not lessened our consumption of oil. They have only succeeded in making us the hostage of foreign oil interests and forever increasing prices. In the hotly-disputed Santa Barbara Channel, geologists tell us that there has been a natural oil seepage occurring for hundreds of years. This far exceeds any amount spilled by oil companies.

A natural question: If this oil spillage is a concern, and natural seepage continues (as it does), why wouldn't it be sensible to pump the oil out as fast as possible?

Sadly amusing is the behavior of some Easterners. They fervently oppose the establishment of offshore drilling because the drilling rigs are not nice to look at. However, it is apparently all right for Gulf Coast residents to look at them, so long as they send the oil to New England. This borders on madness.

POWER PLANTS DRAW CRITICISM

Two Northwest power plants have drawn particular national attention and environmental criticism. These are the coal-fired *Jim Bridger* plant in Wyoming and the *Colstrip* plants in Montana. We wish to develop some facts with relation to these projects.

A unit burning 250 tons of 0.5% sulphur coal per hour may discharge two tons of sulphur compounds per hour. While this sounds like a large amount, it is mixed with 5 million pounds of air which is dispersed into trillions of tons of air over hundreds of square miles.

A 500 megawatt unit would heat a total of approximately 85,000 homes daily. If instead, these homes were heated by oil-fired home furnaces, the total sulphur fallout would be greater than from the coal plant.

Coal plants also discharge nitrogen oxide. The following facts are from a study prepared by the *Stanford Research Institute:*

Nitrogen is the most plentiful element in our atmosphere, 78% by volume. Only two compounds emitted by man are pollutants, nitrogen dioxide (NO^2) and nitrogen oxide (NO). Total emissions amount to 50 million tons annually.

On the other hand, nature itself produces these compounds: nitrogen dioxide (NO^2) — 500 million tons; ammonia (NH^3) — 5.9 billion tons; and nitrous oxide (N^2O) — one billion tons. Less than one per cent of all the nitrogen oxides are man made.

There has been some environmental concern expressed over the discharge of particulate matter by Jim Bridger. To obtain some perspective, consider a natural dust storm covering a 20-mile radius which picks up a 1/32" of dust. This one storm would put as much particulate matter into the air as 1500 of the Jim Bridger power units would discharge in a full year.

(Dr. Pratt's weekly syndicated newspaper column of September 7, 1974, reprinted on the following pages, gives additional environmental and other facts on Jim Bridger.)

COLSTRIP

The steady drumbeat of environmental critics extending even to nationwide television "specials" has singled out the Colstrip project as a "last stand" for concerned environmentalists. Just like General Custer, they couldn't have chosen a worse enemy. Because everything about the Colstrip project makes sense.

Our defense of the Colstrip project rests on two points: (1) Adequate land reclamation and (2) good economic sense.

The Rosebud mine at Colstrip was opened in 1924 by the *Northern Pacific Railway.* In 34 years of mining, 44 million tons of coal were produced. All of this mining disturbed approximately 1000 acres of land. This land is presently being reclaimed by *Burlington Northern,* successor to the *Northern Pacific.* The property was acquired by **Montana Power** in 1959, and, through its subsidiary, *Western Energy Company,* production was resumed in 1968.

Since that time Colstrip has been studied to the point of exhaustion. Since 1972, the *Montana State Agricultural Experiment Station* has conducted a major range resource study. *The Earth Sciences Department* is studying trace elements in the soil. *Environmental Consulting Services* is conducting a wildlife reconnaissance and vegetation survey. The *Montana Bureau of Mines* is making a three year hydrology survey. *Montana State University* is in the sixth year of land reclamation research. None of these studies suggest that the Colstrip project be terminated.

Western Energy Co., a subsidiary of Montana Power Co., plants trees and native grasses on land which was previously surface mined for coal at Colstrip, Montana. Moisture is retained in catchment basins contoured into back-filled material before topsoil is restored and land is reseeded.

To date, Western Energy has mined nearly 20 million tons of coal, disturbing about 500 acres of land, in total.

Concern is also expressed over the use of water in Colstrip power units. Units 1 and 2 will use about 2/10ths of one per cent of the average flow of the Yellowstone River. At the river's all-time historical low, usage would only amount to 1.5%. The water used daily is the same as needed for a sprinkler system on 1600 acres of land. The Colstrip plants will use only 3% as much water as is lost each year by evaporation from nearby Fort Peck Reservoir.

The economics of Colstrip are formidable. From a base population of 100 in 1968, the town of Colstrip will be home for 1700 by 1980. Some 550 new permanent jobs will be created with an annual payroll in excess of $5 million. Construction of Units 3 and 4 alone will provide 1800 jobs with a payroll of $93 million.

By 1980, the four Colstrip power units (at 1973 rates) will produce $9 million in annual state tax revenue. In addition, they will provide $11 million in Rosebud County property taxes.

NORTHWEST INVESTING:
By Shannon P. Pratt, C.F.A.

A VISIT TO JIM BRIDGER

Last week, squarely astraddle the Continental Divide at 7,000 feet elevation in Southwestern Wyoming, I toured one of the modern marvels of engineering accomplishment, the Jim Bridger electric generation plant. When its presently-planned four units are completed in 1978, it will be the largest electric generation facility in the Northwest, with a capacity of 2,000 megawatts.

Both the plant and the adjacent coal mine supplying its fuel are owned one-third by **Idaho Power Company** and two-thirds by **Pacific Power and Light,** who will operate the facility. The first of the planned four units recently started generating electricity on an experimental basis, and they now expect to be in commercial production about the first of November. All power from the first unit will go to Idaho Power. On completion of the second 500 megawatt unit about September of 1975, Idaho and PP & L will share the output equally; and after completion of the third unit about June of 1976, output will go two-thirds to Pacific Power and one-third to Idaho Power. The fourth unit is expected to be finished about June of 1978.

Power from the plant will also be interchanged with the five other companies in the Northwest Power Pool: **Portland General Electric, Puget Sound Power, Washington Water Power, Montana Power,** and **Utah Power.**

The plant is situated at it fuel source, the vast Bridger Coal Mine, which stretches 15 miles long and averages over a mile wide, covering a total area of about 25 square miles. The coal seam is anywhere from a few feet to 200 feet or more beneath the earth's surface, and the seam runs from about 12 to 30 feet thick. A drag line with a boom longer than a football field will remove the earth overburden with a 70 cubic yard scoop, and 16 cubic yard shovels will load the coal into 120 ton trucks to be hauled to the plant.

They are doing an outstanding job of environmental control, but at a substantial cost, which necessarily will become a part of the price of the electricity generated. The precipitators for the final removal of fly ash and other particulate matter from the air emissions are built of components imported from Sweden at a cost of $13 million per precipitator, or $52 million for the four units. The plant's four chimneys rise 500 feet into the desert air above the 14-story structure to diffuse their remaining emissions high into the atmosphere. Waste ash removed will be buried before the land is filled back in where the coal has been mined.

Two PH.D.'s and a team of graduate students from the University of Wyoming have been doing experimental plantings of grasses, trees and shrubs on the site for three years and will advise what will grow and how to do it as part of the land reclamation following strip mining of the coal. About 700 to 1,000 acres will be opened up at a time and fully reclaimed as the mining progresses.

Western Scientific Industries of Fort Collins built and operates a meteorological testing tower which has collected two and a half years of comprehensive data on the air quality, and will continue to collect such data throughout the plant's operations.

Total cost of the project will be over a half billion dollars even in terms of today's price levels. It is being financed in part from 'he two companies' internally generated earnings, plus some municipal pollution control bonds and large offerings of common and preferred stocks and mortgage bonds by Idaho Power and Pacific Power and Light over the next few years.

In money, in sheer size, in engineering complexity, and in contribution of the plant's large output to the region's productive capacity and quality of life, the enormity of the whole thing is hard to grasp and fully appreciate. The region is benefitted immensely by the availability of the vast low-sulphur coal supply making it possible, and by the companies' far-sighted planning, resulting in bringing it into useful production at this time of great need.

From the viewpoint of both the customer and the stockholder, the hugh low-sulphur coal reserves and related electric generating facilities to supplement the companies' hydroelectric power bases place these utilities in a much stronger energy supply position than their counterparts in other parts of the country. Pacific Power stock pays a $1.60 dividend and sold last week at 16 to yield exactly 10 per cent. Idaho Power pays $1.96 and sold recently at 23 to yield 8.5 per cent. The Wyoming Public Service Commission recently approved an Idaho Power $50 million first mortgage bond issue as part of the financing for the Jim Bridger project. The stock and bond issues of both Idaho Power and Pacific Power and Light are listed on the New York Stock Exchange.

This column reproduced from the September 7, 1974 Boise, Idaho *Journal of Commerce.* As this book goes to press, Dr. Pratt's weekly column on "Northwest Investing" appears in the Portland *Oregonian,* the Spokane *Spokesman-Review,* the Boise *Journal of Commerce* and the Seattle *Argus.*

Strip-Mining

I HAPPEN to be one of the many ranchers who believe we can live with controlled strip mining of coal and run cattle at the same time. To Fortify this belief here are a few facts.

The average native range land in southeastern Montana requires 3 acres to run one cow one month. So it takes 36 acres to run one cow one year. An acre foot of coal weighs 1750 tons. A 20-foot seam of coal under one acre weighs 35,000 tons. The 36 acres to run a cow will produce 1,260,000 tons of coal.

At twenty cents a ton royalty, this area, large enough to run one cow, will produce $252,000 to the owner. In addition, the resource now supporting this one cow will benefit the taxpayers of Rosebud County by over $100,000 and the state of Montana by $428,400.

If I decided to sacrifice this one cow, that quarter of a million dollars will go a long way toward making a better home for the rest of my cows.

But I do not have to sacrifice that cow. I can turn her on another 36 acres, reseed it, fertilize it and irrigate it and that cow will have company.

Most ranches are familiar with the old saying "no use to learn anymore about ranching because I don't ranch as well now as I know how." This situation is brought on by money — the lack of it. The history of the cow business is that cows alone, have not generated enough money to do the job of ranching that most ranchers know how to do and would like to do.

This quarter of a million dollars would go a long way toward furnishing better bulls, fertilizing, weed control, levelling, irrigating, better corrals, better fencing and many other things a rancher always needs but has not been able to afford. Beside all of these essentials, it would improve the environment.

I think the efforts of the reasonable environmentalists have been good. I am convinced that these efforts will result in well controlled coal mining operations. I think the environment is as important to me as it is to anyone. My father picked this site in 1882 and I have lived here 71 years. He had traveled from Boston to Nevada, to California to Montana in the years just previous to 1882 so he had quite a choice of environment. He liked it then, I like it now.

I graduated from college with a degree in Geology and wrote my graduation paper on coal because I knew then, in 1928, that we had coal at Birney.

I will be surprised if 10 per cent of our land is mined; that will still leave 90 per cent for the cattle. With the money generated from this 10 per cent for the mined land, I am sure my grandchildren can make a better ranch of this than I have known, and if they did no more than control the noxious weeds along our portion of the Tongue River Valley they would be contributing a major effort toward the environment — especially the environment for a cow. I think it is the environment for a cow that most of us are concerned about, not the environment for hobby ranchers.

Reproduced from Montana
Farmer-Stockman Feb. 2, 1974

—*Burton B. Brewster*
Quarter Circle U Ranch Co., Birney

"The Prophets of Shortage"

The following section is condensed from a speech by Donald P. Hodel, Administrator of the Bonneville Power Administration, before the Portland, Oregon City Club on July 11, 1975.

As a regional energy manager and a lifelong Oregonian, I've become deeply concerned about the future of the environmental movement. What began as a responsible, needed guardian of our natural resources has become something quite different. It is no longer just a conservation movement, but a crusade to stop all development in this country. As such, this new environmental movement is on a collision course with the growing demand for energy, and there's no doubt in my mind as to which will win. The people of this country will not give up their standard of living because someone tells them that the Spartan life is the good life. They will not forego their own aspirations to pay for someone else's nostalgic quest for Walden Pond.

Unless the responsible majority of environmentalists regain control of what used to be their movement, their cause is going to be set back 20 years. When we really feel the energy squeeze — and I think it's almost inevitable — John Q. Public is going to demand somebody's scalp. And the environmental movement will be in for a massive backlash.

The greatest threat to the environmental movement is the environmental movement itself. Over the past several years, it has fallen into the hands of a small, arrogant faction which is dedicated to bringing our society to a halt. I call this faction the Prophets of Shortage. They are the anti-producers, the anti-achievers. The doctrine they preach is that of scarcity and self-denial.

With this as their cause, the prophets of shortage see the energy industry as their prime target. It is our society's Achilles' heel. So while opposing seemingly all progress, these extremists reserve their best efforts for those projects which produce energy. Oil fields, coal mines, refineries, and electric powerplants are their favorite targets. And the closer we come to a real energy crisis, the more pressure they exert to block any and all expansion that could relieve the shortage.

What I am seeking to encourage is a balance. We must avoid **both** excesses — unrestrained development and irresponsible environmentalism.

In the Pacific Northwest we are heavily dependent upon electric energy. We consume about twice as much electricity per capita as does the rest of the nation, at rates about half the national average. More of us heat our homes, more of us depend for our jobs upon electricity than perhaps anywhere else in the world. Consequently, the electric utility industry in this region has drawn the special wrath of the prophets of shortage. By halting the needed expansion of our power supply system, they can bring this region to its knees. I can tell you that they're well on the road to accomplishing that goal.

For nearly a decade now those of us in the business have been predicting an end to the era of cheap, plentiful power — an era which began with the construction of Grand Coulee and Bonneville Dams in the 1930's. It was succeeded by an innovative concept hammered out by the region's utilities and the Federal Government in the late 1960's — the Hydro-Thermal Power Program. The purpose of this original program and of its Phase 2 planning has been to provide the Pacific Northwest with an adequate power supply through at least the mid-1980's — on the most economic basis and with minimum adverse impact upon the environment.

POWER PROGRAM PLAGUED WITH DELAYS

From its outset, the Hydro-Thermal Power Program has been plagued by delays, drastic lengthening of construction leadtimes, and mind-boggling cost escalations. In all fairness, I cannot attribute all of these to environmental pressures. Erratic federal funding, labor disputes and shortages, technical problems — all conspired to upset schedules and impede new generation from coming on line. As a result, this region is now confronted with the prospect of appalling energy deficits over the next decade. For at least 4 of these years, we are forecasting deficits of 2 million kilowatts or more. That's roughly the output of four Bonneville Dams. And since these forecasts were published only a few months ago, environment-related delays have further worsened the situation.

There is no conceivable way in which these deficits can be materially reduced unless we are blessed with a combination of good water conditions and mild winters. It is probable that mandatory curtailments will be required to meet these deficits. Either homes will be cold and dark or factories will close or both because the deficits are no longer manageable.

Powerplants now under construction and on the drawing board cannot be speeded up. To the contrary, experience proves the opposite to be the case. Almost without exception, large nuclear and coal-fired powerplants experience slippages of from several months to a couple of years or more.

The basis for this dire outlook are the regional load forecasts compiled by BPA and the various utilities. Despite their remarkable accuracy over the years, these forecasts are highly suspect in environmental quarters. We are frequently accused of overstating our loads so that we may overbuild and thus make the forecasts "self-fulfilling." I can only say that load forecasts do not create loads any more than tide tables create tides.

In fact there is every reason to believe that not only will there be continued load growth in the future, but I believe the forecasts are decidedly too conservative.

In the Pacific Northwest historically our experience has been essentially the same as for the Nation as a whole. **Total** power requirements have increased more than four times from 1950 to today. The residential load alone is greater than the **total** load in 1950. By 1990 — just 15 years from now — loads will increase nearly three times to about 250 billion kilowatt-hours a year.

It is apparent that loads increase with population, and while this is true, it does **not** tell the whole story. Zero population growth, which has not yet been achieved, does not mean zero energy growth. The age composition of the population will have a dramatic influence on load growth. For example, if we build a population pyramid which shows the 1975 Pacific Northwest population by age groups, the bottom of the pyramid will represent those between 0 and 19 years of age. These persons will be in their prime working years by 1995.

The difference between this number and those now working but who will retire by 1995 is about 1 million. We must provide jobs for more than 800,000 of these young people — **the children who are already here**. It is going to take a lot of kilowatts to provide those jobs.

According to the latest regional utility report, in the next 20 years the firm energy requirements of the Pacific Northwest will more than double — from about 15 million to about 35 million kilowatts. More than 90 percent of this added energy must come from thermal generation.

In an attempt to meet the minimum needs of the region, the public and private utilities and BPA are embarking upon Phase 2 of the Hydro-Thermal Power Program. The utilities propose to construct 13 large coal-fired and nuclear plants over the next 10 years, with a total capacity of about 14,000 megawatts — half again our present capacity. The total cost will exceed $10 **billion.**

I might add that only one of these proposed projects stands a prayer of being completed on schedule. And all of them may go out the window or be held up for years by the barrage of litigation being leveled against them by environmental groups.

ENVIRONMENTAL CONCERNS WARPED

It is the prophets of shortage who are dragging our regional energy system to the brink of disaster. The very real concerns which gave birth to the environmental movement have been warped beyond all recognition by the proponents of the no-growth philosophy. Instead of preserving clean water and clean air, they want to turn back the clock on our society.

I believe that the vast majority of our citizens have a balanced concern about jobs, economic stability and a healthy environment. As such, they should be aware of the utter unwillingness of the prophets of shortage to accept any responsibility for the chaos which could result from their actions. Nor does the environmental extremist have any constructive alternative to offer in place of those energy projects he opposes. He has no program or plan into which he can fit the product of his efforts. He is essentially a negativist — a spoiler rather than the defender he purports to be.

A second trait of the prophet of shortage is his inconsistency. Like Emerson, he evidently feels that "Consistency is the hobgoblin of little minds." A prime example of this was made evident recently by a lawsuit filed here in Oregon. People in my business frequently ask our protagonists for their proposed alternatives to using coal and nuclear material to produce power.

The customary response is that society should, in effect, stop all forward motion until we can develop such clean, nonpolluting resources as geothermal or solar energy. It was therefore ironically amusing to have the *Sierra Club* and a local organization called *The High Desert Study Group* file suit a few weeks ago against the Bureau of Land Management. The purpose of the suit is to halt the issuance of geothermal exploration leases in southeastern Oregon.

This lawsuit against BLM is a favorite tactic of the anti-producers, in that it demands the BLM prepare an environmental impact statement on the grounds that such is required under the National Environmental Policy Act of 1969. This Act in effect requires federal agencies to prepare such a statement prior to taking "a major federal action which will have significant impact on the quality of the human environment." To show the absurd lengths to which environmental attorneys will go in imposing this burdensome requirement upon a federal agency, the complaint against BLM cites a prior law suit as precedent for requiring an EIS.

In a 1971 case in South Dakota against the Department of Transportation, the court held that "the mere existence of a lawsuit is evidence of sufficient controversy as would call for the preparation of an EIS." In other words, regardless of its lack of merit, a lawsuit filed by any individual may force a federal agency to entangle itself in the EIS process.

Before departing from the subject of EIS's, I should note that Bonneville Power Administration last year spent more than $1 million in the preparation of such statements. But this is small potatoes compared to the sums expended by the Washington Public Power Supply System, the sponsor of five nuclear plants now under construction. They report spending well over a million dollars **per plant** on EIS's.

These costs of course must be tacked onto the total project cost, and the ratepayers of the region end up paying them. But the sums I have just mentioned are a drop in the bucket compared to the total price we pay for environmental obstructionism. For example, an optimum-sized nuclear plant now on the drawing board will cost at least $1 billion when it is completed 10 or 12 years hence. Without the additional environmental red tape, litigation, and extended technical clearance time we encounter here, a similar project in Japan can be built in about 6 years. Of the $1 billion we end up paying, about $300 million in additional building costs and carrying charges are directly attributable to these causes.

You and I as ratepayers — and taxpayers — bear the brunt of this obstructionism in more ways than one. The elaborate government environmental bureaucracy which has sprung up takes millions of our tax dollars. To a lesser extent, so do the federal courts where our environmental battles are joined.

And the anti-producers themselves get us coming and going. A substantial portion of their activities are subsidized at the taxpayer's expense. The tax-free environmental organizations receive grants from tax-free foundations. Federal funding also finds its way to the environmental groups. In essence, you and I are paying the bill for hamstringing our economy.

The Magna Carta of the environmental movement was the National Environmental Policy Act, which was signed into law on January 1, 1970. I have no quarrel with that Act or what I believe to be its intent. We have a right to demand both a clean environment **and** economic opportunity. I do have a quarrel with those who, ever since its enactment, have used NEPA to obstruct the orderly progress of obtaining the power supply this region must have if we are to continue to provide for a reasonable lifestyle for ourselves, our children, and the generations to come.

NEED TO MAKE VOICES HEARD

What you and I have to do in the Pacific Northwest is raise the hue and cry among the producers of our society to let them know what is happening.

The anti-producers who are abusing the National Environmental Policy Act by using it as a sword have an avowed purpose — to stop growth in our society. They say "Write an environmental impact statement or we'll take you to court." If we write the Environmental Impact Statement, they then claim it is inadequate and take us to court anyway. If they lose, they appeal. In the meantime, development based on planned growth is delayed, and thereby the full benefit of the planning is lost.

How can our society continue to support, by its silence, the philosophy that we don't need more energy?

How can these people — knowing very well that unemployment in the nation has now passed the 9 percent level — continue to ignore the proven fact that energy means jobs?

How far do they want the nation to regress in pursuit of their society where those who have, keep, and those who are coming along, don't get?

Would they want us to regress to the 19th Century — when the skies of our industrial cities were gray with the smoke of soft coal and soot stuck to the clothes of people walking down the streets?

Or maybe they prefer the Colonial days when they had water power and wind power and animal power and muscle power, and 93 percent of America's population was engaged in farming to support the other 7 percent and to feed the animal power?

Those who are pushing us in this direction should be responsible for assessing the consequences of their actions. Perhaps they should be required to file an **Economic** Impact Statement each time before throwing a roadblock in society's path.

I subscribe wholeheartedly to what Congressman Mike McCormack told the Western Resources Congress at Wenatchee last April:

> "We obviously can and must eliminate wasteful practices in energy consumption. However, there is a point beyond which further reduction will seriously impact the job market. Quite frankly, I am concerned about the stability of our society if energy supplies drop too quickly and too far below normal demand. Energy waste can and must be eliminated, but one man's conservation is all too frequently another man's unemployment.

> "This is one reason why the activities of Ralph Nader and his busy but essentially ignorant supporters present a more serious threat to our society than they do when working for ignition interlocks on seat belts. This nation is truly in mortal danger. Our standard of living, our economic stability, our political institutions, and even the safety of our streets may well hang on whether or not we are able to produce enough energy to maintain the job market and an opportunity for low income Americans and members of minority groups to aspire to and work for a decent standard of living.

> "The new McCarthyism that is becoming a fad in part of our population that is impressionable, sensation-seeking, and uninformed constitutes a real threat. It is directed towards large corporations and utilities, but it focuses most directly on nuclear energy, skipping from one lie or gross exaggeration to the next, living, as Eric Hoffer said of the true fanatic, with no concern whatsoever for fact, and apparently enjoying the ego trip of delaying industrial development and installation of energy systems."

I don't want the kind of nation the doctrine of scarcity would lead to. I can't believe you want it. And I honestly can't believe the prophets of shortage really want it.

What must be established is a mechanism for balancing energy needs and environmental concerns. I do not have a set of pat solutions, but we might consider the following: (1) a legal or regulatory point of final decision where a project is either approved or disapproved, and no further complaints are permitted, (2) an obligation on the part of a plaintiff who abuses the NEPA process to pay the damages caused by his actions, and (3) a statute of limitations on lawsuits which challenge the adequacy of Environmental Impact Statements.

In closing, let me urge you to take up this dialogue. If you belong to an environmental organization, scrutinize its policies and how your dues are being spent. If you have friends who are members, ask them if they know what is being done in their names. Urge them to bend their best efforts to getting their club or association back on its original, constructive course.

Talk to your business colleagues, talk to our State and local office holders. Write to your Congressmen. Tell them these delays are costing jobs now and for the future. Tell them we're jeopardizing our economy and our way of life.

Tell them before the decisions are made by default.

Utilizing Our Forest Resources

"The remainder of the 1970's is a crucial time for action to insure future timber supply. . . . For the truly long run, 2020 and beyond, it is timber growth which is all important; and available timber volume in those decades depends upon measures to increase growth taken in the 1970's and 1980's . . . The panel's considered judgment is that growth on all forests of the nation considered as a whole, might well be doubled by 2020. . ."

> *Report of the President's Advisory Panel*
> *on Timber and the Environment,*
> *September 24, 1973.*

The forest products industry, including pulp, paper, and furniture manufacturing, employs a total of 1.5 million persons. The industry provides an annual payroll estimated at $8.3 billion. Forest products ranks as the fifth largest manufacturing industry.

One would think that such an industry does not need public defenders. But they do, badly.

Although a minority, it seems that hordes of environmentalists, conservationists, students, and others have no other mission in life save to harass the industry.

". . . , the fundamental idea of forestry is in the perpetuation of the forests by use. Forest protection is not an end in itself; it is a means to increase and sustain the resources of the country and the industries which depend on them."

> *President Theodore Roosevelt,*
> *announcing a program that set aside*
> *132 million acres of public lands as*
> *forest reserves, 1901.*

Unfortunately, the ardent wave of environmentalism and the proven ineptitude of our government agencies are wasting these vital national assets.

Worldwide demand for wood products is expected to double in the next 25 years. In that period, the United States alone will require 60 to 75 million new living units to be built and more than two billion tons of paper will be produced. We are concerned that our nation's supply of softwood (the most useful type) will be inadequate.

At present there are about 200 million acres of commercial softwood timberland in the United States. The largest single landholder is the federal government, with 52% of the total softwood inventory. Other public agencies own 12%, private individuals own 20%, and commercial forest product companies own 16%.

The failure of these timberlands to achieve their full potential comes from the fact that only some of this acreage is being properly managed. For example, between 1950 and 1972, forest product companies and some private landowners grew nearly three times as much softwood timber per acre on their lands as did the federal government.

One of the primary reasons for this ineptitude is that Congress fails to provide the Forest Service with sufficient funds to manage its lands properly.

The Forest Service estimates that, under intensive management, the commercial softwood timberlands within the National Forest System could annually yield over 20 billion board feet perpetually with no adverse impact upon the environment. However, the actual annual harvest has averaged less than 11 billion board feet during the last ten years.

Mature trees are allowed to die and rot. Further, much timberland that has been burned or harvested has not been properly restored.

Environmentalists have fought successfully to delay or deny timber cutting rights on public lands. In the deep South, non-commercial timberlands are growing timber at about 50% of the rate of their true potential.

TIMBER CLEARCUTTING

No single term is more of a rallying cry to ardent environmentalists than the word "clearcutting." The word is now a kind of verbal shorthand denoting every kind of evil man can allegedly perpetrate against nature. We will wager that many who decry clearcutting cannot adequately describe the process they so vehemently oppose. We have sought out the following statement which we believe to be a reasoned, impartial description of the subject:

> "Clearcutting is used where it is desirable to reforest an area with trees of a species which grows best under conditions of exposure to full sunlight. This develops an even-aged stand which grows rapidly and is easy to operate and administer. And clearcutting is more than just a method for harvesting a mature stand; it may be used, for example to convert a tract of undesirable vegetation to forest. Clearcutting may be used on tracts logged or burned long ago and since regrown to brush or a species of less than optimum value. On such areas, it serves to salvage what useful material exists and to destroy the rest so that the site may be prepared for regeneration of desirable tree species. It is an appropriate method and sometimes the only method of salvaging timber after fires and for controlling insect and disease epidemics."
>
> James S. Bethel, Dean, College of Forest Resources, University of Washington, as quoted in the book "Clearcutting: A View from the Top"

We feel that the subject would become less emotional if the public would use a different term, "Clearharvest," which we have just coined.

Consider an open field of golden grain, waving gently in a breeze. What could be more attractive? Or a field of ripe corn, tomatoes, or whatever.

We are not aware that anyone is emotionally disturbed at the prospect of clearharvesting these crops. Indeed, the notion of "selectively harvesting" these crops is a strange one. Equally absurd is the thought of leaving valuable, needed crops to rot.

If one accepts the thought that timber is a harvestable crop, then the analogy is abundantly clear.

We maintain, and knowledgable industry sources agree, that timberlands can be clearharvested on a planned, manageable basis. The hangup, for many people, is that the harvest season instead of being six months or one year, lasts for decades. This is understandably hard for an individual to relate to.

ABOVE: In 1956 when Georgia-Pacific Corp. bought this Oregon timberland it looked like this, the desolate victim of lightning fires and old-time logging, now outmoded. BELOW: View from the same point, only 16 years of regrowth later, shows beautiful fir forest with trees large enough for the first thinning and younger trees still coming in.

IMPROVEMENT NEEDED IN FEDERAL FOREST MANAGEMENT

"We again must comment on the management of our National Forests. These forests contain over half the softwood timber used in new home construction. They also have an excessive inventory of older trees which are slowly dying from the ravages of insects and disease. The growth rate of a tree diminishes as it gets older and only the young trees can provide real new growth. Like any other asset that is obsolete and not needed, it should be disposed of. The excessive amount of over mature timber should be harvested in the next 25 years. This will help meet the peak demand we expect for housing during this period. If the government agencies do not change their present policy it will require a century or more to remove this over mature timber, thus delaying intensified forest practices which are essential to proper timber management. This tremendous waste of our wonderful natural resource does not make economic, political, or common sense."

> Howell H. Howard
> President and Chief Executive Officer
> Edward Hines Lumber Co.
> (1974 annual report)

It used to be common knowledge that the growing cycle for Douglas fir trees in the Northwest spanned 80 years. Through modern forestry management, 30 to 40 year growing cycles are now common in the Northwest. In more rapidly growing Southern pine timberlands, 20 to 30 year growing cycles are becoming a possibility.

The next time someone decries "clearcutting", we would suggest "clearharvesting" as a more desirable basis for discussion.

Concerning clear-cutting, naturalist Euell Gibbons has said:

"We came to a tract (in Pennsylvania) that was clear-cut about five years ago, and found second growth already 10 to 15 feet high. I cannot share the anger felt by many ecologists at clear-cutting. Nature never attains a static balance but moves in cycles, and nature always arranged for temporarily clearing areas, through lightning-set fires and storms.

Many species of plants and animals have adapted to these recovering areas and cannot survive without them. The cover furnished by the discarded tree tops and the rejected hollow logs, plus the tremendously increased amount of berries and other growth that springs up due to the newfound sunlight, and the sudden multiplication of the amount of browse available as the swift second growth starts, all tend to vastly increase the wildlife carrying capacity of such areas."

When Columbus first landed in America, there were approximately one billion acres of timber present. Today, almost five centuries later, three-fourths or 750 million acres are still here. Over 250 million of these acres are set aside as parks, monuments, and for public use. And still there is a constant hue and cry to set aside still more productive land. As has been pointed out by Robert B. Pamplin, Chairman of *Georgia-Pacific Corporation*, this 250 million acres is a larger area than all of Norway, Sweden, Denmark, Austria, Switzerland, Holland, Belgium, and Israel combined. How much is enough?

Part II

The Industries

and the Companies

An Oregon Douglas fir being felled.

A slip feeder pulls a log along to the bull chain that feeds logs into the sawmill.

A head sawyer saws each log into huge rough slices that are transported through the mill for further cutting and shaping.

Automatically charged lathe at modernized plywood plant swiftly peels hot Douglas fir peeler block into veneer.

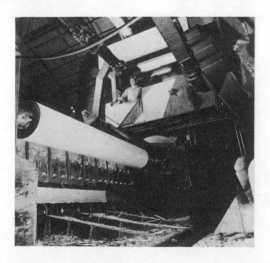

8

Forest Products

The Northwest clearly stands out as the nation's primary supplier of forest products. The region produces about 15 billion board feet of lumber annually, or about 40% of the country's total lumber production, and over 60% of the plywood produced domestically. This production comes from commercial timberlands representing only 15% of total commercial timberlands in the U.S.

The four states of Oregon, Washington, Idaho, and Montana contain more than 75 million acres of commercial timberland. Of this amount 58.4% is held by the federal government, 6.2% by other governments, and 35.4% is under private ownership. Thus, many public investor-owned forest products companies in the Northwest are partially or totally dependent upon cutting rights granted by governmental agencies in order to produce their goods.

The most abundant species of Northwest timber is Douglas fir, with ponderosa pine prevalent in eastern Oregon and Washington, and white fir, white pine, lodgepole pine, hemlock, redwood, alder, and cedar among the other species harvested.

Wood products industry employment in the Northwest normally runs close to 150,000, or about 6% of total employment in the region, and the pulp and paper industry employs approximately 27,000 to 29,000.

The pulp and paper industry has become a substantially larger part of the Northwest forest products industry in the last two decades with paper and paperboard production quadrupling in that period. This growth is destined to continue, as shown by the estimates of capital expenditures for expansion in the 1974-76 period in the accompanying table.

14 INVESTOR-OWNED COMPANIES DISCUSSED

We have identified 14 publicly held forest products companies which are headquartered or prominent in the Northwest. Prior to our discussion of individual companies, we can make some general observations about the entire group.

The ownership of private timberlands varies from company to company. While four of these companies own acreage running into the

NORTHWEST COMMERCIAL TIMBERLAND

Production

	Comm. timber- land thous. acres	Total saw timber volume (thous. ft.)	1974 produc- tion (thous ft.)	1974 est. wholesale volume
Oregon	25,673	457,735,000	7,007,000	$1,210,600,000
Washington	18,401	325,123,000	3,222,000	521,900,000
Idaho	15,192	131,666,000	1,626,000	277,700,000
Montana	15,983	102,018,000	1,165,000	179,600,000
Total	75,249	1,016,542,000	13,020,000	$2,189,800,000

Ownership

	Total comm. forest- land (thous. acres)	Federal owner ship (thous. acres)	% of Total	Other govt. owner- ship (thous. acres)	% of Total	Private owner- ship (thous. acres)	% of Total
Oregon	25,673	14,582	56.8	980	3.7	10,140	39.5
Washington	18,401	7,232	39.3	2,282	12.4	8,888	48.3
Idaho	15,192	11,288	74.3	881	5.8	3,023	19.9
Montana	15,983	10,884	68.1	527	3.3	4,571	28.6
Total	75,249	43,986	58.4	4,640	6.2	26,622	35.4
United States	499,697	107,108	21.4	29,010	5.8	363,576	72.8

[1]As of Jan. 1, 1970

Source: Western Wood Products Association 1974 Statistical Yearbook.

millions, others own practically none. In addition to fee ownership, most of the companies have long-term contractual cutting rights on lands owned by others. In addition to their Northwest holdings, many companies also harvest timber from lands in the southern United States.

The industry has succeeded in diversifying to a great extent in the past decade or so. Companies have added paper and paper products,

PULP AND PAPER CAPITAL EXPENDITURES, 1974-76
(in Thousands of Dollars)

	Production	Environmental			Total
		Water	Air	Total	
Western Idaho	$ 18,380	$ 11,108	$	$ 11,108	$ 29,488
Western Montana	82,060		11,000	11,000	93,060
Oregon	62,087	20,300	9,290	29,590	91,677
Washington	132,202	163,510	28,450	191,960	324,162
Pacific Northwest	$294,729	$194,918	$48,740	$243,658	$538,387

Source: Pulp and Paper, Jan. 1975.

Note: Large expenditures by *Boise Cascade* at St. Helens and Wallula, as well as smaller amounts elsewhere, were not reported, and are not included above.

SUMMARY OF MAJOR NORTHWEST
FOREST PRODUCTS COMPANIES
Ranking in Size by Total Assets

	(1974) Total Assets (000)	Total Revenue (000)	Net Income (000)	Acres Owned (000)
Weyerhaeuser Co.	$2,878,510	$2,529,013	$276,197	5,700
Georgia-Pacific	2,230,670	2,432,350	164,350	4,500
Boise Cascade	1,575,697	1,453,550	104,970	2,200
Crown Zellerbach	1,526,875	1,766,190	124,791	1,900
Louisiana-Pacific Corp.	560,430	460,100	56,600	626
Potlatch Corp.	433,351	487,868	45,289	1,300
Willamette Industries	362,090	388,712	37,516	400
Longview Fibre Company	170,423	199,203	24,315	373
Bohemia	91,963	93,810	7,375	25
Edward Hines Lumber Co.	77,397	169,861	2,781	insignif.
Pope & Talbot, Inc.	73,630	88,415	7,612	125
Brooks-Scanlon	47,528	42,186	4,438	218
Dant & Russell	42,753	89,413	2,286	insignif.
Medford Corp.	41,473	55,904	1,506	87

Return on Average Equity

	1974	1973	1972	1971	1970	5-Year Ave.
Weyerhaeuser Co.	19.2	28.7	15.0	11.3	13.7	17.6
Georgia-Pacific	19.7	22.8	16.1	11.9	14.6	17.0
Boise Cascade	13.4	13.4	3.5	(4.4)	3.9	6.0
Crown Zellerbach	18.1	17.4	8.1	5.8	7.7	11.4
Louisiana-Pacific Corp.	23.7	36.3	20.6	14.8	5.9	20.3*
Potlatch Corp.	18.4	15.8	8.3	5.4	1.2	9.8
Willamette Industries	21.4	22.7	17.2	11.3	10.5	16.6
Longview Fibre Company	19.3	23.4	12.8	7.3	11.3	14.8
Bohemia	14.1	35.9	26.4	17.8	19.7	22.8
Edward Hines Lumber Co.	4.3	22.2	9.3	8.0	(2.5)	8.3
Pope & Talbot, Inc.	14.2	37.5	20.7	13.9	7.4	18.6
Brooks-Scanlon	12.1	15.3	12.9	10.0	7.7	11.6
Dant & Russell	20.1	40.7	12.5	5.3	(2.5)	15.2
Medford Corp	6.3	28.7	16.1	7.5	4.7	12.7

*Reflects 1970-1972 operations as part of Georgia-Pacific.

pulp, plywood, furniture, chemicals, and other products to their dimension lumber operations. While the pattern of rising and falling housing starts clearly affects the industry, it does so to a lesser extent than in prior years. While 1975 has been a dismal year for the construction industry, most forest products companies will show a profit for the year (although down from 1974), which was not necessarily the case in former construction slumps.

Socially, the industry is the target of continuing abuse from environmental and conservation groups. These protestors give little recognition to changes already made by the industry. For example, the use of once-familiar wigwam-type sawmill waste burners, belching smoke and dust, has been eliminated.

Former waste materials such as bark, shavings, wood chips, and sawdust are now utilized in many productive ways. These include the production of particleboard, fiberboard, paper, and other uses. What cannot be used is consumed as fuel in the plants. Whole paper mills have been designed to utilize recycled waste material as their only source of raw material.

Finally, through great research efforts, the industry has developed new, hardy varieties of seedlings which have a greater survival rate and grow better and faster than wild varieties, increasing the already high productivity of the companies' forests.

The investor-owned forest products industry provides much-needed products and employment for hundreds of thousands of workers, and is years ahead of government-owned forest agencies in ecologically sound sustained yield forest management.

In discussing any aspect of forest products, one must begin with the plain fact that the **Weyerhaeuser Company** is the largest publicly owned forest products company in the world, with revenue in 1974 of $2.5 billion.

Weyerhaeuser is one of the largest in every aspect of forest products. It produces wood products (logs, chips, timber, lumber, softwood and hardwood plywood, veneer and doors, particleboard, and hardboard). The company produces all manner of wood fiber products: pulp, paper, paperboard, shipping containers, and cartons.

The varying proportion of wood products and wood fiber products is shown in the following table:

	Wood Products		Wood Fiber Products		Total
1974:					
Sales	$1,264	50%	$1,265	50%	$2,529
Approximate contribution to earnings	294	49	308	51	602
1973:					
Sales	1,432	62	870	38	2,302
Approximate contribution to earnings ..	535	83	111	17	646
1972:					
Sales	1,014	61	662	39	1,676
Approximate contribution to earnings ..	291	92	27	8	318
1971:					
Sales	805	62	495	38	1,300
Approximate contribution to earnings	202	89	25	11	227
1970:					
Sales	688	56	545	44	1,233
Approximate contribution to earnings	159	72	62	28	221

"Approximate contribution to earnings" is defined to be that amount of earings generated before (i) general, administrative and other corporate expenses, (ii) interest expense and (iii) income taxes. Excluded are earnings of the Company's unconsolidated real estate and finance subsidiaries accounted for on the equity method and other unallocable income such as dividends, interest and royalties.

The company was founded in Tacoma, Washington in 1900. The company's original purpose was the purchase of 900,000 acres of timberland in Western Washington from the *Northern Pacific Railway.*

Today Weyerhaeuser owns the largest timber inventory in the world. This includes outright fee ownership of 2.8 million acres in the Pacific Northwest and 2.9 million acres in the South.

In addition, the company has selective harvesting rights on 7.7 million acres in British Columbia, 0.9 million acres in Eastern Canada, and 1.9 million acres in the Far East. The company cuts over 100% of its requirements from its own lands.

The company's domestic timber reserves are estimated at 13 billion cubic feet. (Cubic measurement recognizes the solid wood fiber content of a log.)

Weyerhaeuser has expanded worldwide and has twenty foreign subsidiaries and affiliates. In recent years, about one-third of the company's sales have been to customers outside of the United States.

The only way to adequately catalog Weyerhaeuser's many plants and products is in tabular form. The accompanying tables, supplied by the company, were accurate as of year-end 1974.

Geographic Dispersion of Operations (Includes Facilities Under Construction)

	United States Eastern	United States Central	Western	Canada	Caribbean	Far East-Oceania	Europe-Africa	Total
Major woods operating units	3	8	17	6		5		39
Market pulp mills	1		6	1				8
Paper mills	3	1	1					5
Paperboard mills	2	3	3		1		3	12
Shipping container plants	9	13	7		2		12	43
Carton plants	2	1	2		1		1	7
Lumber mills	3	6	15	6		1		31
Plywood, veneer and door plants	5	7	7	2		1		22
Particleboard plants	2	2	3					7
Hardboard plants		1	1					2
Gypsum wallboard		1						1
Customer service and distribution centers (building materials)	23	26	15			1		65
Sales offices	20	18	16	1		8	10	73

Annual Production (Domestic and Foreign)

Product	Basis	1974 Capacity Additions*	1974	1973	1972	1971	1970
Logs	Hundred thousand cubic feet		8,527	9,087	8,935	8,034	7,743
Market pulp	Thousand air-dry tons		1,220	1,170	938	687	871
Paper	Thousand tons		467	365	262	236	262
Paperboard	Thousand tons		1,814	1,827	1,650	1,066	1,172
Shipping containers	Thousand tons	100	987	1,037	894	807	782
Cartons	Thousand tons		157	174	175	170	167
Lumber	Million board feet	297	2,308	2,405	2,392	2,199	1,938
Plywood	Million square feet (⅜")		1,053	1,293	1,348	1,108	975
Particleboard	Million square feet (¾")	73	350	390	322	187	153
Hardboard	Million square feet (⅛")		226	222	191	188	167
Gypsum wallboard	Million square feet (½")		371	376	376	314	255

*Does not include construction in progress at year-end.

As of year-end 1974, the company's stated total assets were $2.8 billion. Since this includes the book value of timberlands acquired fifty to seventy-five years ago, one can only wonder at the current value of these millions of acres.

Second in size behind Weyerhaeuser is **Georgia-Pacific Corporation.** 1974's sales were $2.4 billion on a base of total assets equal to $2.2 billion.

G-P's operations at 1974 year-end encompass the following:

Sales Offices	134
Distribution Centers	140
Plants	196
Employees	34,275

Incorporated in Georgia in 1927, the company's general offices are now in Portland, Oregon. Starting with timber reserves of about one million acres in 1960, Georgia-Pacific's holdings have increased substantially. The company now owns timberlands, in fee, amounting to approximately 4.5 million acres. In addition, the company has exclusive cutting rights on another 1.5 million acres. These timberlands are dispersed throughout the United States (Pacific Northwest and the Southeast), Canada, Brazil, and Indonesia.

Although it does not need to do so, Georgia-Pacific currently obtains 45 to 50 per cent of its log requirements from governmental and open market purchases. Management estimates that the timber growth on its domestic lands is increasing by about 1.5 billion board feet annually. This is more than the company harvests each year for use in its plants and mills.

MINERAL RESERVES HELD BY G-P

As a result of its extensive land holdings, Georgia-Pacific controls substantial amounts of other raw materials and mineral rights.

In a variety of domestic locations plus Nova Scotia, G-P owns reserves of gypsum rock amounting to 160 million tons. These are used to supply G-P's nine gypsum board plants.

Fossil fuel reserves include coal in Virginia, West Virginia, and Kentucky, gas and oil in Louisiana, and oil in Arkansas. Recoverable coal reserves are estimated at 260 million tons. Under leases to others, 1974 production figures include 3.5 million tons of coal mined and 4.7 billion cubic feet of natural gas produced.

At this writing the company is about to acquire *Exchange Oil & Gas Corp.,* which has holdings close to G-P's petro-chemical operation in Louisiana.

Georgia-Pacific's sales fall into two broad categories: (1) Wood Products and Building Materials, and (2) Pulp, Paper, and Chemical Products. Over the past five years, Building Products have been the dominant element, with Pulp & Paper sales ranging from 27% to 38% of the company's total sales.

Emerging as a major factor in G-P's operations is its chemicals production. Originally intended as an effort at vertical integration (producing needed chlorine for paper, resins for plywood and glues for particleboard), the operation has grown to produce 15% of company earnings on 8% of sales. Chemical sales could double by 1976 to $400

Georgia-Pacific chemical manufacturing complex at Plaquemine, Louisiana.

Using a mobile hydraulic "orchard monkey," this Georgia-Pacific Southern pine harvesting crew in Arkansas is preparing for the next generation of genetically improved "super trees".

million, including inter-company sales, according to management, and may generate 15%-20% of earnings.

In discussing Georgia-Pacific's production figures, within the scope of our study, about all that can be done is to catalog them by various product groups. All figures given are as of 1974's year-end.

Lumber: 2.5 billion board feet of lumber was sold. This includes one billion board feet produced by G-P and the remainder acquired from others. G-P's 42 lumber mills have a total rated annual capacity of 1.424 billion board feet.

Plywood: G-P is the nation's leading producer of both softwood and hardwood plywood. Sales for the year totalled 3.8 billion square feet. Of this amount, about 2.5 billion square feet were produced in G-P's own 23 plywood plants.

Wood Products Specialties: In 1974, 393,100,000 square feet of hardboard, 335,400,000 square feet of panelboard, and 430,700,000 square feet of particleboard was produced. In addition, in 1974, G-P purchased from others 98.9 million square feet of particleboard and 16.4 million square feet of hardboard.

Gypsum Products: Georgia-Pacific produced nearly 14% of all domestic gypsum products in 1974, making it the nation's third largest producer. These products include gypsum board, lath, plaster, joint systems, and gypsum rock. Thirteen G-P plants have the following aggregate annual capacity:

Gypsum Board and Lath	2,080 billion square feet
Plaster	119,000 tons
Joint Systems	92,000 tons
Gypsum Rock Sales	87,000 tons

Pulp & Paper Products: G-P's 25 primary pulp and paper mills have a total annual capacity of 2.25 million tons. In addition, 29 Georgia-Pacific paper converting plants manufacture hundreds of products such as household and industrial paper, waxed paper, grocery bags and sacks, corrugated boxes, folding cartons, milk cartons, paper plates, and labels. G-P's converting plants use about 63% of the company's own production of paper and paperboard, excluding newsprint.

Georgia-Pacific began an ambitious five-year program in 1972 to double both sales and net income. In the first two years, sales have increased by 37% and net income by 67%. The sales goal for 1977 is $3.5 billion.

Louisiana-Pacific Corporation, based in Portland, is the forest product industry's newest major company . . . . and then, again, it isn't.

As the result of the settlement of a government anti-trust suit, Georgia-Pacific Corporation gave birth to Louisiana-Pacific on January 5, 1973. Through a spin-off to stockholders, 20% of G-P's assets were transferred to the new company.

LOUISIANA-PACIFIC SUMMARY OF OPERATIONS

Sales and Contributions to Earnings

By Line of Business:	1974		1973		1972	
Sales						
Redwood lumber	$ 71,000,000	16%	$ 86,000,000	21%	$ 60,000,000	22%
Other lumber	160,000,000	35	162,000,000	39	97,000,000	35
Panel products	85,000,000	18	94,000,000	22	57,000,000	21
Logs, chips, veneer, windows and doors	73,000,000	16	42,000,000	10	33,000,000	12
Pulp	71,000,000	15	33,000,000	8	26,000,000	10
Total sales	$460,000,000	100%	$417,000,000	100%	$273,000,000	100%
Contribution to earnings						
Lumber, panel products and byproducts	$ 40,000,000	42%	$106,000,000	90%	$ 55,000,000	97%
Pulp	39,000,000	40	8,000,000	7	(1,000,000)	(3)
Other products	17,000,000	18	3,000,000	3	2,000,000	6
Total contribution to earnings	$ 96,000,000	100%	$117,000,000	100%	$ 56,000,000	100%
Interest expense	(18,000,000)		(11,000,000)		(7,000,000)	
Corporate administrative expense	(3,000,000)		(3,000,000)		(2,000,000)	
Income taxes	(29,000,000)		(43,000,000)		(17,000,000)	
Net income of Ketchikan Operations, 50% owned	11,000,000		6,000,000		1,000,000	
Net income	$ 57,000,000		$ 66,000,000		$ 31,000,000	
Summary of Production Volumes:						
Redwood lumber, board feet	299,000,000		343,000,000		342,000,000	
Other lumber, board feet	1,203,000,000		982,000,000		757,000,000	
Plywood, board feet, 3⁄8″ basis	674,000,000		722,000,000		545,000,000	
Particleboard, board feet, 3⁄4″ basis	151,000,000		144,000,000		93,000,000	
Hardboard, board feet, 1⁄8″ basis	16,000,000		—		—	
Softwood veneer, board feet, 3⁄8″ basis	39,000,000		30,000,000		—	
Hardwood veneer, square feet	112,000,000		—		—	
L-P pulp, tons	205,000		200,000		205,000	
Ketchikan lumber, board feet	186,000,000		177,000,000		150,000,000	
Ketchikan pulp, tons	186,000		212,000		200,000	
Other Statistics						
Working capital	114,560,000		57,050,000		81,410,000	
Total assets	560,450,000		431,460,000		327,040,000	
Export sales	95,000,000		41,000,000		19,000,000	
Funds generated from operations	91,900,000		96,360,000		51,670,000	
Return on capital employed	13.4%		20.4%		11.1%	
Return on equity	23.7%		36.6%		20.6%	

From its conception, Louisiana-Pacific was probably one of the largest babies ever born. On day one, L-P was the nation's second largest lumber producer, sixth largest manufacturer of plywood, and a major producer of wood chips and other building materials.

As of year-end 1974, Louisiana-Pacific operated these facilities:

Facilities	Capacity
61 Sawmills	2.76 billion bd. ft.
3 Particleboard Plants	285 million sq. ft.
1 Hardboard Plant	140 million sq. ft.
5 Softwood Plywood Plants	793 million sq. ft.
3 Softwood Veneer Mills	270 million sq. ft.
2 Hardwood Veneer Mills	320 million sq. ft.
2 Pulp Mills	430,000 tons
1 Wood Chip Mill	130,000 units
4 Door & Window Plants	——

MANAGEMENT PHILOSOPHY OF L-P UNIQUE

L-P's corporate strategy has confused the management of older, more established forest products companies, because L-P does not recognize the traditional industry goals. For example, L-P is less self sufficient in timberlands than Georgia-Pacific or Weyerhaeuser, owning or leasing 60 per cent of its needs. L-P is not fully diversified. It has only one pulp mill and no paper mills to offset swings in lumber and plywood demand. Rather than viewing export sales as a bonus, L-P considers such sales an integral part of its marketing plan.

All of this suits Louisiana-Pacific's management perfectly well. As articulated by President Harry A. Merlo:

"We're doing things *our own way* when it comes to timber ownership, manufacturing and marketing.
Some have questioned our strategies, but with *performance* the only standard at Louisiana-Pacific, we'll continue to seek whatever flexibility necessary to earn you, our stockholder, the best possible return on your assets."
"To this goal, we're committed."

Louisiana-Pacific's policies are explained further by Donald R. Kayser, vice-president, finance:

"We have become *fiber merchandisers,* for the simple reason that our current strength as a corporation lies more in our abilities than in our possessions ... Fiber merchandising is defined as an L-P management philosophy which breaks down its raw material to its lowest common denominator—fiber—then converts it through efficient manufacturing to the product that represents the best possible return under flexible marketing strategy for that material—be it lumber, pulp, plywood, particleboard, chips, etc. . .
That is why our timberlands are always close to manufacturing facilities. We make certain that the right tree is sent to the right mill. Many in the industry feel that multi-product plant operations give the most efficient conversion operations. L-P takes a slightly different viewpoint. We prefer the highly efficient, single product unit, where the operation is specifically geared to produce the maximum return from a particular log specie and size available in the immediate area. Each production unit is able to concentrate on what it does best."

L-P owns approximately 625,000 acres of timberlands. In addition, L-P holds cutting rights on an additional 924,000 acres. Fifty per cent

Louisiana-Pacific Ketchikan spruce mill.

owned *Ketchikan Pulp Company* has cutting rights to another 840,000 acres in Alaska.

Based in Portland, **Willamette Industries, Inc.** is a major national enterprise and the sixth largest Northwest forest products firm according to total assets. Soundly managed, the company was founded at Dallas, Oregon in 1905 as the *Willamette Valley Lumber Company*. Reorganized into its present structure in 1967, the company has established an impressive operating record.

The company is the fourth largest producer of plywood and the third largest manufacturer of particleboard in the nation. Willamette has no operations in Canada and minimal export sales.

By design, management has diversified so that wood products and paper and paper products each account for about 50% of total sales.

Willamette presently owns more than 400,000 acres of timberland. This includes 200,000 acres in Oregon, 150,000 acres in Louisiana, and 50,000 acres in Tennessee. These lands are intensively managed through thinning, fertilizing, brush control, and planting improved seedlings to increase the yield.

The company's philosophy is to blend its own resources with outside timber supplies whenever they are available at an economic price. Company-owned forests are used as a reserve to provide a flexibility in quality, quantity, and species to meet the varying availability of timber from other sources. These would be primarily purchases of government timber and open market private purchases. For example, in 1974 Willamette purchased about 54% of its timber needs from outside sources.

Full utilization of the company's timber resources has enabled Willamette to grow in a manner not otherwise possible. Since the company was reorganized to its present structure in 1967, annual sales have more than tripled from $114 million to $388 million.

Management believes that the company's strength lies in the fact that wood products and paper products are not dependent upon each other. The demand for paper products usually follows the general business cycle, while the demand for wood products precedes the trend

WILLAMETTE INDUSTRIES

Paper & Paper Products Operations	Rated Annual Capacity	Actual 1974 Production
5 Pulp and Paper Mills	709 thousand tons	606 thousand tons
9 Corrugated Box Plants	5.8 billion square feet	5.3 billion square feet
2 Kraft Grocery Bag Plants	62 thousand tons	57 thousand tons
1 Folding Carton Plant	14 thousand tons	12 thousand tons
2 Business Forms Plants	———	———
Wood Products		
7 Oregon Plywood Plants[1]	736 million square feet (³⁄₈ inch basis)	1,059 million square feet (¹⁄₈ in basis)
4 Southern Pine Plywood Plants[2]	332 million square feet (³⁄₈ inch basis)	388.1 million board feet
7 Oregon Lumber Mills[1]	319 million board feet	295.8 million square feet (¹⁄₄ inch basis)
4 Southern Lumber Mills	123 million board feet	103.1 million square feet
3 Particleboard Plants[1]	365 million square feet (¹⁄₄ inch basis)	———
2 Veneer Plants	112 million square feet	———
1 "Custom Products" Plant (Albany)	———	
7 Retail Lumber Yards (Oregon)	———	

[1]Including 50% owned Brooks-Willamette plants in Oregon.
[2]Including 50% owned Woodard-Walker-Willamette and Wilmar Plywood plants in Louisiana.

in the cycle. Also the company has its own marketing operation, and attempts to sell most of its output before it is produced. The company has been successful in operating at near capacity and avoiding costly plant shutdowns.

Willamette Industries operates a total of 47 plants as shown in the accompanying table.

The company's original paper mill at Albany, Oregon, built in 1955, was designed to make use of otherwise useless wood chips from sawmills and plywood plants. It was the first mill ever built under the concept of close proximity to its sawmill chip source.

Willamette Industries' Albany, Oregon papermill.

WILLAMETTE INDUSTRIES SUMMARY OF OPERATIONS

Summary of Sales: *(000 omitted)*

	Sales	Paper and paper products	Plywood products	Lumber products	Particle-board products	Logs, pulp chips and other	Total
1970	Amount	101,103	43,134	23,107	9,123	9,883	186,350
	%	54	23	12	5	6	
1971	Amount	108,451	52,590	30,643	11,843	9,782	213,309
	%	51	25	14	6	4	
1972	Amount	125,790	67,383	36,832	16,889	10,024	256,918
	%	49	26	14	7	4	
1973	Amount	155,403	75,653	48,677	22,846	20,367	322,946
	%	48	23	15	7	7	
1974	Amount	216,902	72,990	50,380	21,886	26,554	388,712
	%	56	19	13	5	7	

Excluded are sales of 50%-owned companies which are accounted for on the equity method.

Summary of Sales and Earnings: *(000 omitted)*

		Wood Products Amount %		Paper and Paper Products Amount %		Total
1970	Sales	85,247	46	101,103	54	186,350
	Contributions to earnings	6,973	37	11,892	63	18,865
1971	Sales	104,858	49	108,451	51	213,309
	Contributions to earnings	16,228	65	8,595	35	24,823
1972	Sales	131,128	51	125,790	49	256,918
	Contributions to earnings	26,756	68	12,658	32	39,414
1973	Sales	167,543	52	155,403	48	322,946
	Contributions to earnings	39,616	61	25,099	39	64,715
1974	Sales	171,810	44	216,902	56	388,712
	Contributions to earnings	12,003	20	49,370	80	61,373

"Contribution to earnings" is defined to be that amount of earnings generated before (1) "Other income, net" (2) "Interest and debt expense" and (3) income taxes. Also excluded are earnings of 50%-owned companies which are accounted for on the equity method.

The varying proportion of sales of various product groups are shown in the accompanying table.

Now, through its *Western Kraft* Division, Willamette produces corrugated containers in a wide variety of types, shapes, and designs for use by food manufacturers and other industries, nationwide.

Business forms are produced for computer firms, banks, insurance companies, industry, and governmental agencies. Willamette also produces quality long-run custom and stock carbon interleaved continuous forms, optical scanning forms, and custom snap-out forms.

At the company's Port Hueneme, California mill, more than 320 tons of waste paper are recycled daily. This mill relies entirely on consumer waste materials for its production.

Only partially dependent upon new housing starts, Willamette produces building materials for a variety of markets. Besides residential construction, these include institutional, commercial, and industrial building, furniture, mobile homes, recreational vehicles, and home remodeling. To serve the home remodeling market, Willamette purchased five retail building outlets in Oregon in 1974.

Boise Cascade Corporation is another major diversified forest products company headquartered in the Northwest. Boise is one of the largest concerns in the industry. Its timber reserves of 7.3 million acres (owned or controlled) also rank it as a leader. Boise is believed to be the largest supplier of office products in the nation as well.

Unfortunately, Boise Cascade is best known to many investors because of the company's massive write-offs and losses in the 1971-1972 period. These were the result of expansion into unrelated fields, including real estate and investments in Latin America. These unrelated operations were sold or discontinued in 1972, and Boise is midway through a five-year liquidation program of its real estate projects. The company is also converting Latin American investments to cash or to investments in its paper and building materials businesses. Long-term debt associated with the real estate holdings has been reduced from $422 million in 1970 to $134 million in 1974. In fact, Boise's total long-term debt for all purposes was just $455.8 million at the end of 1974, compared to nearly $1 billion in 1970.

COMPANY WELL-BALANCED

Investors' focus now should be on the more positive aspects of Boise Cascade's present situation. Boise is well balanced between forest products and paper manufacturing. The company is vertically integrated from timber ownership through manufacturing and distribution. Resources of the company and its affiliates at year-end 1974 included ownership of 10.9 billion board feet of sawtimber and 57 million cords of pulpwood.

Boise's 1974 net income was three times that of 1970. The cash dividend on the company's common stock has been increased to double that of 1970, on a per share basis. At the same time, because of a company stock repurchase, there are 1.6 million fewer common shares outstanding than in 1970. In spite of the intervening write-offs, losses, and discontinued operations, shareholders' equity at year-end 1974 was $822 million versus $885 million in 1970.

In 1974 Boise Cascade produced 615 million board feet of lumber. Plywood and veneer production came to 1,651 million square feet ($3/8''$ basis). Boise's plants also manufactured 126 million square feet of particleboard and 501 million square feet of fiberboard. Revenue of the division came to $432.7 million.

Not to be confused with mobile homes, "manufactured housing" involves the pre-finishing of wall units, inset windows and other housing components before their arrival at conventional construction sites. Even in 1974's depressed housing market, Boise's manufactured housing plants delivered a total of 8,512 units.

In addition, the division manufactured over 530,000 kitchen cabinets and 500,000 door units. Including Builder Service Centers and Wholesale branches, the Building Materials Division produced 1974 revenue of $323.8 million.

The company makes a wide range of paper products: printing and publishing papers, business papers, converting papers, paperboard, and newsprint, and market pulp. Boise's ten paper mills had a total 1974 production of 1,407,224 tons of paper products. The year's revenue came to $418.8 million.

Boise Cascade is the world's largest manufacturer of composite cans. These are spiral wound containers with layers of paper in combination with foil, metal, or plastic. Typical uses are for frozen orange juice containers, motor oil cans, and hundreds of other everyday uses.

Basic 1974 output of the company's packaging operations was as follows:

Composite Cans	3,138,833 (thousands of units)
Corrugated Containers	4,729,298 (thousands of square feet)
Envelopes	6.609 (millions)

Net sales of Packaging and Office Products for 1974 totaled $424.3 million.

Total annual sales for the company on an ongoing basis have increased from $835.6 million to $1.4 billion over the past five years. At the same time, net income from continuing operations (excluding real estate) has increased from $23.3 million to $103.6 million in 1974.

In summary, each of the business areas contributed the following percentage of Boise's total 1974 sales:

Timber and Wood Products	27%
Building Materials	20%
Paper	25%
Packaging & Office Products	26%
Other	2%
Total	100%

Boise Cascade's product diversification is represented by (top row) veneer, corrugated boxes, and paper production, and (bottom row) envelopes, composite cans, and manufactured housing.

> ## BOISE CASCADE SUMMARY OF MAJOR OPERATIONS
> ### (12-31-74)
>
> *Wood Products Manufacturing and Sales*
>   18 Lumber mills
>   24 Plywood and veneer plants
>   2 Particleboard plants
>   1 Fiberboard plant
>   7.3 Million acres timberland—*
>   (owned or controlled)
>
> *Building Materials Fabrication, Distribution*
>   11 Wholesale distribution branches
>   34 Builder service centers
>   13 Manufactured housing plants
>   4 Kitchen cabinet plants
>   2 Door plants
>
> *Paper Manufacturing and Sales*
>   10 Pulp and paper mills
>
> *Packaging and Office Products Distribution*
>   20 Composite can plants
>   17 Corrugated container manufacturing plants
>   6 Envelope plants
>   26 Office products distribution centers
>   22 Retail office supply stores
>
> *Includes joint ventures and affiliated companies.

All divisions were profitable. The accompanying table summarizes Boise Cascade's major operations.

Boise Cascade is involved in several joint ventures, the largest of which is *Boise Southern Company*. The Boise Southern complex in DeRidder, Louisiana operates one of the most modern and efficient pulp and paper facilities in North America, producing approximately 450,000 tons of newsprint and paperboard annually. The venture with *Southern Natural Resources, Inc.* also has a pulp and paper mill in Elizabeth, Louisiana, which it acquired in 1974, a plywood plant, a pole plant, and a sawmill at DeQuincy, Louisiana. Boise Southern also owns 50% of *Vancouver Plywood Co.* with two plywood plants, two sawmills and a hardwood milling facility.

Miramichi Timber Resources Ltd. is another 50% owned venture in New Brunswick, Canada, which produced 220,000 tons of kraft pulp in 1974.

Headquartered in San Francisco, the **Crown Zellerbach Corporation** is another fully integrated forest products company. In addition, it is one of the largest paper manufacturers in the world.

Wood Products: Principal products produced by the division are logs, lumber, plywood, piling, and poles. The company sells building materials through independent dealers in the United States and through its own stores in Canada.

Wood Fiber Utilization at Crown Zellerbach

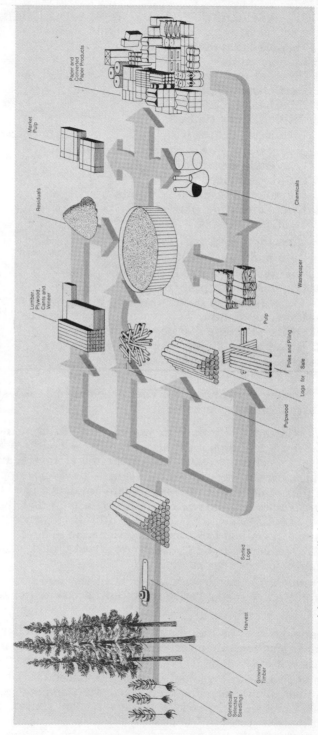

Artwork by Crown Zellerbach

The process of forest management at Crown Zellerbach begins with forest genetics, which involves the development of superior seedlings for forest planting. As trees reach maturity and are harvested they are converted into multiple end-products to obtain optimum economic utilization from the available fiber.

Crown Zellerbach owns or controls more than 3.4 million acres of timberlands, 39% in British Columbia, 26% in Oregon and Washington, 35% in Mississippi and Louisiana.

In the past five years, sales of the company's wood products division have grown at a compound annual rate of 26%. Nevertheless, actual 1974 wood products sales of $322.6 million amounted to just 18.2% of Crown Zellerbach's total revenue.

Pulp and Paper: Crown's largest division, pulp and paper products, accounted for 40% of the company's total sales in 1974. This division produces a multitude of diverse products.

The company is a major supplier of newsprint and printing papers of all types. CZ also supplies papers for business machines, office copiers and computers. Crown produces tissues and sanitary papers as well as containerboard and 'bag paper (multiwall bags, grocery bags, and sacks). The five year annual compound growth rate of sales of these products is 13%.

Containers and Packaging: Crown's container plants in the United States and Canada produce about 20% of the company's total sales. Corrugated and solid fiber shipping containers are the mainstay of the container division. However, the sale of both flexible and rigid plastic packaging materials has grown steadily over the years. Flexible packaging products are used for plastic film packaging of processed foods, polyolefin grocery bags and special wrapping papers and tapes.

Distribution: Crown Zellerbach, through its subsidiary *Zellerbach Paper Company,* is a major wholesaler of its own products as well as those of some 2600 other manufacturers.

The company operates 28 distribution centers in 13 Western states, including Alaska and Hawaii. In addition, Crown's Canadian subsidiary operates eleven other wholesale centers. These centers all distribute printing papers, packaging supplies, commercial stationery, school supplies, and other related merchandise. 1974 sales of $374.6 million were 21% of company revenue and have been increasing at an annual compound rate of 17%.

A GLANCE BACKWARD

Knowing the splendid record of **Potlatch Corporation,** it is interesting to pause and delve into the company's more modest beginning.

In 1901, the *Edward Rutledge Timber Company* began acquiring timberlands in Idaho. It happens that Mr. Rutledge had been a companion of Frederick Weyerhaeuser in Wisconsin, and the two had traveled West together. Meanwhile, the *Potlatch Lumber Company* was incorporated in 1903, with Charles Weyerhaeuser as its first president. Potlatch Lumber acquired the timber holdings of two other companies, and proceeded to build the mill and town of Potlatch, Idaho in 1906. The word Potlatch comes from the Indian expression "potshatl" which means "the giving of gifts". An Indian potlatch was a ceremonial con-

Products of Potlatch's Wood Products, Paperboard and Packaging Divisions.

vention involving feasting, speeches, and gift giving. Still a third company, the *Clearwater Timber Company,* was founded in 1900 with Frederick Weyerhaeuser as vice president. In 1931, the three companies merged with the name, **Potlatch Forests, Inc.**

Seemingly, the woods were full of Weyerhaeusers. John P. Weyerhaeuser became president of the Clearwater company until the merger in 1931. When Rutledge built the Coeur d'Alene sawmill, R. M. Weyerhaeuser was named president. Following World War I, George F. Jewett, Sr. (a grandson of Frederick Weyerhaeuser) joined Rutledge and became vice president and general manager in 1928. In 1925, John Phillip Weyerhaeuser, Jr. came to Lewiston and later served as the first president of Potlatch Forests, Inc. One would have to conclude that there was no lack of management candidates during the formative years of Potlatch Forests. The present company name, Potlatch Corporation, was adopted in 1973.

Potlatch is now an integrated forest products company ranking sixth in the Northwest industry with sales of $487.9 million in 1974. The company ranks 345th in Fortune's top 500 U.S. companies by sales, and by net income ranks 203rd. The Company's 9.3% return on sales in 1974 and 17.1% return on stockholders' equity put it in 51st and 104th places respectively on Fortune's list according to those measures.

Approximately 30%-40% of Company sales are from wood products, and paper and related products account for 60%-70%. Total company sales have grown at a compound annual rate of approximately 10% over the last 10 years, while earnings have grown at a 20% rate. A sales summary for 1974's operations is as follows:

Wood Products	$152,448,000	31.2%
Paperboard	64,173,000	13.2
Printing & Business Papers	140,804,000	28.9
Packaging	69,996,000	14.3
Consumer Products	45,345,000	9.3
Paper Merchants ·	15,102,000	3.1

The company's Wood Products Group operates 15 sawmills, three plywood plants, a hardwood veneer plant in Samoa, and a new particleboard plant that began operations this past May.

Potlatch's Paperboard Group manufactures bleached kraft paperboad, used primarily for certain kinds of food packages such as folding cartons and milk containers. Bleached paperboard accounts for about one-half of total company paper and paperboard capacity. In 1974, the company's Lewiston, Idaho facility operated at 102% of average capacity, and shipments had to be allocated. The company believes it is the third largest manufacturer of bleached kraft paperboard in the U.S. The Northwest Paper Division manufactures bleached papers for commercial printing business, and converting and labels markets.

The two basic product lines of the Packaging Division are folding cartons and liquid-tight packaging primarily for dairy products. The company operates seven folding carton plants and three dairy service plants, located mostly in the East, South and Midwest. Two Potlatch shipping container plants were recently sold to *Willamette Industries*, and a third to another party.

Shipments of the Consumer Products Division are contributed approximately 75% from tissue and toweling and 25% from paper plateware. The Division's products are sold primarily as private label products to large retail chains.

LOW-COST TIMBER BASE MAJOR ASSET

Potlatch owns approximately 1.3 million acres of timberland in Idaho, Arkansas, and Minnesota, with current inventory estimated at 2.36 billion cubic feet. Cutting rights are also held on about 140,000 acres in three states. A significant portion of Company timberlands was acquired around the beginning of the century and are stated at that cost (plus subsequent additions, less cost of timber harvested) equalling $41,646,767 at year-end 1974, or about $32 per acre. In 1974 approximately 61% of the Wood Products Group's timber requirements was cut from fee-owned land (versus 54% in 1973), with the remainder cut mostly from U.S. Forest Service and State of Idaho land.

In order to make more efficient use of its low-cost timber and land resources, Potlatch has begun a capital expansion program costing an estimated $300 million through 1977. New projects which have been completed in 1975 include the St. Maries, Idaho small log mill and chipping facility; Lewiston, Idaho small log mill with chipping facility to begin operation in the fourth quarter; Post Falls, Idaho particleboard mill; and replacement of the Prescott, Arkansas sawmill. The largest single project in the program is a new $150 million bleached pulp and paperboard mill in Arkansas. Additional projects in the program include expansion of the Lewiston mill's sawdust pulp capacity, modernization of the Cloquet, Minnesota pulp mill, and construction of a plywood core mill in Lewiston. A comparison of the capacities of Potlatch's operations at January 1, 1975 with capacities at completion of the current program is as follows:

	January, 1975	1977
Lumber	626,500,000 bd ft	736,500,000 bd ft[1]
Particleboard	—	50,000,000 sq ft[1]
Plywood & Veneer	410,400,000 sq ft	490,400,000 sq ft
Bleached Pulp	561,200 tons	740,000 tons
Bleached Paperboard	310,600 tons	468,600 tons

[1]Current Capacity

Management says that "these projects will provide good earnings opportunities for the company as demand for our products picks up and we move concurrently out of the expensive start-up phase." A minimum of a 10% after-tax rate of return is expected by management on its projects.

A relatively small and highly conservative forest products company is the **Longview Fibre Company** of Longview, Washington. The company is an integrated manufacturer of kraft papers and containerboard. It converts about one-half of its production into paper bags and fibre shipping containers.

The company's sales and production in fiscal 1974 were as follows:

Sales		Production	
Paper, Paperboard	$ 57,940,000	Paper, tons	219,000
		Paperboard, tons	323,000
Converted Products	116,106,000	Converted products, tons	330,000
Logs	25,157,000	Logs, thousands of board feet	138,000
Total	$199,203,000		

Longview's conservative nature is apparent in reviewing the financial figures. The company has no bank debt or long-term debt at all. As of year-end, 1974, the company's total assets were stated at $136 million, of which $10.2 million was in marketable securities. Over the past ten years, annual cash flow has averaged $25 million. In eight of the past ten years, the company has made repurchases of its common shares, reducing the shares outstanding, by more than 13%.

Annual sales for Longview Fibre have increased from $88.8 million (1964) to $199.2 million in 1974. Similarly, net income has grown from $9.8 million to $24.3 million.

Headquartered in Portland, **Pope & Talbot, Inc.** is a firm which has operated in the Northwest for the past 125 years. Of historical interest, Pope & Talbot's sawmill at Port Gamble, Washington, is the oldest continuously operating sawmill in North America. Started in 1853, the mill currently produces about 90 million board feet of lumber annually. Pope & Talbot owns and manages approximately 125,000 acres of prime commercial timberlands in Oregon and Washington. This timber lies in three managed forests containing Douglas fir, hemlock and lodgepole pine. In addition, the company owns one of the largest private holdings of alder hardwood in the Northwest. Altogether, these forests have an inventory of about 1.4 billion board feet of commercial timber.

Pope & Talbot acquired *Boundary Forest Products, Ltd.,* a Canadian company, in 1969. This added two sawmills at Grand Forks and Midway, British Columbia. The purchase gave Pope & Talbot access to more than one million acres of British Columbia timberlands with sustained yield rights to harvest timber producing approximately 165 million board feet of lumber per year.

Pope & Talbot manufactures dimension lumber, specialty plywood, industrial hardboard, plywood veneer, and wood chips. In addition to the Canadian sawmills, the company operates a specialty plywood plant and sawmill in Washington, and a sawmill, veneer plant, and hardboard plant in Oakridge, Oregon.

Under a ten-year export agreement, the company delivers wood chips to a Japanese paper manufacturer. Six full vessels of wood chips were shipped in 1973, ten in 1974, and an additional ten are scheduled in 1975.

POPE & TALBOT SUMMARY OF OPERATIONS

Wood Products Production Statistics

	Rated Capacity	1974 Production	1973 Production
Lumber			
(millions of bd. ft.)			
Domestic			
Oakridge, Oregon	98	47	60
Port Gamble, Washington .	80	82	81
Canadian			
Grand Forks, B. C..	70	66	71
Midway, B. C.	95	81	99
Hudson, Ontario*	75	21	24
Total	418	297	335

*Hudson sawmill was sold effective July 31, 1974.

Plywood Veneer			
(millions of sq. ft. ⅜ " basis)			
Oakridge, Oregon	70	55	76
Specialty Plywood			
(millions of sq. ft. ⅜ " basis)			
Kalama, Washington . . .	86	61	90
Industrial Hardboard			
(millions of sq. ft. ⅛ " basis)			
Oakridge, Oregon	230	190	231
Export Wood Chips			
(thousands of B.D.U.)			
Oakridge, Oregon	60	47	44

Abundant and well-balanced log inventory is in concert with production requirements of Pope & Talbot's Midway, British Columbia sawmill.

Port Ludlow easily ranks as the most complete recreational and residential development on Washington's Puget Sound.

Pope & Talbot is remarkable for the size and low cost of its timber holdings. With some of its domestic holdings purchased in the 1850's, the actual value of these lands is substantially above that stated on the company's books. For example, the average cost of Pope & Talbot's Oakridge area timber is less than $2 per thousand board feet. Figures published by the U.S. Forest Service show that purchases of government timber of comparable quality averaged $200 per thousand board feet in 1974.

SUSTAINED YIELD FOREST MANAGEMENT

In the Oakridge, Oregon tract the company is accelerating the cut of old-growth, over-mature timber to position these holdings into a complete second-growth cycle. This particular stand of timber, because of its age, inability to reproduce, and vulnerability to storms, fire and insect infestations, has literally stopped growing.

Shortly after harvest, the company begins replanting with genetically superior trees commonly called "super trees." Special nursery-grown seedlings, a one-year-old superior seedling is five times the size of a natural seedling.

In 1974, the company started the first phase of an advanced forest genetics program on all of its tree farm properties. They planted well over 50,000 superior seedlings on harvested land. In 1975, the company plans to plant 800,000 super trees on its Oakridge and Hood Canal property.

Pope & Talbot owns about 85,000 acres of timberland on Puget Sound, mostly on the Olympic Peninsula. This is prime real estate which the company plans to sell or develop gradually.

Included in this area is the town of Bangor, Washington, with about 10,000 residents at present. This is the planned home base of a new fleet of 28 to 30 *Trident* missile submarines. The Navy's $15 billion project will increase the area's population by some 25,000, obviously affecting real estate values.

Pope & Talbot's major recreational development is at Port Ludlow, Washington, known as the *Admiralty*. There the company has established a second-home community with a golf course, beach club, restaurant, convention center, and marina. Over 150 condominium units have been constructed to date.

Based in Bend, Oregon, **Brooks-Scanlon, Inc.** is a land and timber company with virtually all of its manufacturing and production facilities located in Oregon.

The company owns 218,000 acres of timberland in Central Oregon. While Brooks' reserves amount to about 800 million board feet of timber, the company relies heavily on purchases from U.S. Forest Service sales.

In the past five years, Brooks-Scanlon and *Brooks-Willamette,* a 50% owned subsidiary, harvested a total of 855 million board feet of timber. Some 206 million of this total was from company holdings and 649 million board feet was purchased from the U.S. Forest Service.

Brooks' Bend Division mills logs into lumber and by-products. In 1974, the division shipped 130 million board feet of lumber and 75,000 tons of by-products from its large and small log mill complex. Included in byproducts are wood chips for paper manufacture, planer shavings and sawdust for particleboard manufacture, and decorative bark for the landscaping market.

A new long-term contract was recently signed calling for Brooks-Scanlon to ship about 2,200 railroad cars of chips per year from its Bend plant.

At Redmond, Oregon, the company's Whittier Division remanufactures Ponderosa pine lumber into mouldings and millwork products. These include solid and fingerjointed door jambs, door casings, exterior door frames, and many moulded wood patterns. Whittier produced 110 million lineal feet of wood mouldings in 1974. Due to poor market conditions, this was down from 153 million feet manufactured in the previous year.

Brooks-Willamette Corporation, 50% owned by *Willamette Industries, Inc.* produces lumber, plywood, and particleboard from timber

Truck driver tightens binder on truck loaded with Ponderosa pine.

Fully-loaded Brooks-Scanlon truck heads for Bend, Oregon.

From Brooks-Scanlon's Black Butte Ranch condominiums one can enjoy the scenery of Oregon's Three Sisters Mountains.

supplied by Brooks-Scanlon. 1974 sales were: plywood—114 million square feet; lumber—26 million board feet; and particleboard—96 million square feet. Total sales for Brooks-Willamette in 1974 amounted to $29.6 million with net earnings of $3.4 million.

The company's *Black Butte Ranch* near Oregon's Cascade Mountains is a prime real estate development. Black Butte includes a golf course, tennis courts, other recreational activities, and a deluxe dining hall, all in a pleasant rustic setting. The project consists of 1250 dwelling sites, of which more than half have been sold. Completion of the entire project will probably not occur until 1980.

Sales and net income in 1974 were the second highest year in the company's history, next to 1973's record year. Over the past ten years, the company's total assets, now $47.5 million, have grown at an annual rate of 12.5%.

The **Medford Corporation** (Medford, Oregon) has been an expanding integrated forest products operation since 1935.

Medco operates the following facilities: two plywood operations manufacturing approximately 250 million square feet (3/8″ basis); a lumber operation with an annual capacity of 85 million board feet; two kitchen cabinet plants (*Diamond Industries*); a priming and coating operation (*Sierra Wood Products*); a pallet and crate manufacturing plant in Portland (*D&M Wood Products*) and a specialty overlay plant (*Sel Ply Products*) in White City, Oregon.

A major addition to Medco's building materials operations was completed in the spring of 1975. This is a new $13.5 million plant which has the annual capacity to produce 110 million square feet of "MEDITE," a new medium density fiberboard, best described as a mixture of hardboard and particleboard technology. Former waste material from the company's sawmill and plywood plants and other area operations is utilized in its production. Medite board has workability and machining characteristics which are superior to industrial grade particleboard.

Aerial view of Medco's expansive Medford, Oregon complex, with new MEDITE plant in lower right.

Medite's primary applications include furniture, cabinet, and millwork manufacturing. The company estimates that sales of Medite should reach about $1 million per month in 1976.

The Medford Corporation's Diamond Industries Division manufactures kitchen cabinets in Grants Pass, Oregon. In mid-1975, Diamond acquired another cabinet manufacturer, *Noblecraft Industries* (Hillsboro, Oregon) from *Columbia Corporation.* The purchase price was in the area of $2 million. Medford's management believes that Noblecraft has the capacity to generate $10 million in annual sales in 1976, although it had not been doing that before Medco's purchase.

Medford Corporation owns in fee approximately 87,000 acres of timberland in Southern Oregon within proximity of its major manufacturing plants at Medford and Grants Pass. It is the company's policy to manage its timber and timberlands on a sustained yield basis, which has provided approximately 26% of the sound log requirement for its plants over the past 10 years. The remaining logs are purchased from private lands and from federal and state agencies in competitive bidding.

One forest products company active in the Northwest is unique in many respects. That would be the **Edward Hines Lumber Co.** The company is headquartered in Chicago, Illinois. The company has practically no timber reserves of its own. And finally, with annual sales approaching $200 million, the company has no long-term debt whatever.

Edward Hines started his lumber business in Chicago at what is called the "Main Yard" in 1892. The company headquarters is still there today. Today, the Hines Main Yard is the largest lumber yard in the Midwest. It houses millions of board feet of lumber on more than 25 acres of land. On an average day, there is enough lumber in the Main Yard to build 1500 homes.

The company began its Oregon operations in 1928. This was a

We started with a fresh marketing concept

When Mr. Edward Hines decided to start his own business, Chicago was in the midst of a building boom. As soon as trees could be cut and shipped into the city, buyers were ready and waiting. The Chicago lakefront was jammed with ships, decks stacked high with ungraded rough timber. Lumber

wholesalers had to bid for a ship's entire cargo, and almost always took a big chance on quality.

Mr. Hines made a significant move. He went directly to the sawmill and contracted to buy its entire production, insisting on uniform high quality. The next step was inevitable—the

purchase of sawmills to give his company complete control over delivery, quality, and cost. The groundwork for a program of careful quality control and dependable customer service had been laid and the forest-to-sawmill-to-customer concept of Hines was created.

At the turn of the century, Chicago was bustling with lumber activity.

Mr. Edward Hines in his office at the Main Yard.

result of the U.S. Forest Service's request for help in managing the growth of one of the largest stands of Ponderosa pine in the country. This long-neglected tract was located in the Malheur National Forest, which was rapidly becoming unsuitable for wildlife and recreation. Today, this forest has more trees growing than when the harvest first began. The company's plant at Hines, Oregon has grown into a complex including sawmills, a millwork factory, and a plywood plant. More Ponderosa pine lumber is produced in this complex than at any other single place in the world . . . more than 150 million board feet per year.

Edward Hines also harvests Douglas fir in Oregon, southern pine in Louisiana, Mississippi, and Arkansas; and Lodgepole pine and spruce in the forests of Idaho, Wyoming, and Colorado. The company operates its own railroad, the *Oregon and Northwestern,* between Hines and Seneca, Oregon, a distance of 51 miles.

In 1973, Hines purchased the *Stauter Lumber Company* of Hill City, South Dakota, which receives its Ponderosa pine from the Black Hills National Forest. This brings the number of Hines' sawmills to thirteen. Scheduled for completion in 1975 is a 50 million board feet sawmill at John Day, Oregon.

Essentially all of Hines' timber in the West and Northwest is purchased from the U.S. Forest Service. In the South, timber cutting rights are purchased from private landowners.

Edwards Hines' retail activity is conducted through the operation of a chain of home improvement centers. *Hines Home Centers* offer wood products, power tools, *"True Value"* hardware, electrical and plumbing supplies and similar items. Presently, there are 26 retail Home Centers in operation, all in the Greater Chicago area.

Bohemia, Inc. of Eugene, Oregon manufactures and markets a variety of wood products, many of which are specialty, non-commodity items, and is involved in specialized marine-oriented construction through its Umpqua Division. In fiscal 1975 ended April 30, Wood Products contributed 69.5% of company sales and 73.3% of pre-tax income, and Specialized Construction accounted for 28.6% of sales and 25.5% of income. Other sales (including non-contract gravel, ready-mix concrete and rock, equipment rental, repair service, glue extender and wax) contributed 1.9% of sales and 1.2% of earnings.

Bohemia's wood products operations include five sawmills with total annual capacity of about 203 million board feet, two plywood mills, a particleboard plant, a laminated beam plant, a cedar fencing plant, two veneer plants, and a bark processing plant.

Approximately 60%-70% of Bohemia's wood products sales are to industrial and commercial construction markets, meaning less dependence on residential construction markets than it would experience if it produced strictly commodity lumber products. Specialty wood products produced by the company include such items as ladder stock, laminated beams up to 120 feet long, decking for ships, railroad ties, crossarm and transmission arm stock, bridge stringers, and bleacher seats.

Construction of the Lost Creek Dam (left) by Bohemia's Umpqua Division nears completion. Bohemia's bark plant (above) has launched a new industry with unlimited potential.

In the fourth quarter of fiscal 1975 Bohemia's new $4.3 million bark plant adjacent to its veneer plant and sawmill at Coburg, Oregon began production, launching an entirely new industry with unlimited potential. Using Douglas fir bark, which was formerly a waste material, Bohemia technicians are obtaining commercially marketable products through a unique extraction process on which Bohemia holds a patent. The highly automated process enables Bohemia to produce vegetable wax and cork — both of which had not previously been available from any domestic source. While markets for these two products are developing slowly, plywood glue extender is the bark plant's primary commercial product at this writing, with shipments being made to about 40 plywood plants. The plant has the capacity to use 80 million pounds of Douglas fir bark annually, which is to be supplied primarily from the Company's nearby veneer plant.

Bohemia's timber requirements are supplied almost entirely from purchases from federal and state agencies and open market log purchases. In 1975 federal and state agencies accounted for 75% of its needs; open market log purchases, 17%; private contracts, 7%; and fee timber, 1%. Bohemia owns about 25,000 acres of timberlands in the Willamette Valley, which are carried on its books at about $35 per acre. Management has no intention of cutting any substantial amounts of this timber in the near future.

Company policy is to maintain a minimum of two to three years of its annual timber requirements (207,055 thousand board feet (MBF) in 1975) in cutting contracts. At April 30, 1975 the total volume of timber held under public contracts over the next six years totaled 343,000 MBF.

Bohemia holds an additional 127,000 MBF under private contracts, and its total contracts represent the most timber the company has ever had under contract.

Bohemia's specialized construction operations are involved mostly in marine-oriented construction projects for public agencies in Oregon, Washington and California. While all contracts are on a fixed price basis, the *Umpqua Division* has not had to recognize any losses on major projects during the inflationary climate of the last couple of years. In order to achieve this record, the Division operates quite efficiently, as evidenced by its on-schedule operations at the four-year, $48 million *Lost Creek Dam* project on the Rogue River, and early completion expected at the *North Jetty Rehabilitation* at Grays Harbor, Washington. The company's huge rock quarry east of Vancouver, Washington on the Columbia River provides it with an assured supply of high density rock for use in its marine construction activities.

Unlike most other Northwest forest products companies, **Dant & Russell Inc.** does not own any timberlands nor does it seek any. All timber is acquired through open market purchases from federal, state, and private sources.

With a company history dating back to 1904, Dant & Russell's primary business is the conversion and distribution of timber products. The company's three sawmills are located at Warrenton, Oregon; Marysville, Washington; and Haines, Alaska.

About five years old, the modern Warrenton mill has a capacity of approximately 95 million board feet on a two-shift basis. Marysville, 35 miles north of Seattle, specializes in cutting Western red cedar and specialty products. Annual capacity (two shifts) comes to 20 million board feet. The Haines mill cuts Western hemlock and Sitka spruce for Japanese export, as well as for Alaskan and Yukon Territory markets.

Dant & Russell also operates several other facilities. These include a wood treating and preserving plant at North Plains, Oregon; a pole peeling and storage yard at Vadis, Oregon; and a custom millwork plant in Miami, Florida.

Dant & Russell is a firm believer in the use of water transportation. The company's principal domestic markets are on the East Coast, where company-owned distribution yards are located at Baltimore, Maryland and Port Everglades, Florida. Some 40% to 50% of Dant & Russell's domestic sales are transported by the *Terminal Steamship Company,* a wholly owned subsidiary, and chartered U.S. flag vessels.

The company still views the Japanese log market, currently depressed, as an important world market over the long term.

It isn't easy to impress an influential investment advisory firm. And, under ordinary circumstances, it should be next to impossible if you're less than a year old.

It should be. But you ought to read what some are saying about Louisiana-Pacific.

Now we're not about to put words in anybody's mouth, so please, don't ask us what they said. Go to the source. But if you want to know why we feel so confident about our future in forest products, we'd have to say it's because we came at the right time, in the right places, with all the right kind of people.

We were born in January 1973, in the middle of a boom for building materials. And we came with just the right strength and market position to take advantage of it. In six months we parlayed $327 million in assets into more than $387 million. That's an 18 percent increase. We were also the country's third largest producer of lumber and the sixth of plywood. But, by mid-year, we had increased our capacity in lumber by 46 percent and jumped into the number two spot. We upped plywood capacity another 38 percent and became the sixth largest producer of particleboard in the nation by more than doubling our small initial capacity.

And we burst on the scene with all our operations right where they should be. Next to substantial timber supplies and with flexibility for distribution to the most profitable markets, either foreign or domestic.

But most important, we came along with the right people. Some of the most experienced in the industry. They're filled with the ambition, vitality and ideas we need to keep Louisiana-Pacific performing and growing like few others.

Now, potential alone doesn't impress anyone. But when you deliver, people get the message.

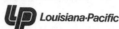 Louisiana-Pacific

Louisiana-Pacific / 1300 S.W. Fifth Avenue
Portland, Oregon 97201 / NYSE Symbol: LPX

"Louisiana-Pacific is bullish on you too, Merrill Lynch. And Bache, Blyth Eastman Dillon, Clark Dodge, Dean Witter and the others."

Harry A. Merlo —President

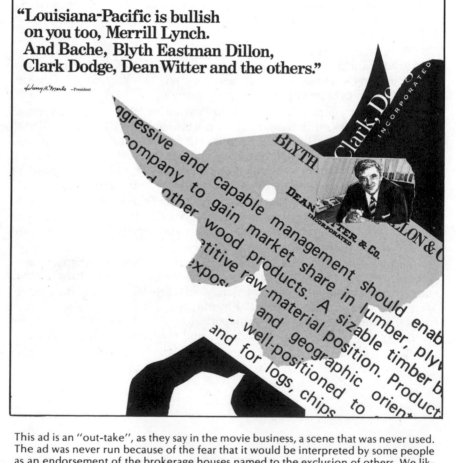

This ad is an "out-take", as they say in the movie business, a scene that was never used. The ad was never run because of the fear that it would be interpreted by some people as an endorsement of the brokerage houses named to the exclusion of others. We liked the ad as a typical representation of Louisiana-Pacific's flamboyant style. By printing it here for posterity we are keeping it from falling into oblivion.

9

Building Materials,
Construction and Real Estate

One of the three largest Oregon-based corporations, which also is one of the nation's largest retailers of building materials, as well as a major manufacturer and lessor of railcars and other transportation equipment, is **Evans Products Company.** In spite of the company's record 1974 revenue of $1,132,892,000 (a significant portion of which was generated by building material manufacturing and wholesaling operations which have subsequently been permanently closed or sold), the petulant economy treated Evans no better, and, in fact, much worse than the other construction-related companies in the Northwest. The combination of reduced housing starts and record high interest rate levels, which in turn prompted Evans to drastically alter its operations, stuck the company with a $44.4 million net loss in 1974. (By contrast, the next largest 1974 loss by any of the 200-plus companies discussed in this book was less than $6 million.)

One reason for the severity of Evans' loss was the mobile home industry's dismal performance. Evans had diligently sought dominance in supplying mobile homes with materials and equipment. The drop in 1974 mobile home industry sales from 567,000 units (1973) to 329,000 (1974) was not pleasant news for Evans.

Under Chairman Monford A. Orloff, who has reassumed the Presidency of Evans, the company is being completely reorganized. The goal is to reduce long-term debt, eliminate marginally profitable or losing operations, and concentrate company assets in those areas which show the promise of greatest return on assets in the future. The plan has been implemented as follows:

OPERATING ENTITIES RESTRUCTURED

Management's objective for 1975 and beyond is to concentrate company efforts and resources in the Transportation Systems and Industrial Group and the Retail Group. Operating groups have been reorganized and now consist of the following:

(1) *Homes Group*—Seven of the Group's eleven precut homes plants have been closed, and management says the remaining four plants have a "proven capacity for profitable operations and are situated in relatively strong market areas." These homes are marketed under the names of "Capp Homes" and

Evans serves "do-it-yourselfers" and professional building craftsmen through its chain of Grossman's and Moore's retail building materials stores.

"Ridge Homes" to individual lot owners, who can realize substantial savings by doing all or some of the finishing work themselves.

(2) *Shelter Products Group* — Divisions consist of Door Systems Division, Heating and Cooling Division, Paint Division, Plastics Division, Riveria Division (kitchen cabinets and countertops), and Remington Division (aluminum doors and windows). A number of the building products manufactured by the Shelter Products Group are merchandised by the Retail Group or used in the construction of homes by the Homes Group.

(3) *Forest Products Division* — This Division is successor to certain operations of the former Building Materials Group, including *Evans Products Co., Ltd.,* manufacturing lumber, plywood and shingles in Canada; *U.S. Wood Products,* manufacturing plywood, plywood specialties, lumber, and particleboard; and *Maderas Centro America S.A.,* manufacturing hardwood lumber in Nicaragua. Management indicates that continuation of operations of the division "will be contingent upon industry conditions and, for the most part, upon the ability to produce an acceptable return on capital invested in the Division's facilities." A pretax return on invested capital of 25% is management's target. According to Orloff, prior to reorganization there were approximately $175 million of assets involved in building materials operations which have subsequently been sold or are being considered for sale.

(4) *Fiber Products Group* — This new Group also is successor to certain operations of the former Building Materials Group and Technology and Engineering Groups. Its divisions consist of the Battery Separator Division; the Hardboard Division; the Permaglas Division, manufacturing glass fiber roofing materials; and the Glassfiber Technology Project, engaging in glassfiber research and development.

(5) *Retail Group* — The Group consists of 239 retail building material sales outlets carrying over 4,000 items for home construction, remodeling, maintenance, and repair. For the near term the company plans to add only a few new outlets. One of the nation's largest building materials chains, Evan's retail stores operate in the Northeast, Midwest, and California under the names *Grossman's* and *Moore's* in the Southeast. These stores carry such items as lumber and plywood, hardware, wall panels, floor coverings, electrical supplies, plumbing and heating equipment and hand power tools.

(6) *Transportation Systems and Industrial Group* — Evans' second major line of business, transportation and industrial equipment and services, has experienced consistent revenue growth and profitability over the past five years. Evans owns a fleet of approximately 24,000 freight cars *(United States Railway Equipment Co.)* and 1,200 truck trailers *(Evans Trailer Leasing Company)* which are leased to others. Evans manufactures, rebuilds and repairs railcars in seven plants. The company's truck trailer manufacturing division is the nation's leading producer of fiberglass-reinforced plastic trailers. In addition,

the Transportation and Industrial Group operates two foundries which manufacture engineered steel and alloy castings. These are sold to original equipment manufacturers of farm, construction, and transportation equipment. The foundries also make specialized castings vital to the mining industry.

Results of this radical reorganization have already become apparent. Since the third quarter of 1974, a number of Evans properties have been sold or permanently closed. These were primarily facilities which were generating high sales, but marginal income, or in several instances losses. This includes operations which generated $268 million in sales in 1974's first nine months and $14 million in 1975. Proceeds from these sales have been an important element in repayment of nearly $100 million in debt in the first nine months of Evans' 1975 year.

The third quarter of 1975 saw net income of $5.3 million for Evans Products, compared to the $12.7 million net loss reported in the same period of 1974. This was on a much smaller sales base — $224 million compared to $317 million the previous year. Management is convinced that the company's turnaround is established.

Pacific Western Industries, Inc. is a Northwest building products manufacturer which is also dependent upon the vicissitudes of the construction market. Sales grew in each of four years through 1974 to $29.6 million, and earnings grew considerably faster than sales until 1974 when earnings declined on a year-to-year basis to $244,399, still very respectable under the adverse conditions of that year. Pacific Western's plants, services and subsidiaries are organized into five main operating divisions.

Plywood—Timberland Forest Products (Seattle) is a plywood and lumber wholesaler. The company buys from Northwest producers into their warehouses in Seattle and Spokane, and sells and ships to customers in the Midwest and Eastern United States. Timberland also is an active participant in the *Chicago Board of Trade,* which allows hedging of their inventories through futures contracts.

Housing—Western Modular Corporation (Kent, Washington) was established in mid-1974 to manufacture modular homes and panelized housing packages. Western Modular sells through a dealer network operating in Washington, Oregon, Idaho, and Alaska.

Millwork—Western Cabinet and Millwork (Boise, Idaho and Seattle) offers a complete prefinished millwork package to single family and multi-unit residential builders in Washington, Oregon, Idaho, Alaska and Hawaii.

Doors—Cal-Wood Door (Santa Rosa, California) manufactures flush wood doors for commercial and residential markets. The products consist of door panels, prefinished and machined for hardware, and include the matching frames. These are sold by distributors in the eleven Western states serviced by Cal-Wood's own truck fleet. Midwest and Eastern markets are serviced by factory representatives.

Paneling—Welsh Panel (Longview, Washington) manufactures plywood paneling for the home improvement market and mobile home manufacturers. They also prefinish particleboard in a wood-grain look for the furniture industry.

Lindal Cedar Homes, manufacturer of pre-cut houses to be assembled on site, was seriously affected by the 1974-75 recession. In the 1970-1973 period, annual sales had increased rapidly from $4.6 million to $18 million. Racing to meet this booming demand, Lindal incurred substantial increased overhead and expense in completing two new Canadian sawmills.

Upon completion, the company experienced a 33% drop in 1974 sales to $12 million, leaving considerable excess capacity. Lindal reported a 1974 loss of $2.4 million, and was in default on a number of its loan restrictions. New management, facing a loss of $568,541 at March 31, 1975, has made profits in two consecutive quarters on revenue levels that in previous years were unprofitable.

Moduline International manufactures a wide range of mobile homes from a network of nine plants. Three of these plants are in the Northwest—two near the company headquarters at Chehalis, Washington and one in Aumsville, Oregon. Others are located in Arizona and Minnesota, plus four plants in Canada.

In spite of the fact that manufacturers' shipments of mobile homes to dealers in 1974 amounted to 329,000 units compared to 567,000 the previous year, annual sales for Moduline have increased each year — from $4.7 million in fiscal 1969 to $41.4 million in fiscal 1975 (fiscal year ending March 31). In addition, the company has been profitable in each of those years, although net income fell from $1,489,000 in 1974 to $832,000 in 1975.

While not pleased with current events, Moduline's president, L. C. "Bud" Merta, points out these facts which are optimistic for the future: There are about four million mobile homes currently in use; these serve as primary year-round dwellings for more than nine million people; mobile home industry shipments have increased at a compound annual rate of 6% over the past ten years. According to the *Manufactured Housing Institute,* the industry now provides more than two-thirds of all new single family housing units under $30,000. Moduline has steadily increased its share of the market over these recent difficult years.

Several of the companies discussed in our Forest Products chapter have been involved in manufactured housing, but most of them have either discontinued or sharply curtailed their manufactured housing activities.

Trus Joist Corporation is a Boise, Idaho company which is well known in the construction field, although the name may not ring any bells with most investors. Trus Joist manufactures and markets all-wood and combination wood and steel structural components for use in the floor and ceiling structures of buildings in the light construction classification.

The company's *TJI* joist is an all-wood joist, which is used in apartments, condominiums, townhouses, residential dwellings, and commercial buildings. A new series of Trus Joist's light, medium, and

The "Hearthside" mobile home, manufactured by Moduline International, has three bedrooms, sufficient for growing families.

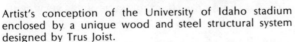

Artist's conception of the University of Idaho stadium enclosed by a unique wood and steel structural system designed by Trus Joist.

Two of Trus Joist's all wood and wood and steel joists.

heavyweight open-web wood and tubular steel joists use revolutionary new *MICRO-LAM* wood top and bottom chords. These are joined together by tubular steel webs connected to the chords with steel pins.

MICRO-LAM is a new proprietary lumber product consisting of many layers of thin wood veneer laminated together. The main advantage of *MICRO-LAM* lumber is that it utilizes low-grade veneers to produce structural lumber that is much more predictable and uniform in strength than ordinary lumber. Using exclusive company-designed machinery, thin sheets of veneer are glued, heated, and pressured into long strips of lumber with uniform strengths and handling characteristics. All of the irregular imperfections of natural lumber are eliminated. There is no shrinkage or warping. Every piece of *MICRO-LAM* is straight. The board comes out 1½ inches thick, 24 inches wide, and 80 feet long.

The company pointed out to us the significant conservation of wood products possible with *MICRO-LAM*. In 1972, for example, 880 million board feet of wood joists were used in multi-family dwellings — mainly sawn 2x8's and 2x10's. If it had been possible to substitute the company's *I* joist, 587 million board feet of lumber would have been saved. This is equal to the total amount of timber which can be grown in any one year on 4,700 square miles of Pacific Coast timberland. The savings is possible because the *I* joist contains 44% less wood than a 2x10, and is superior in strength, so that the joists can be placed further apart and span greater distances.

Founded in Boise in 1960, the company presently operates eight plants located in Boise, Idaho; Hillsboro, Oregon; Eugene, Oregon; Dubuque, Iowa; Fort Lupton, Colorado; Claresholm, Alberta, Canada; Delaware, Ohio; and Chino, California. Four additional plants have been temporarily closed until construction activity reaches a higher pace. While Trus Joist's president, Peter T. Johnson, expects lower sales in 1975, growth over the past five years has been commendable. Annual sales advanced from $11.3 million in 1970 to $41.6 million in 1974, with each year profitable.

Alaska Interstate Company (AKI) is a diversified company with wholly-owned subsidiaries engaged in the transmission and distribution of natural gas in Alaska, as well as manufacturing and service businesses in other states. The Company holds an interest in a major Indonesian oil and gas venture. The headquarters of AKI is in Houston, Texas.

Wholly-owned *Alaska Pipeline Company* is an intrastate natural gas company headquartered in Anchorage, Alaska. Alaska Pipeline operates a 116 mile gas transmission line from the Kenai Peninsula to Anchorage. *Alaska Gas and Service Company,* a 14-year old division of Alaska Interstate distributes natural gas to consumers in the greater Anchorage area. Reflecting Alaska's growth, expansion of gas service increased 13.6% to 25,100,000 mcf in 1974.

Alaska Interstate owns 7.5% of the common stock of *Northwest Energy Company* (See Chapter on Utilities).

Following are Alaska Interstate's manufacturing and service subsidiaries, some of which relate directly to the Northwest economy:

Lockwood Corporation — Manufactures potato harvesters and center pivot irrigation systems. Also manufactures sugar beet, bean harvesters and orchard spraying equipment. Major facility is in Gering, Nebraska with branch sales offices throughout the country.

Delta Engineering Corporation, with offices in Houston, Calgary, and London, England performs engineering and construction services for the petrochemical industry.

The Anlin Companies operate desulfurization and pollution control facilities at two major oil refineries in Illinois and New Jersey.

Kranco, Inc. — Located in the Southwest, Kranco manufactures overhead traveling cranes and gantry cranes capable of carrying loads up to 400 tons. Kranco is one of the five largest U.S. crane manufacturers.

National Aircraft Services, Inc. — performs overhaul and maintenance service for both jet and piston aircraft engines. Facilities are in Dallas, Texas and Miami, Florida.

Stardust Cruiser Manufacturing Co. — A regional manufacturer of houseboats.

Sauder Industries, Inc. — Manufactures steel pressure vessels, water storage facilities, and industrial heat treating furnaces.

Baldwin Properties, Inc. owns real estate properties in Alaska, California, Texas and Louisiana.

In addition to the above, Alaska Interstate holds substantial equity interests in *Roy M. Huffington, Inc.* and *Virginia International Company,* which in turn are participants in a joint venture called the Huffco Group. The joint venture is developing a major oil and gas field in Indonesia. Sales of natural gas are under contract to a Japanese consortium for delivery in 1977.

Basic to the building and construction industry is the use of cement. **Oregon Portland Cement Company** serves the Pacific Northwest with three cement manufacturing plants — Lake Oswego and Lime, Oregon and Inkom, Idaho. Cement and related construction materials are marketed through nine distribution centers in Oregon, Idaho, and Washington.

The economic disruptions in 1974 affected Oregon Portland's operations in several ways. Freight costs increased considerably — railroad rates increased 30% and truck freight rates climbed 15%. Fuel costs soared dramatically — a 56% increase. In turn, following the expiration of federal price controls, the company was able to increase its sales prices. Thus, company sales rose 14% in 1973 and 20% in 1974. However, unit shipments of cement increased just 2% and 8% in those years.

In addition to its usual Northwest markets, Oregon Portland Cement has contracts to supply the *Ririe* and *Teton* Dams in Idaho and the *Jim Bridger* Power Plant in Wyoming.

OPC also markets other products which contribute to the company's profitability. Agricultural lime products are used extensively

The new Government Services Administration Building in Portland, Oregon is clad with precast panels utilizing light gold quartz aggregate and OPC Lime*Lite cement.

OPC manufacturing plant at Inkom, Idaho.

Test plot liming with OPC agricultural lime.

throughout the Willamette Valley for soil enrichment. Sales of these products have increased 100% over the past five years. Chemical limestone from the company's Durkee, Oregon quarry is used principally by the beet sugar industry in its sugar refining process.

OPC is also the major producer of pozzolan in the Pacific Northwest at its Lime, Oregon location. The company's pozzolan is a natural volcanic ash that may be used in combination with cement in concrete or with cement and lime in a mixture that is being used for sand stabilization. Pozzolan is being used in concrete presently at the third power plant completion at *Grand Coulee Dam* and the additional units at *Chief Joseph Dam*. A combination of pozzolan with lime and cement was recently used to stabilize the sub-base at *John M. Fulton Marine Terminal* and *Portland International Airport*.

HIGHWAY CONSTRUCTION ACTIVITIES

The activities of two Northwest companies relate to highway construction and maintenance, although neither firm would be classified as a "road builder." **Fentron Highway Products, Inc.** is active in the Northwest in the fabrication of highway sign structures, transmission poles, railings and metal buildings. The company also makes component parts for the air pollution control industry.

In 1969, Fentron diversified somewhat by acquiring the Portland Swan Island heavy steel fabrication plant which makes structural and marine products. Fentron is also supplying a new line of bus shelters for the mass transit field. These are currently sold to Seattle, Portland, Spokane, and San Francisco, among others. Fentron's sales in fiscal 1975 topped $5 million, with a net income of $303,386.

An altogether different sort of company is **Transportation Safety Systems, Inc.** based in Salt Lake City. Research resulting from the growth of jet airliner traffic has created the demand for new safety features in paving work. Cutting small grooves in the paving surface helps to eliminate dangerous hydroplaning when the surface is wet.

Transportation Safety Systems (TSS) operates specialized equipment engaged in highway and runway grooving, concrete planing and texturing, and specialized sawing and coring on construction projects. A 1973 acquisition is California-based *Modern Alloys, Inc.* which (1) installs highway guard rails, signs, and fences, (2) constructs concrete barrier walls on highways and (3) fabricates guard rail and sign components.

Transportation Safety Systems operates international subsidiaries in England, West Germany, Sweden and France. Although TSS reported a net loss for 1974 ($224,495), annual revenue in the past five years has expanded from $4.2 million to $9.6 million.

REAL ESTATE DEVELOPMENT

Pacific Northwest Development Corporation is involved in the complete development, marketing, and management of real estate in the Pacific Northwest. Typical projects include commercial and professional buildings, mobile home parks, residential subdivisions, and apartment complexes. All phases of the real estate process are handled — feasibility and analysis, property acquisition, construction, marketing, financing, and mortgage servicing, as well as property management. Since 1969, the company has also been active in the mortgage brokerage and loan servicing business.

Pacific Northwest's main subsidiary is *Pete Wilson Realty,* an 11-year-old commercial real estate brokerage firm which derives its income from sales commissions.

Another important subsidiary of Pacific Northwest Development Corporation is *Pioneer Industries.* Pioneer handles the construction and development of multiple dwellings, commercial and professional complexes, mobile home parks, condominiums and townhouses and recreational facilities. Through the related *Commercial Supply Division,* Pacific Northwest is able to purchase items such as carpets, furniture, and appliances at substantial discounts.

Finally, in the field of mobile home park development, Pacific Northwest is creating these communities: *Deer Creek Estates* (Aurora, Oregon); *Green Tees* (Gresham, Oregon); and *Lakeside Village, Greentree Estates, Surfwood Village,* and *Sleepy Hollow Village* — all in Salem, Oregon.

For more than 35 years, **Edwards Industries** has been primarily engaged in real estate construction and sales in Oregon, with some additional revenue from building materials and glass operations. During the past three years, sales and earnings contributions from auto glass, contract glass, and building materials have combined for a more significant share of the business. These operations accounted for 74% of 1975's $20.3 million in revenue, and 49% of operating income, and are expected to play an increasingly important role in Edwards' future.

Windows and exterior doors are stocked at Edwards Industries building materials outlets.

One of Edwards Industries 14 auto glass outlets in Washington and Oregon.

Edwards sells auto glass through four outlets in Oregon and 10 in Washington, primarily Seattle. Four more residential and commercial glass and paint outlets in Oregon specialize in contract work, but also sell flat glass and auto glass as well as selected other lines of building needs on a retail basis.

Since you can't *really* own "a piece of the rock," how about owning "a piece of the island"?

Hayden Island, Inc. is one of the Northwest's most unusual public companies. Its primary line of business is real estate development, and its main asset is ownership of property on a very well-situated island lying in the Columbia River between Portland, Oregon and Vancouver, Washington. Interstate Highway 5 carries 90,000 cars per day across the island between the two cities, and contributes significantly to the island's commercial and residential development, virtually all of which is owned or at least 50% owned and controlled by Hayden Island, Inc.

Of the island's 1,200 acres, the company owns about 375 acres. To date, the company has developed or reserved for expansion only 160 acres (47%) of its holdings. Further development of the land will extend over the next five to ten years.

JANTZEN BEACH NAME RETAINED

While the property is properly known as "Hayden Island," the area is more popularly known to Oregon and Washington residents as *Jantzen Beach*. The world-famous *Jantzen Beach Amusement Park* operated for several decades on this island. The park is gone now and in its place is one of Oregon's most modern shopping centers.

The initial development phase of *Jantzen Beach Shopping Center* climaxed with the opening of 39 stores in September 1972. By the end of 1974, the Center had grown to over 75 shops and services, including department stores operated by *Montgomery Ward* and *Liberty House* (an *Amfac* subsidiary) and a *Pay Less Drug Store*. Proposed plans for further expansion include a third department store and 30 additional mall shops.

The shopping center is surrounded by a growing number of other commercial and residential developments, including the Jantzen Beach *Thunderbird* motel-restaurant complex, a cluster of condominium units and apartments and mobile home parks. Gross business volume on Hayden Island's property exceeded $50 million last year, and is projected at $75 million for 1975. Gross volume at the shopping center alone will approximate $45 million for 1975.

Property rentals and Hayden Island's 50% venture participation in the *Thunderbird Motor Inn* have accounted for nearly all of the company's net income during the past five years. Revenue from property rentals has increased 270% during the past four years from $682,000 in 1970 to $2.5 million in 1974.

In addition to the above, two Jantzen Beach Mobile Home Parks provide permanent space for 360 homes and overnight space for 50, with more under construction. Jantzen Beach Moorage, one of the largest in

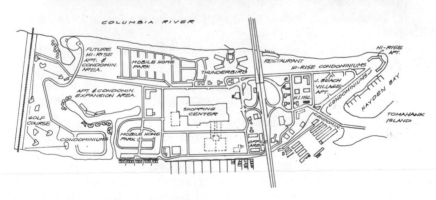

Hayden Island is realizing its potential as a planned commercial-residential development.

Oregon, provides space for about 700 pleasure boats plus 150 houseboats.

Year-round customer traffic count on the island is about evenly divided between Oregon and Washington residents. The current 1,600-person work force is similarly divided. The island's residential population is now more than 1,800 persons. Upon completion of Hayden Island's projects, this island will provide residences for about 3,000 people and employment for some 5,500.

Investors may not realize that one of the world's largest and most diverse design engineering and construction firms is based in the Northwest. This is **Morrison-Knudsen Company, Inc.** of Boise, Idaho.

A very complex company, M-K has numerous wholly-owned subsidiaries, one 90% owned subsidiary and two partially-owned affiliates. The company has completed projects in all 50 states and 70 foreign countries.

Morrison-Knudsen engages in all kinds of construction — industrial heavy, municipal, building, transportation, pipeline, pipe-coating, marine, utility and energy-related fields. With 1974 sales of $678 million, M-K currently has an order backog in excess of one billion dollars.

The complexity of the company's work can best be shown by a few examples:

(1) the design, planning and completion of a major new mine — *Sarpy Creek Mine* — in Southeastern Montana with 800 million tons of coal reserves.

(2) the laying of 21 miles of natural gas pipeline off the coast of Holland.

(3) Construction of a gymnasium and Olympic Pool (6000 spectators) in Brazil.

(4) Erection of a 52-story office building in Singapore.

(5) A 260,000 acre irrigation project in Bangladesh.

(6) Rebuilding or repair of 43 railroad locomotives in 1974 for U.S. railroads.

(7) Design and construction of a $43 million beet sugar factory in Minnesota.

While hundreds of examples such as those above could be cited, two instances in particular will be meaningful to Northwest investors.

In 1974, Morrison-Knudsen was awarded a $125 million construction contract by the *Alyeska Pipeline Service Company*. This is for the construction of 145 miles of the trans-Alaska pipeline between a point known as Sourdough and the port of Valdez. Under other contracts worth more than $32 million, the company completed 35 miles of roadway paralleling a remote northern stretch of the pipeline, and is carrying out an extensive program of excavation and grading at Valdez to prepare the site for marine terminal facilities.

Another example of Morrison-Knudsen's diversity is its 90% owned subsidiary. *Morrison-Knudsen Forest Products Company, Inc.* The company has exclusive rights to an improved method of forming "oriented" fiberboard from wood particles. The process involves dropping wood fibers through a high-voltage electrical field that aligns (orients) the fibers so that they point in the same direction. The fibers are then pressed into a board that has a significant increase in strength in the direction of orientation. A commercial scale former machine has been installed by M-K in a new northern California plan owned by the *Louisiana-Pacific Corporation*. The plant is designed to produce medium-density fiberboard for wall panels, door skins, and furniture products. While not yet fully operational, this new process would seem to have a very exciting future.

Morrison-Knudsen lays cross country and offshore pipelines for transmission of oil and gas, remanufactures railroad locomotives, co-owns the largest shipbuilding firm in the west (National Steel and Shipbuilding Co. of San Diego), and has become widely recognized for its expertise in the field of design and construction of mine facilities.

M-K's 50% owned affiliate *National Steel & Shipbuilding Company* (NASSCO) based in San Diego, contributed over $2 million to total company earnings of $9.3 million in 1974. A 2-year expansion of NASSCO's shipyards, permitting construction of tankers of up to 190,000 dwt, is being completed in 1975.

M-K is also heavily involved in coal mining through its 24% partnership interest in *Westmoreland Resources.* The partnership owns the *Sarpy Creek Mine,* an 800-million-ton coal resource near Hardin, Montana. As mentioned earlier, M-K designed and constructed the mine and operates it under a 20-year contract awarded by Westmoreland Resources. Production in 1975 is expected to reach 4 million tons, mostly to be shipped to Midwest utilities.

It seems that there is literally nothing that Morrison-Knudsen's staff of more than 2,700 professional engineers and technicians cannot do, given the time and resources.

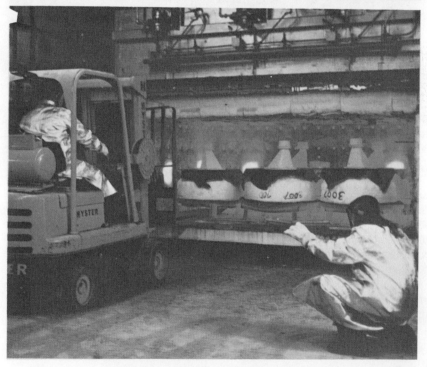

Vacuum furnace (at top) for remelt alloy production is shown under construction at Precision Castparts. Burn-out furnace (bottom) heat treats investment castings.

10

Manufacturing

As an industry, manufacturing is not as dominant in the Northwest as in some other regions of the country. Indeed, the original components were lumber and wood products, which we discussed under forest products.

Aerospace and Electronics

By the mid-1950's, the aerospace industry had grown to the point of surpassing all other manufacturers. Aerospace means just one thing to many people in the Northwest — The *Boeing Company*. Even after substantial employment reductions following cancellation of the *SST* program, Boeing is still the largest employer and has the highest annual sales of any company in the Northwest. A number of supportive industries (electronics, controls, metal castings, exotic metals, aluminum fabrication, etc.) were originally attracted to the region by Boeing's presence. Now, in the mid-1970's, Boeing's activities, while still as significant as before, are no longer quite as dominant.

Manufacturing in the Northwest has matured and diversified into various self-sustaining components. In addition to Aerospace, Electronics and Instrumentation, we can identify a number of other industrial classifications which are worthy of separate discussions. These are (1) Exotic Metals, (2) Recreational Boating, (3) Heavy Industrial, and (4) Consumer Goods and Miscellaneous Manufacturing.

Originally geared to domestic markets, a number of companies now thrive on foreign sales as well. These would include among others, *Boeing, Tektronix, Hyster, Omark Industries, Western Marine Electronics,* and *Jantzen.*

In summary, Northwest manufacturing companies now produce goods ranging from aircraft to boats, boxcars, medical and electronic instruments, tools, clothing, and dental equipment. We have identified more than thirty-five publicly-owned firms of interest to Northwest investors.

In the aircraft and aerospace industry, most investors recognize that the **Boeing Company** is the nation's and the world's leader.

Boeing's fortunes are inextricably tied to changes in airline traffic

121

loads and the financial condition of its client airlines. Boeing is also dependent upon such things as fuel shortages and military-political decisions of the United States and many foreign governments.

In 1967 Boeing's total employment peaked at 142,700 workers, and rapidly declined to a low of 37,200 in 1971. Many investors concluded that the company was terminally ill. However, the financial record suggests otherwise. Boeing has been profitable in each of the past ten years, and has paid dividends in each of those years. In fact, in 1969, the company paid cash dividends in excess of earnings for that year. Net stockholders' equity has increased in nine of the last ten years, and was $954,967,000, at the end of 1974.

While the 1975-1976 period will not set any sales records for commercial aircraft, the business remains a healthy one.

Estimates Of Commercial Model Aircraft Deliveries*

	1974 Actual	1975 Estimated	1976 Estimated
707	21	10	15
727	91	90	72
737	55	50	36
747	22	22	26
Total number of aircraft	189	172	149
Total Commercial Sales (incl. parts, modifications etc.) (in millions)	$2,192	$2,175	$2,100

*Includes military versions

Table courtesy of Foster & Marshall, Inc. (research report dated 8/11/75)

Through June, 1975, a total of 1,225 aircraft of the 727 type have been sold, making it the most popular commercial model of all time. Sales of the Boeing 737, which was introduced in 1967, had reached 454 units as of that same date.

The only imminent new aircraft product for Boeing is the 747 SP (Special Performance) plane, which was first test flown on July 4, 1975. A modified version of the original 747, the SP is 47 feet shorter and will carry about 290 passengers, compared to 360 or more on the standard 747. Weighing 115,000 pounds less, the 747 SP can fly faster than the 747, and has a 6,900 mile maximum range (the equivalent of New York to Tokyo) non-stop.

Boeing's President, Malcolm Stamper, has predicted that the company will eventually sell about 300 of the $30 million 747 SP's. Four airlines — *Pan American, South African, Iran* and *Syria* — have already placed orders for a total of 13 *747 SP's.*

Most investors know that the aerospace industry has had its problems (ups and downs, if you will) in the past decade.

Heath Tecna Corporation (Kent, Washington) has endured this pattern along with other such companies. The company's sales declined in 1972, were up in 1973 and 1974, and were down again in fiscal 1975 (fiscal years ending April 30). However, investors should note that the

Two Boeing 747's in the final assembly stage.

Rocket Research is working on a number of NASA contracts such as the Space Shuttle Orbiter.

Heath Tecna's new Model 750T Speedway passenger loading bridge won airline orders soon after its introduction in 1974.

company's "bottom line" has shown steady improvement. Although net losses totaled $10.6 million for 1971 and 1972 combined, the company has shown improvement in each of the last four years, and recorded a $3 million net profit in fiscal 1975, including $1.5 million in tax loss carry-forward benefit.

Last year Heath Tecna's Air Transportation Products operations (one Division, two subsidiaries) accounted for 60.4% of company sales and 52.1% of its pre-tax and pre-extraordinary earnings. These operations manufacture commercial aircraft interiors, fiberglass reinforced plastic structures and assemblies, and aircraft ground support equipment. In 1975 Heath Tecna began producing interior systems for the new Douglas DC-9-50's. *United Airlines* has purchaed Heath Tecna interior conversion systems for 56 DC-8's and 114 727's. Heath Tecna is the nation's leading independent producer of aircraft interiors, with systems available for DC-9's, DC-8's, and for Boeing 707, 720, 727, and 737 aircraft.

Heath Tecna's Building Products and Protective Finishes operations (two Divisions and one subsidiary) provided 43.2% of fiscal

1975 pre-tax, pre-extraordinary income, based on 32% of total company sales. The company's main subsidiary in this division is *Fentron Industries, Inc.* of Seattle, Washington (not to be confused with *Fentron Highway Products,* discussed elsewhere). In 1975 Fentron Industries received a contract to manufacture and install aluminum and glass curtain wall for a new *Fourth and Vine* office building in downtown Seattle, as well as the new *Equitable Center* in Salem, Oregon. In Alaska, Fentron has new contracts for three office buildings and a 7-story community hospital.

Heath Tecna's smallest line of business, Defense and Electronics, (two subsidiaries) produced 7.6% of 1975 sales and just 4.7% of pre-tax, pre-extraordinary earnings. Primary activity in this business line is the manufacture of TACAN (Tactical Air Navigation) Beacon Simulators and related equipment.

A very recent development is Heath Tecna's purchase of *Maico Hearing Indstruments, Inc.* (Minneapolis, Minn.). Maico is a leading producer of hearing aids, with annual sales in excess of $7 million. According to company president Martenson, "This is the first acquisition in our program to enter new markets and expand Heath Tecna's business base from our present position in the capital goods and air transportation fields."

One Northwest company deeply involved with exotic aerospace and other high technology products is **Rocket Research Corporation** of Redmond, Washington. Rocket Research (RRC) can best be described by identifying some of the products and projects it is involved with.

The company is a sub-contractor to *Sundstrand Aviation* for the *NASA* Space Shuttle orbiter. Rocket makes integral components of the three auxiliary power units employed on each Space Shuttle orbiter vehicle to generate hydraulic power for the vehicle's nose wheel steering, wing flaps, and other hydraulically actuated equipment.

Also in the field of space technology, RRC has been selected to provide a low-cost thruster for the *Mariner-Jupiter-Saturn (MJS)* spacecraft currently under development at the *NASA/Jet Propulsion Laboratory.* This initial program involves development, qualification, and production of flight hardware for the MJS mission. It also provides opportunities for follow-on orders, since the Rocket Research thruster has been selected by *NASA* as a standardized component for future *NASA* spacecraft.

Among many other projects under development by Rocket Research, investors may be interested in RRC's tire sealant program. The company has been working for several years on an apparently successful new process. The RRC tire sealant has been extensively tested and proven to be effective in sealing tire punctures over a broad range of test conditions. The sealant is unique in that it effectively seals punctures caused by nails up to and including ¼ inch diameter. It does not creep or flow at the elevated tire temperatures caused by excessive loads and high speeds. It is unusually resistant to degradation from aging.

The first eighteen months of this research was performed under contract to *General Motors Corp.* GM's ultimate objectives include the elimination of the spare tire to effect a reduction in automobile weight and an increase in trunk space. A working agreement with GM gives RRC a non-exclusive, royalty-free license to any inventions conceived by RRC under the contract. Incidentally, Edward N. Cole, former president of General Motors, became a Rocket Research director in 1974.

Sales for Rocket Research grew from $10.8 million in 1970 to $16.4 million in 1974, with net earnings of $621,888 in 1974.

A success story of interest to Northwest investors is the record of **John Fluke Mfg. Co., Inc.** The company was begun in 1948 by John Fluke and one other employee. They designed and manufactured a device called a VAW meter (voltage, amperes, and wattage). The company was profitable in its first year on sales of just $20,000. The VAW meter became an industry standard, and, without redesign, remained a part of the company's product line until 1972.

John Fluke makes a multitude of precision electronic instruments for testing and measuring purposes. These include such products as multimeters, high voltage power supplies, voltmeters, frequency synthesizers, and calibrators. Frequency synthesizers provide carrier signals for many communication applications such as satellite transmission. Multimeters are used to measure the electrical characteristics of electronic circuits such as current, voltage, and resistance.

The company has a new line of digital thermometers, which are finding commercial applications in industries such as steel, plastics, food, and petrochemicals. Although Fluke was formerly dependent on military and aerospace markets, these markets currently account for about 20% of revenues each. Fluke's commercial business now includes a customer list of some 14,000 companies and individuals. John Fluke's sales in fiscal 1974 (ending September 30) were $33.4 million, and the company has never experienced an unprofitable year.

Another interesting Northwest electronics company is **Western Marine Electronics Company** (Wesmar) located in Seattle. The company designs and manufactures marine sonar equipment and industrial ultrasonic measuring devices and equipment. These are all based on the principle of measuring distances by means of sound traveling through water or air. In addition, Wesmar makes vapor detection equipment for monitoring hazardous vapors in industrial or other locations.

Wesmar's marine sonar devices are widely used by commercial fishermen to locate and home in on schools of fish. Pleasure fishing boats are also beginning to use this equipment to locate all varieties of fish. Recent sales have been concentrated in the U.S., Canada, Norway, and Spain. Over one-third of Western Marine's sales are to foreign markets.

Western Marine's ultrasonic industrial models can be used to electronically measure the level of material or liquid in large containers such as coal or metal bins, oil tanks, or grain silos. This means that they can be adapted for automated materials handling systems. For example, in automating coal-fired utility plants, Wesmar devices have been installed in ten such plants during fiscal 1974. The company had orders in hand for seven more utility plants and others are anticipated.

Products of the **Heinicke Instruments Company** (Portland, Oregon) serve two principal markets: (1) medical and scientific equipment and (2) the aviation industry.

Heinicke produces two basic types of incubators. One type is used for controlling growth of tissue cultures in the medical research area. The other is used for controlling the growth of pathogenic bacteria in the hospital clinical laboratory. Drying ovens, which are used in chemistry applications for non-destructive drying, tissue embedding, and curing electronic components are produced in ten different models by the company. Other Heinicke products include autoclaves (pressurized vessels using steam to sterilize contaminated surgical instruments), washers providing pulsonic cleaning of hospital and medical research laboratory glassware, and large walk-in environmental rooms and chambers.

Heinicke's acquisition of the *Jet Avion Corporation* in October, 1974 contributed the company's other major line of products. Jet Avion manufactures over seventy replacement parts for *Boeing, Douglas, Lockheed,* and *General Dynamics* aircraft engines.

The world's largest manufacturer of oscilloscopes is **Tektronix, Inc.** located in Beaverton, Oregon. The markets for Tektronix's equipment is seemingly universal. Over three-fourths of the companies rated as the 500 largest by *Fortune* magazine are Tektronix customers. The total customer list is about 35,000 commercial accounts in science, industry, and education.

Oscilloscopes are basic test instruments which display electrical

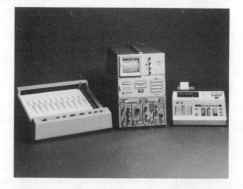

Wesmar's SS 110, the world's first small boat sonar, penetrated the pleasure boat market in the U.S. as well as in many overseas countries.

The signal acquisition capabilities of Tek's wide-band laboratory oscilloscope, computational power of a modern programmable calculator, and the stability and accuracy of a digital X-Y plotter are combined to form a powerful system to meet the ever growing measurement needs in many varied fields.

current into visual pictures on cathode ray tubes (CRT). These electrical currents can be triggered by heat, pressure, sound, strain, nuclear events, velocity, or biochemical signals. Virtually every testing laboratory in the country uses some form of oscilloscope.

Tektronix has been the leader in developing new types of such equipment and inventing new uses for it. For example, the newest wrinkle is the "storage" oscilloscope. The CRT viewing screen normally displays the electronic data visually with a snake-like curve continuously moving across the screen. "Storage" is much the same as freezing the image on the screen. Thus, irregularities in a moving pattern which would otherwise be missed by a technician can be stored and later studied at length. Tektronix has also developed a multitude of other related oscilloscope products — hand held, portable, microscopic, etc. — which make the company the unquestioned leader in this field.

Tektronix is an international operation, with three manufacturing operations in Europe and one in Japan. In addition, marketing subsidiaries or representatives are located in more than fifty locations worldwide. Annual sales for Tektronix have risen in nine of the past ten years, from $102.1 million in fiscal 1966 to $336.6 million in 1975, while annual net income increased from $11.1 million to $26.3 million. About 40% of sales now come from markets outside the United States.

A fact that probably goes unnoticed by many Oregonians as well as other Northwest residents is Tek's impact on employment in the region. Tektronix is the largest industrial employer in Oregon with 8,950 people presently employed in the state. This is particularly surprising and noteworthy considering the predominance of forest products and related industries within the state's economy. Employment figures for other major companies in Oregon include 7,400 people for Weyerhaeuser and 3,800 for Georgia-Pacific. Approximately 13,800 personnel out of Weyerhaeuser's 49,000-total work force and 1,450 personnel out of Georgia-Pacific's 34,500-total work force are employed in the State of Washington.

A new, inventive Northwest company is **LRC, Inc.** of Riverton, Wyoming. Organized in 1971, the company did not become operational until November, 1973. LRC designs and develops various types of electronic and electro-mechanical products for use with computers, business machines and related devices. LRC also offers contract research and development and engineering services to other manufacturers. (LRC is a computer shorthand term for "Longitudinal Redundancy Check" — a measure of reliability and accuracy).

The company's initial efforts were focused on the development of a multi-character high-speed impact matrix printer for use with computers and communications-related equipment. Other company research has gone into the development of a low-speed impact matrix printer for use in calculators, the development of low-cost computer mass memory mechanisms, and an inexpensive "floppy disc" mechanism for computer data storage and retrieval.

The **A T & E Corporation** (formerly *Gemini Venture Corp.*) moved its headquarters and production facilities from Salt Lake City, Utah to San Francisco during 1974. A T & E is engaged in the design, manufacture and sale of telephone and industrially oriented electronic products. A line of advanced measurement systems, which include large scale integrated (LSI) circuits is produced by *Counsel Corporation,* a division of A T & E. Counsel Corp.'s ESCAL and ESPRINT calculator product lines are distributed by K & E (*Keuffel & Esser Co.) and Ricoh of America,* whose dealer networks in engineering and office supply companies exceed 4,500 outlets in the U.S. alone. Foreign distribution is supported through A T & E International. Products of A T & E Systems, another division, also utilize LSI systems and include a variety of telephone-related apparatus, such as *Comdial* (a rotary dial replacement assembly) and *Faxfone* (for use with a business facsimile unit).

Tally Corporation (Kent, Washington) is a manufacturer of computer peripheral equipment. The company markets medium speed line printers, paper tape equipment, and data communication terminals. Tally's products are geared to serve the fast-growth, low-cost, medium-capacity minicomputer and microprocessor systems business. Tally printers are low-cost, high-reliability machines with speeds ranging from 125 to 400 lines per minute. Tally has also introduced a new perforator/reader combination system. This paper tape unit is ideally suited to the data input/output needs of microprocessor systems.

Tally has overseas offices in England, Germany, Italy, and France. The company's sales have been relatively flat in the past five years, from $13.3 million in 1970 to $17.8 million in 1974. While the 1971-73 period was an unprofitable one, management is hopeful that growth will be resumed in the near future.

The **Systems Corporation** sells and services under contract minicomputer business systems, primarily its TSC-1000 system. With its executive offices in Portland, the company operates a sales and service office in Honolulu and, under joint venture agreements, has other offices in Oregon and Iowa. The company teams up with established EDP service companies to build, sell, and service turnkey mini-business systems. The Systems Corporation buys mini-computers from leading manufacturers and adds its own controllers and proprietary software to produce low-cost, on-line data processing systems. The systems have been particularly useful to medical groups, distributors, memorial parks, retailers, manufacturing companies, and construction firms, among others.

Physio-Control Corporation (Redmond, Washington) is the leading manufacturer in the Northwest of sophisticated electronic medical equipment. The company's line of defibrillators presently accounts for 80% of corporate sales.

There is increasing awareness that coronary disease is the largest single cause of death in the United States. This has led to substantial improvements in diagnostic and therapeutic facilities for heart disorders, including the establishment of special coronary care and inten-

Coronary disease is the nation #1 killer—Physio Control is doing its best to combat this with defibrillators and other medical equipment.

sive care units (CCU and ICU) in hospitals, equipped with specialized patient monitoring systems for emergency treatment. Emphasis is being placed on programs which provide immediate medical attention to those suffering from heart attacks and other forms of coronary disorder. Such programs provide for treatment of the patient where stricken, as well as constant monitoring of the patient while being transported to the hospital for care in a CCU.

According to the *National Electrical Manufacturers Association,* Physio-Control is the largest manufacturer of defibrillators in the world. These and other instruments combining a defibrillator and a cardioscope are used to diagnose, monitor, and on certain occasions, resuscitate heart attack victims by applying precordial shock. This equipment is used in hospitals, clinics, doctors' offices, emergency first aid vehicles, industrial plants, sports arenas, and other locations where heart attacks are likely to occur.

Physio-Control has also developed a peritoneal dialysis system in conjunction with Dr. Heinrich Tenckhoff and the *University of Washington Medical School.* Peritoneal dialysis is a method of cleansing the blood of patients suffering from kidney disorders. In association with the University of Washington Medical School, the company manufactures the *Thomas Femoral Shunt.* These shunts are surgically installed in a large artery and vein in the upper thigh of kidney patients to facilitate blood flow to and from an artificial kidney machine.

Another product developed by Physio-Control and the *University of Washington Center for Bioengineering* is a solid state oximeter. This continuously monitors the percentage of oxygen in the blood stream by means of a fiberoptic catheter inserted through a vessel to a point in or near the heart. The oximeter eliminates the need for periodic blood withdrawals during major surgery and postoperative recovery by continually displaying the oxygen saturation percentage in the blood on a digital readout.

Physio-Control's sales have increased steadily each year, from $1.1 million in 1969 to $10 million in 1974. The company has been profitable in each of the past five years, with net income of $1,051,000 in 1974.

Exotic Metals

As an outgrowth of specialized research and development of commercial processes for handling titanium and other specialized ore which took place in Portland and the Willamette Valley in the 1950's, a rather interesting exotic metals industry has grown up in the area. The largest publicly held company in the group is **Precision Castparts,** located in Portland. Information provided by the company best describes the nature of their work:

"Precision Castparts Corp. is a manufacturer of precision investment castings to customer specifications. The company specializes in complicated and large investment castings requiring high performance reliability and meeting rigid quality standards. These castings are produced from stainless steels and alloys of nickel, cobalt and titanium, using air and vacuum melting processes.

Investment casting is a highly specialized segment of the foundry industry. The manufacturing process consists essentially of these steps: (1) Making a wax reproduction of the object, (2) Surrounding the wax reproduction with a ceramic mold material, called the "shell" or "investment," (3) Melting out the wax leaving a hollow mold, (4) Pouring molten metal into the mold, (5) Removing the old material, and (6) Removing excess metal, finishing and inspecting the casting.

Investment casting can produce complex metal parts to closer tolerances and better surface finishes than other methods of casting. Depending upon the application, investment castings may require little or no subsequent machining.

Investment casting is used where the part to be formed is difficult, if not impossible, to machine, forge or weld, due either to the nature of the alloy from which it is to be made or the complexity of the part."

The company is a principal manufacturer of castings for large industrial gas turbines, primarily for electrical power utilities. Castings for small industrial gas turbines are produced for use in gas line transmission and compression systems. These are also used in oil ex-

Fluorescent penetrant inspection shown here is only one of the techniques employed to verify that Precision Castparts' products meet the exacting standards of its customers.

ploration, drilling, and pumping operations, such as Alaska's North Slope activity.

Precision Castparts also has extensive aircraft markets. New military aircraft programs (U.S. Navy F-14 and U.S. Air Force F-15 and F-16) make extensive use of the company's turbine castings. According to President E. H. Cooley, the company is currently selling to every major jet engine manufacturer in Europe. A decision in June, 1975 by a European group (Belgium, Denmark, Holland, and Norway) to purchase new F-16's as their basic equipment will mean upward of $30 million in new business for Precision Castparts stretching into the 1980's. The company now has a market share of 8% of the investment casting industry's total business, up from 4% just five years ago.

Another Oregon company that has developed special skills in handling rare metal castings is **Rem Metals Corporation.** Curiously enough, the company's principal product—the result of high technology metals casting—is an expensive line of stainless steel golf club heads. Sales boomed steadily from $1.2 million in 1969 to $8.6 million in 1974. About 64% of 1974's sales were in the golf club line.

However, Rem Metals has fallen upon evil times. A large customer has defaulted on its purchases from Rem. This left Rem with (1) the loss of one of its biggest accounts, and (2) an uncollectible (to date) trade debt in excess of $600,000. While Rem Metals has a lot of potential in the future, it has not yet solved its present dilemma.

In a happier position is the **Oregon Metallurgical Corporation** (OREMET) of Albany, Oregon. Oremet's 1973 revenue, $12.2 million, inceased to $22.2 million in 1974. Net income soared from $466,881 to $2,837,173 in the same period.

Founded in 1956, Oremet is believed to be the industry's second largest melter of titanium ingot. Titanium's principal use is in the aircraft and aerospace industries. However, other markets are developing. One use is the casting of large pump parts for hydrofoil boats. A new application is the use of titanium in a copper extraction process using low-grade domestic ores. This new process is necessary to meet more stringent federal and state regulations concerning environmental pollution.

Oremet also operates the only magnesium reduction plant in the Northwest. Producing pure magnesium and its by-product, chlorine, the plant's entire output has been sold under contract for the next five years.

Investors might find it interesting to note the major shareholders in Oremet. They are: (1) *Armco Steel Corporation* — 23.6%, (2) the *First National Bank of Oregon*—19.2% and (3) *Ladish Company* (a Wisconsin manufacturer of valves, fittings, and forgings)—18.5%. It would seem that private investors in Oremet are in good company. (First National acquired their Oremet stock in satisfaction of a $1 million Oremet debt to the bank at the time that Armco and Ladish invested $900,000 in the company.)

Other Albany, Oregon companies involved in the exotic metals industry include *Wah Chang,* owned by **Teledyne; Zirconium Technology,** acquired by **Kawecki Berylco** in 1975; and **Tiline,** acquired by **Whittaker Corp.** in the early 1970's.

Recreational Boat Builders

The Northwest is headquarters for four of the nation's publicly-held boat manufacturers, excluding divisional operations of multi-line companies also located in the region. All four companies are based in Washington, and include **American Marine Industries (AMI), Reinell Industries, Tollycraft Corp.** and **Uniflite, Inc.**

AMI and Reinell have concentrated on production of inboard-outdrive (or stern-drive) boats, while Tollycraft and Uniflite have primarily produced luxury inboard cruisers. Reinell and Uniflite each have a second plant operation outside of the Northwest, to tap key Eastern markets.

Of the four companies, Reinell has the largest revenue base, which approximates $27-$28 million; but Tollycraft has demonstrated the most stable earnings and rate of return among the four companies in recent years. Although its earnings will be lower in fiscal 1975 compared to the previous year, Tollycraft has not been hindered by its relatively smaller size, its production of a luxury line of boats, or its one plant operation which serves a worldwide market.

During the past five to ten years, the boat building industry has experienced strong growth with the increased popularity of boating as a leisure-time activity. Approximately 10 million boats and 47 million people used the country's waterways in 1974, and the popularity and usage has probably increased at least 5% or better since then.

Since the 1973 oil embargo, a variety of factors have impacted the sales and earnings picture of most recreational boat builders, including those headquartered in the Northwest. Fast-rising material costs, slackening in demand for power-boats, and materials shortages all contributed to production cutbacks.

Boat builders have experienced good sales increases during previous years of economic recovery. If the nation's economy continues to improve in 1976 and beyond, each of the four manufacturers will have further opportunities to expand in their respective markets.

NORTHWEST BOAT BUILDERS

| | | Latest Fiscal Year | | |
	Year	Sales (000)	Net Income (000)	Reported E.P.S.
American Marine Industries	12/31/74	$ 4,118	$(366)	$ .65Def.
Reinell Industries	7/31/74	25,969	45	.04
Tollycraft Corp.	8/31/74	6,366	270	1.58
Uniflite, Inc.	10/31/74	15,838	(36)	.07Def.

While rising costs have made profits somewhat elusive for many boat builders, boat owners have often experienced a more fortunate out-

Tollycraft takes great pride in the high standards of quality built into their luxury offshore cruisers.

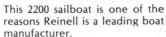

This 2200 sailboat is one of the reasons Reinell is a leading boat manufacturer.

come. Many owners, in fact, now view their craft as investments, rather than expensive luxuries. The market for quality used stern-drive and inboard cruisers remains steady, and owners are realizing as much as, and sometimes more than, their original cost, even if their boats are a year or two old.

American Marine Industries manufactures and distributes *Sabre Craft, Bell Boy* and *Fairliner* pleasurecraft, which range in length from 19 to 36 feet. Most models are stern-drives, but AMI's line also includes a limited number of outboards. Manufacturing operations employ AMI's patented *Web-cor* hull construction process, which aids in positive flotation as well as structural strength and reduced engine noise. These craft are distributed primarily through dealers along the West Coast.

American Marine consolidated its manufacturing operation into the former Fairliner facility in Tacoma, Washington during 1974. Annual sales have been in the $4-$5 million range for the past few years, as the company has redesigned a number of boat models and retooled to enter the larger-sized pleasurecraft market.

Uniflite has enjoyed a reasonably steady growth in sales of its luxury inboard cruisers during the past five to ten years. With its headquarters in Bellingham, Washington, the company launched a second plant operation in Swansboro, North Carolina during fiscal 1974.

Uniflite introduced sailboats into its line in 1974. However, luxury motor yachts, primarily in the 26 to 48 foot range, continue to account for the majority of its commercial sales. About 80% of Uniflite's $15 million in sales is made to commercial markets, and the other 20% to the U.S. government.

For the inboard cruiser market, total manufacturers' volume has approximated $100 million annually in recent years, according to industry sources. Uniflite's share is currently more than 10%. High quality standards in safety, service, and equipment, as well as construction, are characteristic of the cruiser market. Uniflite has been an industry pioneer in this respect through use of fire-retardant fiberglass resins. The company has used such resins extensively for years on contract orders for U.S. Naval patrol boats as well as on its commercial craft.

Tollycraft's 150,000 square foot manufacturing facility is located at Kelso, Washington. The company's line of 26 to 40 foot luxury cruisers features both stern-drive (moveable prop) and inboard engine systems. Primary markets are Pacific Coast states and Vancouver, British Columbia, with some sales in eastern states and foreign countries. Despite its size and somewhat regional market area, Tollycraft has generated a good earnings record during the past four years. One reason for its success during this unsettled period is maintenance of a high utilization of plant and equipment.

Customers are trading up to larger boats, which generally carry a slightly higher dollar margin of profit. Board Chairman R. M. Tollefson keeps in touch with owners for ideas on new boat designs and improvements. Personal interest and attention to customer preferences has contributed significantly to repeat business, especially in trading up existing owners to larger models.

Reinell Industries is considered the nation's largest manufacturer of trailerable stern-drive boats, and overall the fifth or sixth largest producer of all types of pleasure boats. Plants at Marysville, Washington and Poplar Bluff, Missouri distribute family pleasure boats nationwide and to Canada, Europe and Africa. In Japan, production is licensed through another manufacturer. Reinell's line of fiberglass craft includes sailboats and outboard models, as well as stern-drives, and range from 15 to 30 feet in length.

A network of some 200 franchised dealers supports the national sales program. In addition, the company has initiated its own retail operations on a very limited basis. This retail program is designed to obtain information for further training and improvement of dealer operations. Reinell also intends to expand its own retail operation into potentially profitable market areas where successful independent dealers have not been found for its line.

Industrial Equipment and Supplies

A number of nationally and internationally known industrial manufacturers are headquartered in the Northwest, as well as several smaller, regional companies. Their products include heavy-duty trucks, railroad cars, fork lift trucks and a variety of other heavy materials handling equipment, steel, specialized control valves for various purposes, and many other items.

MAJOR NORTHWEST HEAVY INDUSTRIAL MANUFACTURERS
Comparative Financial History

	1974		1970	
	Sales (000)	Net Income (000)	Sales (000)	Net Income (000)
Paccar, Inc.	$ 907,987	$ 23,340	$442,714	$ 14,760
Hyster Company	342,273	10,133	214,399	9,833
Omark Industries, Inc.	115,339	9,834	80,467	5,966
Cascade Corporation	49,692[1]	3,015[1]	24,156[2]	735[2]
Cascade Steel Rolling Mills, Inc.	27,442	4,238	4,383	(1,084)
Total	**$1,442,733**	**$ 50,560**	**$766,119**	**$ 30,210**

[1]Fiscal year ended Jan. 31, 1975
[2]Fiscal year ended July 31, 1970

A seventy year old company, **PACCAR Inc.** began in 1905 as the *Seattle Car Manufacturing Company,* which produced horse and oxen-drawn trucks for the logging industry. In 1907, the company began production of railroad logging cars.

This original business was relocated at Renton, Washington and the name changed to the *Seattle Car & Foundry Company* in 1911. The division's present name *Pacific Car & Foundry Company,* was adopted in 1924. Railroad cars have been produced continuously ever since. Pacific Car and Foundry produces plain box cars and cabooses as well as specialty cars. The division is the nation's leading manufacturer of poured-in-place polyurethane foam insulated box cars and mechanical refrigeration cars. Pacific Car also produces the *CARCO* line of winches for wheeled vehicles and crawler tractors.

PACCAR's other principal division and now by far its largest is truck manufacturing. Anyone experienced in the trucking industry will readily concede that PACCAR's two truck brands, *Peterbilt* and *Kenworth,* are among the top values in quality trucks. These heavy duty (Class 8) trucks are basically custom built and modified to individual customer orders.

Peterbilt trucks are constructed at Newark, California and Nashville, Tennessee. Kenworth plant facilities operate in Seattle; Kansas City, Missouri; and Chillicothe, Ohio. These heavy duty trucks are used in the freight, logging, construction, and petroleum industries.

Peterbilt and Kenworth, both part of
Paccar's truck manufacturing division,
are among the best values in quality
trucks.

One of Hyster's 87 different types of lift
trucks.

Two other specialty truck manufacturing subsidiaries of Paccar are
the *Dart Truck Company* (Kansas City, Missouri) and *Wagner Mining
Equipment, Inc.* (Portland).

Dart has produced custom-engineered off-highway trucks since
1903. These are used by logging, construction, airline and mining industries. A Dart aviation refueler was the first vehicle capable of servicing *Boeing 747* aircraft. Dart also makes a 45,000 pound capacity
front-end loader used in the construction and mining industries. The
timber industry uses Dart's massive log stackers with up to 120,000
pounds capacity.

Wagner manufactures rubber-tired diesel-powered vehicles to load,
haul and dump ore, rock, and coal in underground mines. Wagner
produces over 30 standard models to serve the mining industry.

PACCAR produces about 5% of all freight cars built in the U.S.,
15% of all U.S. trucks in its category, and 18% of the Canadian truck
market.

Hyster Company, whose home base is Portland, is a worldwide
manufacturing and marketing enterprise. Since the company's founding in 1929 to serve the Northwest logging industry, Hyster has grown
to the point where an international network of distributors and dealers
serve markets in some 130 countries.

The company was organized in Portland by Ernest G. Swigert, who
served as President until 1961 and Chairman until 1971. Mr. Swigert
continues to serve the company as a director. The company's original
name, *Willamette Ersted*, was later changed to *Willamette Hyster
Company,* and now **Hyster Company.**

The term "Hyster" comes from a slang word "hyst", a Pacific
Northwest logging colloquialism meaning "to hoist." Hyster was first
used as the trade name for a tractor hoist, or winch. Eventually it was
selected as the company name because of its simplicity and familiarity.

The company manufactures sixteen models of solid cushion tire internal combustion lift trucks, thirty-seven pneumatic tire lift truck models, and thirty-seven types of electric fork lift trucks. The company's extensive line of industrial forklift trucks has accounted for 87%-88% of total company sales in each of the past five years. Construction items manufactured include compaction equipment, logging equipment, and an assortment of cranes and heavy equipment hauling trailers.

The company's registered trademarks include *Hyster, SpaceSaver, Load Grab, Straddle Truck, Karry Krane, Grid, Yardmaster, Monotrol, Order Master, SitDrive, StanDrive,* and *LandSaver.*

Hyster products are sold to a wide variety of industries. These include the retail building material distribution field; transportation industry; forest product, stone, clay, glass and concrete industries; food manufacturers; and the primary metals industry. No single end-use commercial customer accounts for as much as two percent of the company's consolidated sales.

Hyster operates seven U.S. manufacturing plants and seven international plants. The foreign plants are located in Scotland, Canada, The Netherlands, Brazil, Belgium, South Africa, and Australia. In 1974, foreign sales were about 41% of Hyster's total revenue. Hyster's revenue has increased in four of the past five years — from $215.9 million in 1971 to $348.9 million in fiscal 1975.

Omark Industries, Inc. is the successor to a Portland firm established in 1947 as the *Oregon Saw Chain Corp.* While Omark has since diversified its operations, saw chains are still the company's sales leader (45% of sales), and contribute the bulk of company profits (87%).

Omark operates five divisions, which contributed the following percentages of fiscal 1975 sales:

Cutting Chain for chain saws	
Oregon Chain Saw Division	45%
Hydraulic Loaders and Cranes	
Hydraulic Materials Handling Division	14%
Industrial Fastening Systems	
KSM Fastening Systems Division	22%
Precision Fastening Division	10%
Sporting Equipment Division	9%

Management estimates that sales to professional loggers and pulpwood harvesters, worldwide, account for about 55% of the annual saw chain sales. Farmers, tree surgeons, construction workers, public utilities, and homeowners account for the remainder.

Chain is an expendable product which wears out regularly, requiring replacement. Consequently, manufacturing chain for the replacement market and for original equipment on chain saws increases Omark's opportunity to stabilize its long-term sales and earnings growth. In addition to cutting chain, Omark manufactures saw bars and sprockets at plants in Portland, Oregon; Bayamon, Puerto Rico; and Guelph, Ontario, Canada.

While the company does not manufacture any chain saws, Omark

KSM Safeguard welding gun is used to attach shear connectors to deck of Sears Tower in Chicago.

Omark's Hydraulic Materials Handling division is the leading U.S. producer of hydraulic log loaders.

In Brazil, lumberjacks don't wear lumberjackets (or indeed much of anything), but they've been quick to adapt North American aids to timber harvesting. The Oregon Saw Chain division of Omark Industries markets its chain world wide.

is by far the leading supplier of chain for original equipment on power saws made by the nation's largest manufacturers. Omark sells private brand saw chain and chain bearing the company's *Oregon* brand to both saw manufacturers and dealers serving the replacement market. Omark's proprietary brand of chain is distributed worldwide through a variety of retail outlets, including home and garden supply stores, hardware stores, and chain saw dealers. *Oregon* brand chain accounted for about 60% of saw chain footage sold during fiscal 1975.

Prentice hydraulic log loaders are the chief product line of the Materials Handling Equipment Division. During fiscal 1975, this division sold about 90% of its loaders and cranes to the pulpwood and timber harvesting industry.

During the fall of 1974, Omark combined its Construction Tool and KSM Welding divisions. KSM manufactures and sells stud welding systems, including equipment and fasteners, to many industries. A significant share of its sales are to the nonresidential construction industry.

The Sporting Equipment Division has tripled its sales since its acquisition in 1967. The division produces loads for the company's powder-actuated fastening systems, and also produces a line of .22 caliber rifle ammunition and "CCI" brand primers for reloading sporting rifle cartridges and shotgun shells. Omark, in 1975, purchased *Speer, Inc.* of Lewiston, Idaho, a well-known name in the bullet manufacturing field. Omark-CCI, also based in Lewiston, took over operations of Speer, which had sales in 1974 of about $3.9 million.

Now an international enterprise, Omark products are manufactured at 16 plants in four countries. These products are sold through a worldwide marketing network to customers in over 100 countries.

Cascade Corporation is a prospering materials handling manufacturer that seems to have been overlooked by most investors. The company makes a specialized line of attachments for fork lift trucks as well as hydraulic components (hose reels).

Cascade produces a wide variety of accessories designed to improve the speed or efficiency of fork lift equipment. The types of equipment can best be described by their functions: A "Load Push/Pull" lift truck attachment eliminates the need for palletizing loads. Cascade "Paper Roll Clamps" lift and stack massive paper rolls in warehouses without damage. "Rotators" allow automatic dumping of waste and storage bins by lift trucks. Cascade "Quad-Lift" masts allow overhead stacking of heavy loads up to a height of 22 feet.

While the company's products are hard to describe, Cascade Corporation's financial record is easy to understand. Sales have more than doubled in the past five years, from $24.1 million in 1970 to $49.7 million in fiscal 1975. In the same period, net income has quadrupled, from $735,000 to $3 million.

In addition to the domestic market, Cascade Corporation has facilities in Canada, Australia, Europe, South Africa, and Japan.

The smallest of the five industrial manufacturers, **Cascade Steel Rolling Mills, Inc.** had 1974 sales of $27.4 million. Cascade's stock was first offered to investors in 1968, and the company commenced production in November, 1969.

High, tight stacking of paper rolls is made possible by thin profile arms and secure "holding" ability of Cascade Paper Roll Clamps.

Cascade's business is the manufacture of steel reinforcing bars (rebars). Rebars are a necessity in many types of construction work. The company's raw material is scrap steel — old trucks, autos, and railroad cars. Cascade's mill processes scrap at a rate of 300 to 400 tons per day. This is equivalent to about 500 automobile bodies.

Recycling is an essential part of Cascade Steel's business. The company takes what was junk and turns it into useable goods for the construction of roads, buildings and other projects which require reinforced concrete. An additional social payoff is in the conservation of energy. Making steel by recycling scrap uses just 16% of the energy needed to make steel from raw iron ore.

Headquartered in Provo, Utah, **Valtek, Inc.** is a small company manufacturing top quality specialized valves. While sales in fiscal 1974 were just $2.6 million, president Charles Bates announced in early 1975 that the company's sales backlog had reached a record $4 million.

Valtek's specialized valves are used in chemical plants, petroleum refineries, and nuclear reactors. Serving some 900 different valve customers, Valtek's biggest customers have been *General Electric* and *DuPont*. The company presently has licensees in England and Australia, as well as a 30% interest in a Canadian plant.

Process Systems, Inc., headquartered in Salt Lake City, manufactures DigiCon valves, steam valves for surface ships and submarines, and microcomputers. The company's first year as a fully operating company was 1974, although it had been in a developmental stage for three years prior to that time.

A company with a checkered history and changing fortunes is **Golconda Corporation.** Incorporated in 1927 in Idaho, Golconda operated a famous silver and lead mine in the Coeur d'Alene Mining District. The company was then known as *Golconda Lead Mines.* This lasted from 1928 until 1957, when the mine's ore reserves became depleted.

Golconda then began acquiring mining companies, properties, and mining securities of other companies in the Coeur d'Alene District. From 1966 until 1971, the company operated as a non-diversified closed-end investment management company. On September 15, 1970, a concern named *Astro Controls, Inc.* was merged into Golconda, and the company assumed its present name. All of this is a roundabout way of stating that Golconda is now primarily a manufacturing company.

Golconda's *RegO Division* designs and manufactures: (1) pressure regulators, valves and other equipment for LP-Gas and anhydrous ammonia; (2) pressure regulators, cylinder valves, manifolds and other control equipment for atmospheric and other compressed, liquefied and dissolved gases; (3) gas welding and cutting equipment, (4) medical oxygen and chemical equipment; (5) electrical welding products; (6) pneumatic control devices; and (7) cylinder valves and regulators for self-contained breathing apparatus. A common characteristic of RegO products is the control or regulation of the flow of gases, either into or out of containers in which the gases are stored, or into piping systems.

Golconda's *Anderson Copper and Brass Division* manufactures a line of fittings for use with copper tubing. This includes flare fittings, compression fittings, inverted flare, double compression and brass pipe fittings, and garden hose and air hose fittings.

In early 1974, the **Cerro Corporation** obtained ownership of about 85% of the voting control of Golconda. The remaining 15% of the stock is held by some 1,500 stockholders and traded on the *Pacific Stock Exchange.*

Consumer Goods and Other Manufacturers

Located far from the textile and garment industries of the East, Portland, Oregon is world headquarters for the famous **Jantzen Inc.** which has a long history and a very successful record.

The company was founded in 1910 as the *Portland Knitting Company* for the manufacture and marketing of heavy woolen sweaters, hosiery, scarves, and gloves. In 1913 Jantzen developed the first rib-knit bathing suit. (Bikini lovers should note that the ladies' one-piece wool bathing suit weighed eight pounds when wet.) By 1918 the company had achieved national distribution of its swimwear and the name was changed to *Jantzen Knitting Mills.*

In 1938 Jantzen began making both men's and women's sweaters. In the 1940's and 1950's the company diversified into sportswear and intimate apparel (brassieres, girdles, etc.). The company adopted its present name, *Jantzen Inc.,* in 1951.

Today, Jantzen's production is divided among three divisions — Men's, Misses' and International. The basic swimsuit lines contribute less than 20% of the company's present annual sales.

Founded in 1910 in Portland, Oregon, Jantzen products are sold in many countries around the world.

After the mid-1920's, Jantzen manufactured swimwear exclusively and adopted "Red Diving Girl" as a trademark. The Jantzen trademark is one of the most widely recognized in the world.

Jantzen currently employs about 5,000 men and women in the U.S. and Canada. Apparel is manufactured in 15 plants containing 995,000 square feet of floor space for spinning, dying, knitting, fabric finishing, cutting and sewing. The company has three distribution centers with a total floor space of 454,100 square feet.

Jantzen products are sold in more than 11,000 domestic retail outlets. Foreign licensees and export agents sell Jantzen products in a total of 97 foreign countries. In the ten years ending in fiscal 1974 (fiscal year ending August 31), annual sales have grown from $59.5 million to $113.9 million. Net income in the same period increased from $1,154,000 to $5,254,000.

Moore Clear Co. (Portland, Oregon) is involved in two aspects of manufacturing in the Northwest. Since 1927, Moore Clear's subsidiary, *Northwest Foundry & Furnace Co.*, has produced grey iron, ductile iron and allied castings in automated foundry facilities. These castings range in size from four ounces to more than four tons. They are sold primarily to manufacturers of pumping equipment, materials handling equipment, and forest products.

Moore Clear's other operations produce electric furnaces and air conditioning equipment. The company has produced a new type of solid state forced air electric furnace, the *WESCO VEM*. The VEM is the only electric furnace manufactured in the United States that offers true energy-saving modulation of the heating elements and accurate temperature control with an electronic thermostat. The VEM electric furnace will maintain the temperature in a residence within one-half degree of the thermostat setting.

In the past five years, Moore Clear's sales have advanced each year from $2.5 million in 1970 to $7.9 million in 1974. Earnings have also improved each year, from a loss of $220,434 in 1970 to positive earnings of $199,304 in 1974.

The business of **Interface Mechanisms** (Intermec), located at Mountlake Terrace, Washington, is the sale of bar code printers to other original equipment manufacturers. The largest application for Intermec products is the printing of *Universal Product Code* (UPC) symbols on labels for in-store attachment to grocery items. Intermec printers create labels for use on random weight packages such as fresh meat and produce and other products which do not have preprinted symbols.

Bar code labels are becoming increasingly common as they are easily read by computer devices. Bar code systems are currently in use in a wide variety of applications — library systems, filing, photofinish invoicing, and industrial inventory control. About 30 supermarkets are now testing the use of these codes at checkout stands prior to making their usage standard industrywide.

In fiscal 1975 (fiscal year ending March 31), Intermec earned its first operating profit, $89,556, on revenue of $1,388,839.

Audiscan, Incorporated is a Bellevue, Washington manufacturer of 16 mm filmstrip projectors in various models. These use a synchronized filmstrip and sound tape cartridge of a proprietary Audiscan

RED SHOES $12.93 PR.

||||||||||||||||| |||||||||||||||
a 1 35972846 $12.93a

More and more stores are realizing the
value of uniform price coding.

design. Audiscan projectors are primarily marketed to other commercial companies which use them for instructional training and as sales aids.

Audiscan's other principal business is 80% owned *Gem East Corporation,* located in Seattle. Gem East manufactures diamond, pearl, and other lines of precious stone jewelry. Gem East sells to individual jewelers as well as to retail jewelry chains.

A small Salt Lake City firm, **Centralarm International, Inc.** operates a central station silent alarm system in that city for more than 600 residential and industrial subscribers. Centralarm also manufactures the transmission and control equipment used in the system. This equipment detects intrusion, fire, burglary and other events by means of various sensing devices in the premises being protected. These sensors are continuously monitored at a central station via specially installed telephone lines reserved for that purpose.

The company's Alarm Control division sells fire alarm and burglary alarm systems which do not involve the continuous monitoring activity. This alarm receiving equipment has been installed in police and fire departments throughout Utah, Nevada, Idaho, and Wyoming. The division has also installed fire detection systems in thirteen Salt Lake City schools.

Four years old on April 30, 1975, Centralarm did not show a profit during its first three years. However, the first six months of fiscal 1975 have been profitable.

Silver Metals, Inc. (Salt Lake City, Utah) is a company with a somewhat misleading name. While Silver Metals was founded six years ago to develop some silver mining leases, the company's principal revenues and future prospects come from manufacturing operations. In 1972 a subsidiary named *W. B. & H. Fine Furnishings Company* was acquired. Management changed the name to *Commercial Fixtures and Furnishings,* or *Com-Fix.*

Com-Fix specializes in the millwork and manufacture of high quality wood fixtures. Com-Fix provides custom designed interiors for commercial establishments, churches, and offices. One example is the company's contract to produce the woodwork in the interior of the new Salt Lake *Hilton Hotel.* Com-Fix provided over 1,000 doors, as well as the complete registration desk area, contoured lobby staircase, handrailings, vanities, displays, and restaurant interior wood fixtures. In addition, extensive beam work in the lobby and convention center were prefabricated in the company's milling facility. Com-Fix's revenues from this one project amounted to more than $400,000, and the solid woodwork gives the hotel interior a beautiful effect.

Silver Metals' chief mining properties consist of 42 unpatented claims near Eureka, Nevada known as the Kent project. Exploration of the project has revealed a silver-lead-zinc-gold deposit in excess of 30,000 tons of ore in addition to a sizeable barite deposit. Studies are underway to see if this area can be mined economically.

Western United Resources is a relatively new manufacturing company (started in 1971-1972) whose business is the manufacture and marketing of a line of specialty agricultural chemicals — herbicides, insecticides, fungicides, and fertilizers. President Phillip C. Mozer says that the company's plan is to capitalize on the opportunity resulting from patent protection running out on a number of important chemical compounds originally developed by *DuPont* and other large companies.

Western United's *Colorado International Corporation* subsidiary holds about 500 E.P.A. (*Environmental Protection Agency*) approved brand labels, believed to be one of the largest portfolios of labels held by an independent operator. Management believes that it would cost potential competitors more than $5,000 per label to begin registering similar labels at this time.

Using the company's *Best-4-Servis* brand name, these products are marketed through distributors for commercial use as well as through retail lawn and garden stores. The table below shows some of the products sold under the *Best-4-Servis* brand name.

Insecticides	Herbicides	Cattle Sprays
Chlordane	Amrol	Ciodrin-DDVP (TM)
DDVP	Amine 2,4-D	Toxophene formulations
Dimethogon	Butyl Ester	Mal-Thox
Malathion	Diuron	Poly-Coat
Lindane	2,4-Dichlorophenoxy	
Parathion	Acetic Acid Ester	**Seed Treaters**
Toxaphene	Pentachlorophenol	Captan formulations
	formulations	Diazinon-Heptachlor
	Crop Oil	Polyran (TM)
	Concentrates	

Western United's sales expanded from $2.6 million in fiscal 1974 to $9.8 million in 1975 (fiscal year ending February 28), while related income increased from $99,726 to $268,486.

Normarc, Inc. of Tangent, Oregon processes seed for grass seed markets and farms some crops, including wheat, for future sale on a contract basis. Since August, 1974 the company has sold the assets of two subsidiary operations, *Union Seed Company* and *Beal Seed Company* which processed alfalfa, clover and vegetable seed. Sales of continuing operations in the fiscal year ended May 31, 1975 were $16.8 million, and earnings $253,000 before receipt of a special dividend of $96,000 from the former Union subsidiary.

Located in Spokane, **Noble Metals, Inc.** is in the silver recovery and refining business. Recovery comes from films, (medical x-ray, photo, litho, industrial x-ray) and from the dissolved particles in fixer solutions. Noble also buys and sells silver bars. In addition, Noble is in the manufacture of lumber re-manufacturing equipment including twin rip saws, cut-off saws, trim saws, conveyors, turn tables, wood boring equipment, router equipment, slotting and notching equipment and overhead cranes.

Kirkman Laboratories, Inc. (Portland, Oregon) manufactures a variety of dental and pharmaceutical products. The company's *Flura Tray* preventive dentistry delivery system treats children's teeth with a fluoride gel and fluoride rinse. Kirkman also distributes *Doublegard,* a patented contact athletic mouthpiece. Another dental product is *Endoragard,* a device used for tooth protection during anaesthesiology and electroshock therapy. Kirkman Laboratories also produces a variety of vitamins under the trademarks *Multi-Jets, Cabnet,* and *Nu Thera.*

Another Northwest manufacturer in the medical-dental field is **Marco Dental Products, Inc.** of North Plains, Oregon. Originally incorporated in Minnesota in 1967, the company relocated in the Northwest in 1971. Marco manufactures and sells, under its own label, high quality dental chairs, chair-mounted over-the-patient delivery systems, mobile units, utility carts, and component parts.

Sales are generated primarily through dental supply dealers and include dental schools, other equipment manufacturers, and government sources. International sales account for about 10% of the company's total revenue. Although small, $1.9 million revenue in fiscal 1974 (fiscal year ending July 31), Marco has been profitable in each of the past three years.

Increasing sales of Marco Dental Equipment's high-quality products has produced profits in each of the past three years.

Deseret Pharmaceutical Co., Inc. is a specialized manufacturer of hospital and surgical supplies. Two of Deseret's principal products are *Filtermask* which filters and collects up to 96% of airborne organisms to protect both patient and surgeon; and *E-Z Scrub* a sponge-brush combination offering a choice of antiseptic agents with surgical detergent to efficiently cleanse the hands and arms of the surgical team before surgery.

New products developed by Deseret are a surgical wound drain and an arterial blood sampling kit.

Deseret's annual revenue has advanced in each of the past six years from a base of $5.1 million in 1968 to $28.7 million in fiscal 1975 (ending August 31). Net income in 1975 was $2,595,000.

Olympia Brewing invites visitors to tour their brewery when passing through Olympia, Washington.

11

Food and Beverage Processing

The Great Northwest is, of course, an area of agricultural abundance. Anyone traveling through Washington, Oregon, Idaho, Montana, or Utah during the various harvest seasons would find fruits, vegetables, and grain in bewildering profusion. It is logical, then, for investors to take note of those publicly held corporations which process and distribute these products.

For example, the *Great Western Malting Company* (Vancouver, Washington and Los Angeles, California) is a wholly-owned subsidiary of the **Columbia Corporation**. (See chapter on Multi-Line Companies.) Great Western supplies malt, the principal ingredient in beer, to virtually every brewery on the West Coast. Great Western is the fourth largest commercial malting company in the United States. Malt is composed of specialty barleys which were once grown only in the Midwest. Over the past 15 years, Great Western has stimulated the growing of these barleys in the Northwest, thereby reducing their cost to Western breweries. In 1974, Great Western processed over eleven million bushels of these barleys.

Following these thoughts, there are two publicly-held breweries situated in the Northwest. The first is the **Olympia Brewing Company** of Olympia, Washington. Olympia markets its beer through distributorships in eighteen western states, including Alaska and Hawaii. In addition, its product is exported to civilian and military markets throughout the Pacific Basin area.

Olympia's annual production has increased during the past ten years from 2,460,715 barrels in 1965 to 4,300,940 in 1974. During 1975, Olympia acquired Hamm's Brewing Company. The 1974 combined production of the two organizations was just under 7 million barrels, thus making Olympia the 6th largest brewing company in the United States, with 3% of the nation's market.

It is interesting to note that the total of federal, state and local taxes paid by the company have ranged between $14 and $20 per share annually for the past ten years. By comparison, net earnings per share in 1974 amounted to just $0.79 per share.

The second publicly-owned Northwest brewery is **The Rainier Companies, Inc.** of Seattle, Washington. Rainier's 1974 production was

At your next party or picnic, add the flavor of the Great Northwest.

During the harvest time, mountains of sugarbeets such as this are commonplace sights at U & I processing plants.

875,500 barrels, about a fifth the volume produced by Olympia. At this level, Rainier ranks 20th among the nation's brewers. Rainier could expand at its present location to over two million barrels from its present 950,000 barrel capacity. The company serves a nine state marketing area (Washington, Oregon, California, Idaho, Montana, North Dakota, Wyoming and Hawaii).

In addition, Rainier owns 75% of the Robert Mondavi winery and 100% of the Robert Mondavi vineyards in Northern California. Annual wine sales have increased steadily from $1.2 million (1970) to $4.8 million (1974). Having undergone a major expansion program in the last few years, the winery is not presently profitable. However, management looks to this area for good long-term growth.

There are two other Northwest brewers, *Blitz* and *Lucky Lager,* but they are not publicly owned.

Two Northwest companies are major beet sugar producers. The **Amalgamated Sugar Company** has processing facilities in Oregon, Idaho and Utah. **U & I, Inc.** (formerly the Utah-Idaho Sugar Company) has its headquarters in Salt Lake City, with processing plants in Washington, Oregon and Utah.

Both companies experienced the effects of a roller coaster commodity market in 1974.

WORLD SUGAR
(metric tons)

Year	Consumption	Production	Consumption In Excess of Production
1970-1971	74,518,000	72,771,000	1,747,000
1971-1972	76,105,000	73,852,000	2,253,000
1972-1973	78,099,000	77,173,000	926,000
1973-1974	81,068,000	81,021,000	47,000

As shown, worldwide sugar consumption has exceeded production for some years. When the U.S. Congress failed to renew the Sugar Act (which imposed tariffs and quotas) in 1974, sugar prices soared. This is apparent in the sales figures of the two companies. Amalgamated's sales rose from $129 million to $202 million in one year, while U & I's sales leaped from $142.5 million to $237.4 million. Both gains were substantially due to price increases.

However, as commodity prices will do, the trend changed abruptly. One hundred pounds of granulated sugar brought $61.85 in November, 1974 and then subsided to $31.35 in March, 1975. Prices at this writing in late 1975 are still above their long-term historical levels, even though well below last year's highs.

U & I's management has elected to diversify into the expanding potato processing industry. In February, 1975, the company acquired a 55% controlling interest in *Gourmet Food Products, Inc.,* headquartered at Boardman, Oregon. Gourmet operates two processing plants — at

Metolius and Boardman, Oregon which produce frozen French fried and hash brown potatoes. U & I also conducts extensive farming operations in Southeast Idaho and Southeast Washington.

Also of interest is the *California & Hawaiian Sugar Company,* which is the only cane sugar refiner west of the Texas Gulf Coast. With an annual production of 11 million tons, C & H is the nation's second largest sugar company. A cooperative venture, C & H is privately owned by 16 Hawaiian sugar producers including *Amfac, Alexander & Baldwin,* and *Castle & Cooke, Inc.* Amfac also owns Portland-based *Lamb-Weston Co.,* a potato processor based in Idaho Falls. (These operations are discussed more fully in the Chapter on "Multi-Line Companies".)

An altogether different type of Northwest food processor is a Seattle company with the paradoxical name of **New England Fish Company.** Rich in history, New England Fish Company (NEFCO) was founded in 1868 in Boston. The company was originally a membership club of wholesale fish dealers. In the 1880's, the Northern Pacific Railroad opened its tracks to Tacoma, Washington. NEFCO then began delivering and selling West Coast halibut in the Eastern United States. Rapidly expanding, the company appointed its first Canadian agent in January, 1894.

In 1907, a cold storage plant was constructed in Ketchikan, Alaska. A number of acquisitions put NEFCO in the fresh salmon business. In 1918, the company's first salmon cannery was built in Vancouver, British Columbia. NEFCO's first U.S. salmon cannery was opened in Alaska in 1923. By 1931, NEFCO's Boston head office was moved to Seattle, Washington, which has been headquarters for the last 45 years for what has now become a worldwide enterprise.

New England Fish operates salmon, crab, shrimp and groundfish plants in the Northwest; salmon, herring and groundfish plants in Western Canada; a groundfish station in Nova Scotia; and a shrimp plant in Miami. The company processes its own catch as well as imports from South America, Europe, Africa, and the Orient. Products include, among others, canned tuna, salmon, shrimp, seafood soups, crab, and pet food; and frozen sole, perch, halibut, oysters, and trout. The company also maintains a large fresh fish business.

Investors should be aware of a very interesting group of small specialty food processors, all based in Northern Oregon. The annual sales of the largest of these companies is less than $20 million, but each company has the capacity for future growth.

SPECIALTY FOOD PROCESSORS

Smoke-Craft, Inc. produces a wide variety of meat snack impulse items. These include products such as beef jerky, Hickory Stick sausage, Polish sausage, salami, pepperoni, and similar goods.

Smoke-Craft markets its meat products to a large number of supermarket chains, other grocers, and convenience store outlets in the Western states, and has annual sales in excess of $11 million. The company's plant is located at Albany, Oregon.

In keeping with the environmental concern of the Northwest, Gregg's Gold-n-Soft margarine is packaged in reuseable containers.

Light, long-lasting and easy-to-store, Oregon Freeze Dry Foods are a favorite of Northwest campers and back-packers.

With operations around the world, here NEFCO processes live Dungeness crab caught from the Oregon coast.

Smoke-Craft's wide variety of meat snacks are found at home in an hors d'oeuvre dish, lunch pail, or back pack.

Reser's Fine Foods, Inc., headquartered in Beaverton, Oregon, manufactures about 200 specialty and convenience foods, which include smoked sausage products, ready-to-serve salads, salad dressings, sour cream, dips, desserts, tortilla and taco shells. Reser's has 12 company distribution centers in Oregon and Washington. A system of 197 independent distributors serve 23 other Western and Midwestern states including Hawaii and Alaska. Since 1973, as the result of an acquisition, Reser's also distributes a variety of pizza products. Sales for fiscal 1975 were $12,104,548.

Gregg's Food Products, Inc. has operated in the Pacific Northwest since 1931. Originally a manufacturer of mayonnaise, the company has been primarily a producer of margarine since 1965.

Gregg's soon switched to a soft margarine (the *Gold-n-Soft* brand). In an innovative marketing move, Gregg's began packaging their margarine in reuseable plastic containers. These gaily colored plastic dishes are now sought after by housewives for their own worth. This led Gregg's into the business of private label packaging for other manufacturers, a profitable business in itself. Gregg's also manufactures the plastic containers for outside sales for dairy products, candy, fruits, and vegetables.

Serving all of the western states, Gregg's holds a 49% market share in soft margarine sales, and is the largest producer and marketer of soft margarine in the Northwest. The company's expansion extended to North and South Dakota in 1974 and to Minnesota in 1975. Annual sales have advanced in each of the past ten years to the $18.5 million point at the end of 1974.

Another unique food processor located in Albany, Oregon is **Oregon Freeze Dry Foods, Inc.** According to President Ellis Byer, the company has the largest totally integrated freeze drying plant in the world. They are capable of freeze drying completely cooked casseroles, egg dishes, meats, fruits, vegetables, coffee and specialty products. Except for coffee, Oregon Freeze Dry supplies most of the freeze dried food used in the United States. They have supplied food for the NASA space programs, Apollo flights, Sky Lab, and the joint U.S.-Russian space mission.

Investors will recognize that freeze dried foods could have significant growth potential. They do not require refrigeration. If properly sealed, they can be stored for many years. Weight is reduced to 10% of the fresh weight, in most cases. Freeze dried foods can be prepared with hot or cold water in less than five minutes without further cooking. When reconstituted with water, the foods regain most of their original texture and flavor.

The company's sales in fiscal 1974 were a record $8,905,994. At the same time, net income of $383,842 represented a 103% increase over the previous year. Oregon Freeze Dry markets its goods under the *Teakettle* brand name as well as *Mountain House,* a special line for campers and backpackers.

Centennial Mills, another subsidiary of a multi-line Northwest company, **Univar,** is the largest flour miller on the West Coast. Established in Spokane, Washington in 1889, Centennial now has three flour mills, located in Los Angeles, Portland (the Division's headquarters) and Spokane, with a combined capacity of 19,000 cwt. per day. Scheduled expansion of the Los Angeles mill, to be completed in 1976, will double the capacity of that facility from 4,000 cwt. to 8,000 cwt. per day.

If you've ever been across Eastern Washington and Montana, you must have noticed a grain elevator at almost every town on the railroad. Six of these belong to Centennial to supply their flour mills.

The primary market for Centennial's flour is commercial bakeries, and distribution facilities are operated in Seattle and San Francisco.

12

Silver and Metals Mining

The Northwest is blessed with an abundance of mineral reserves of many kinds. We pointed out previously that the capital investment per worker for the nation's major industries averages over $25,000 per job. In the mining field, due to the extensive heavy equipment involved, this figure exceeds $70,000 per worker — almost three times the national average. In fact a new project of Hecla Mining Company (Lakeshore Copper) will involve an investment of more than $135,000 per worker. Many areas in the Northwest support various mining activities.

A key state in the Northwest's mining industry, the total value of Idaho's mining production in 1974 was estimated to be $195-$200 million. A wide range of ores are commercially produced. These include phosphate rock, beryllium, thorium, titanium, tantalum, antimony, vanadium, mercury, sand, gravel, and cement. However, the allure of Idaho's mining industry has always been the vast quantities of metals, primarily silver, lead, zinc, and copper present in the northern Coeur d'Alene mining district.

COEUR D'ALENE AREA RICH IN SILVER

Mining in Northern Idaho's Coeur d'Alene area has been continuous since the gold mining days of the 1880's. Since that time, some $2.5 billion worth of minerals have been produced in the Coeur d'Alene district. All underground, present day mining is primarily at levels of 4,000 to 6,000 feet. These are among the deepest mines in North America. The Coeur d'Alene region produces about 19 million ounces of silver each year — almost 45% of all United States mine production. In addition, the district produces about 12% of the nation's lead and 8% of its zinc.

All three of the nation's largest silver mines are located in the Coeur d'Alene district. These are: (1) The **Sunshine** mine, (2) The **Galena,** and (3) The **Lucky Friday** mine. The Sunshine mine has been the nation's leading silver producer regularly since the 1930's and is capable of producing 5 to 6 million ounces of silver or more annually. The Sunshine is also the country's leading producer of antimony, and operates an antimony plant near Kellogg, Idaho.

SUMMARY OF LEADING IDAHO
SILVER MINING COMPANIES (1974)

	Mkt.	Total Assets (000)	Total Revenue (000)	Net Income (000)	Approximate Total Reserves (tons)[1]
Sunshine Mining Company	NYSE	$ 58,698	$59,948	$5,039	729,794
Hecla Mining Company	NYSE	102,909	29,934	8,441	1,210,000
Silver Dollar Mines	PSE	3,340	1,872	1,047	98,200
Day Mines	ASE	10,925	7,382	1,435	396,000
Coeur d'Alene Mines	OTC	1,445	non-operating at present		834,000

[1]Including, for Sunshine, Hecla and Silver Dollar, each company's proportionate share of the Sunshine Mines' unit area reserves.

IDAHO SILVER MINING COMPANIES

The five companies in the accompanying table, discussed individually later in the chapter, are all companies of substance with proven properties, currently in production with one exception, and having assets in the millions of dollars.

The companies discussed are primarily silver companies, although quantities of other metal are also produced. As such, the price of silver and future price trends are of keen interest to potential investors. For a variety of reasons, silver prices have moved significantly higher in recent years, and the trend established seems likely to continue for some time in the future.

Causes of the rapid rise in silver's value can be traced to several factors:

1. Concern about runaway inflation and worsening economic conditions. Some investors have lost confidence in paper currencies and put their money in precious metals as a hedge.

2. Increased speculation and emotional buying, which result from day-to-day political and business occurrences. These short-term influences can cause substantial swings in the metal's prices. Commodity-type price swings encourage more speculative trading in metals markets.

3. Ever-tightening supply/demand conditions. In 1974, world-wide consumption of silver totaled approximately 448 million ounces, compared to total new mine production of 240 million ounces, leaving a gap of 208 million ounces to be filled by scrap refining, coin refining, and dwindling accumulations of above ground supplies. Over the past ten years, mining production has been increasing at an annual rate of less than 2%, while industrial usage has grown at the rate of about 6%.

Both the monetary inflation hedge and industrial use have a long-term effect on silver's price, with month-to-month price movements fluctuating, sometimes violently, in response to outside influences. In most industrial uses, silver accounts for just a small fraction of the product's ultimate selling price. Silver substitutes duplicating the metal's unique properties are not being developed, which would indicate that higher silver prices are not likely to cause a change in industrial demand. Also contributing to continuing high demand for silver is the consumption of silver in coinage (37.6 million ounces in 1974) and photographic films.

Although production is likely to increase in response to higher

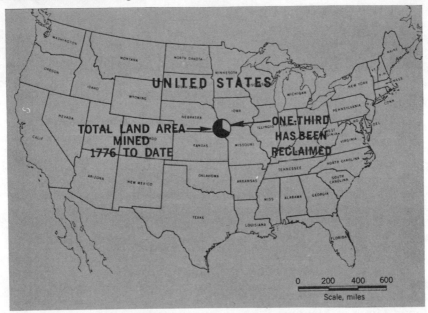

Source: "What Mining Means to the United States," American Mining Congress. The mining industry has disturbed less than .3% of the land area of the United States including Alaska and Hawaii to produce all the mineral materials since 1776 including coal, oil, gas, stone, sand, gravel, cement rock, and metal and nonmetallic ores. One-third of the disturbed area has been reclaimed.

prices, with increased scrap refining, coin melting and, to a degree, new mining, we estimate that it will not be sufficient to close the gap between supply and demand. Above-ground stocks will continue to be tapped. As the supply/demand deficit continues to draw from these supplies, remaining stocks will be worth considerably more.

This positive long-range outlook has good implications for the Coeur d'Alene area mines, where the value of silver constitutes over one-half the value of all ore mined. The Coeur d'Alene mineralization, which spreads over an area 25 miles long, varying in width from 4 to 15 miles, is one of the greatest concentrations of silver in the world, and is unique for its richness and the characteristic of ore persisting at great depth. The bottoms of many veins, which have been traced down to 8,000 feet, have yet to be reached, whereas most silver mines in other areas tend to close after exhausting silver-containing ores at the 400 to 500 foot level.

At present silver prices, exploration for new silver mines is being stepped up, as opportunity to realize better profits is recognized. Investors must realize, however, that several years are required to bring a new mine into production. The mining companies are also reopening mining areas in which the grade of ore was previously unprofitable to recover.

SUNSHINE MINING COMPANY

The company is the operator of the Sunshine Unit mine, the largest silver mine in the United States. Annual silver production has kept the Sunshine number one since the 1930's. The Sunshine mine is operated as a consolidated unit, with ownership divided among three mining companies. Sunshine's ownership of the Sunshine Unit is approximately 58%.

Although the fact is little known, Sunshine owns extensive properties in addition to the Sunshine Unit Mine. Immediately adjacent to and surrounding the present mine, Sunshine has a 50% interest or more in a number of promising silver mining properties. These include the *Silver Syndicate, Sunshine Consolidated, Big Creek Apex, Silver Surprise*, all of which management estimates to have considerable reserves, and the so far untested *"Metropolitan area"*. Sunshine Chairman Irwin Underweiser and Chief Geologist Don Long told us at press time that Sunshine is driving some drifts in these areas and "finding some very good ore."

Sunshine is also pursuing exploration outside the Coeur d'Alene area, including a joint venture with *Anaconda* in Alaska, a joint venture with *Terra Mining and Exploration* in Canada, and a joint venture with *Hanna Mines* in Montana.

Sunshine also has other manufacturing subsidiaries in addition to its mining properties. These include *Anchor Post Products*, a national leader in the production of chain link fencing; *Piezo Crystal*, supplier of components for manufacturers in the communications industry; and *Premier Metal Products*, a leading manufacturer of electronic cabinets and accessories. Sunshine also receives income from Canadian oil and gas production and sales of garnet by its Idaho Garnet Division.

Following is a breakdown of the contributions by the Company's three business areas to the latest five years' revenues and earnings:

	1974	1973	1972	1971	1970
Revenues:					
Mining and Oil[1]	21.1%	14.1%	10.2%	19.6%	24.3%
Fencing Products	68.6	74.9	77.4	69.0	62.0
Electronic Products	10.3	11.0	12.4	11.4	13.7
Income[2]					
Mining and Oil	39.1	51.0	47.0	39.6	72.6
Fencing Products	49.2	38.9	20.0	49.8	22.5
Electronic Products	11.7	10.1	33.0	10.6	4.9

[1]Sales of silver concentrates accounted in the aggregate for approximately 17%, 12%, 7%, 16% and 20% of the Company's sales in 1974, 1973, 1972, 1971 and 1970 respectively. It should be noted that the Sunshine Mine was closed by a fire on May 2, 1972 and did not reopen until late in 1972, and was shut down by a strike from March 11, 1973 to July 16, 1973.

[2]Before income taxes and general corporate administrative expenses, interest expense, misc. income, and realized loss and provision for unrealized loss on investments.

While non-mining revenue is substantial, the main attraction of Sunshine as an investment is its position as the nation's number one silver producer.

Lift truck loads supplies into the four-foot by five-foot metal "cage" at the top of the Jewell Shaft in the Sunshine Mine. This shaft is the main vertical artery through which all men, supplies, and ore are hoisted into and out of the first 4000 feet of depth of the Sunshine Mine.

Anchor Post Products, a subsidiary of Sunshine Mining, is a national leader in the production of chain link fencing.

Eimco Rocker Shovel loading broken ore from a drift at the 4800 ft. depth level of the Sunshine Mine.

ARGUS

April 11, 1975

Sunshine Silver Mine
Back at Full Speed

By SHANNON P. PRATT

LAST WEEK I toured the Sunshine Mine in Kellogg, Idaho, where a disastrous fire took the lives of 91 miners in May of 1972. Today, after millions of dollars have been spent on rehabilitation and improvements, the work force finally is back to its full complement of about 450 men underground. Morale is excellent, and production is on the increase, with over 1.1 million ounces of silver mined from the Sunshine already in 1975.

On arrival at the mine at 7 a.m. we changed into coveralls, rubber boots, a short rubber raincoat, hardhat and safety belt. From the belt hangs a canister which can filter out carbon monoxide gas and a large battery with a cord running to our "miner's lamp," attached to the front of our hardhat like a headlight.

Thus equipped, we walked to the top of the "Jewel Shaft," where as many men as physically possible jammed into a four by five foot metal cage. The hoist quickly lowered our cage to a depth of 3,700 feet, where we boarded a small train. The miniature train (18 inches between rails, engine powered by a series of 12-volt batteries) took us about a mile through narrow tunnels to another shaft. Every so often the engineer pulled a cord and a set of doors opened to reveal the next set of caverns, much like a ride at Disneyland. (Actually, the doors are a fire safety precaution.)

The cage in the "number eleven shaft" took us down another 1,100 feet to the 4,800-foot level. Since the surface of the Sunshine Mine is at 2,700-feet elevation, we were now 2,100 feet below sea level. Here we sat down on a tiny flatcar and one of the little engines pulled us another mile. Then, walking through a series of tunnels, we examined an "exploration face," where miners were exploring with long, diamond-tipped drills to determine which way the veins of silver ore lie in the rock ahead, and a "development face," where they were preparing to extract ore.

We then went to another level (like most hardrock mines, the Sunshine has a network of tunnels at about every 200 feet of elevation), walked through more tunnels, and descended a ladder 50 feet to a "stope," a small cavern where ore was being extracted. Men worked in teams of two, taking out the ore with a "mucking machine" powered by compressed air, dropping the ore through another shaft about 150 feet to the level

Sampling for silver

below, where ore cars carry it to the main hoist to be lifted to the surface.

The miners are very skilled in their specialized art, using substantial judgment and a variety of heavy equipment in extremely cramped quarters in an underground world totally unknown to most. In spite of elaborate ventilation, the mine was hot and humid, with water dripping from the tops of the tunnels in many places. We had been sweating and damp for several hours, and so on returning to the surface, the hot shower and dry clothes felt very welcome.

Our host on the tour was Sunshine Vice President Clint Miller, a 25-year mining veteran who joined the Company five months ago to serve as chief operating officer of the Sunshine Mine. Miller is planning silver production at 5 to 6 million ounces annually, mining intensively and doing new exploration and development work along the way to sustain the production level for many years to come.

In addition to the mine, Sunshine also owns other manufacturing operations in the East. Listed on the New York, Spokane, and three other stock exchanges, Sunshine stock is very actively traded, selling recently around 14.

Last week Sunshine reported 1974 operating earnings of $.85 per share, up from $.58 in 1973 and deficits in 1971 and 1972. Sunshine's Chief Executive Officer Irwin Underweiser told me he hopes the improved silver operations will result in further earnings gain in 1975.

The improved efficiency and production level at the Sunshine Mine will also benefit Hecla Mining Company, which owns a 33.25 percent interest in the output of the Sunshine Mine, and Silver Dollar Mining, with 9.61 percent interest in the Sunshine's production.

The Sunshine Mine is back into profitable and stable production after years of difficulties, to the benefit of both the stockholders and the area's economy.

Reprinted from Shannon Pratt's weekly *"Northwest Investing"* column ·

CAPSULE HISTORY
OF THE SUNSHINE MINE

Gold caused the first mining excitement in Idaho's Coeur d'Alene District in 1860, first discovered by miner E. D. Pierce, at what is now Pierce, Idaho. Gold mining remained the area's principal activity until 1884, when a multitude of silver lode claims were first staked out. On September 24, 1884, the *Yankee Lode* was discovered by two brothers, True Blake and Dennis Blake. The Yankee Lode later became the nucleus of the present Sunshine Mining Company holdings.

The Blakes worked their mine for thirty years, patenting their claims in 1909. They had built a mine shaft and ten tunnels without the aid of any hired men. The Sunshine was not a "rich" orebody at shallow depths, and the Blakes sometimes worked veins less than an inch thick. The Blakes sold out in 1914, and the mine limped along under various owners until purchased by the Sunshine Mining Company in 1918.

Better ore grades at a 500 foot depth, called the "Chinatown" region, were found in the mid-1920's, and insured the mine's success. After 1927, the Sunshine never again faced serious financial difficulties.

In 1931, the company struck a bonanza at the 1,700 foot level. A silver vein was uncovered which was 20 to 23 feet wide in places and sometimes solid high grade. In that year, Sunshine ranked as the largest silver producer in Idaho and the second largest in the United States. Production increased each year, until 1937, when the Sunshine produced 12,147,719 recoverable ounces of silver. This made Sunshine the largest known producer of silver from any ore mine in the world.

The Sunshine is now producing on the 5,400 foot deep level, 2,700 feet below sea level and 6,300 feet below the uppermost tunnel.

The Sunshine Mine has been the largest single producer of silver in the United States for thirty years and of metallic antimony for half as long. Its total silver production far outstrips that of the famous *Comstock* mine in Nevada, and indeed, of all the mines on the Comstock Lode combined.

Starting twenty years after its discovery by the Blake brothers, recorded production from 1904 through 1974 is:

Tons Produced	8,989,589
Ounces Silver Recovered	276,768,152
Pounds Lead Recovered	141,614,012
Pounds Copper	86,233,443
Pounds Antimony Recovered	54,317,963
Smelter Returns	$294,724,550

If all of the Sunshine's recorded silver production had been minted into silver dollars, the resulting 286,250,000 dollars would form a single stack 508 miles high. If all of this silver were drawn into a wire of nearly 1/16th inch diameter (American Wire Gage #15) it would stretch from the surface of the earth 275,035 miles, or 35,486 miles beyond the far surface of the moon.

Truly, a monumental mine.

Condensed from *"History of the Sunshine Mine"*, paper by R. L. Anderson, assistant to the president, Sunshine Mining Co.

HECLA MINING COMPANY

Headquartered in Wallace, Idaho, Hecla's primary property is the famous *Lucky Friday* mine, which is 100% owned. Lucky Friday is the third largest silver mine in the United States. Hecla also owns 33.25% of the Sunshine Unit Area, the number one silver producer. The company's third major property is a 30% interest in the *Star Morning* Unit Area, owned by the *Bunker Hill Company.*

A new mining property of major importance to Hecla's future is the *Lakeshore Copper Project,* a new venture in Southern Arizona, 50% owned by Hecla and 50% by *El Paso Natural Gas.* Scheduled for opening in late 1975, the Lakeshore project is planned to produce 65,000 tons of copper per year at maximum capacity.

HECLA'S LAKESHORE COPPER MINE

A Wagner Scooptram loading 13 tons into a 25-ton Teletram truck.

A Scooptram transporting 8 cu. yards of broken rock from the face of one of the 15° declines to the surface.

Hecla also owns 35.4% of *Granduc Mines, Ltd.,* in British Columbia, which is currently operating at one-half capacity due to the combination of poor copper prices and adverse British Columbia taxation policies. Hecla has one non-mining subsidiary, *Ace Concrete Company,* a ready mix concrete sand and gravel producer in Spokane, Washington.

ANNUAL METAL PRODUCTION
HECLA MINING COMPANY

	1974	1973[1]	1972	1971	1970
Tons of Ore Mined	300,236	295,462	419,441	495,776	463,297
Ounces of Gold	1,026	1,271	48,037	59,974	52,103
Ounces of Silver	3,579,872	3,853,939	4,468,989	6,369,914	6,245,087
Tons of Lead	19,791	23,202	26,970	32,170	27,467
Tons of Zinc	6,638	7,074	10,034	10,323	9,479
Tons of Copper	454	438	1,939	2,214	1,906

[1]The Mayflower Mine was closed December 31, 1972. The Sunshine Unit Area was closed because of labor strike from March 11, 1973 to July 15, 1973.

SILVER DOLLAR MINING COMPANY

Silver Dollar is the third partner with Sunshine-Hecla in the Sunshine Unit Area mine. Silver Dollar's interest in the Sunshine Unit Area is 9.61%. This is the company's principal asset.

Silver Dollar's share of the Sunshine's production was 13,948 tons (1974) versus 9,914 tons in 1973. Comparable market values were $1,-707,990 and $763,903. 1974's ore production for Silver Dollar amounted to: silver—345,000 ounces; antimony—900,600 pounds; and copper—135,000 pounds.

Silver Dollar's other primary holding is a 9.45% interest in the *Consolidated Silver Company.* An 80-year lease to develop the *Silver Summit* mine, owned by Consolidated Silver, is held jointly by *Hecla Mining* and the **American Smelting and Refining Company.** For several years, operations have been inactive. However, continued higher silver prices may substantially improve the value of this property.

DAY MINES

Organized in 1947, Day was the result of the consolidation of 12 separate mining companies operating in the Coeur d'Alene district. Day is the largest owner of patented mining claims in the Coeur d'Alene mining district. Day Mines owns, leases, or operates some 19,000 acres of mining properties in Idaho and Washington, plus some holdings in British Columbia and Montana.

A well-integrated operation, Day is the only mining company of its size that has its own metallurgy, engineering, and exploration departments. Financially strong, Day Mines has no long-term debt and about $10 million in stockholders equity.

Owner of the once-rich *Dayrock Mine,* the company had the misfortune to see the mine's known reserves depleted in mid-1974. However, extensive exploration along the fringes of the mine and in previously un-tested regions show promise of eventually restoring the mine's operations. While exploration continues at Dayrock and on numerous other properties, production continues at a number of other fully developed mines.

Wholly-owned *Monitor Mine* produces silver, lead, and zinc and has 1½ years of proven reserves. Day owns 25% of the large *Galena* silver-copper mine where reserves for more than six years have been proved.

METALS AS A PERCENTAGE OF DAY MINES SALES

	1974	1973	1972	1971	1970
Silver	57.2	48.9	42.8	43.9	47.8
Lead	15.4	26.9	30.2	26.9	17.1
Gold	15.7	13.2	12.6	13.6	17.8
Zinc	7.7	7.4	9.5	10.8	10.8
Copper	4.0	3.6	4.9	4.9	6.5

In addition to being an operating company, Day Mines holds a diversified portfolio of shares in other mining companies, worth a little over $2.5 million at year-end 1974.

COEUR D'ALENE MINES

This company is different from those previously discussed in that operations have been inactive up until this point. CDA owns property

Head shaft of the Coeur project which supports the cables that lift the hoist up and down. Coeur d'Alene Mines holds 40% interest, Day Mines 5%, Callahan Mines 5%, and operator ASAR-CO 50% interest in the project.

midway between the Sunshine and the Galena, the nation's two largest silver mines. Unlike other mines in the area, known silver deposits exist much closer to the surface. Present development work is at 1,900, 2,200, and 3,500 foot levels.

Development work, including a mill, ventilation shafts, hoists, etc., are all nearing completion. In exchange for a 50% interest, the *American Smelting and Refining Company* will complete and operate the new *Coeur Silver Mine* at an initial cost of about $10 million.

A new mine, Coeur will rank as the fourth largest silver mine in the nation when in production. Assays indicate possible aggregate ore reserves in excess of 1,000,000 tons, assaying twenty-five ounces of silver per ton and 1% copper. American Smelting has announced that they anticipate production of 2.2 million ounces of silver annually, giving the mine a minimum life of 10 years.

It is interesting to note that the production and reserve figures cited pertain only to tests made down to a depth of 3,700 feet. No tests below that level have yet been made. By contrast, we should point out that the Sunshine and Galena mines have been extremely productive at levels of 6,000 to 8,000 feet.

The *Bunker Hill Mine,* one of the oldest and richest mines in the Coeur d'Alene district, is owned and operated by **Gulf Resources and Chemical Corporation,** headquartered in Houston, Texas. In March 1974 Gulf also acquired *Pend Oreille Mines and Metals,* formerly headquarted in Spokane.

Callahan Mining, headquartered in New York, has a 50% interest in the operating income of the *Galena* silver-copper mine. Another company headquartered elsewhere that has important interests in the Coeur d'Alene district is **American Smelting and Refining Company** (ASARCO), which owns a 25% interest in the Galena and is the operator of the Galena.

OTHER MINING ACTIVITIES

According to information furnished to us by the *Utah Power & Light Company,* Utah ranks high in the nation's extractive industries. In copper, Utah is the nation's number one producer, mining 20% of all U.S. production and 8% of the world's annual supply. In addition, in 1974, the **Anaconda Company** initiated a $135 million mining operation in western Utah that will increase copper production by 112 million pounds per year beginning in 1979.

Utah is also the United States' leading producer of beryllium. Other mining activity in the state involves the production of zinc, potash, sodium chloride, selenium, tungsten, cadmium, tellurium, gold, silver, uranium, iron ore, lead, gilsonite, and molybdenum.

One region (Southeast Idaho, Southwest Wyoming, and Northeast Utah) contains some 43% of the country's phosphate rock reserves. Among the many uses of phosphate, fertilizer production is being expanded to meet a critical world shortage. Some of the major producers of phosphate rock in this region are *Monsanto Company, J. R. Simplot, Earth Sciences, FMC Corporation,* and *Stauffer Chemical.*

Wyoming mineral production is summarized in the accompanying table:

SELECTED WYOMING MINERAL PRODUCTION

	1974P Quantity	Value ($000)	1973P Quantity	Value ($000)	National Ranking 1974
Sodium Carbonate					
(000 lb)	W	W	W	W	1
Uranium (000 lb)	3,800	W	10,060	65,390	2
Iron Ore (000 long tons)	2,075	W	2,070	W	4
Petroleum (crude) (42,000					
gal. barrels)	147,825	983,086	141,914	541,820	5
Natural Gas					
(000,000 ft)	256,169	64,298	357,731	64,745	7
Gemstones (000					
short tons)	NA	142	NA	142	8
Coal	18,887	113,320	14,886	60,939	9

W-Withheld to avoid disclosing individual company confidential data.

NA-Not Available.

P-Preliminary.

Source: "Mineral Industry Industry Surveys Preliminary," U.S. Department of Interior, Bureau of Mines, Division of Fossil Fuels, December 31, 1974.

Montana is a major producer of copper, primarily in the Butte region. The *Anaconda Company* is the dominant producer of copper in the state along with related amounts of lead, zinc, and silver as by-products.

Alaska's mineral production potential is still in the future. Massive iron ore deposits exist in Southeast Alaska. Controlled by *Mitsubishi* and *Marcona* corporations, present development has been deferred due to the presence of less expensive ore in Australia. A major deposit of nickel at Glacier Bay is owned by **Newmont Mining.** However, environmental questions are delaying its development. Another ore body of large economic significance is the *Lost River* fluorite mine on Alaska's Seward Peninsula. Lost River is estimated to contain one-third of the world's reserves of fluorite.

In the Ambler District of Alaska, the *Sunshine Mining Company* has been developing mining claims (copper, zinc, and silver) on 24,000 acres of land since 1972. The Ambler District is situated about one hundred miles east of Alaska's west coast and north of the Arctic Circle. The *Anaconda Company* will acquire a 75% interest in this claim by spending $11 million in development work over the next several years.

What we might term a "start-up" potential mining operation, **Bannak** was incorporated in Nevada on June 7, 1974. Subsequently it merged with *Westlake Silver Inc.*, an Idaho corporation with Bannak the surviving company. *Mineral Ventures, Ltd.*, the company's wholly owned natural resources subsidiary, was acquired by Bannak in December 1974, through a stock exchange. Dr. Mead LeRoy Jensen,

Professor of Geological and Geophysical Sciences at the University of Utah and a well-known consulting geologist, is president of Bannak.

Mineral Ventures holds a number of properties, including 3,526 unpatented mining claims covering 70,520 acres in Western Wyoming and 75 contiguous lode gold mining claims known as the "Hi Ute" claims in the famous Skylab area in White Pine County, Nevada. This latter area received national publicity in 1974 when a photograph taken by the Skylab II astronauts suggested that a huge potential mineralization might exist in an area of post ore volcanic cover.

Brandonstreet, another Bannak subsidiary, has 1,089.5 acres of undeveloped ground in a growing residential area in Southwest Salt Lake County under long-term written and oral options or contract. Brandonstreet plans to sell lots to the public and construct homes on some lots.

ALUMINUM REDUCTION & FABRICATION

While no aluminum mining of substance takes place in the Northwest, the aluminum industry does have a definite impact on the economies of Oregon, Washington, and western Montana. Because of the abundant water resources and availability of economical interruptible power supplies, substantial investment has taken place in the Northwest in the form of aluminum reduction plants.

The Western Aluminum Producers Association consists of seven companies, all publicly held or divisions of publicly held corporations. These companies are *Aluminum Company of America, Amax Pacific Aluminum Corporation, Anaconda Aluminum Company, Intalco Aluminum Corporation, Kaiser Aluminum and Chemical Corporation, Martin-Marietta Aluminum,* and *Reynolds Metals Company.*

All of these enterprises are international corporations not headquartered in the Northwest. Since the focus of our study is upon the investment in Northwest companies, we have little comment on the above group of corporations other than to identify them.

These western aluminum producers employ some 12,000 workers in the Northwest, with a direct annual payroll of about $140 million. Over the years, the companies have spent or budgeted more than $160 million for pollution abatement equipment related to their plants.

In one year alone (1973) the western aluminum producers purchased supplies and services worth $86 million from Northwest firms. In the same year, $71.5 million was spent on freight and transportation services in the region. Aluminum fabrication in the Northwest is at an annual rate of about 1.5 million tons. This is about one-third of the nation's output, and an amount greater than that produced by any other nation at present.

13

The Energy Resources

In this era of critical nationwide energy shortages, Wyoming has tremendous surpluses of coal, oil, shale, natural gas, and uranium. For example, Wyoming ranks first among the 50 states with her 545 billion tons of known coal reserves — 17% of the country's total. She ranks fifth in the nation in oil production. Increasing exploration and drilling with major new discoveries reported almost weekly may well rank her even higher. In the production of natural gas (which is often discovered as a by-product of oil drilling) Wyoming ranks seventh, and in oil shale reserves, third. In addition, the state's uranium reserves, representing 35.7% of the nation's total are second only to those of New Mexico.

Wyoming's coal reserves are located in 10 major regions of the state, and mining is currently being carried on in six. The Hanna Field, the Hams Fork Region and Powder River Basin account for over 90% of the state's annual production. 99.5% of Wyoming's explored coal reserves remain unmined after more than a century of mining. Approximately 136 billion tons, or 25% of her estimated reserves, are classified as mapped within 3,000 feet of the land surface. The greatest potential for production lies in the Powder River Basin, where almost 90% of Wyoming's strippable coal reserves are located. Most of the state's coal production is currently used by public utility electric generating plants, both in-state and elsewhere. Construction of the 4-unit *Jim Bridger* power plant near Rock Springs by *Pacific Power & Light* and *Idaho Power* points up the growing effort to develop a vast system of coal-fired electrical power generating facilities.

RAILROADS DOING RECORD EXPANSION IN WYOMING

Prompted by increased demand for the state's coal, several major railroad companies serving Wyoming and the West have invested millions of dollars in new hauling equipment. *Burlington Northern,* in connection with *Chicago and Northwestern,* is undertaking to build a $32.5 million, 126-mile rail line through the Powder River Basin to expedite coal shipments to the nation. This is the longest stretch of new railroad constructed in the United States since 1931.

Wyoming's number one mineral export, however, continues to be crude oil, as large amounts are shipped by pipelines to be refined and marketed in the Midwest and East. Ten refineries are located within

COMMON OIL AND GAS TERMS

"Gross" and "Net" Acreage

As is the case with mining companies, the oil and gas companies have many joint ventures and other interrelationships. If a company has a ¼ interest in 1,000 acres, that would be described as 1,000 *"gross acres,"* or 250 *"net acres."* A company spreads its risk by having small interests in many different properties.

"Overriding Royalties" and "Net Working Interests"

An *"overriding royalty interest"* means that a company gets a certain percentage or dollar amount of what is produced and sold "off the top," regardless of production costs. A *"net working interest"* means that the company has a percentage participation in the net profits, if any, after costs associated with the particular production are paid.

the state's boundaries, however, and Wyoming is the refining capital of the Rockies, with 70,000 barrels refined daily just in Casper's three refineries.

EXPLORATION INCENTIVES STEPPED UP

There are approximately 400 oil-affiliated companies operating in the area, with Casper as the service headquarters. The industry spends $200-300 million annually in the search for and development of oil and gas wells. Although the area has never been a prolific producer of natural gas, increased price incentives have stimulated exploration of Wyoming's seven trillion cubic feet of proven reserves. The vast oil shale deposits in the Green River Formation of Colorado, Utah and Wyoming offer great potential for the production of large quantities of low-cost, low-sulphur oil.

The increased demand for uranium to fuel nuclear reactors for electrical power generation has resulted in substantially increased prices for the fuel. Recent forecasts indicate that by 1980 one-third of the country's electrical generating capacity will be nuclear, and by 2000 one-half. Currently there are approximately 25 exploration companies involved in the mining of Wyoming's U_3O_8 (uranium oxide) reserves.

While the huge costs of exploration on Alaska's North Slope have pretty much dictated that exploration and development there be carried out by the large, major oil companies, the industry has relied on the smaller, independent companies for much of the exploration and development work in Wyoming and the surrounding Rocky Mountain area. The following pages describe a number of such companies of potential interest to investors who wish to participate in this exciting phase of our country's energy development.

Shut-in gas well in Western Colorado. Rainbow has interests in over 100 such gas wells in Colorado, Montana, and Wyoming, with negotiations in progress for sale of gas and commencement of production.

Oil and Gas

RAINBOW RESOURCES, INC.

The largest Wyoming-headquartered independent oil and gas exploration and development company, Rainbow Resources has working interests in over 4 million acres plus royalty interests in over 2.5 million acres of oil and gas prospect acreage, mostly in the Northern Rocky Mountains most productive areas. The company's method of operation is to assemble blocks of oil and gas prospect acreage, and then to sell interests in the acreage to companies willing to commit development funds. This gives Rainbow spot cash from lease sales, plus percentage interests in a large number of oil and gas wells, without the risks of huge losses from often unsuccessful wildcat drilling. The company expects to participate in hundreds of new wells in the next five years.

Approximate current net production from Rainbow's interests amount to 1,100 barrels of oil per day, which compares favorably with the 850 barrel rate of 1974. In addition, the company has participations in over 100 successful gas wells which have been drilled and will commence production as soon as gas sales contracts are negotiated. Income derived from production as opposed to lease sales amounts to about one-third of the company's operating revenue as compared with only 10% in fiscal 1971. President Don Carpenter says this trend will continue as the company "will orient a lot more to oil and gas drilling and production" as its major source. Of 54 wells drilled in fiscal 1975, 27 were producers.

In the fourth quarter of fiscal 1975, one of the largest exploration projects ever assembled in a major Rocky Mountain Basin was put together, providing Rainbow with about $1.7 million in income. *Farmland International Energy Co.*, subsidiary of *Farmland Industries, Inc.*, purchased from Rainbow and Claud B. Hamill, as equal interest partners, a 50% working interest in 1.1 million net acres of undeveloped oil and gas leases in the Williston Basin of North Dakota, South Dakota, and Montana. Farmland has the right to earn an additional 25% interest by spending $7 million in exploration over the next three to five years. The group expects to be involved in 150-200 exploratory wells during the term of the agreement. Management says the project is the largest single such program Rainbow has ever been involved in and represents enormous future potential for the company.

Another sizeable exploration program, involving a $1.7 million seismic and drilling program on 608,000 acres in Southeastern Colorado is currently underway. Rainbow's financial position is strong, with over $4 million net working capital, a current ratio over five to one, and no long-term debt.

DOUBLE EAGLE PETROLEUM AND MINING COMPANY

Double Eagle Petroleum and Mining Company is participating in the development of petroleum, coal, uranium and other mineral resources in Wyoming and North Dakota. Currently the company has completed a drilling and trenching program in its zeolite deposits, confirming substantial reserves of 90% pure clinoptilolite (used in sewage treatment processes). The company has acquired ownership of two additional zeolite deposits, bringing reserves to more than 100 million tons.

Drilling on uranium claims has shown mineralization, although substantially more drilling will be required to determine whether a commercially mineable ore body is present. A preliminary drilling program on the company's Powder River Basin claims has established the presence of potentially valuable coal beds. More drilling is required to determine whether the leases contain economically exploitable reserves.

ECHO Oil Corporation was formed in May, 1968 as an oil and gas exploration company with offices in the First National Bank Building, Casper, Wyoming.

ECHO, with few exceptions is primarily involved within the state of Wyoming and more specifically in the Powder River, Green River and Wind River Basins of Wyoming. Their non-producing leasehold inventory currently consists of approximately 37,000 net acres under some 127,000 gross acres. They also presently have on their books some 22,000 net non-producing royalty acres under 135,000 gross acres which are under lease to other parties. They have 2,644 net producing acres of leasehold under 5,800 gross acres and over 1200 net producing royalty

Outfit on left is drilling rig, and outfit on right is tank truck which supplies water as lubricant for drilling operation. This combination of vehicles is a common sight in Wyoming whether drilling is done for oil or coal or other minerals.

acres under over 8,000 gross producing acres under lease to other parties.

Since its beginning in 1968 with 110,000 acres of non-producing leasehold and the proceeds of an intrastate stock sale totaling $150,000 and no producing income, ECHO has grown steadily to a company with gross revenue in excess of $1,000,000 annually of which some $800,000 annually are from the sale of oil and gas from 15 separate fields.

Since 1969 ECHO has participated, directly or indirectly, in the drilling of over 130 total wells. Included in this was their participation with 12.5% of the Amoco #1 Bitter Creek II Unit in Sweetwater County, Wyoming, which at 21,323 feet was, until recently exceeded by the Union Oil Company, the deepest well ever drilled in the region. The outcome of this well, plagued by mechanical problems, is not determinable at this time. ECHO also originated and is participating with 12.4% of the costs in the PanCanadian #22-25 Fuller Reservoir II Unit well in Fremont County, Wyoming, which is a 17,500 foot test directed to the Mississippian Madison Formation as a final objective at total depth. This well was commenced October 23, 1975.

Although ECHO continues to pursue these ultra deep and large size objectives, the shallower portions of the Powder River Basin is thought of as ECHO's "Bread and Butter" country and is where all of ECHO's present production is located.

EAGLE EXPLORATION COMPANY

Eagle Exploration Company (Casper, Wyoming) was founded in 1972 and first publicly offered to investors in March, 1973. Since that time, Eagle has assembled working interests and overriding royalty interests in over 1,000,000 acres of oil and gas leases.

Eagle Exploration's lease interests are in Wyoming, Utah, Montana, Louisiana, Colorado, and Oklahoma, with the bulk of the acreage in Wyoming. At year-end 1974, Eagle had interests in 42 producing or produceable wells, up from 37 the prior year.

WULF OIL

A seismic program is underway on 250,000 gross acres in the Northern Denver Basin, central Sioux County, Nebraska, in which Wulf holds a 25% working interest. Wulf and the two other independent oil operators, who hold the remaining interest in the properties, are presently seeking joint venture partners to begin a drilling program on the acreage.

Wulf is currently drilling a second well on its Water Creek Prospect in Washakie County, Wyoming. The company's first well on the prospect, the "No. 1 State," is now in production. Geologic studies indicate that as many as 15 development locations may possibly be productive on the Prospect.

EMC ENERGIES

Overall, EMC Energies has interests in 76,000 gross acres of oil and gas properties in Wyoming, Colorado, New Mexico, Montana, and North Dakota. The company currently has oil production of 210 barrels per day net to the company, of which approximately 85% is classified as "old oil." This is selling at $5.00 per barrel, but could go up considerably if price controls on old oil are dropped.

DISCOVERY OIL, LTD.

Discovery Oil has interests in 85 producing oil and gas wells generating approximately $30,000 per month cash flow off its 112,678 net acres in the Rocky Mountain area, primarily in Wyoming and Montana. Discovery also has about 42,000 acres of Wyoming coal leases. The company's business is acquiring leases on potential oil, gas, and coal producing lands, which are then assembled into packages of properties for sale to others. The company usually retains an interest in the leases, but does drill with its own funds, and promotes its properties to companies in the oil and gas industry.

Total assets at September 30, 1975 were $2.9 million compared to nearly $2.1 million at December 31, 1974. Revenue for the first nine months of 1975 was $843,000 compared to $438,000 in 1974. Net income more than doubled to $357,000 in the same 1975 period compared to $143,000 in 1974's first nine months. Acquisition of the assets of *Arman Oil Company* was completed by mid-1975.

BURTON/HAWKS

Burton/Hawks holds interests in 361,000 gross acres of oil and gas properties in nine Rocky Mountain states and Alaska. Of this amount, 4,000 acres are producing properties, returning to the company approximately 350 net barrels of oil and natural gas equivalent per day.

Oil and gas sales by the company more than tripled during 1974, reaching $745,798, compared with $228,506 the year before. This in-

Among the 32 oil producing states, Utah and Wyoming are well situated to serve many important regions. Oil well pumps such as the one at right are visible signs of this vital industry. Natural gas fields, also found in region, are supported by storage facilities such as one at left.

crease is the result of both higher prices for crude oil and increased production.

Burton/Hawks' most successful drilling venture to date is in the Lone Pine Field, which the Company discovered in 1971, in the North Park Basin in north central Colorado. Here the company has working interests in 17 producing wells. In 1974 these wells produced 277,644 barrels of oil, of which 75,938 barrels were net to Burton/Hawks.

The company is entering the third year of a five-year joint venture with *Husky Oil Company.* Under the agreement, Burton/Hawks contributed a 50% interest in certain of its nonproducing oil and gas properties to the venture and Husky contributes $750,000 per year for the five-year period for venture funds. Burton/Hawks is operator for the venture.

The strongest asset and potential for future growth of the company continues to be its undeveloped oil and gas prospect acreage on more than 60 separate prospects. The company is concentrating on getting these prospects drilled, according to company President Bill Hawks.

OIL RESOURCES, INC.

Oil Resources, Inc. is an exploration and development company with its principal interests in the Rocky Mountain and Alaskan regions.

Oil Resources has about 37,600 gross acres of producing properties with 11,000 net acres attributable to the company. As of the end of the company's 1974 fiscal year, 207 oil and gas wells were in place, with the company's net ownership amounting to 38.58 wells.

The company's property interests are in Montana, Utah, North Dakota, Wyoming, Colorado, Alaska, and Alberta and Saskatchewan, Canada. Oil Resources, has total leases of about 672,082 gross acres amounting to 273,447 net acres.

CHAPARRAL RESOURCES, INC.

Another company with heavy Wyoming involvement is Denver-based Chaparral Resources, Inc. Founded in January 1972, Chaparral is off to a fast start. Annual revenue in 1972 and 1973 was less than $60,-000, as the company was busy acquiring leases and properties for later exploration. This began to pay off in fiscal 1974 (fiscal year ending November 30), when revenue was $817,156 versus $22,222 in 1973. 1974 profits of $75,447 reversed a 1973 loss of $69,464.

Chaparral operates drilling rigs for itself as well as other companies. In 1974, 32 wells were drilled on the company's properties. These resulted in 27 producers or indicated producers and only five dry holes. As of February 15, 1975, Chaparral owned working interests in 139,948 gross acres and 47,222 net acres. In addition, the company has overriding royalty interests in 25,833 gross acres and 23,036 net acres.

In late 1973 the joint venture Chaparral Resources and *American Quasar Petroleum* "No. 1 Patterson," a deep exploratory well 65 miles northeast of Casper, Wyoming, drew national attention when it blew out, caught fire and was battled for 33 days before being brought under control. The *Red Adair Company* of Houston, Texas, which had charge of battling the blaze, said it was "the most difficult onshore oil well fire we have fought in the United States." The epilog to that spectacular holocaust is that the well was brought into production in 1974, and, through July of 1975 had already produced 254,000 barrels of oil and 660 million cubic feet of gas, generating gross revenue of almost $3.5 million.

BRONCO OIL COMPANY

Another new company, Bronco Oil, has acquired working and royalty interests in several undeveloped oil and gas prospects in Wyoming. Bronco has 1,120 acres in Washakie County in which it owns 100% interest. The company intends to drill or cause to be drilled a 10,300-foot Phosphoria test in the near future. In Fremont County, the company owns a 1¼% overriding royalty, convertible at payout to a 5% working interest, in 2,207 acres known as the Beaver Creek Prospect.

The company also has an interest in two properties in Big Horn County, Wyoming. One, the Southeast Byron Prospect, consists of 120 gross acres in which the company holds a 0.625% overriding royalty during payout, convertible at payout to a 15% working interest. The other property, the Table Mountain Prospect, consists of 4,835 gross acres of undeveloped oil and gas leases upon which the company holds a ½ to 1% overriding royalty.

EQUITY OIL CO.

Equity Oil, based in Salt Lake, is a long-established exploration and production company. In 1974, an active exploration year, Equity drilled a total of 58 wells. This resulted in 23 completions, 18 oil wells and 5 gas wells. 50 to 60 new wells were scheduled for drilling during 1975. Equity's 1974 revenue of $7,646,897 and income of $3,337,549 were the highest in the company's 52-year history.

The spectacular 1973 blow-out of the No. 1 Patterson Well took 33 days to bring under control. Chaparral Resources participated on a joint venture basis with American Quasar Petroleum in the exploratory drilling phase of this oil and gas discovery.

Equity's production of oil and gas during the past five years is shown below:

	1974	1973	1972	1971	1970
Oil (Bbls.)	911,515	928,838	724,555	625,270	660,814
Gas (Mcf.)	586,560	541,300	483,040	268,075	175,133

Also worth mentioning is Equity's involvement in some of the pioneering work in oil shale development. In Colorado's Piceance Creek Basin, Equity Oil has a net ownership of 4,488 acres. This is estimated to contain 1.3 billion barrels of oil reserves in place as oil shale.

Since 1970, **Altex Oil Corporation,** based in Vernal, Utah, has taken a growing and active interest in exploration, development and oil and gas production in the Greater Altamont-Bluebell area, a major producing region located in Utah. In 1974, this area was ranked as the tenth largest onshore producing field in the U.S., and was producing 1.9 million barrels of crude oil and 1.8 billion cubic feet of natural gas per month.

Altex has participated in the area's development through ownership of minority leasehold, overriding royalty, and minority interests under 262,830 gross (46,582 net) acres of oil and gas leases in Utah. Altex owned interests in 77 producing wells with other wells either drilling or scheduled for drilling during 1975.

Paiute Oil & Mining Corp. (Pomco) has a 25% interest in five producing wells in a northern New Mexico gas field, and additional sites under evaluation for mining and drilling prospects in Nevada and Utah. The Salt Lake City headquartered company formed a joint venture with *Basin Petroleum Corp.* of Oklahoma in 1974 to develop Pomco's coal leases in southwestern Utah. Through its subsidiary *Trans-Western Tankers, Inc.,* Pomco also operates specially-equipped trucks to supply water and drilling fluids under pressure to various oil field operations.

Headquartered in Salt Lake, the **Bingham Silver Lead Company** is a 46-year-old mining company with a highly confusing name. Periodic work on the company's mining claims in the Oquirrh Mountains have not been productive to date, although substantial copper deposits are believed to exist in the area. Meanwhile, the company has developed a number of oil and gas joint ventures which are producing revenue currently.

Uranium

The United States requires massive amounts of electrical power — more and more each year. Energy is needed, not only for industry, but for governmental and consumer use as well. The choices available to us are few. Foreign supplies are tenuous, at best, as recent world events have shown.

For practical purposes, most hydroelectric dam sites have been fully utilized. Coal is an abundant energy source but possesses some drawbacks. Underground mining is hazardous work, and strip mining is upsetting to environmentalists. For technological reasons, we don't expect solar power systems (highly praised by environmentalists) to be workable on a commercial scale until the year 2000, if then.

One of the most workable answers lies in the increasing use of nuclear power plants. The technology exists. Commercial plants are in operation, and their record of safety and economy is proven.

As of June, 1975, some 157 nuclear power plants were in operation worldwide (including naval vessels). These plants have a combined capacity of 66 million kilowatts of power. They have a total of 2,000 nuclear experience years among them without a single instance of harm to a member of the public due to a nuclear reactor accident.

The entire fuel cycle of an average coal plant discharges 24,000 tons a year of sulphur dioxide releases. A similar size nuclear plant discharges just 720 tons per year. Another point to consider is fuel conservation. In 1974, U.S. utilities generated 125 billion kilowatt hours of electricity with nuclear power. This represented a saving of 185 million barrels of oil (that would otherwise have been imported) or the equivalent of 45 million tons of coal.

The conclusion is inescapable — like it or not, the U.S. is going to become increasingly more dependent upon nuclear fuel plants as a primary source of energy. This being the case, producers of uranium oxide concentrate (U_3O_8), commonly referred to as "yellowcake," have to be of interest to thoughtful investors.

American Nuclear Corporation, based in Casper, Wyoming, appears to have a solid future as a uranium producer. With a large amount of potential reserves, American Nuclear has done extensive exploration in Wyoming's Gas Hills Area, Sweetwater Area and Powder River Basin of eastern Wyoming. The company owns working interests in some 400,000 gross acres of upgraded land holdings.

American Nuclear has a strong financial partner in developing its properties. The *Tennessee Valley Authority* (TVA) has acquired a 50% interest in about 257,000 gross acres of the company's properties. This involved the payment of $5 million at intervals from 1972-1974. TVA will control the first ten million pounds of ore produced, and American Nuclear will control the second 10 million pounds.

In December, 1974 TVA agreed to assume $498,000 of American Nuclear's outstanding debt and to finance an additional $498,000 for the company to be paid out of future production. Further, TVA is advancing all necessary monies for exploration and development until production has begun. While actual production of uranium yellowcake may not begin until 1977-1978, the future prospects of American Nuclear have brightened considerably.

American Nuclear also has a 40% interest in a partnership with *Federal Resources* of Salt Lake, known as *Federal-American Partners.* This partnership has owned and operated a 950-ton per day uranium mill in the Gas Hills since 1959. The partnership has leased all its

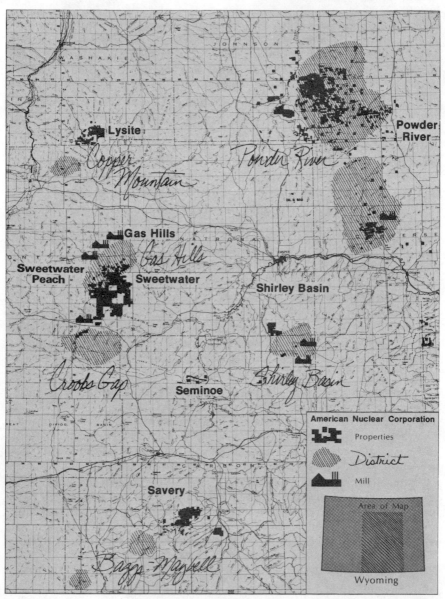

The above map, courtesy of American Nuclear Corporation, shows most of the major mining districts in Wyoming as well as the company's own properties.

prospective uranium property to the Tennessee Valley Authority, and the partnership is operating the exploration and development program for TVA on an operating cost plus royalty formula.

American Nuclear also holds 100 per cent of the working interest in approximately 95,000 acres of prospects in three states, principally in

Wyoming. At this writing American Nuclear is seeking a joint venture partner to explore and develop these properties.

In contrast to American Nuclear, Spokane-based **Midnite Mines, Inc.** has been mining and selling uranium concentrate for a number of years. Uranium was discovered in 1954 on Lookout Mountain near Spokane, Washington. This discovery became the *"Midnite Mine,"* so-called, the story goes, because it was found near midnight by two Indians, James and John LeBret, exploring with a Geiger counter. *Dawn Mining Company* (51% owned by *Newmont Mining, Inc.* and 49% by Midnite Mines, Inc.) was formed to operate the mine.

Dawn Mining's processing plant was built in 1957 at a cost of $3 million, plus $1 million to expand capacity in 1969. Currently processing 500 tons of ore per day, this mill has processed about 9.2 million pounds of uranium oxide from its inception through the end of 1974. Milling operations are carried out at Dawn's concentrator on a year-round, 24 hours a day, seven days a week basis.

As mentioned, 1975 has seen renewed demand for uranium oxide on a worldwide basis. Midnite's management has reported the following sales:

December 1974 to *General Public Utilities* @ $10 per pound

March 1975 to a West German purchaser @ $16 per pound.

May 1975 to *Florida Power & Light Co.* @ $20 per pound

Midnite has computed the following ore reserves, as of April 30, 1975:

	Tons	Containing Pounds U_3O_8
Company Stockpiles	115,000	537,000
Positive Reserves	460,000	985,800
Inferred Reserves	750,000	

Midnite also owns the *Polaris Mine* near Dillon, Montana. Polaris is a silver mine which has been dormant for more than fifty years. A recent sample shipment of ore from this mine assayed at 31.8 ounces of silver and 0.02 ounces of gold per ton. Some estimates of positive and probable reserves in the Polaris total more than one million ounces of silver. While the mine would involve higher than normal operating costs, Midnite's management is considering returning the Polaris to full production.

Power Resources Corporation (POWERCO) of Casper, Wyoming, is at this writing one of the newest of those energy companies primarily engaged in uranium exploration. Its shares were first publicly underwritten in September, 1974. To date, the company has no proven uranium reserves and minor oil and gas revenue.

The company is taking a "home run" approach, and is attempting to discover a major new uranium district rather than to chew around the edges of known properties. Powerco has assembled uranium leases on two major areas. One, in eastern Wyoming (Goshen Hole Project) involves 104,000 acres. The second is in northeastern Colorado (Pawnee Project) and amounts to a 50% interest in about 125,000 acres.

Western Standard Corp., Riverton, Wyoming, recently signed a mining agreement with *U.S. Energy* also of Riverton, for a mining operation on Western's Kaycee uranium property in the Powder River Basin of Wyoming. Western controls 70,000 acres in the area covering the Tertiary, Fort Union, Lance, and Wasatch formations. Chemical solution fronts totaling over 200 miles have been delineated in two formations by wide spaced drillings and a sizeable amount of vanadium-uranium mineralization located. U.S. Energy will begin mining operations as soon as it receives a mining permit.

The company has leased its Shirley Basin, Wyoming properties near Casper to *American Nuclear Corp.* under terms of annual payments plus a fixed fee per pound of yellowcake produced. Western claims in the basin cover 9000 acres.

Coal properties held by the company have been leased for cash considerations and a royalty on coal produced. Western also receives about $10,000 per month from oil and gas production on properties which it owns. Most of the producing wells are in the Powder River Basin.

U.S. Energy Corp. is engaged in the contract mining business, both as an independent contractor and as a contractor who receives its income in the mined product, rather than on a fee basis. Its present principal business is contract mining and drilling services performed for other companies, the production of minerals from properties leased from others and the acquisition and resale of mining properties. During 1974, 65.8% of its revenue remitted was from contract mining.

The company is currently operating four underground uranium mines in Wyoming for *Western Nuclear, Union Carbide,* and *Exxon.* It recently entered into a mining venture with *Western Standard* to mine and share in the profits of Western's Kaycee uranium properties in the Powder River Basin. This venture has a commitment to furnish 3 million pounds of uranium oxide (yellowcake) over a five year period.

U.S. Energy has entered into a joint venture agreement with *Gulf Oil Corporation* on 250,000 acres of mining claims in Arizona, Wyoming, and California whereby Gulf has a right to earn up to 75% interest in the properties through conducting an exploration program. Gulf will be the operator of the program and U.S. Energy has agreed to perform the drilling on locations designated by Gulf.

Coal

In view of the vast reserves of Wyoming coal known to exist, we should mention the **Wyoming Coal Corporation** (Gillette, Wyoming). A new issue in May, 1974, 4,750,000 shares were placed at $0.10 share. There are a total of 8,000,000 shares outstanding. To our knowledge, the company has no proven reserves at present. The company is acquiring and testing various leases in the hopes of establishing commercial reserves.

Much more substantial is the mining activity of **Morrison-Knudsen Company.** In Kemmerer, Wyoming, M-K has been actively mining coal for 24 years. M-K is presently operating under a 20-year contract granted by the *Kemmerer Coal Company* in 1971. Two million tons of thermal coal was initially produced in 1972 and production was up to 3.3 million tons in 1974. Further expansion is underway.

An even more ambitious coal project exists at the *Sarpy Creek Mine* in southeastern Montana near Hardin. There, 800 million tons of coal reserves are owned by *Westmoreland Resources,* a partnership in which Morrison-Knudsen has a 24% interest. During 1972-74, M-K engineered and constructed Sarpy Creek facilities, and commercial production began on July 1, 1974. The mine is operated by M-K under a 20-year contract.

In the last half of 1974, 1.5 million tons of thermal coal was shipped from Sarpy Creek to Midwest utility customers under a contract calling for delivery of 76.5 million tons over a 20-year period. Production in 1975 is expected to reach 4 million tons, and existing mining equipment has an annual capacity of about 6 million tons. When coal storage capabilities are expanded, the Sarpy Creek mine will have the capacity to handle at least 13 million tons of coal per year.

Southeastern Montana contains a significant amount of the nation's reserves of low sulphur coal. Some of the publicly-held companies besides M-K owning coal reserves in this area are *Burlington Northern, Westmoreland Coal,* and *Western Energy,* a wholly owned subsidiary of the **Montana Power Company.**

Mining at Colstrip, Montana near the Sarpy Creek mine, has been underway since 1924. However, the entire property was acquired by Montana Power in 1959, and subsequent acquisition of additional leases give Montana Power coal reserves currently estimated at about 850 million tons.

Recent increases in coal production have been dramatic, as shown below:

COLSTRIP COAL PRODUCTION
(Western Energy Company)

Year	Tons produced	Year	Estimated Future Production
1968	150,000	1975	6,800,000
1969	521,000	1976	9,700,000
1970	1,658,000	1977	11,800,000
1971	5,161,000	1978	13,400,000
1972	5,500,774	1979	13,800,000
1973	4,253,781	1980	16,600,000
1974	3,211,851		

Source: Montana Power Company.

Montana Power, through its subsidiary, Western Energy, has been active in the land reclamation of this strip mining area. This includes the restoration of 450 acres of land disturbed prior to the time that Western Energy arrived on the scene. This land has been contoured and planted with a scientifically selected mix of new vegetation. Present mining operations at Colstrip involve a total of just 85 acres, of which 25 acres are now in the reclamation process.

WHERE OUR ENERGY COMES FROM

(Trillions of BTUs)

	1972		1977		1980		1985	
Coal	12,495	17.3%	15,125	17.6%	16,140	16.8%	21,470	18.4%
Petroleum	32,966	45.7	39,730	46.3	42,190	44.0	50,700	43.5
Natural gas	23,125	32.1	25,935	30.2	26,980	28.0	28,390	24.3
Nuclear	576	0.8	4,224	4.9	6,720	7.0	11,750	10.1
Other	2,946	4.1	3,738	4.4	3,990	4.2	4,320	3.7
Total	72,108		88,752		96,020		116,630	

Source: FEA, Project Independence Blueprint, November 1974

WHERE OUR ENERGY GOES
(Trillions of BTUs)

	1972		1977		1980		1985	
Household and commercial	14,696	20.5	16,657	19.4	17,500	18.2	18,960	16.3
Industrial	20,561	28.5	23,704	27.6	24,840	25.9	27,520	23.6
Transportation	18,058	25.0	22,127	25.8	22,840	23.8	27,090	23.3
Electrical generation	18,560	25.7	22,983	26.8	29,970	31.2	40,390	34.6
Synthetics	233	0.3	387	0.4	870	0.9	2,670	2.2
Total	72,108		85,880		96,020		116,630	

Source: FEA, Project Independence Blueprint (Table F 15)

The table above gives some idea of the huge increases in energy use from all sources just in the next few years. Although all sources must increase on an absolute basis, the increase in the use of nuclear power is most significant in the changing *proportions* of energy sources. It is also apparent that the proportion of energy supplied through electricity will rise markedly.

14

Utilities

The Northwest has historically been an area of power abundance. The extensive river systems of the Snake and Columbia led to the early development of hydroelectric plants. The presence of coal in Montana, Wyoming and Utah also aided utility development. Today, nuclear power generation is under extensive development in the region, as well. One system, unique to this region, is the *Northwest Power Pool.*

Formed in 1942 as a result of war-time needs for efficient usage of power supplies, the Northwest Power Pool is comprised of seven private and eleven government utilities. Its geographical range includes Utah Power and Light in the southeast corner, Montana Power in the northeast, British Columbia Hydro & Power Authority in the North, and Portland-based Pacific Power & Light, with a service area in California on the South. Other participants are Idaho Power Company, Washington Water Power, Puget Sound Power & Light, Portland General Electric, U.S. Bureau of Reclamation, three Public Utility Districts in Washington, Seattle City Light, Tacoma City Light, the Bonneville Power Administration, the U.S. Corps of Engineers, Eugene Water & Electric Board, and West Kootenay Power & Light Company in British Columbia.

The Pool is not a legal entity, and its operating committee has no contractual authority to do anything. Rather, it is a completely voluntary group, whose purpose is to encourage mutual cooperation in providing the area with needed energy, acting as one entity but maintaining the individuality of members. The utilities operate independently except where bilateral transactions dictate otherwise. The Pool's activities are confined to operational aspects of power generation. (Planning and coordination of plant construction is handled by the *Pacific Northwest Utilities Conference Committee.)*

The Pool's coordinating group, with a small office of five engineers located in Portland, serves as a clearing house of information from members, keeping data on power systems conditions. They use the information to coordinate systems operations, including the scheduling of maintenance work on plants to avoid simultaneous shutdowns, keeping tabs on systems protection, seeing that hydro energy is not wasted, and the coordination of many other aspects of interactive systems operations. Conference calls are held weekly with the participants.

This coordinating group also helps reconcile differences among participants, represents the Pool in the *Western Systems Coordinating Council* (made up of utility and agency representatives from 11 Western states and British Columbia), and, within the provisions of the Pacific Northwest Coordinating Agreement among most of the Pool members, budgets the usage of water stored in the Northwest region's reservoirs. The coordinating group takes on new functions continually, including 1973's coordination of members energy conservation efforts.

In addition to the organization of the Northwest Power Pool, the *Intercompany Pool (ICP),*, now made up of the seven investor-owned utilities, was also formed about the same time as the larger pool. The purpose of this group is also to effect a more economic and efficient generation of energy, and attempting to achieve more intense cooperation with a new contract agreed to in 1974.

NORTHWEST POWER PRODUCTION TO DOUBLE

The magnitude of the electric power supply program the utilities and government agencies must undertake in the Pacific Northwest during the next decade through 1986 is indicated by the fact that the new hydroelectric installations (mostly at existing government projects on the Columbia River basin) and new coal-fired or nuclear-fueled steam-electric plants scheduled by the utilities must add as much new generating capability as the region had available in mid-1975. Expressed in another way, the *region must develop as much power production capability in the next ten years as it developed in the ninety years or so since the pioneering utilities of the region started supplying consumers.*

At the beginning of 1975, the inter-connected power generating capability installed in the five Pacific Northwest states of Oregon, Washington, Idaho, Utah and Montana totaled almost 27 million kilowatts. Plants now under construction or scheduled will add approximately 28 million kilowatts to supply the total of approximately 55 million kilowatts of generating requirement forecast for 1985-1986. Of the new capability, almost 20 million kilowatts at the installations will be coal or nuclear-fueled steam-electric plants scheduled by the utilities as part of the Pacific Northwest Joint Hydro-Thermal Power Planning Program. Much of this steam-electric capacity will be at large developments exceeding 1,000,000 kilowatts at each location.

U.S. NUCLEAR ELECTRICAL GENERATING CAPACITY*

	1973	1980	1990	2000
Megawatts	25,660	120,000	475,000	1,090,000
Total electric in U.S.	429,456	680,000	1,160,000	2,020,000
Nuclear's per cent of total	5.6	16	41	55

Source: Office of Planning and Analysis, Atomic Energy Commission, April 24, 1974.

*These forecasts are part of a range of projections with the above table viewed as the most realistic.

Even if all of the power developments are completed on schedule, there still could be months in certain years of the decade when the Pacific Northwest will be deficient in generating resources because precipitation on the main Columbia River watershed and other streams of the region is below normal and the hydroelectric reservoirs cannot sustain optimum production of power at the river plants. In those periods the degree to which power consumers are able to conserve electric energy will be significant in terms of how the region manages its primary energy resource.

NUCLEAR POWER — FUEL OF THE FUTURE

An informed study of the utility industry nationally as well as in the Northwest leads to one inescapable conclusion . . . For the forseeable future, our reliance on nuclear power is going to increase steadily.

There are only a very few acceptable sites left for hydroelectric dams. The cost of fuel oil and natural gas is escalating rapidly with no assurance of future supplies. While thermal plants (coal-fired) will increase, nuclear power is both environmentally cleaner and lower in cost. One of the biggest problems with developing nuclear power plants is the very long lead time required for all the steps from planning through construction and becoming operational.

The tables on the accompanying pages clearly illustrate our growing reliance on electrical energy. At the same time, the projected increase in nuclear power usage is unmistakable. While extreme environmentalists and some others may fret over these projections, there is, literally, no other alternative.

The *Atomic Industrial Forum* is an international non-profit association of 625 organizations interested in the peaceful uses of nuclear power. A study has been released by the AIF comparing the cost of nuclear powered plants with those using fossil fuels. They found that one kilowatt hour (Kwh) produced by a nuclear plant costs, on average, 6.5 mills less (including amortized capital allocations) than a Kwh produced by a fossil plant.

In 1974, there were 56 operable nuclear power plants in the U.S. which generated more than 125 billion kilowatt hours. This resulted in a national saving of more than $810 million in total electric generating costs, compared to generating the same kilowatts via fossil fuel plants. Without these nuclear plants, the bulk of this saving would have been spent upon increased imports of oil.

The Electric Utilities

Pacific Power & Light's service area is the most widely spread among Northwest electric utilities. Approximate geographic distribution of electric operating revenues, including 550,000 customers, is Oregon 61%, Wyoming 18%, Washington 12.5%, California 5.2%, Montana 2.5%, and Idaho 0.8%. The company also provides water and steam heat service to customers in a number of communities. Through its 80% plus interest in *Telephone Utilities,* a holding company head-

Snow cover on the Cascade Range augers well for hydroelectric production as evidenced in this aerial view of Pacific Power's 204,000 kilowatt Swift project on southwestern Washington's Lewis River.

quartered in Ilwaco, Washington, with 25 operating subsidiary units, PP&L is involved in serving the telephone needs of customers in Washington, Oregon, Montana, Idaho, and Nevada.

Pacific Power & Light controls coal reserves totaling a substantial 1.8 billion tons, which is far more than enough to meet company needs, and provides considerably more fuel supply flexibility and cost protection to the company than is available to most other utilities. The company's strip coal reserves are located in Washington, Wyoming, and Montana.

Decker Coal Company, in which a PP&L subsidiary, *Western Minerals, Inc.* has a one-half interest, controls approximately 750,000,000 tons of low-sulphur reserves near Decker, Montana. In 1974 it shipped over 6.5 million tons, and expects shipments to increase by one-half million tons in 1975. Major contracts include shipments by Decker to *Commonwealth Edison Company* in Chicago and *Detroit Edison* and, beginning in 1978, to the *Lower Colorado River Authority* and the City of Austin, Texas. PP&L also has 400 million tons of wholly-owned coal reserves near Decker and plans to open a new mine within several years for its own needs and sales to others.

Well over one-half of PP&L's generating capacity comes from plants fueled by the low-sulphur western coal. The company's *Dave Johnston* plant near Glenrock, Wyoming receives its coal supply from a nearby field from which 117 million tons of coal is dedicated, and the jointly-owned *Jim Bridger* plant, near Rock Springs, Wyoming is supplied by adjacent reserves of which about 200 million tons are dedicated to the plant. Another 50 million tons in the Bridger field are unassigned.

NORTHWEST ELECTRIC UTILITY
YEAR-END 1974 COMPARISONS

	Customers Served	Maximum Generating Capacity (kilowatts)	Total Revenue (000)	Net Income (000)	Return on Stock-holders Equity
California Pacific Utilities	120,346	NA[1]	$40,312	$2,377	8.54%
Idaho Power	198,027	1,494,700	100,427	24,783	13.13
Montana Power	294,300	1,145,000	124,009	22,765	13.06
Pacific Power & Light	550,000	2,659,000	246,979	45,722	13.16
Portland General Electric	393,411	2,467,000	146,001	26,341	14.03
Puget Sound Power & Light	409,000	2,513,000	142,393	18,071	12.02
Utah Power & Light	349,910	1,787,000	152,585	24,173	10.39
Washington Water Power	267,590	1,111,500	110,098	14,351	10.46

[1]Company purchases its power from other suppliers.

INVESTOR-OWNED UTILITY POWER PLANTS
PROPOSED & UNDER CONSTRUCTION
OR COMPLETED SINCE 1974

Plant Name	Type	Owners	Megawatt Capacity	Completion Dates
Huntington (Utah)	Fossil	UP&L	846	1974,77
Wood River (Idaho)	Comb.	IP	50	1974
Jim Bridger (Wyo.)	Fossil	IP,PP&L	2000	1974,75,77,79
Beaver (Ore.)	Comb.	PGE	614	1974,77
Whitehorn (Wash.)	Comb	PSPL	67.5	1974
Colstrip (Mont.)	Fossil	MP,PSPL, PP&L,PGE,WWP	2060	1975,76,79,80
Trojan (Ore.)	Nuclear	PGE,Eugene, PPL	1130	1975
Wyodak (Wyo.)	Fossil	PP&L, Black Hills P&L	330	1978
Emery (Utah)	Fossil	UP&L	800	1978,80
Boardman (Ore.)	Fossil	PGE	500	1980
Pioneer (Idaho)	Fossil	IP	1000	1981,83
Naughton (Wyo.)	Fossil	UP&L	800	1982,84
Pebble Springs (Ore.)	Nuclear	PGE	2520	1983,86
Skagit #1&2 (Wash.)	Nuclear	PSPL,PP&L, WPPSS, WWP	2576	1982,85
WNP #3 (Wash.)	Nuclear	WPPSS, PP&L PGE,WWP,PSPL	1240	1981

Eugene-Eugene Water & Electric Board; IP-Idaho Power; MP-Montana Power; PP&L-Pacific Power & Light; PGE-Portland General Electric; PSPL-Puget Sound Power & Light; UP&L-Utah Power & Light; WPPSS-Washington Public Power Supply System; WWP-Washington Water Power.

Comb.-Combustion Turbine.
WNP—Washington Nuclear Project

After all commitments to existing plants and plants under construction and Decker's present contracts are accounted for, over 1.3 billion tons of coal controlled by PP&L are available for future contracts or company needs. Since the definition of coal reserves refers to coal

ELECTRIC UTILITIES—SALES BY CLASS OF USER (1974)

	Residential		Commercial		Industrial		Gov't and Other[1]		Totals	
	Dollars (000)	KW Hours (000)	Dollars (000)	KW Hours (000)	Dollars (000)	KW Hours (000)	Dollars (000)	KW Hours (000)	Dollars (000)	KW Hours (000)
Idaho Power	32,652 37.7%	1,927,320 25.4%	20,695 23.9%	1,146,370 15.1%	18,959 21.9%	3,126,740 41.1%	14,374[2] 16.6%	1,401,604 18.4%	86,680 100.0%	7,602,034 100.0%
Montana Power	25,655 38.1%	1,043,593 24.2%	20,448 30.4%	930,212 21.6%	18,668 27.7%	2,171,066 50.3%	2,547 3.8%	168,926 3.9%	67,318 100.0%	4,313,797 100.0%
Pacific Power & Light	87,465 44.6%	5,653,332 39.0%	58,146 29.7%	3,418,127 23.6%	47,526 24.3%	5,286,592 36.5%	2,803 14.3%	141,144 1.0%	195,940 100.0%	14,499,195 100.0%
Portland General Electric	73,123 52.5%	4,700,025 43.5%	41,881 30.1%	2,632,272 24.4%	20,888 15.0%	3,364,222 31.1%	3,320 2.4%	105,822 1.0%	139,212 100.0%	10,802,341 100.0%
Puget Sound Power & Light	72,722 55.4%	5,039,751 53.6%	36,230 27.6%	2,043,167 21.7%	15,146 11.5%	2,050,080 21.8%	7,189 5.5%	274,252 2.9%	131,287 100.0%	9,407,250 100.0%
Utah Power & Light	53,939 40.4%	2,377,442 31.2%	33,762 25.3%	1,572,138 20.6%	40,401 30.2%	3,274,481 42.9%	5,471 4.1%	399,989 5.3%	133,573 100.0%	7,624,050 100.0%
Washington Water Power	25,805 48.4%	2,141,425 43.9%	16,188 30.3%	1,166,787 23.9%	10,369 19.4%	1,532,762 31.4%	988 1.9%	33,743 0.7%	53,350 100.0%	4,874,717 100.0%

[1]Sales for resale have been excluded.
[2]Consists almost entirely of energy used for irrigation.

Coal for the Jim Bridger power plant near Rock Springs, Wyoming, is being scooped from the top half of a 28-foot thick seam at the rate of 110 tons every 2½ minutes.

which is currently economical to extract, there is the possibility that the reserves could be even larger upon increased demand and higher prices.

Of total coal reserves, about 85% contain less than 1.0% sulphur content. New emission standards adopted in Wyoming could prevent the usage in Wyoming of coal reserves with a sulphur content over 1.0%.

Generating facilities owned by PP&L include 33 hydroelectric plants with a rated capacity of 863 megawatts and four steam-electric generating plants, including the four-unit Dave Johnston plant with a total 1,433 megawatts capacity. The company is a 47.5% owner and operator of the Centralia, Washington steam-electric generating plant, and is participating with Idaho Power in the construction of four 500 megawatt coal-fired units at the Jim Bridger plant.

The aggregate rated capacity of PP&L's plants and interests in plants is 2,659 megawatts, and company-owned plant generation accounts for approximately 59% of total generation requirements. Approximately 27% of company energy requirements are met through long-term purchase contracts, primarily from hydroelectric generating facilities, and 14% through interchange and other purchase agreements. The company also has contracts to purchase firm peaking capacity from the *Bonneville Power Administration*.

Construction expenditures by PP&L in 1974 amounted to $241 million, with 1975's anticipated expenditures at $213 million; 1976's are expected to be $277 million. Management anticipates a 4.2% load growth in 1975 and about 6% annually thereafter. In the years 1970-74 the average yearly increase in energy sales was 6.5%.

The company's major construction project presently is the previously-mentioned four-unit 2,000 megawatt Jim Bridger plant being constructed with Idaho Power (one-third interest). The company's portion of the total cost of the plant and associated transmission lines and coal mine is about $675 million, of which $152 million is for air and water pollution control facilities.

During 1974, primary foundations were completed for the 330 megawatt coal-fired plant known as the *Wyodak Project* east of Gillette, Wyoming. PP&L expects to have an interest of up to 90%, with the remainder belonging to the *Black Hills Power & Light Company*. Coal for the plant will be supplied from nearby deposits controlled by Black Hills. The cost of the plant, scheduled for completion in 1978, is estimated at $680 per kw.

PP&L also has a 2½% interest in the 1,130 megawatt *Trojan Nuclear Plant* being constructed by Portland General Electric near Rainier, Oregon.

The first three units of PP&L's Dave Johnston plant, which were built prior to adoption of state and federal air quality standards, also require construction of precipitators at an estimated cost of $60 million. In 1975 about $15.5 million will be spent for continuation of the construction of the emission control units.

New regulations adopted in January 1975 by the *Wyoming Environmental Quality Council* are imposing much stiffer restrictions on sulphur dioxide stack gases than those imposed by federal regulations. Whether the new regulations will require the addition of still more emission control equipment at the Dave Johnston plant is yet uncertain, but if "scrubbers" are required, management predicts substantial capital expenditures and increased operating costs. Court action against the regulations is being sought by the company and others.

Reclamation of land mined by PP&L in Wyoming has been going on since 1965, four years before it was required by state law. Management points out that because of extensive research and experimentation, reclaimed acreage is even exceeding the productivity of native terrain. The approximate cost per acre of the reclamation project is $2,000 as compared with the $30 surface value, which is allocated to the value of the coal mined, adding about $.05 per ton to over-all costs.

Financing of PP&L's construction program over the next five years is expected by management to require over $1 billion in new financing.

In 1973 PP&L acquired 1.8 million shares of the common stock of Telephone Utilities in return for TU's acquisition of *Northwestern Telephone Systems, Inc.*, a PP&L subsidiary. Together with other TU stock acquired previously by a tender offer to TU stockholders, PP&L gained control of over 80% of the outstanding shares. The remaining approximate 922,000 shares are distributed among some 3,000 stockholders. The telephone systems now service approximately 122,000 stations. 1974 revenue of TU was $25.6 million, and consolidated net income was up 12% to $3.7 million.

Idaho Power Company began service in 1916, and now supplies electric energy in Southern Idaho, Eastern Oregon and Northern Nevada, serving a total population of about 555,000 persons. The economy of its service area is solidly based on diversified agriculture, including electric-pump irrigation which is steadily increasing. Idaho Power also supplies a wide variety of commercial and industrial customers ranging from elemental phosphorus electric-furnace plants to year-round recreational developments like Sun Valley. Because of the predominantly agricultural industries served, Idaho Power is unique among Northwest utilities in that peak load comes in the summer rather than the winter. Therefore, they can trade power with neighboring utilities through interconnected transmission systems to the advantage of all.

Economic activity in Idaho Power's service area has experienced steady growth in recent years, coming from expansion of existing industries, additional location of light, diverse industries in the area, and irrigation and development of land for productive farm use. The company is experiencing a customer growth rate about double the national average for electric utilities. From 1968, when the accelerated rate of increase in new customers started, to the end of 1974, total customers served increased by 28%. Accounting for this rise is not only the area's share of the nation's population growth, but also an influx of families from outside the area, according to Idaho Power President James Bruce.

Jim Bridger

The Jim Bridger steam generating plant, one-third owned by Idaho Power and two-thirds owned by Pacific Power & Light, began commercial operation in 1974 upon completion of the first of four units.

Another major factor in Idaho Power's steady load growth is increasing average use by residential customers. In the latest 12-month period for which figures were available, the company's gain in average home use of electricity was the second largest of 139 major U.S. utilities. It rose by 958 kilowatt hours (Kwh) to a total 12,835 Kwh for the 12 months. This compares to an average annual usage of 8,111 Kwh for all 139 companies.

Energy sales to general business customers over the 1968-1974 period increased by 37%. Idaho Power's annual revenue topped $100 million for the first time in 1974.

IRRIGATION ELECTRIC NEEDS GROWING

An important contributor to the area's rising energy demands is the rapidly increasing use of electric pumping to open new desert land to productive farming and conversion of existing systems to more efficient high-pressure sprinling. In 1975 approximately 97,660 horsepower for new pumps to irrigate an additional 115,048 acres were added to the company's irrigation load, which now totals 13,000 pumps and 962,885 horsepower irrigating 1,505,600 acres. Irrigation revenues in 1974 increased by about $2 million, or 19.9% over the previous year. Management sees no immediate end to land reclamation, with approximately three million prime acres available for development.

Until 1974, Idaho Power was one of the nation's few all-hydro systems, operating 16 plants on the Snake River and tributaries that still are its chief source of supply. These plants have a dependable generating capacity, at summer peak and under adverse river flow conditions, of 1,136,000 kilowatts. Faced with limited opportunities for additional hydro developments, the company must rely increasingly on coal and, eventually, on nuclear-fueled plants. The company became a combination hydro-thermal system when, in the last quarter of 1974 it commenced commercial operation of the first of four 500,000 kilowatt units at the *Jim Bridger* coal-fired plant in Wyoming. It owns these units jointly with Pacific Power & Light Company. Idaho Power is receiving the first unit's entire output, and will be entitled to a total of 667,000 kilowatts, or a one-third share, when all four units are in operation.

Additional plans are in the making for a 1,000 megawatt coal-fired steam generating plant to be built 24 miles southeast of Boise near Orchard, Idaho. Idaho Power has filed an application with the Idaho Public Utilities Commission for construction at that site, after having considered over 20 sites. The units, the first of which is tentatively scheduled to begin service in the early 1980's, and the second as load growth requires, will be fueled by low-sulphur coal contracted for earlier last year from *Black Buttes Coal Company* in Wyoming.

The addition of coal-fired plants to the company's predominately hydro system will enable the company to eliminate problems created by water fluctuations. Management plans to use the coal plants for base loads, and hydro sources as peaking sources. One of management's main reasons for emphasizing coal rather than nuclear plants in the short run is because of the shorter lead time required to bring them on line to meet the area's rapidly-rising energy demand.

Construction expenditures are estimated to total approximately $500 million in the five years 1974-1978. For 1974, $83.6 million was spent, with about $46.4 million going for the *Jim Bridger* project.

Idaho Power is a very well-managed company, and its 16 hydro-electric generating plants and large coal reserves give the company a strong base as we enter a period of critical energy supply needs.

The **Montana Power Company** (Butte, Montana) encompasses a service area including a population of about 596,000. This covers about 65% of the land area of Montana and 81% of the state's total population. Montana Power operates thirteen hydroelectric projects and two thermal generating plants.

The area's economy is primarily agricultural, including livestock. Other major industries are nonferrous metal and coal mining, forest products, petroleum refining, and tourism. Unlike other Northwest utilities, Montana Power has one dominant industrial customer. In 1974, the operations of *The Anaconda Company* accounted for 11.5% of the utility's revenues.

An important new link in the *Northwest Power Pool* is under construction at Colstrip. Two 330,000 kw mine-mouth coal fired steam generating plants are scheduled to go into service in 1975 and 1976. These are each 50% owned by Montana Power and *Puget Sound Power & Light*.

Colstrip units "3" and "4" are planned for construction soon thereafter. These vitally needed new facilities have become the focal point for attack by virtually every environmental group in the country that is capable of forming a committee. (See chapter on "Environment and the Economy" for our discussion of the Colstrip project and related environmental questions.)

LOW-SULPHUR COAL RESERVES HELD

The construction of Colstrip would not be feasible without the resources of *Western Energy Company,* Montana Power's wholly-owned subsidiary.

At Colstrip, Western Energy has coal mining leases covering approximately 610 million recoverable tons of coal reserves. This is low-sulphur content coal averaging 0.7% by weight, far less than the sulphur present in eastern coal fields. About 490 million tons are reserved for the use of Colstrip units 1-4. Leases are pending on other reserves at Colstrip amounting to approximately 180 million tons. At other locations in eastern Montana, Western Energy holds leases on an additional 250 million tons of low-sulphur coal.

The company's coal mining production in 1974 was 3,212,000 tons. Deliveries are estimated to increase to more than 6 million tons in 1975 and 13 million tons by 1977. Most of these sales are to other parties under long-term contracts.

Montana Power has a massive construction program under way.

1974 expenditures were $76.2 million and will rise to $91 million in 1975. For the 1975-1979 period, the company has budgeted $464 million in capital improvements. Western Energy will spend an additional $48.5 million in the same period.

These are heady figures for a company which had just $549.7 million in total assets as of March 31, 1975.

Puget Sound Power & Light Company serves an area of approximately 4,500 square miles, principally in the Puget Sound region of Western Washington. The primarily suburban and rural service area includes the cities of Bellevue, Olympia, Bellingham, and Bremerton. The company has in excess of one million people in its region, and customers amount to about 412,000.

Approximately 94% of the company's energy requirement is supplied by hydroelectric generation, with about 80% obtained through long-term contracts with several of the Washington public utility districts' projects on the Columbia River. The balance of hydroelectric generation is supplied by the company's six hydroelectric plants and purchases from other utilities. Puget Power also owns a steam-electric plant on Lake Washington, and a 7% interest in the Centralia, Washington coal-fired steam-electric plant. Puget is a 50% partner with *Montana Power Company* in the *Colstrip* mine-mouth coal-fired steam generating plant. (See section on Montana Power Company.)

Puget Power's construction expenditures for 1974 were $94.4 million, and are estimated at $97.7 million in 1975. Projections for 1976-77 construction call for the disbursement of an additional $320 million.

The **Washington Water Power Company,** based in Spokane, serves eastern Washington and northern Idaho. This area of about 550,000 population includes the city of Spokane, the Coeur d'Alene mining district, and extensive timberlands and farmlands.

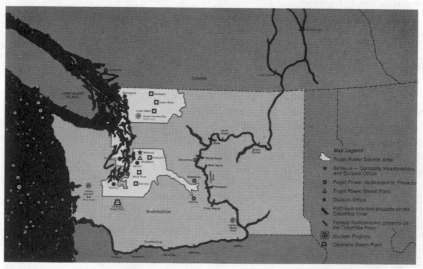

Puget Sound Power & Light's service area.

This plant on the Spokane River in Spokane, Washington was the first plant built by Washington Water Power.

Washington Water Power (WWP) traces its history back to its founding in 1889. Originally a system of hydroelectric plants on the Spokane River, WWP produced a number of "firsts" in the utility industry.

The company's 60,000-volt transmission line to Burke, Idaho, completed in 1903, was the longest transmission line in the world at that time. In addition, WWP's Long Lake Dam, built in 1915, was the highest spillway dam and had the highest capacity turbines in the world at that time.

In 1958, Washington Water Power purchased various natural gas distribution properties to become a combination utility service company. The company's 1974 revenue was divided as follows: Electric — 67.7%, Gas — 30.5%, and 1.8% from steam heat and water service. (The gas portion of WWP's business is discussed under the section on natural gas utilities.)

65% of the electrical power distributed by the company is generated at its own facilities, which include six hydroelectric generating plants in Washington, two in Idaho, and one in Western Montana; the 15%-owned thermal plant in Centralia, Washington, and a fuel-oil fired combustion turbine generator in Othello, Washington (used primarily for peaking capacity). Remaining generating needs are purchased from the Public Utility District's Columbia River projects and other utilities. The company estimates these sources to be sufficient to supply its estimated requirements through 1978.

Coal required to operate the 15% owned Centralia thermal plant is supplied from adjacent coal fields jointly owned by *Pacific Power & Light* and by WWP's wholly-owned subsidiary, *Washington Irrigation and Development Company,* manager of the operations.

SOPHISTICATED TROJAN PLANT
ALSO ENHANCES ENVIRONMENT

The Trojan plant will use a pressurized water reactor, rather than a boiling water reactor. (About one-half the nuclear reactors in the country are of the pressurized variety.) What this means is that the water which flows through the reactor, picking up heat from nuclear fission occurring in the cores, is kept constantly under pressure to prevent boiling. This heated water then transfers its heat to a second water system, not under pressure, which then boils, creating steam to turn the turbines. The pressurized water continues back through a pump to start its closed cycle to the reactor again. After the second system's water does its job of making the turbines turn, it goes through a condenser, which is kept cool by a third water system, and as it is reconverted to water, is pumped back to be heated and reused by the turbines.

The third water system, which keeps the condenser cool, is itself cooled by the 499 foot tall natural draft cooling tower. Its water is pumped by engines with power equivalent to those of two large train locomotives, sprayed through the asbestos cement boards of the heat exchanger at the base of the tower where it is cooled, and then returned to the turbine generator building to cool the condenser. An advantage of the use of the pressurized water system is that, because the primary water system passing through the reactor does not go very far, it requires less shielding and protective equipment than a boiling water reactor.

PGE's efforts to maintain and enhance the environmental quality in the area around its Trojan plant site are considerable. Plans include ultimate development of recreational facilities, including picnic grounds, nature trails, public boat landings and warm water swimming area. In addition, half the area will remain in its natural state, except for more than four miles of nature trails connecting the various points of interest. Water warmed by the plant will be used by the Oregon Fish and Game Commission to rear salmon and steelhead fish in facilities set aside for that purpose. The total project not only preserves but appreciably enhances the environment of which it is a part.

Safety precautions required in the construction of the plant are extensive. Seismic supports of all key cable structures and piping will prevent any dangerous disruptions or breakage in the event of earth tremors. The reactor containment structure, completely housing the nuclear reactor and reactor coolant system, is steel lined, reinforced concrete, and has walls 3½ feet thick and roof 2½ feet thick. Auxiliary equipment exists for major operational equipment.

Although a very small amount of coolant water from the condenser coolant system is returned to the Columbia River, it causes no measurable temperature increase in the river downstream. A well-done introduction to the nuclear plant prepared by PGE and distributed at the elaborate Visitors Information Center near the plant also points out to worried individuals that natural background radiation level near the plant is only five millirems annually, considerably less than the amounts of 100 millirems from a chest X-ray or 131-175 millirems annually in the natural background of the city of Portland.

Washington Water Power places very high priorities on customer service and community service, and is outstandingly well regarded in the territory it serves.

Portland General Electric provides electrical service to 42% of Oregon's electric customers, including Portland and Salem, the state capital. The company, together with its predecessors, has been furnishing electric service for 84 years. PGE is the Northwest's pioneer in nuclear power generation, with its construction, operation and 67.5% ownership of the *Trojan Nuclear Plant* near Rainier, Oregon on the Columbia River west of Portland.

The Trojan Nuclear Plant built by Portland General Electric on the Columbia River is a familiar sight to motorists on Interstate 5.

Generating facilities owned by the company include eight hydroelectric generating plants with net capability of 661,000 kilowatts, and minor steam-electric and diesel engine generating capability. In 1973 the company installed six jet-engine type combustion turbines with capability of 385,000 kilowatts. In addition, 439,000 kilowatts of industrial type combustion turbine capacity was installed in August of 1974 at the Beaver site on the Columbia River 60 miles northwest of Portland. The turbines can operate on crude oil, a variety of petroleum distillates, or natural gas. Management has approximately 1,550,000 barrels of petroleum distillates in storage, and the company's storage capacity is being increased to 1,750,000 barrels. Both the jet type and industrial type turbines are primarily for peaking and emergency purposes, but can be used to provide base load energy in the event of any prolonged hydro-power shortage.

As a member of the *Northwest Power Pool,* the *Intercompany Pool* and the *Western Systems Coordinating Council,* PGE supports and participates in joint coordination of planning and operations of the region's power plant facilities in an effort to provide the most efficient and economic electric generation. Long-term contracts with Washington Public Utility Districts, owning hydroelectric projects on the Columbia River, are providing PGE with varying percentage outputs of four hydro plants, which currently total approximately 874,717 kilowatts.

The inability to develop new sources of hydroelectric power, which has historically been the Northwest's primary electric energy source (in 1973 it was 95% of PGE's energy source), is forcing Northwest utilities to place increased emphasis on nuclear energy and coal-fired sources, evident in PGE's current construction plans. The company has concluded negotiations with the AMAX Coal Company which has coal sources in Wyoming for 1.2 million tons of coal per year for 20 years to be used for fueling a planned coal-fired unit. Recently the company announced it has received coal prospecting permits from the State of Alaska for core drilling on 46,000 acres about 100 miles north of Anchorage. Tentative plans call for rail transportation of the coal, which is extremely low in sulphur content, from the surface mine approximately 225 miles south of Seward, and then water transport to Oregon by barge. PGE believes the coal could be mined as economically as in Wyoming or Montana, and since the major transportation would be by water, these costs would be competitive.

$1.4 BILLION CONSTRUCTION PROGRAM 1975-1979

In its effort to continue to meet the area's growing electrical energy needs, PGE has embarked on a construction program which will cost approximately $1.4 billion in the 1975-1979 period. *Not* included in this figure is the major portion of the cost of the company's 67.5% share of the *Trojan Nuclear Plant* estimated at about $300 million (total cost of the plant is $443 million). The originally predicted cost of the plant in 1969 of $235 million was increased due to additional interest, labor, and engineering costs, and design changes. An additional $32 million will be incurred for the initial nuclear core.

Contracts for the mining, milling and conversion of uranium for Trojan's core needs through 1980 have been signed with *Kerr-McGee*. The most crucial element of the nuclear fuel cycle, a contract for the enrichment of the uranium with the *Energy Research and Development Administration,* will provide all needed enrichment services for uranium for 30 years. *Westinghouse Electric* will provide fabrication services for the first core and nine reload batches, and *Allied General Nuclear Services* will take care of spent fuel reprocessing and transportation. Estimated life of the plant is 30-40 years. PGE's share of Trojan's 1,130 megawatts (equal to 1.1 billion watts) will provide approximately 34% of the company's energy requirements in 1977-78.

Compliance with environmental regulations on air and water pollution, as well as other ecological concerns, cost PGE $20.6 million in 1973, and the company estimates 1974's expenditures were at least $15 million. Estimates for 1975, 1976, and 1977 are $30 million, $55 million, and $65 million, respectively.

State agencies to which PGE answers on environmental considerations are *Department of Energy*, the *Environmental Quality Commission* (EQC), the *Department of Environmental Quality* (DEQ), and the *Energy Facilities Siting Council.* The Governor of Oregon has designated the DEQ as the state agency authorized to give certification required by the Federal Water Pollution Control Act Amendments of 1972. Under the Rivers and Harbors Act of 1899, PGE must also obtain permits from the U.S. Army Corps of Engineers to construct facilities on navigable waters. Even with all these agencies to please, PGE not only provides adequate energy to its service area, but does so at a cost about half that of the nation's average.

Utah Power & Light serves parts of Utah, southeastern Idaho, and southwestern Wyoming. The service area comprises approximately 79,000 square miles extending approximately 500 miles from Ashton, Idaho to the Arizona border and from central Utah to the Colorado border. Utah Power serves Salt Lake City, Ogden and some 438 other cities and towns, in addition to eighteen wholesale customers serving other communities.

The area involved is a residential, agricultural, and diversified industrial territory. It has a large reserve of natural resources, including coal, uranium, oil, oil shale, tar sands, elemental phosphorus, copper, and a variety of hard metals. Agricultural products include potatoes, sugar beets, grain, and livestock.

Recent industrial development in Utah has produced many new customers for Utah Power. These include manufacturers of plumbing fixtures, plastics, clothing, missile engines, fabricated steel, fertilizer, packing seals, medical apparatus, frozen foods, and electronic controls. The Utah economy is one of the fastest-growing of the Northwest/Intermountain states.

In 1974, the company generated 81% of its own energy requirements and purchased or interchanged the remaining 19%. In 1975, management expects to generate about 76% of its own energy needs.

Utah Power is different from other utilities in the *Northwest Power Pool* in that it generates very little hydroelectric power. With an abun-

Utah Power & Light Huntington first unit with covered coal conveyor.

dance of coal reserves in its area, Utah Power has a higher proportion of steam generation than other utilities as shown below:

	Actual 1974	Estimated 1975
Coal	88%	92%
Hydro	9%	6%
Natural Gas & Oil	3%	2%
	100%	100%

With all types of energy supplies a national concern, Utah Power appears to be in a very favorable position. The company has contracts, letters of intent, and options covering approximately 410 million tons of high-quality coal with a sulphur content of about one-half of one percent by weight. Additional high-quality coal reserves available from company-owned lands and leased interests amount to about 18 million tons.

Also, the company estimates that there are several hundred million tons of low-sulphur coal in reserves on which it has pending preference right lease applications. Thus, it is estimated that the company has adequate coal to fuel all its steam plants planned for construction to the year 2000 and for their 35-40 year life thereafter.

The only investor-owned electric utility serving a portion of the Northwest that is not a member of the Northwest Power Pool is **California-Pacific Utilities Company** of San Francisco, California. Unlike the other utility companies discussed, California-Pacific is a diversified public utility, providing electric, natural gas, telephone and water service. It also distributes liquefied petroleum gas in Oregon.

Since the founding of California-Pacific in 1928, the company has sought to acquire profitable utility properties serving rural communities in western states. Present operations cover portions of California, Oregon, Nevada, Utah, and Arizona.

Widely diversified, the company's operations are dispersed as follows:

Revenue by Service		Revenue by States	
Electric	42.2%	Oregon	56.0%
Gas	33.6%	California	20.9%
Telephone	17.5%	Nevada	14.6%
All Other	6.7%	Utah	8.2%
Total	100%	Arizona	0.3%
		Total	100%

California-Pacific Utilities provides electric, natural gas, telephone and water service.

Natural Gas Suppliers

In recent years the Pacific Northwest, like other parts of the nation, has been affected by shortages in natural gas supplies coupled with increasing prices. The total supply problem, however, is less severe in the Northwest than in many other areas of the U.S.

Northwest Pipeline Corporation, a wholly-owned subsidiary of Northwest Energy Company, Salt Lake City, Utah, is the wholesale supplier of all the gas used in Washington, Oregon and Idaho. Approximately two-thirds of the company's annual deliverability comes from Canada, principally the Province of British Columbia.

In September, 1973 Northwest Pipeline's Canadian supplier, Westcoast Transmission Co. Ltd., announced that deliveries would be partially curtailed due to production difficulties in certain gas producing fields in western Canada. Westcoast advised that there had been no change in proven gas reserves, but that production was being reduced until additional wells were drilled. Later, Westcoast announced that in imposing the curtailment required, it would first serve the contract demand requirements of its existing Canadian distributor companies. Thus, U.S. gas users in the Pacific Northwest had to carry the burden of the entire shortfall. Curtailment of contracted deliveries to Northwest Pipeline at the company's major import point near Sumas, Washington, averaged approximately 142 million cubic feet per day during the 1973-74 winter heating season. This resulted in curtailment of firm sales by Northwest to its customers of an average volume of 80 million cubic feet per day during the same period.

In November 1974, curtailment of deliveries at Sumas began again and averaged approximately 240 million cubic feet of gas per day during the 1974-75 heating season. As a result, curtailment of firm sales by Northwest Pipeline to its customers averaged nearly 190 million cubic feet per day during the same six-month period.

Although Northwest Pipeline anticipates continued curtailments

---

BRITISH THERMAL UNITS

One British thermal unit (BTU) is equal to the amount of heat energy necessary to raise the temperature of one pound of water one degree Fahrenheit. The following table shows the number of BTU's available from each of the common measures of our major energy sources:

	Common measure	BTU's
Oil	Barrel*	5,800,000
Natural gas	ThousandCubic Feet	1,031,000
Coal	Short ton	24,000,000
Nuclear fuel	Pound	360,000,000

Sources: National Petroleum Council and AEC.
*1 barrel of oil equals 42 gallons of oil.

NATURAL GAS DISTRIBUTORS
SALES BY CLASS OF USER (1974)

	Residential		Commercial		Industrial	
	Dollars (000)	Therms (000)	Dollars (000)	Therms* (000)	Dollars (000)	Therms* (000)
Cascade Natural Gas	$12,700	68,152	$12,248	89,382	$40,384	500,800
	19.4%	10.4%	18.8%	13.5%	61.8%	76.1%
Intermountain Gas	$14,888	80,787	$10,665	82,660	$15,638	219,328
	36.1%	21.1%	25.9%	21.6%	38.0%	57.3%
Montana Power	$14,602	123,694	$ 7,155	72,013	$16,397	270,907
	38.3%	26.5%	18.7%	15.4%	43.0%	58.1%
Northwest Natural Gas	$37,141	192,715	$17,607	101,488	$52,309	618,062
	34.7%	21.2%	16.4%	11.1%	48.9%	67.7%
Washington Natural Gas	$40,667	239,162	$20,777	134,604	$33,699	455,853
	42.7%	28.8%	21.8%	16.2%	35.4%	55.0%
Washington Water Power	$12,694	80,467	$ 7,176	59,596	$13,569	183,556
	38.0%	24.9%	21.4%	18.4%	40.6%	56.7%

*Firm and interruptible power usage.

of Canadian gas supplies during the 1975-76 winter heating season, the company feels that, barring an extended spell of unseasonably cold weather in the Pacific Northwest, the effects of such curtailment will be less severe than last year. To help offset the shortages this winter, the company is purchasing on an emergency short-term basis as much as 55 million cubic feet of gas per day from Alberta, Canada. It has also entered into an emergency gas exchange agreement with another pipeline company, *Pacific Gas Transmission Co.*, under which PGT would deliver to Northwest on a best efforts basis as much as 150 million cubic feet of gas per day, or up to a total of 1.2 billion cubic feet during the 1975-76 winter heating season in order to help meet peak-day requirements.

In addition, the company is making additional purchases of domestic gas reserves to further ease the impact of curtailment. Further, Westcoast Transmission reports that drilling has increased substantially in western Canada in recent months, and it is possible that significant volumes of new reserves may be added to its system for export this winter.

While supplies of natural gas imported from Canada have been decreasing in recent years, the price for this premium fuel has been increasing steadily. Since the fall of 1973 the import price for gas from British Columbia has risen from 33 cents per thousand cubic feet to a current level of $1.60 per thousand cubic feet. Virtually all of the significant price increases to Pacific Northwest gas users in the last two years have been a direct result of higher border prices. Canadian export prices, however, are now regulated by the federal government at Ottawa, rather than by the individual provinces. This change in authority, it is hoped, will be a moderating influence on future price increases.

Turning to alternatives for supplying Northwest and Intermountain natural gas customers, one runs into a problem of lack of producer incentive to develop additional domestic supplies. Not until the U.S. government's artificial price ceiling on wellhead gas prices is abandoned, and the wellhead price is allowed to seek its own market clearing level, will "the industry be able to attract the capital necessary to develop the potential domestic gas reserves needed to insure U.S. self-sufficiency," says John G. McMillian, Chairman and Chief Executive Officer of Northwest Energy Company.

According to McMillian, 52 cents per thousand cubic feet is the most an interstate pipeline company, such as Northwest Pipeline, currently is allowed to pay for new gas. The Congress is now considering various proposals to raise, or lift entirely, the ceiling on wellhead prices. If deregulation should come about, it will provide the financial stimulus needed to explore for and develop vitally needed new gas reserves in the Rocky Mountains and elsewhere, McMillian says.

The companies serving the Northwest's natural gas needs are making strong efforts to alleviate gas shortages through as much exploration as feasible, construction of storage facilities, and long-range plans for development and transportation of natural gas from Alaska, as well as investigation of coal gasification and other means of producing and transporting gas. Capital needs are obviously going to be high.

Descriptions of gas operations of *Northwest Energy*, the Northwest's wholesale distributor, and seven retail distributors (*Northwest Natural Gas, Intermountain Gas, Washington Water Power, California-Pacific Utilities, Cascade Natural Gas, Washington Natural Gas*, and *Montana Power*) are found in the following pages.

NORTHWEST ENERGY CO.
(Named changed from *Northwest Pipeline* 3/1/75)

Northwest Pipeline Corporation is now the principal operating subsidiary of Northwest Energy. Northwest Pipeline's system extends from the Canadian boundary near Sumas, Washington to the San Juan Basin in northern New Mexico, providing natural gas to distribution companies, municipalities and industrial customers in Washington, Oregon, Idaho, Utah, Wyoming, Colorado, and northern Nevada. Five Northwest distributors, Cascade Natural Gas, Intermountain Gas, Northwest Natural Gas, Washington Water Power, Washington Natural Gas, receive *all* their gas supply from Northwest Pipeline.

Other utilities which are partially supplied by Northwest Pipeline include *Colorado Interstate Gas Company, Mountain Fuel Supply Company, Peoples Natural Gas Company, Rocky Mountain Natural Gas Company, Inc., Southwest Gas Corporation, Utah Gas Service Company*, and *Western Slope Gas Company*. In addition, Northwest Pipeline supplies the municipalities of Naturita, Colorado and Buckley, Enumclaw, and Ellensburg all in Washington.

Northwest Pipeline was formed in February, 1974 as a result of a U.S. Supreme Court Order which required *El Paso Natural Gas Co.* to divest itself of its Northwest Division, which, before El Paso's 1957 purchase, had been known as *Pacific Northwest Pipeline Corp.*

The system's facilities now consist of 3,113 miles of main line and branch transmission pipelines; 1,191 miles of field gathering and supply pipelines; main and field compressor units and stations with a total

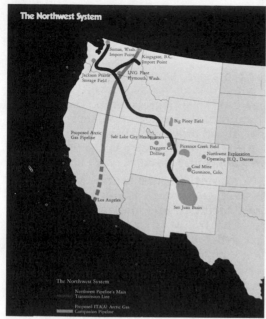

The Northwest Energy supply system extends from British Columbia to New Mexico.

rated capacity of nearly 190,000 horsepower; four gas dehydration plants with combined daily inlet capacity of 433 million cubic feet; and two liquid hydrocarbon extraction plants with an aggregate daily inlet capacity of 550 million cubic feet of gas. Northwest Pipeline also has one-third interest in the Jackson Prairie Field underground storage project near Chehalis, Washington. The other two-thirds is shared between *Washington Water Power* and *Washington Natural Gas*.

A proposal approved February 27, 1975 by Northwest Pipeline stockholders restructured the ownership of Northwest Pipeline so it is now owned by a holding company, Northwest Energy Company. Northwest Pipeline stock was exchanged share for share with that of Northwest Energy. Management's reasoning for the new organization is to facilitate expansion into other unregulated energy areas.

Approximately 67% of Northwest Pipeline's annual gas supply comes from two long-term purchase contracts with *Westcoast Gas Transmission Company Limited* of Canada, one of which covers up to 809 million cubic feet of gas per day expiring in 1989, and the other covering up to 152 million cubic feet expiring in 1981. Westcoast Gas Transmission is a wholesale gas pipeline distribution company, and receives gas from various Canadian producers. The company plans to purchase additional gas amounting to 55 million cubic feet of gas per day from *Pan-Alberta Gas Ltd.* on an emergency basis during the next two winter heating seasons. Management also is seeking long-term contracts with independent Rocky Mountain producers in an additional effort to reduce dependency on Canadian gas.

The company's gas reserves are currently about nine trillion cubic feet, half of which are located in Canada, 29% in San Juan Basin in New Mexico and Colorado, and the remainder in various fields in Colorado, Utah and Wyoming. 84% of these reserves are controlled under long-term gas purchase agreements and 16% are owned under leasehold interests. It has a reserve life index — a ratio of reserves to annual production — of 19.7 years, nearly double the gas transmission industry average of 9.9 years.

An exploration program aimed at developing new reserves in the Rocky Mountain sedimentary basins, with estimated undiscovered reserves of several hundred trillion cubic feet of gas, as well as in the Pacific Northwest, is underway. The company plans to spend at least $25 million on these activities over the next five years, and will spend an additional $25 million on the development of existing wells and leaseholds over the same period.

Construction of a $17 million liquefied natural gas (LNG) plant in Benton County, Washington was completed in December, 1975. Liquefaction of gas has commenced and the plant will be in full operation prior to the 1976-77 winter heating season. Other company projects being considered in energy areas include a proposal to build one of three U.S. companion pipelines to the Alaska-Arctic Gas Pipeline system, a coal slurry pipeline from the Rockies to the Pacific Northwest, and a coal gasification plant to supplement normal gas requirements.

Earnings for the 11 months of operations in 1974 came in at $14.7 million. For the nine months ended September 30, 1975, Northwest reported net income of $17.1 million, or $4.92 per share, on revenue of $333.1 million. Earnings for the 12-month period ended September 30, 1975 totaled $22.1 million, or $6.34 per share, based upon revenue of $427 million. Northwest Pipeline has established an initial dividend policy of paying out 50% of earnings available for dividends under the company's debt indenture restrictions. We consider this company a strong situation that has not been fully appreciated by the investment community to date.

CHANGING CORPORATE STRUCTURE

The evolution of Northwest Pipeline and Northwest Energy is likely to be confusing to most investors. As mentioned earlier, El Paso Natural Gas Company was required by the U.S. Supreme Court to divest its Northwest Division properties, which became known as the Northwest Pipeline Corporation.

A group of four oil and gas companies was allowed to form a joint venture, known as the APCO Group, to purchase Northwest Pipeline. The companies and their respective percentages of ownership are: Alaska Interstate Company (7½%); Apco Oil Corporation (7½%); Gulf Interstate (3%); and Tipperary Corporation (2%).

The remaining 80% of Northwest Pipeline's ownership was distributed to stockholders of El Paso Natural Gas Company in the form of non-voting trust participation certificates. The Voting Trust will be in effect for five years from the date of divestiture. John G. McMillian, Northwest Chairman, is the voting trustee and is empowered to vote the stock represented by the participation certificates at the direction of the company's Board of Directors.

As mentioned previously, a holding company, Northwest Energy, was formed in February, 1975. At this time Northwest Pipeline became a wholly-owned subsidiary. Among its other subsidiaries are: *Northwest Exploration Company, Northwest Coal Corporation, Northwest Alaska Company,* and *Northwest International Company,* which is involved in a gas exploration and development project in Ecuador.

Among the company's major investments is a 49% interest in *Phillips Pacific Chemical Company,* which owns and operates a chemical fertilizer plant near Kennewick, Washington.

Northwest Energy also recently completed a cash tender offer for 1.5 million common shares, or approximately 48% of Apco Oil Corporation, Houston. The company has assumed working control of Apco and is formulating a plan for the complete liquidation of its assets. In making the successful tender offer, Northwest Energy outbid another member of the APCO Group, Alaska Interstate Co., which was seeking to gain control of Northwest via purchase of Apco Oil.

Incorporated in 1910, **Northwest Natural Gas Company** distributes natural gas to customers in Western Oregon and Southwestern Washington. The company and its predecessors have supplied gas service to the public since 1860. Northwest Natural Gas supplies Oregon's Willamette Valley as well as several coastal and Columbia River communities in Oregon and Washington.

Some 216,000 customers in 98 cities are served. The company's exclusive service areas approximate 15,000 square miles, with a population of more than 1,800,000, including about 77% of the population of the State of Oregon.

Although the number of customers served has been increasing steadily for years, a temporary moratorium stabilizing the number of customers served during the 1974-75 winter season was imposed by Oregon's Public Utility Commissioner. New customers were up by about 6,000 in 1974 versus an increase of about 8,000 in 1973. The moratorium was lifted on April 15, 1975. Since it was of such short duration, it had no appreciable adverse impact on earnings.

COMPANY OPERATES AREA'S FIRST LNG PLANT

Service agreements with the company's supplier, Northwest Pipeline, provide for a maximum daily delivery of 2.7 million therms to Northwest Natural, and for peak day purchases of 390,000 therms and an annual purchase of 12 million therms from the Jackson Prairie storage facility near Chehalis, Washington. The company also draws peaking capacity from its liquefied natural gas (LNG) plant in Portland, which Northwest Natural Gas has been operating since 1969. It was the Northwest's first liquefied natural gas plant and one of the first in the West.

Plans for the purchase and transport to Oregon of LNG from the Kenai Peninsula in Alaska cleared a major hurdle in January, 1975 when an administrative law judge for the Federal Power Commission

Designed to blend the best qualities of environment with utility, the proposed "Flanders Square," being built by Northwest Natural Gas for its Portland headquarters, will provide much needed space for the firm, as well as a number of commercial stores.

(FPC) ruled that it had no jurisdiction over the wellhead price nor transport of the gas. However, in June 1975 the FPC issued an Opinion which reversed some of the findings of the administrative law judge and contained such onerous and burdensome jurisdictional rulings that *Phillips Petroleum Company* and *Marathon Oil Company* found it necessary to withdraw their applications before the FPC and to cancel their agreements for the sale of LNG to Northwest Natural. The producers nevertheless expressed the hope that events may develop in the future which would make the project feasible so Northwest Natural continues to be confident that a supply of LNG from Alaska can be obtained in the foreseeable future. Company plans include transport of the LNG by tanker from Alaska to Newport on the Oregon coast, where receiving, storage and vaporizing facilities were to be constructed. Interim shipments before the new tanker is completed would have to be made by a foreign flag vessel. Once the project was underway, Northwest Natural's year-round gas supply would have been increased by about 15%, and peak demand capability materially improved. In the interim, the company is proceeding with construction of the LNG plant at Newport which will be used as a winter peaking plant until the Alaska delivery problem is resolved.

Washington Natural Gas traces its past back to 1873, when the first of nearly two dozen predecessor companies, the *Seattle Gas Light Company*, was organized to manufacture gas to make Seattle's steep, ungraded streets safe after dark. 1873 was 16 years before the Territory of Washington became a state. It was only 21 years after the founding of Seattle and 81 years after the discovery of Puget Sound. Seattle Gas Light began service with gas made from coal, which was stored in wooden holders and delivered to users through bored-out fir logs.

Gas lamps lit Seattle's unpaved streets (circa 1884).

The year 1956 began Washington Natural's modern era, when the company switched from manufactured to Natural gas. Then the company served 48,500 customers in 19 communities. Now, as of mid-1975, the company has 217,500 customers in 58 communities, a service area encompassing more than 50% of the state's population. In the same period, Washington Natural's annual revenue has increased from $8.4 million to $95.1 million.

The company's firm service agreement with Northwest Pipeline entitles the company to 2.9 million therms per day, expiring in 1986. To meet peak day needs the company purchases natural gas from underground storage and produces propane-air gas at two company-owned plants.

The company has expanded its propane stations with the addition of new tanks, which will enable the facilities to increase the equivalent amount of natural gas that can be delivered from storage over a three-day peak demand period to 53 million cubic feet. The company believes that this expansion, along with purchase of a committed share of gas from Northwest Pipeline's LNG plant under construction in Benton County, Washington, and continued expansion of the Jackson Prairie underground storage project, will enable it to take care of anticipated growth of residential and firm commercial customers for the foreseeable future.

INVOLVED IN EXPLORATION PROJECTS

Through wholly-owned subsidiary *Thermal Exploration, Inc.*, the company is participating with *Intermountain Gas* and *Washington Water Power* in the exploration for gas reserves in the Rocky Mountain area. Washington Natural, through Thermal, is also involved in an exploratory drilling venture carried on by *McCulloch Oil Corp.* in south-central Montana. Evaluation of the results of the initial exploratory drilling is continuing and part of the acreage has been farmed out for future drilling at no additional cost to the venture. Thermal's investment in the limited partnership is about $400,000.

Washington Natural has found it necessary to request rate increases simply to stay even with the game. Request for a general rate increase was filed on May 22, 1974. Not until April 1, 1975 was an increase of $2,686,600 approved. Such regulatory delays are the despair of the utility industry, and many states are moving toward decreasing this devastating "regulatory lag." The revenue lost in the interim periods is never made up.

Capital expenditures budgeted for fiscal 1975 amount to $12-$13 million, approximately the same level as for 1974. A substantial portion will go for the continuing expansion of the Jackson Prairie storage facility.

Cascade Natural Gas' service area includes 75 communities in Oregon and Washington with approximately 79,000 customers. The company receives all its natural gas supply under contracts with Northwest Pipeline, the latest expiring in 1989. Curtailments during the winter of 1975 did not affect Cascade's firm customers, although substantial curtailments were experienced by the company's interruptible customers. Efforts to meet firm demand have been supplemented with natural gas from the Jackson Prairie facility under terms of its contracts with Northwest Pipeline, and with gas from the company's propane-air peak shaving plant at Yakima, Washington. The plant, which was completed in 1973, has played an important role in maintaining firm service deliveries both years.

Cascade has no major construction projects in the offing, and construction expenditures in 1975 will be down to about $3 million, compared with $5.4 million in 1974. The expenditures will be essentially for extension of Cascade's distribution system.

Incorporated in 1950, **Intermountain Gas** is the sole supplier of natural gas to Southern Idaho, serving a total of 93,000 customers. Intermountain Gas provides natural gas service to approximately 64 communities in Southern Idaho encompassing nearly 50,000 square miles, with over 4,100 miles of transmission, distribution and service lines. The company's service area has a total population of about 500,000 and includes the cities of Boise, Nampa-Caldwell, Pocatello, Idaho Falls-Blackfoot, and Twin Falls. The territory described is larger than the combined states of Connecticut, Delaware, Maryland, Massachusetts, New Hampshire, Rhode Island, and Vermont. Intermountain's service area is one of the largest in size of all natural gas distribution companies.

The company's new LNG plant in Nampa, Idaho was completed in 1974, and management does not hesitate to point out that it came in on schedule within budget. Management feels this resource will be invaluable in meeting winter commitments and will allow the company to

Intermountain Gas liquefied natural gas plant.

attach 60,000 additional residential customers without contracting for another cubic foot of additional supply. During the 1974-75 winter Intermountain Gas experienced peak day curtailment of its gas supply of 34% versus 11% the previous year.

The company also purchases gas from the Jackson Prairie storage facility. The company intends to purchase gas from Northwest Pipeline's LNG plant being constructed near Plymouth, Washington, beginning in winter 1976-77. Management describes the company's long-term supply outlook as excellent, in that Intermountain is strategically located with respect to new supplies from Canada, the Rocky Mountain region, and Alaska.

Intermountain is investigating the use of coal gasification plants as an energy source, although no specific plans have been made. Other areas of research include high BTU coal gas (versus low BTU coal gas technology which is now available), fuel cell research, and solar research.

Capital expenditures in 1975 and 1976 are budgeted at $6 million each year, substantially lower than the $11 million spent in 1974. The company's long term goal is for a more conservative capital structure (see capital structures table), reducing reliance on long-term debt.

Montana Power derives approximately 37% of its revenue from supplying retail natural gas service to about 99,000 customers in 90 communities in Montana, and from selling gas at wholesale to four communities in Montana and two in Canada.

Over 80% of the company's gas supply comes from Alberta, Canada, and the remainder comes from Montana producers. For the 12 months ended December 31, 1974, the company's wholly-owned subsidiary, *Canadian-Montana Gas,* produced 34% and purchased the remainder. The company's total gas reserves and gas dedicated under import authorizations are approximately 962 million Mcf.

Under licenses with the *National Energy Board of Canada* (NEB), which expire from 1985 to 1993, the company is authorized to purchase 29.2 million cubic feet annually.

Montana Power's situation vis a vis natural gas supply is unique among the other gas distributors in this survey, a result of different political problems in dealing with the Alberta government instead of the British Columbia government. Although producers in Alberta are receiving more incentive from the government to produce, red tape involved in receiving authorization to export is obviously a crucial factor.

Washington Water Power receives approximately 30% of its business from supplying natural gas service to nearly 70,000 customers located in Spokane, 32 other Eastern Washington communities, and 24 Northern Idaho communities. Company properties relating to natural gas service include approximately 1,965 miles of gas distribution mains.

The availability of gas from the Jackson Prairie Storage Project has been very helpful in meeting load requirements on peak days. In mid-January on 1975's coldest day, with temperatures ten degrees below zero, 40% of the company's supply came from this storage. On that day WWP met all its firm load plus minor "hardship" requirements of interruptible customers. The company says "the Canadian supply deficiency is resulting only in some additional curtailment of interruptible customers over that normally experienced."

Washington Water Power has contracts with *Northwest Pipeline* for two types of firm gas service and one type of interruptible service. Pipeline firm gas is purchased under a service agreement extending to October 31, 1986, and should provide an adequate supply of gas for estimated growth through 1978. WWP is totally dependent upon Northwest Pipeline as its source of supply. The company owns a one-third interest in an underground storage field near Chehalis, Washington, where storage capacity is being increased from 20 billion cubic feet to 34 billion cubic feet. *Columbia Gas Company,* formerly a subsidiary of *Hardrock Oil Company* of Great Falls, Montana, was merged with Washington Water Power in 1975, resulting in the addition of 1,334 customers in Eastern Washington to the company's gas service as well as the combining of Columbia's Northwest Pipeline gas supply contract with the company's.

Washington Water Power's efforts in investigating new supply sources include participating in a three company gas exploration venture in the Rocky Mountain area, which early this year discovered gas in a well in Moffat County, Colorado.

California-Pacific Utilities furnishes at least one of four utility services — electric, gas, telephone and water — in 132 communities in Oregon, California, Nevada, Utah, and Arizona. Approximately 35% of its operating revenue and 24% of operating income come from supplying gas service to approximately 42,000 customers.

The company's most extensive natural gas system is in Southern Oregon, but the company also provides natural gas to customers in Union County in Eastern Oregon; in the town of Henderson, Nevada and South Lake Tahoe, and Needles, California. Approximately one-half of natural gas revenue is received each from residential and commercial-industrial customers.

Gas for the Oregon division's customers is supplied under contracts with Northwest Pipeline, one of which provides firm service up to a maximum daily delivery of 308,710 therms through October, 1986 and year to year thereafter. The company also receives winter withdrawals from the Jackson Prairie storage facility, and from a propane-air plant at Medford, Oregon, which is owned by the company.

California-Pacific has no reserves other than that of its Medford facility and is not involved in any exploration activities, and so is totally dependent on the progress of its suppliers in obtaining reliable and new sources of natural gas.

Telephone Companies

By far the largest telephone company operating in the Northwest is **Pacific Northwest Bell**, headquartered in Seattle. An integral part of the "Bell" system, Pacific Northwest Bell (PNB) operates in Washington, Oregon, and Idaho.

The impact of PNB's operations on the Northwest's economy can be seen clearly in the table below:

Pacific Northwest Bell Five-Year Summary

	1974	1973	1972	1971	1970
Total Operating Revenue	$688,833,000	$601,099,000	$530,721,000	$463,537,000	$438,186,000
Net Income	$78,316,000	$67,004,000	$59,637,000	$49,680,000	$48,664,000
Telephones in Service	2,952,380	2,822,287	2,684,275	2,561,494	2,462,111
Number of Local Calls	4,973,005,249	4,665,885,652	4,440,739,819	4,208,796,339	4,002,639,298
Number of Long Distance Calls	306,614,656	281,185,338	248,314,247	226,146,514	218,557,752
Number of Employees	19,614	19,442	18,517	18,830	18,557
Total Wages Paid	$241,431,111	$220,861,000	$195,852,000	$180,008,000	$159,486,000
Construction Expenditures	$244,935,000	$200,505,000	$199,373,000	$183,163,000	$180,972,000
Average Plant Investment Per Telephone*	$633.99	$610,32	$589.01	$562.26	$540.03

*Excludes telephone plant under construction.

PNB's chief problems are the effects caused by almost continual inflation and the attendant problem of receiving adequate rate relief from the necessary regulatory authorities.

In terms of internal efficiency and providing good value to the customer, Pacific Northwest Bell has done an excellent job. For example, the Consumer Price Index rose 75% from the annual average of 1960 to the end of 1974. Other consumer items increased as follows: Transportation — 60%; Housing — 77%; and food — 93%. In contrast PNB's telephone service (including long distance and local calls) rose just 20%. In terms of worker productivity, in 1970 the company required 75.37 employees per 10,000 phones in service. By 1974, just 66.43 employees were necessary for the same 10,000 phones.

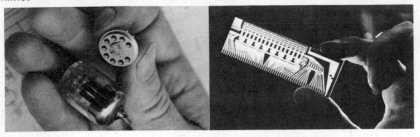

(Left) PNB is replacing about 154,000 vacuum tubes with solid state devices. (Right) Exotic circuit pattern machined by laser light.

Because of past experience, and good management techniques, PNB is able to project future demand with reasonable accuracy. By 1981, there will be about 179,000 new households to serve. By 1991, the company expects to add some 544,000 new business telephones. Intrastate long distance calls are projected to increase from 202 million in 1974 to 355 million in 1981 and about 857 million by 1991.

The telephone service industry is very capital intensive and requires continual doses of new financing. The costs are of such magnitude ($245 million for construction in 1974 alone) that they cannot be financed out of retained earnings and other internal sources. Thus, debt financing — bank loans and long-term bonds — are a necessity. Periodic equity financing is also required in order to maintain a balanced capital structure.

Such financing is not available to Pacific Northwest Bell (or any other company) unless the company is sufficiently profitable to insure that debt costs will be paid and sufficient income remains to compensate stockholders adequately.

Thus, relief in the form of higher rates is required when the company's costs rise and earnings diminish due to inflation. Over the past six years, PNB has filed for rate increases amounting to $134 million in Washington and $108 million in Oregon. Only 57% of the Washington requests and 55% in Oregon have been granted to date.

In a national study of corporate profits conducted by Investor's Management Sciences, Inc., for the twelve months ending in September, 1974, the following percentage returns on common equity were found: All industries — 16.2%; Manufacturing — 18.0%; Non-Manufacturing — 12.9%; and Mining & Petroleum — 21.4%. However, Pacific Northwest Bell's return on equity was just 9.7%, far below all of these groups.

In terms of conservation and efficiency, Pacific Northwest Bell has done a good job. PNB was the first Bell System company to begin replacing vacuum tubes in central offices with energy saving transistorized devices. This alone will save the company about 3.4 million kilowatt hours of electricity per year. Altogether in 1974, Pacific Northwest Bell used 5.4% less electricity than the previous year, 8.2% less gasoline, and 1.5% less fuel oil, natural gas and steam.

The second largest provider of telephone service in the Northwest is

Part of the electronic switching system being installed throughout the Bell system.

General Telephone of the Northwest, headquartered in Everett, Washington. The company is a wholly-owned subsidiary of **General Telephone and Electronics Corporation** of Stamford, Connecticut. In fact, if you consider all of General Telephone's subsidiaries operating in the Northwest, Hawaii, and British Columbia, the total annual revenues are nearly as great as those of Pacific Northwest Bell. However, the aggregate of these revenues constitutes only 10.9% of General Telephone's total national revenue.

There are two other investor owned independent telephone companies operating in the Northwest. **Telephone Utilities, Inc.**, based in Ilwaco, Washington is a telephone holding company which owns 25 subsidiary operating companies. These companies provided telephone services to a total of 115,757 telephone stations during 1974. These stations were located primarily in the states of Washington, Oregon and Montana and, to a lesser extent, in California, Idaho, and Nevada. Total 1974 revenue for Telephone Utilities, Inc. amounted to $25.6 million, with net income of $3.7 million. Eighty percent of the stock of Telephone Utilities is owned by Pacific Power & Light and the remaining 20% is distributed among over 3,000 stockholders.

The remaining independent publicly-owned telephone company is **Ellensburg Telephone Company** (Ellensburg, Washington). Serving the counties of Kittitas and Yakima in Washington, the company had 16,587 telephones in service in 1974. Revenues for Ellensburg Telephone in 1974 came to $3.4 million with a net income of $538,000.

While American Telephone & Telegraph's Bell System is certainly

General Telephone Northwestern Subsidiaries
Five-Year Summary

Company	Annual Revenue (000)					Annual Compound Growth Rate
	1974	1973	1972	1971	1970	1970-1974
Hawaiian Telephone Co.	$144,545	$136,245	$116,613	$ 96,671	$ 87,088	13.5%
General Telephone Company of the Northwest	149,368	131,927	114,132	99,999	89,350	13.7
Other Domestic Companies*	18,874	18,403	18,542	14,849	16,377	3.6
British Columbia Telephone Company	302,873	259,326	˙228,438	195,894	167,549	16.0

Annual Net Income (000)						
	1974	1973	1972	1971	1970	%
Hawaiian Telephone Co.	$18,204	$15,670	$11,261	$ 8,615	$10,530	14.7
General Telephone Company of the Northwest	19,669	17,314	14,506	12,034	9,916	18.7
Other Domestic Companies*	4,231	4,700	3,661	3,277	290	—
British Columbia Telephone Company	19,418	19,518	18,380	16,531	14,182	8.2

*Includes General Telephone Company of Alaska

the largest by far in the industry, there are still well over one thousand independent telephone companies operating in the United States.

UTILITIES INDUSTRY NEEDS RATE AND TAX RELIEF

In the face of massive requirements for new capital formation over the next few years, 12 of the 14 Northwest utilities in the accompanying table are selling below book value. The aggregate book value of the equity of the 14 companies totals $2,781,161,000 while the combined present market value is only $2,434,728,000, a shortfall of $347,433,000 or 12.5%. per cent.

In spite of the higly vocal but frequently poorly informed antagonists, the urgent need for developing new energy and communications facilities is generally recognized. In a time of high unemployment, many jobs that would have been available have been lost by postponements of important plant construction. What is more important in the longer run, however, is the potential loss of jobs in industry because of lack of adequate energy to develop and operate industrial plants to serve our expanding economy.

Utilities cannot finance new facilities by debt alone, because an inadequate equity base weakens the financial stability of the individual companies and the industry as a whole. Neither, however, can utilities solve the equity problem by continuing to issue new stock below book value.

Every time new stock is issued below book value, without prospect of an adequate rate of return, it lowers the book value of all the previously issued shares outstanding. This can appropriately be regarded as a confiscation of the prior investors' capital. Unless stock investors become convinced that this deterioration of the value of their capital, experienced frequently in recent years, will not continue, new equity capital for utilities will cease to be available in the market.

In addition to the implications of the future capital availability, the negative effect on existing stockholders is serious. The aggregate stockholders of the 14 utilities in 6 Northwest states in the accompanying table total over 468,000. Many of them are retired people who cannot afford to lose their capital and who need to have their dividends increased at least enough to offset inflation.

A recent report issued by **Blyth Eastman Dillon** stated:

". . . even the fair minded intervenors against utility rate increases are willing to concede that utilities should be able to float new common stock above book value."

It is generally agreed that a normal premium above book, very reasonably 20 to 25 per cent, should be achieved in normal market trading in order to allow for market discount and financing costs associated with an equity offering.

The solutions to the problem lie primarily with the ability and willingness of the regulatory bodies of each of the states to take appropriate actions regarding utility rate-making, and with Congress' propensity to enact proposed tax legislation to facilitate the utilities' capital formation process.

The primary issue at the state level is adequate rate of return, especially on equity. The adequacy of return on equity as viewed by the capital market is measured in two dimensions: (1) the *amount* of the earnings, generally measured as a percentage return on the book value of investors' equity, and (2) the *quality* of the earnings, measured as compared with other businesses competing for capital.

15% RETURN ON EQUITY NEEDED

Seven to ten years ago, when capital costs were much lower, there was a general consensus among utility commissioners that a 10 to 12 per cent rate of return was appropriate for electric utilities, and the capital markets responded satisfactorily to the securities of utilities achieving that rate at the time. The recent Blyth report, however, stated, "In our judgment, a 15% return is minimum to meet longer-term investor expectations." This opinion is important, because they act as manager or co-manager of a significant proportion of all public utility offerings.

State utility commissions traditionally have defined the base on which they allow an over-all rate of return to include only the part of a utility's plant that is actually in service. This is no longer adequate, with large amounts of investors' funds tied up in facilities under construction on which no return is allowed at all, especially nuclear power plants with extremely long lead times to achieve operational status. The definition of the rate base should recognize that funds tied up in facilities under construction are also part of the invested capital on which a return must be earned. This will have the effect of improving the quality of earnings as viewed by the capital markets by removing an

SUMMARY OF NORTHWEST UTILITY STOCKS
(As of September 30, 1975)

Mkt.	Symbol	Company	Recent Price[1]	Book Value[2]	Price/ Book	Ind. Div.	Current Yield	Number Stock-holders	Shares (000)	Long Term Debt	Pfd. Stk.	Common Stk.
NYS	CLP	California-Pacific Utilities	15¼	$24.56	−37.9%	$1.52	10.0%	6,454	1,153	52%	10%	38%
NYS	CGC	Cascade Natural Gas	8	11.27	−29.0	.92	11.5	7,220	1,931	64	12	24
OTC	—	Ellensburg Telephone	17	16.14	+ 5.3	1.00	5.9	390	280	49	—	51
NYS	IDA	Idaho Power	27¼	27.13	+ 0.4	2.06	7.6	18,671	7,530	59	6	35
OTC	INMT	Intermountain Gas[4]	12¼	17.68	−30.7	1.28	10.4	5,110	1,114	60	10	30
NYS	MTP	Montana Power	22⅞	22.44	+ 1.9	1.80	7.9	36,710	8,747	51	5	44
NYS	NWE	Northwest Energy Co.	26	29.45	−11.7	1.80	6.9	111,000	3,491	67	—	33
OTC	NWNG	Northwest Natural Gas	7½	10.45	−28.2	.80	10.7	18,020	6,111	46	14	40
ASE	PNB	Pacific Northwest Bell	13⅝	16.27[3]	−16.3	1.20	8.8	35,622	49,723	45	—	55
NYS	PPW	Pacific Power & Light	18⅛	18.75	− 3.3	1.70	9.4	77,935	23,111	55	9	36
NYS	PGN	Portland General Electric	15¾	17.92	−12.1	1.58	10.0	45,000	15,500	51	12	37
NYS	PSD	Puget Sound Power & Light	26	33.23	−21.8	2.16	8.3	25,370	4,998	59	10	31
OTC	TPHN	Telephone Utilities	5¼	9.06	−42.1	Stk.	—	3,280	4,728	52	1	47
NYS	UTP	Utah Power & Light	26¼	33.21	−21.0	2.36	9.0	31,556	8,158	53	12	35
OTC	WGAS	Washington Natural Gas	10⅜	15.17	−31.6	1.08	10.4	10,446	3,264	56	9	35
NYS	WWP	Washington Water Power	18¾	20.14	− 6.9	1.52	8.1	32,011	7,230	66	—	34

1. Close or asked as of Tues. 9/30/75.
2. Per share as of end of latest fiscal year;
3. As of May 31, 1975.
4. Fiscal year end Sept. 30.

adjustment commonly known as "allowance for funds used during construction."

Where accelerated depreciation is used, normalization rather than flow-through of the resultant tax reduction should be allowed for reported earnings, as is the common conservative practice in other businesses.

At the Federal level, the utilities' capital plight would be alleviated some by Congressional approval of a number of proposals, including the following: (1) a 12 per cent investment tax credit as funds are spent for new plant, (2) an allowance for depreciation as funds are spent rather than when plant goes into service, (3) deductibility of dividends as an operating expense to the company (same treatment as interest on bonds), or non-taxability to the recipients, and (4) deferral of taxes to recipients of cash dividends reinvested in the stock of the issuing company.

On the basis of assuming a rational market environment, a reasonable regulatory environment, and proper tax incentives, the Blyth report concludes that they expect the ailing utility industry to recover. There are enough encouraging signs of increased awareness of the utilities' problems and constructive actions by regulatory bodies that we continue to recommend investment of reasonable portions of portfolios in Northwest utilities, which are soundly-based and well managed.

15

Transportation

With the huge open spaces that characterize the Northwest, the vast natural resources (especially timber and coal) and agricultural output produced in the region, plus the people and materials required for Alaskan development, transportation is big business in the Northwest.

Motor Transportation

From the investors' point of view, two trucking companies are prominent in their service to the Northwest region. These companies are **Consolidated Freightways, Inc.** and **Lynden Transport, Inc.**

We include Consolidated Freightways (Con Freight) because its origins are rooted in the Northwest and because it blankets the Northwest region with its network of common carrier routes. However, the company's involvement with the region as a per cent of its total business is difficult to define.

Con Freight's routes extend from the East Coast to the West Coast, including Alaska, and from the Great Lakes to the Gulf of Mexico, and Canada. With $800 million in annual revenues (57.5% from the motor carrier division), Con Freight is the second largest trucker in the nation in general freight revenues, with 3.5% of the industry total.

One of the company's major divisions, based in Portland, is the wholly-owned *Freightliner Corporation*. The subsidiary manufactures the White-Freightliner, a heavy duty diesel truck or truck-tractor (Class 8, over 33,000 pounds Gross Vehicle Weight), as well as lighter trucks on special orders.

These trucks are marketed by the *White Motor Corporation* through over 300 dealerships in the U.S. and Canada. The Freightliner Corporation had $311.5 million in 1974 sales. New capital investments by Freightliner in 1974 totalled $6.7 million. Company sales total about 9% to 10% of the industry's sales of this class of equipment.

The other trucking company prominent in the Northwest is **Lynden Transport, Inc.** a concern quite different in both size and scope when compared to Consolidated Freightways. Based for years in Lynden, Washington, the company moved its headquarters to Seattle

A motor carrier highway unit of Consolidated Freightways, Inc.

in 1975. Lynden's total service area involves Portland, Oregon, the state of Washington, and Alaska, which is served by means of the 1,500 mile Alaskan Highway passing through western Canada. Lynden is by far the largest carrier of motor freight between Seattle and Anchorage as well as between Seattle and Fairbanks.

Lynden Transport is also a major motor carrier of freight and of bulk fluid milk within the State of Washington. Lynden has approximately 300 employees and operates freight terminals in Lynden and Seattle, Washinton; and Anchorage, Fairbanks, Valdez, and Juneau, Alaska.

During 1974, over 13 million vehicle miles were logged, of which 1.9 million miles involved the hauling of milk. Central Alaska is the focus of the company's major operation in terms of freight transported, number of trips, and capital investment.

Lynden's service to Southeastern Alaska involves both general freight and mail, and combines both overland and water transportation to provide shippers with more departures and faster service than

The 1500-mile Alaska highway tests the capabilities of men and equipment; LTI tractors will log 250,000 miles a year on this run.

provided by barge lines and steamship companies. Lynden trucks make the trip from Seattle to Alaska in 75 hours.

Lynden's intra-Alaska operating authorities are broad, allowing freight transportation between Anchorage and Fairbanks, Fairbanks to Prudhoe Bay, and from Anchorage to the oil fields in the Kenai Peninsula. Another route is from Anchorage to Seward and Valdez, the future southern terminus of the pipeline from Alaska's North Slope.

On June 27, 1975, Lynden received a new four-year contract from the U.S. Postal Service for the hauling of mail between Seattle, Anchorage, and Fairbanks. The new contract could amount to revenues of $12 million during this period.

Reflecting the new Alaska boom, Lynden Transport's 1974 revenues were $16.4 million, up from $7.9 million in 1973. The gain in net income was even more sharp — $1.7 million compared to $489,000 the previous year.

Air Transportation Companies

Investors who may be searching for a "special situation" involving participation in the Alaskan boom would do well to consider **Alaska Airlines.** Having experienced rocky years in the past financially (losses totaling $19 million over 15 years), the company now stands to be a major beneficiary of the increased commerce between Alaska and its sister states. (See the section entitled "Alaska—The New Economic Dimension" in the general discussion in Part I.)

Steadily improving operations over the past four years brought Alaska Airlines' operations into the black in 1973, and 1974's performance confirmed the turnaround in the company's fortunes.

In 1974, Alaska Airlines was the leading carrier in passengers transported between the Mainland and Alaska for the entire year, with 33.6% of the total revenue passengers in that market. Competitors on these routes are *Northwest, Pan American* and *Western Air Lines.* Within the state, Alaska Airlines is the sole carrier serving Southeast Alaska and competes with Wien on other routes. Alaska Airlines has nearly 6,000 miles of unduplicated routes, and serves 90% of the state's population.

In 1974 one Boeing 727-100C was converted to cargo and cargo/passenger charter use. Primarily for oil field use, the plane operates between Anchorage, and Fairbanks, to Prudhoe Bay. As a result, charter operations for the first five months of 1975 topped $1 million, more than for all of 1973 and 1974 combined.

An innovative "Pipeline Express" was instituted on May 15, 1975 and is proving highly successful. This is a joint service between Alaska and *Braniff* which provides a daily round trip flight between Alaska and Texas with no change of planes — a useful service for oil company executives.

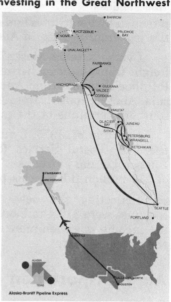

Alaska Airlines—beneficiary of the oil boom.

As shown below, 1974 saw vastly improved results in every operating category.

ALASKA AIRLINES FINANCIAL HIGHLIGHTS

	1974	1973
Airline Revenues	$51,202,454	$36,875,920
Net income	$ 2,811,040*	$ 442,811
Net income per share—Primary	$ 0.75*	$ .11
Net income per share—Fully diluted	$ 0.71*	$ .11
Total assets	$37,309,314	$24,447,337
Shareholders' equity	$ 3,006,544	$ (868,021)
Average shares outstanding	3,645,148	3,669,925
Revenue passenger miles	455,101,000	353,970,000
Available seat miles	865,968,000	690,488,000
Revenue passenger load factor	52.6%	51.3%
Average fuel cost per gallon	28.5¢	18.3¢

*excludes special credit of $1,357,284 resulting from change in accounting method

Further, the improvement in operations has continued into 1975. For the first nine months of 1975, Alaska Airlines reported revenues of $51.1 million, up 32.1%, and net income of $5,330,000, a 92.6% increase over the previous year.

During 1973 and 1974 Alaska Airlines and Wien Air Alaska laid some tentative plans that might have led to a merger of the two companies, but the efforts were terminated in June of 1974. Merger interest has also been expressed by Braniff, but the last time we talked to Alaska management they said they wanted to "rebuild the company's financial strengths before considering any more merger possibilities."

Alaska Airlines also owns the "Golden Nugget" motels in Fairbanks and Nome, and the Alyeska Ski Resort south of Anchorage. Management plans to sell its motels in Fairbanks and Nome.

SERVING ALASKA FOR
HALF A CENTURY

Wien Air Alaska, Inc. (Formerly *Wien Consolidated Airlines*) is really a pioneer in the Northwest transportation industry. The company began with Noel Wien's first commercial flight in Alaska, from Anchorage to Fairbanks, in 1924. Later, in 1935, Mr. Wien and Raymond I. Petersen piloted the first commercial flight from Seattle to Fairbanks. Mr. Petersen is now the Board Chairman and President of the company.

Wien Air Alaska provides scheduled passenger, cargo, and mail service to some 175 points in Alaska over a 10,000 mile system. Wien is the only federally certificated carrier providing scheduled service to the North Slope of Alaska. On its major routes, Wien operates Boeing 737-200C jet aircraft. 1974 revenues for the company were $38.4 million, with net income of $3.8 million.

In 1975 Wien completed new terminal facilities at Aniak and Dellingham, as well as at Deadhorse airport on the North Slope. They also expanded their facilities at Anchorage and Fairbanks.

Alaska International Industries, Inc., recently reorganized as a holding company, is involved in Alaskan transportation on two scores, air freight and trucking.

Alaska International Air, Inc. (AIA) operates a fleet of Lockheed Hercules L-100 air freighters. Having 6,000 cubic foot cargo bays, these specialty aircraft can carry up to 24 tons of cargo. Hercules craft can land on unimproved, short, rough runways such as the ice and sand found on Alaska's North Slope. Between four and nine Hercules were operated during 1974, with seven in service at year end.

Acquired by Alaska International in November 1973, *Weaver Bros., Inc.* is a scheduled trucking line which primarily serves the areas of Anchorage, Fairbanks, Homer, Kenai, and Seattle. Weaver also serves Prudhoe Bay and various Alaskan points from Portland. New terminals have been established at Valdez, Alaska and a major terminal and maintenance shop in Seattle.

Two other subsidiaries that the company believes have good long term-term growth potential are *Valdez Alaska Terminals, Inc.*, acquired in June, 1974, and *Alaska International Construction, Inc.*, a new enterprise formed in January, 1975.

Capitalizing on the current Alaskan boom, Alaska International's 1974 revenues of $45.1 million displayed a 254% gain over the previous year. Even more impressive, net income ($7.7 million) registered a 451% increase.

Freight Forwarding

Two other freight transportation companies are based in Seattle, even though their operations are not confined to the Northwest. In fact, the activities of these companies are both national and international. These are **Airborne Freight Corporation** and **WITS, Inc.**

Both companies are air freight forwarders. As such, they assemble and consolidate freight from shippers and assume the responsibility for transporting it from the point of origin to the destination. This involves helping the shipper select from among a maze of airline schedules and routings as well as varying domestic and international rates.

While the shipper pays the normal published rate for his freight, the freight forwarder earns his income through discounts from the airlines for the volume of traffic handled.

Airborne Freight is the second largest freight forwarder among more than 250 companies authorized by the *Civil Aeronautics Board*. WITS ranks about seventh or eighth. By way of comparison, 1974 revenue for Airborne was $108.9 million while WITS generated sales of $19.7 million.

16

Retailing and Wholesaling

The concept of retailing has undergone dramatic and exciting changes during the past two decades. As a result of changes in consumer needs and the economies of retailing, today's retail outlets offer more complete selections of merchandise and include the most modern and up-to-date customer conveniences and merchandising equipment. However, the key to success in retailing is attracting top personnel and developing training programs to serve the customer and to develop future store managers. Good operating results are important to both management and shareholders, and *people* continue to make a significant difference in achieving these results. Superior employees are an integral part of the foundation for a retailer's growth.

Much of the success of many Northwest-headquartered retailers is attributable to their people, as well as to the strong growth of the region's economy. The same holds true for Northwest companies primarily engaged in wholesale trade. Several Northwest retailers also have wholesale operations, covered separately at the end of this chapter.

The tables on the accompanying pages present a summary of the six-year sales and earnings records for most of these companies. Records of five out of the 21 companies were excluded from the tables for one of the following reasons (1) a substantial change in store operations during the past one or two years which would make past operating results not particularly comparable to current operations (*Baza'r, Millers International* and *Weisfields*); or (2) company does not have six years of operating history in its present mode of activities as a publicly-traded entity (*Alpine International* and *Laser Link*).

Food-Variety Stores

Fred Meyer, Inc. has posted record sales and earnings each year since going public in 1960. Based in Portland, Fred Meyer's marketing territory is Washington, Oregon, and Montana, with some wholesale distribution activity in Idaho. Few, if any, food retailers nationally have been as successful in their diversification into non-food lines of merchandise.

Retail sales from its 50 Pacific Northwest stores increased 29% in

NORTHWEST RETAILERS AND WHOLESALERS ...

Albertson's, Inc.

Jan. 31	Sales (000)	Net Income (000)
1975	$1,046,105	$11,702
1974	852,491	9,138
1973	681,623	7,470
1972	550,175	6,257
1971	487,933	4,815
1970	449,313	4,912

Fred Meyer, Inc.

Dec. 31	Sales (000)	Net Income (000)
1974	$536,760	$8,251
1973	425,620	8,191
1972	349,268	7,045
1971	298,354	5,794
1970	261,654	4,649
1969	244,411	4,299

Pacific Gamble Robinson Co.

Dec. 31	Sales (000)	Net Income (000)
1974	$481,518	$4,884
1973	391,466	3,864
1972	315,918	3,094
1971	287,392	3,268
1970	267,769	2,859
1969	256,873	2,218

Skaggs Companies, Inc.

Dec. 31	Sales (000)	Net Income (000)
1974	$498,677	$10,008
1973	412,324	7,202
1972	357,418	4,582
1971	319,973	5,124
1970	183,439	5,155
1969	172,244	4,681

Pay Less Drugs Stores Northwest, Inc.

Jan. 31	Sales (000)	Net Income (000)
1975	$172,888	$4,621
1974	150,314	4,048
1973	128,707	3,518
1972	110,325	2,944
1971	101,422	2,289
1970	91,299	2,204

Pay 'n Save Corporation

Jan. 31	Sales (000)	Net Income (000)
1975	$223,566	$7,283
1974	181,723	5,304
1973	147,825	3,932
1972	120,598	3,369
1971	97,277	2,806
1970	84,335	2,664

Grand Central, Inc.

July 31	Sales (000)	Net Income (000)
1975	$128,605	$1,585
1974	99,478	2,016
1973	85,520	1,874
1972	63,285	1,503
1971	48,412	1,098
1970	41,400	863

Consumers Building Marts, Inc.

Dec. 31	Sales (000)	Net Income (000)
1974	$5,737	$344
1973	4,872	450
1972	3,947	401
1971	3,166	298
1970	2,457	71
1969	2,135	61

... SUMMARY OF SALES AND EARNINGS RECORDS

Nordstrom, Inc.

Jan. 31	Sales (000)	Net Income (000)
1975	$128,768	$5,165
1974	101,434	4,372
1973	88,337	3,924
1972	79,637	3,529
1971	67,666	2,876
1970	64,857	2,998

Pay 'N Pak Stores, Inc.

Feb. 28	Sales (000)	Net Income (000)
1975	$61,471	$2,226
1974	51,894	1,857
1973	42,397	1,460
1972	30,928	1,132
1971	21,806	664
1970	18,097	559

Discount Fabrics, Inc.

Sept. 30	Sales (000)	Net Income (000)
1974	$13,937	$507
1973	10,609	560
1972	8,717	420
1971	6,559	476
1970	4,417	317
1969	2,469	202

Fabric Wholesalers, Inc.

Dec. 31	Sales (000)	Net Income (000)
1974	$5,432	$(21)
1973	4,540	(272)
1972	4,462	(71)
1971	4,869	332
1970	3,387	335
1969	2,053	234

International King's Table, Inc.

June 30	Sales (000)	Net Income (000)
1975	$11,025	$303
1974	8,803	224
1973	5,736	174
1972	3,506	106
1971	2,602	59
1970	1,219	22

JB's Big Boy Family Restaurants, Inc.

Sept. 30	Sales (000)	Net Income (000)
1974	$19,066	$840
1973	13,441	654
1972	11,552	566
1971	9,436	392
1970	7,342	350
1969	5,842	290

Palmer G. Lewis Co., Inc.

Jan. 31	Sales (000)	Net Income (000)
1975	$41,121	$635
1974	30,663	412
1973	25,029	339
1972	20,659	275
1971	16,789	192
1970	17,238	211

Trailer Equipment Distributors, Inc.

Sept. 30	Sales (000)	Net Income (000)
1974	$15,487	$171
1973	15,558	324
1972	12,244	444
1971	8,100	312
1970	6,800	87
1969	6,134	178

MAJOR LINES OF BUSINESS FOR
NORTHWEST RETAILERS AND WHOLESALERS

Line(s) of Business / Company	Food stores	Department stores	Drugs	Variety	Home improvements	Sporting goods	Apparel	Shoes	Fabric	Jewelry	Restaurants	Consumer electronics	Building materials	Groceries	Electronic parts/equip.	Rec. Vehicle supplies
		Retail Trade											Wholesale Trade			
Albertson's	●		●	●	●	●	●				●			●		
Baza'r	●	●	●		●	●	●				●					
Consumers Bldg. Marts					●											
Discount Fabrics									●							
Fabric Wholesalers									●							
Grand Central		●	●		●	●	●	●		●						
Internat'l King's Table											●					
JB's Big Boy Restaurants											●					
Laser Link												●			●	
Fred Meyer	●		●	●	●	●	●			●	●	●		●		
Millers International											●					
Nordstrom							●	●								
Pacific Gamble Robinson	●													●		
Palmer G. Lewis													●			
Pay Less Northwest			●	●	●	●										
Pay 'N Pak Stores					●	●										
Pay 'n Save			◉	●	●	●	●									
Skaggs Companies	●		●	●	●	●	●				●					
Trailer Equip. Distrib.																●
Weisfield's		●									●					

1974. A wide diversity of food, drug, apparel, housewares, building materials, cosmetics, hardware, and other lines account for the more than 60,000 items stocked. Even so, the breakdown of sales has been remarkably stable. For the past five years, general merchandise has produced 54%-55% of sales, while food sales accounted for 45%-46% of revenues.

In a successful effort to maintain cost and quality control, Fred Meyer also processes and sells a substantial amount of food and non-food products under proprietary names, in addition to stocking national and regional brand name items. Company-owned family brands include *"Hostess Pride"* meat, pork, poultry, fish, and a full line of *"My-Te-Fine"* canned goods. Fred Meyer's company owns six processing plants, which include a dairy, bakery, candy kitchen, photo processing plant, pharmaceutical laboratory and central kitchen. The company's multi-faceted business also covers other areas, such as wholesaling and home improvement supplies, which are treated in other sections of this book.

Probably the most exciting new development at Fred Meyer is the acquisition of a savings and loan institution and the opening of branch outlets in several stores. While the concept of "one stop shopping and saving" is still in an experimental stage, the company cashes the most customer checks of any retailer in Oregon, and a surprising number of

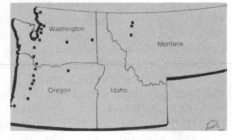

Fred Meyer, Chief Executive Officer, founded the Company when he opened the first Fred Meyer store on Fifth and Yamhill in Portland, 1922. Today, the company operates 50 stores in Oregon, Washington and Montana. Modern shopping centers opened during the 1960's and 1970's feature a broad line of food and non-food merchandise. More recent store openings also include home improvement centers.

customers do not have checking accounts, not to mention savings accounts, anywhere. The concept has great appeal and potential for Fred Meyer and other retailers, considering the electronic age that we live in and the present availability of equipment to electronically transfer funds from a customer's account to the check-out stand. The courage to try new innovations is a characteristic of today's leadership in the retail field, and Fred Meyer himself, at age 90, still looks for ways to improve business and customer convenience.

Based in Seattle, Washington, **Pacific Gamble Robinson Co.** is an example of one of the many hybrid companies headquartered in the Northwest. Almost totally involved with the food industry, Pacific Gamble's business is divided about evenly between the wholesaling and retailing of food items. Other operations such as shipping and trucking are mostly supportive to the main food business. We will consider the company's wholesale activities later and discuss the food retailing aspect for the moment.

Pacific Gamble Robinson owns and operates two types of grocery chains. The *Tradewell* chain consists of 33 conventional supermarkets located in Washington and Oregon. A few new stores are opened each year, and the results have been profitable.

Prairie Markets, a newer development, have grown rapidly from zero to 71 units in the past ten years. Prairie Markets are wholesale-type bare-bones stores open to the public for a small membership fee. Selling goods in case lots in low-cost buildings with a minimum of services, Prairie Markets have attracted a loyal following of customers. Prairie Markets are located in Oregon, Washington and California.

Less successful in retailing has been **Baza'r, Inc.,** a Portland-based company. Baza'r operates food and variety-department stores in Washington, Oregon, California and Arizona. Management has been unable to cope with rapidly changing events during recent years. Multi-million dollar losses have been sustained in each of the past three years. Food operations are considered profitable, but variety departments have not generated sufficient volume and turnover of merchandise. The company has divested itself of many of its stores that management did not feel would contribute to prospects for a turnaround in profitability.

The companies discussed above are a mixture of retail-wholesale, food, variety, and department stores. For the investor seeking a specific company mainly in the food supermarket field in the Northwest and nationally, **Albertson's Inc.** is the one obvious candidate. Head-quartered in Boise, Idaho, Albertson's had 246 modern supermarkets operating in the Western states in fiscal 1975 (ending in January).

Concentrated near its home base, Albertson's distribution of stores in the Northwest is as follows: Idaho (18); Washington (50); Oregon (32); Montana (6); Wyoming (6); and Utah (27). The company plans to add 20 new supermarkets in the region during fiscal 1976. In the past five years, this rapidly-growing company has opened 71 new supermarkets, upgraded and remodeled 75 units, and replaced or sold 37 less suitable units.

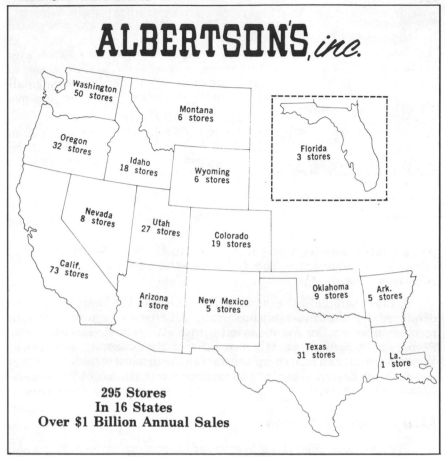

ALBERTSON'S,inc.

Washington 50 stores

Montana 6 stores

Oregon 32 stores

Idaho 18 stores

Wyoming 6 stores

Florida 3 stores

Nevada 8 stores

Utah 27 stores

Colorado 19 stores

Calif. 73 stores

Arizona 1 store

New Mexico 5 stores

Oklahoma 9 stores

Ark. 5 stores

Texas 31 stores

La. 1 store

**295 Stores
In 16 States
Over \$1 Billion Annual Sales**

An excellent example of the public benefits derived from successful private enterprise, the new stores opened by Albertson's in fiscal 1975 provided 3,200 jobs for new employees in addition to 175 new managerial positions. Total employment for all of Albertson's divisions is approximately 16,500.

In 1970, Albertson's formed a 50/50 partnership with *Skaggs Companies,* which has fired the imagination of the retailing industry. The concept was simple and at the same time a radical one. *Skaggs-Albertson's* has opened a chain of superstores which are a combination supermarket and super drug store under one roof. Both stores operate as one unit with common checkout stands, parking lot, etc., with no visible line of demarcation. These stores, averaging 53,000 to 55,000 square feet, are considerably larger than Albertson's normal 28,000 to 30,000 square foot food store.

Located in a new marketing territory (the South), some 49 Skaggs-Albertson's stores operated from Texas across to Florida in fiscal 1975. Twelve new units are opening in fiscal 1976. In the first five years, the

Skaggs-Albertson's super drug-grocery combination units are located in five states.

partnership's sales have grown from 3% to 13.5% of Albertson's total sales. More importantly, the 13.5% of sales now contribute 17% of Albertson's net income.

A good example of the management talent and industry leadership displayed by Northwest businessmen, Albertson's is now receiving recognition as a major American enterprise with annual sales exceeding $1 billion. Alberton's growth also reflects the economic strength of Western states, and is in sharp contrast to the lacklustre performance of several large Eastern-based supermarket concerns in recent years, most notably that of *A&P*.

Drug-Variety Stores

We have identified three Northwest based drug-variety chains and one general merchandise chain which merit serious attention from investors. The three drug-variety chains are also referred to as "super drug chains" because of their historical development within the drug store industry. The fourth retailer operates self-service outlets, and also offers a broad range of general merchandise, somewhat comparable to that of the other three chains.

The drug store industry produces annual sales in the United States of $16.7 billion, of which $6.4 billion comes from drug chain operations. With annual sales in 1974 of $500 million, **Skaggs Companies, Inc.,** headquartered in Salt Lake City, ranks second in size in the United States only to the *Walgreen* system. Skaggs operates 228 stores in a 22-state area (October 1975), including 59 combination Skaggs-Albertson's stores.

The new Skaggs-Albertson's partnership units are producing record sales. In just five years, the Skaggs-Albertson's partnership sales have zoomed from a standing start to over $280 million annually. The importance of these sales to Skaggs is clear. Their share of 1974 joint revenue was $140.9 million, 28% of Skaggs' total revenue.

Over 75 Pay 'n Save Drug stores operate in West Coast states, Hawaii and Canada.

Pay 'n Save Corporation, based in Seattle, Washington is more diversified than most other super drug chains regionally and nationally, with 134 stores in operation at the end of September, 1975. Pay 'n Save's operating territory includes the states of Washington, California, Oregon, Alaska, Hawaii, Idaho, and Canada. Over 90% of the company's present stores are in Washington and California.

In addition to the 77 drug-variety stores operated under the Pay 'n Save name, the company operates 13 *Bi-Mart* drug stores, which were acquired in mid-1975. Other store operations include 27 *Ernst-Malmo* home centers, nine *Lamonts* apparel stores, and eight sporting goods stores. Fiscal 1975's company-wide sales were divided as follows: Drug Division—67.2%; Hardware Division—24.6%; and Apparel Division—8.2%.

Both Pay 'n Save and the next retailer in this section rank among the top five drug chains in the country in terms of annual growth in earnings per share for the past five years, according to *Financial World* magazine. The high performance rankings are as much a tribute to management ability as they are to the stength and viability of the region's economy.

The other drug-variety chain maintaining one of the best growth records in the country is **PAY LESS Drug Stores NORTHWEST, Inc.** (NYSE). Pay Less Northwest is headquartered in Portland, Ore. and presently operates 50 stores, mainly grouped around its home base. All but five stores are located in Oregon and Washington. There are two stores each in Northern California and Western Idaho. In addition, Pay Less Northwest has opened one store in Colorado (near Denver), a new area destined for further company expansion. Stores in that state will operate under the name *Harts Super Drug.*

Pay Less Northwest stores average 29,900 square feet in size and offer a "Super Drug Store" line of merchandise including drugs,

Pay Less Northwest Super Drug stores sell a broad line of nationally-advertised and brand-name products at popular prices. Below, the district manager and store manager of the Company's first Colorado store review plans before grand opening in 1975.

cosmetics, toys and games, small appliances, cameras, sporting goods, hardware, etc. and other household and garden supplies.

In 1975, Pay Less Northwest opened its new Distribution Center in Portland. It is the last phase of a four-year program to streamline the company's storing and ordering system. Two miles of conveyor belt serve the new 140,000 square foot warehouse facility.

Similar to other successful drug chains, Pay Less Northwest stores sell primarily basic consumer goods that are subject to high repeat sales and volume purchases by customers. Emphasis is placed on efficient turnover of capital invested in all merchandise to achieve an adequate rate of return on a relatively low margin of profit to sales.

In keeping with the objective of an adequate return, Pay Less Northwest converted its clothing sales space to leased departments in 1975. An experienced and successful privately-owned Seattle firm will operate the departments. The change affects 18 stores, and is expected to lower store operating costs, free-up additional capital, and further improve corporate earnings.

Grand Central, Inc. is based in Salt Lake City, and operates a total of 21 stores in Idaho, Nevada, Wyoming, and Utah. A junior department store self-service operation with a broad range of general merchandise, Grand Central stores average more than 80,000 square feet in size — larger than the other drug-variety chains in the Northwest. *The Great Atlantic & Pacific Tea Co.,* (A&P) headquartered in New Jersey, has proposed the acquisition of Grand Central for an exchange of stock valued at $18.5 million.
(Latest word at press time—merger called off.)

Home Improvement Centers

The Northwest is the center of the forest products industry. The many facets of this industry involve construction, plywood, lumber, and related materials. Therefore, it seems natural that the development of a corollary industry—home improvement centers—would also have firm roots in the Northwest.

In this field, investors should consider **Pay 'N Pak Stores, Inc.** based in Kent, Washington. Pay 'N Pak stores are designed for the economy-minded do-it-yourselfer. Retail merchandise includes a full line of building materials, plumbing, electrical, and lighting fixtures. Ten of Pay 'N Pak's stores also stock automotive parts, accessories, and sporting goods.

Pay 'N Pak presently operates 58 retail stores in eleven western states. Future plans call for expansion into three additional states: Wyoming, North Dakota, and Hawaii. However, at the company's 1975 annual meeting, Chairman David J. Heerensperger observed that the stores located "closer to home" seem to be the most successful, and that the company was interested in further expansion of its primary markets in Washington, Oregon and Idaho.

Pay 'N Pak's store in Lynnwood, Washington is one of 58 serving do-it-yourselfers.

In the past five years, Pay 'N Pak's annual sales have grown from $21.8 million to $61.5 million. Similarly, net income in that period increased from $663,840 to $2,226,045.

One other Northwest company is totally committed to the retail home improvement market, although on a much smaller scale. Based in Portland, Oregon, **Consumers Building Marts, Inc.** operates six retail stores under the *"Mr. Plywood"* name in Portland, Seattle, and Denver. As the Mr. Plywood name suggests, the company is primarily a plywood and wood products specialty retailer.

Each store carries about 80 to 100 varieties of prefinished wall panels together with prefinished mouldings, siding and sheathing. Limited space is given to related materials such as nails and panel adhesive, ceiling tiles, and decorator items. In recent years, painting materials and carpeting have been added in some stores. As we go to press, Consumers Building Marts has announced plans to be acquired by *Erb Lumber Company*.

Several other Northwest companies operate home improvement type stores. These include previously mentioned *Fred Meyer* and *Pay 'n Save* (Ernst-Malmo home centers) and others mentioned at the end of the chapter.

Specialty Merchandisers

Considering the diversification moves of many retailers today, the future of the specialty retailer may not appear particularly bright to the casual observer. It seems that by the time a specialty retailer has developed successfully in his chosen area, any number of big variety and general merchandise retailers will want to start their own departments in the same field. While some retailers shy away from this kind of business climate, others thrive on the competition. The Northwest is headquarters for several specialty retailers, who concentrate on one or two basic lines of merchandise.

One retailer that has been eminently successful in specialization is

Nordstrom stores sell fashion apparel and shoes for women, men and children.

Nordstrom, Inc. The Seattle-headquartered retail chain sells a full line of medium to better quality apparel, accessories and shoes for women, men and children. The company operates 12 retail specialty stores and two retail shoe stores, all located in Washington and Oregon.

In addition, Nordstrom operates leased shoe departments in 29 department stores in seven western states, including Hawaii. These shoe departments are under a licensing agreement with *Amfac, Inc.,* operator of the *Liberty House* department stores.

On February 25, 1975, the management of Nordstrom made a significant acquisition which greatly enhances their future sales growth and profit potential. Three major department stores in Alaska were purchased from the *Northern Commercial Company.* Nordstrom had previously leased the shoe departments in these stores. Located in Anchorage, Fairbanks, and Kenai, Alaska, these have been Alaska's leading retail stores for some 70 years. Nordstrom's management estimates that this acquisition will add $20 million to the company's annual sales, which already exceed $100 million.

Two specialty merchandisers which serve the home sewing market with a full line of fabrics and sewing notions are also headquartered in the region. **Discount Fabrics, Inc.,** located in Portland, operates a chain of retail fabric stores in Washington, Oregon, Idaho, Montana, Utah, California, and western Canada. The number of fabric stores has increased each year, from 6 in 1966 to 56 in 1974. Discount Fabrics has been profitable each year.

Somewhat similar in its operation is **Fabric Wholesalers, Inc.,** also of Portland. However, Fabric Wholesalers operates on a smaller scale, having 25 retail outlets in the four states of Oregon, Washington, California and Idaho (one unit in each of the latter two states).

As indicated in its name, the company also supplies some 300 wholesale accounts in 30 states plus Canada and Australia. However, the importance of wholesale sales has declined—from 56% of revenues in 1970 to 13% in 1974. Although Fabric Wholesalers had a deficit in 1974, they have turned into the black at this writing, and posted a solid profit for the first half of 1975.

JEWELRY STORES

Weisfield's, Inc., a Seattle company, presently operates 67 retail stores in ten states, primarily in the Northwest. Established in 1917, Weisfield's mainstay is a chain of 67 retail jewelry stores. Prior to 1974, the company also operated a chain of 16 discount department stores under the *Valu-Mart* name. Having turned unprofitable, some Valu-Marts were closed and the remainder converted to junior department stores and operated under the name *Leslies.* By the latter part of 1975, substantially all department store operations were discontinued and most of these stores sold to other retailers. However, Weisfield's principal operation, the retail jewelry stores, is profitable and, in fact, expanding.

Another retailer in the jewelry field is **Millers International, Inc.** Millers creates, manufactures and sells fine jewelry, including dia-

mond, gold and precious stone jewelry, primarily rings. Its manufacturing facility and only retail outlet are adjacent to the home office in
Portland. Wholesale operations contribute a relatively small percentage
of sales.

Restaurant Chains

Two growing restaurant corporations, **International King's
Table, Inc.** of Eugene, Oregon and **JB's Big Boy Family
Restaurants, Inc.**, based in Salt Lake City, Utah have many
similarities, although each operates a distinctly different type of
restaurant.

Both offer low-priced family type meals, and each is expanding
rapidly. King's Table, just 10 years old, had 48 restaurants in service at
the end of fiscal 1975 (fiscal year ending June 30) including 21 units
franchised to other operators, and plans the addition of 5 more
company-operated restaurants in the current year. In fiscal 1977 IKT
plans to open 6 more, and after that its goal is 12 per year. JB's began
with a single restaurant in 1961, and had 58 in operation at the end of
1974. Both companies have had flawless financial records, with higher
sales and net income in each of the past five years.

International King's Table operates a specialized "American
smorgasbord" style self-service restaurant. Since they are typically
located in suburban communities, the IKT restaurants have a high
volume of repeat customer business, and are not generally subject to the
vagaries of tourism and highway traffic.

JB's Big Boys are coffee-shop short order type restaurants
somewhat similar to *Denny's or Sambo's* chains. JB's is a franchisee of
the national Big Boy chain of more than 700 restaurants. The "parent"
company that issues the franchises nationally is the *Marriott Corporation,* which is headquartered in Atlanta.

JB's has units in 15 states, including all of the western states except
Oregon. King's Table has 14 restaurants open in Oregon, its home state,
plus operations in Washington and Idaho. Outside of the Northwest,
the company has locations in 11 other states, primarily the South and
mid-South.

IKT president Wilbur W. Houmes expresses "the IKT philosophy"
in part as follows:

> "Our goal is to provide a place where the whole family can once again sit
> down together and enjoy genuinely good food in comfortable, wholesome
> surroundings, and, at a price that is easily within the reach of the average
> family. Each of our wide variety of dishes is prepared from top quality
> fruits and vegetables, choice meats, poultry, and fish, and the freshest
> dairy products. Every dish is cooked and presented with the skill and atten-
> tion that characterized the home kitchen of yesteryear.
>
> International King's Table has been successful, we believe, primarily
> because we have tried to put service and good citizenship first as an objec-
> tive. We depend primarily on the trade of the community, and we want to be
> a permanent and constructive part of each area we serve."

One other Northwest restaurant chain, Boise-based **Red Steer**,

International King's Table serves communities through 48 restaurants in 13 states.

Inc. was publicly traded during the early 1970's, but the major stockholders made a successful tender offer to repurchase the company's publicly-held stock in 1975, returning the company to private ownership.

Wholesalers

Investors who are seeking new ways to participate in the Alaskan boom would do well to consider wholesaler **Palmer G. Lewis Co., Inc.** of Auburn, Washington.

The Palmer G. Lewis Company is a distributor of a wide range of building materials. They serve retail building material dealers, large general merchandise chains, roofing and drywall companies, and industrial and government accounts.

The company serves all of the Pacific Northwest and Alaska through 10 Palmer G. Lewis branches in Washington and Alaska and three *Pacific Yard Service* branches in Oregon. In addition, the company owns 70% of *Superior Building Supply, Inc.,* which services the Kenai Peninsula in Alaska with three retail outlets.

Supplies wholesaled by Palmer G. Lewis include these:

Doors	Plywood
Floorcovering	Prefinished Wood Panels
Hardware	Rigid Insulation
Insulation Board	Roofing
Lumber	Soft Insulation
Marlite	Specialty Building Products
Nails & Steel Products	Wallboards
Plasterboard	Wood Mouldings

In 1975 the company doubled the size of its Anchorage, Alaska covered warehouse storage space, to 72,000 square feet, a $500,000 expansion project.

Fiscal 1975's sales for Palmer G. Lewis were $41.1 million, an increase of 2.4 times in five years and 4.6 times compared to 10 years ago. Cash dividends have been paid in each of the past 15 years.

As stated by Palmer G. Lewis Company's president, Robert D. Peterson:

"We do have many, many positive factors going for us. First of all, Alaska is booming, and Alaska is an important part of our total picture. Secondly, the balance of our trading area—the Pacific Northwest—is much stronger, economically, than the rest of the country."

Three other companies engaged heavily in wholesale distribution are headquartered in the Northwest. One distributes electronic components, another distributes recreational vehicle parts and accessories, and the third company sells softwood veneer to wood products manufacturers. Each company is treated separately below.

A research and development company prior to 1974, **Laser Link Corporation** became an operating company in that year through the acquisition of Seattle-based *Almac Electronics,* which is now the *Almac/Stroum* Division. The company is the largest distributor of industrial electronic components in the Pacific Northwest, representing 10 major manufacturers and distributing the lines of another 50 electronics firms.

Laser Link has created a strong channel of distribution along the entire West Coast through a series of acquisitions, which, to date, include *Western Electromotive* of Los Angeles, *Shephard Components* of Van Nuys, and *Yukon Radio Supply* of Anchorage. Sales for 1975, including contributions from acquisitions, probably will exceed $13 million.

Samuel N. Stroum, Laser Links' president, expresses confidence in his growing organization and its ability to serve a market that is fast-changing in technology. A sampling of items distributed includes integrated circuits, micro-processor components, solid state devices, switches, potentiometers and resistance devices, digital read-outs, indicator lights, power supplies, wire, cable, and other electronic hardware.

Acquisitions have increased the company's total assets to $8.5 million as of September 30, 1975. As a result of its Yukon Radio acquisition, Laser Link has also become more active in the retail field. The company now has four consumer electronics stores in Alaska — Anchorage (2), Fairbanks, and Valdez — and one store adjacent to its distribution facility in Seattle.

Trailer Equipment Distributors, Inc., headquartered in Seattle Washington, has benefited from the growth of recreational vehicle and related leisure-time industries, particularly in the Northwest region and Canada. Trailer Equipment (TEDCO) is a supplier to virtually all of the nation's manufacturers of travel trailers, mobile homes and motor homes. In addition to new equipment installations, TEDCO now receives 70% of its sales in the aftermarket, to owners of existing camper equipment. TEDCO carries a line of about 10,000 items, ranging from replacement parts to accessories and doodads. These include such diverse items as trailer hitches, awnings, air conditioners, and television antennas. Recently TEDCO began supplying equipment for pleasure

Pacific Gamble Robinson distributes Snoboy and Standby products throughout the West.

boats as well. This includes heating, plumbing, electrical, and propane equipment for boats. Expansion into Canada in the mid-60's has resulted in 40% of TEDCO's wholesale sales now coming from that country.

Alpine International Corporation (Portland), through its subsidiary *Alpine Veneers, Inc.* and its subsidiaries, manufactures and wholesales wood products. Alpine Veneers owns and operates a plywood manufacturing plant at Portland, and a newly acquired veneer manufacturing plant at Klamath Falls, Oregon. In addition, Alpine Veneers has two wholly-owned subsidiaries — *Cantree Forest Products Ltd.* and *RDI, Inc.* doing business as *Cress Ply*. The Cantree operation consists of a plywood manufacturing division and a wholesaling division. Cress Ply is a plywood manufacturing plant. Besides plywood and veneer manufacturing, Alpine has a longstanding reputation in the veneer, plywood, and lumber wholesaling trade. Total gross sales exceeded $74 million for the fiscal year ended August 31, 1974. Although wholesale operations account for the majority of gross sales, revenue from commissions earned is considerably less than manufacturing revenue. Plant and equipment at manufacturing operations account for at least 80% of fixed assets.

FOOD WHOLESALERS

The largest food wholesaler in the Northwest is **Pacific Gamble Robinson Co.** Nationwide in its coverage, Pacific Gamble operates 79 branch warehouses in 16 Northwest states and three provinces of Canada. With a system of 600 trucks, the company supplies 16,000 retail grocery stores and 12,000 institutional food service accounts. Pacific Gamble has established its own brand names — *SNOBOY* (frozen foods, fresh fruits and vegetables) and *STANDBY* (canned goods). These two brands account for more than 25% of the company's wholesale sales.

Much of the wholesaling activity in the Northwest is carried on by companies which do not devote 100% of their resources to this activity. Thus a company such as **Fred Meyer, Inc.,** which we discussed as a retailer, also makes its presence felt in wholesaling through its *Roundup Grocery Co.* subsidiary. In the past five years, the company's wholesale division has produced revenue amounting to 23%-25% of Fred Meyer's total sales. Wholesale sales now are in excess of $100 million annually.

Fred Meyer's wholesale sales consist almost entirely of food items, which are sold to various food chains, hotels, schools, hospitals, and restaurants. Based in Spokane, Washington, Roundup Grocery Company's primary marketing area is Eastern Washington and Oregon, Idaho and Montana.

Albertson's, Inc., the Northwest's largest retail grocery chain, is also beginning to enter food wholesaling in a big way. In 1972, Albertson's acquired the *Mountain States Wholesale Company* in Boise, Idaho. In addition to supplying Albertson's stores, Mountain States sells to outside customers in Idaho and Southern Oregon. In 1974, sales to these outside accounts amounted to $39.8 million. Albertson's opened a new 200,000 square foot wholesale distribution center in Brea, California in 1973, to supply stores in Southern California, Southern Nevada, and Arizona. A wholesale meat processing and fabricating plant (126,000 square feet), also in Brea, California, was opened in 1975.

OTHER COMPANIES IN RETAILING AND WHOLESALING

Many other companies described elsewhere in this book also operate substantial retailing and wholesaling chains, discussed along with other operations of the companies in their respective chapters. **Amfac,** for example, owns *Liberty House* and *Rhodes* department stores, *Joseph Magnin* specialty stores, *Fred Harvey* restaurants, and other retailing operations. Amfac is also heavily involved in both electronic and drug wholesaling.

Columbia Corporation operates the *Thunderbird* chain of home improvement stores. **Evans Products** is one of the largest home improvement retailers in the United States through its *Moore's, Grossman's and Hubbard & Johnson* chains. **Willamette Industries** recently entered the building materials retailing field through an acquisition. **Edwards Industries** distributes building materials through *Edwards Building Supply* in Oregon as well as through *Fircrest Supply* in Tacoma, and also has eight auto glass outlets in Oregon and ten in Washington.

Hillhaven operates a national chain of retail pharmacies and retail optical stores. **GranTree** retails furniture through its "rental return outlets."

Univar distributes industrial chemical supplies through its *Van Waters & Rogers* subsidiary, laboratory supplies through *VWR Scientific,* and photographic supplies through *Treck PhotoGraphic.* **Wayne's Photo** also wholesales photographic supplies and equipment.

Most of the forest products companies are involved in wholesaling, especially in the field of paper products. These include *Boise Cascade, Crown Zellerbach, Georgia-Pacific, Potlatch,* and *Weyerhaeuser.*

Many of the manufacturing companies are "vertically integrated," in that they also operate their own wholesale and/or retail distribution systems. Most of the food and beverage processors operate wholesale distribution systems.

All in all, the retail and wholesale merchandising segment accounts for a very significant part of the total economic activity, and dozens of the region's publicly-traded companies are involved.

17

Services

Recreation

While recreational activities are very much a part of the Northwest, there are few publicly owned companies available to the investor.

One Northwest concern that has grown to national prominence in the past ten years is **Kampgrounds of America, Inc.** In 1962, a privately owned campground was opened at Billings, Montana, to serve travelers visiting the Seattle World's Fair. The apparent demand shown led to the formation of KOA and the franchising of the first seven KOA campgrounds in 1964. Ten years later, at the end of 1974, 765 KOA campgrounds were in operation.

Presently, according to company officials, more families stay in KOA campgrounds each year than in all of the campgrounds of the *National Park Service* and the *U.S. Forest Service* combined. In association with the U.S. Forest Service, KOA campgrounds now operate exclusive information centers for the campground and motel industries concerning pollution control by the camping public.

KOA CAMPGROUNDS OPERATING

	1974	1973	1972	1971	1970
Franchised campgrounds	747	687	582	492	352
Company-operated campgrounds	18	20	14	10	4
Total	765	707	596	502	356

The adverse economic conditions of 1973 and 1974 affected KOA in various ways. The oil embargo and resulting fuel shortage obviously affected pleasure travel for a period of time. High interest rates and the scarcity of construction funds adversely affected the opening of new campgrounds. Finally, the recession and resulting increase in unemployment caused less vacation travel. All of this resulted in lower sales during 1974 for the first time in five years for KOA as well as its first earnings deficit.

KOA's Chairman Darrell Booth regards this condition as temporary, and sees renewed growth and profits in the future.

One recreational company that stands to receive lasting benefits from the renewed interest in Alaskan tourism is **Westours, Inc.** of Seat-

243

Westours motorcoach on scenic Canadian Rockies highway.

tle. Westours is one of the nation's largest tour wholesalers, a business not generally familiar to the public.

As a wholesaler, the company plans and organizes so-called "package tours," which are offered to the public through retail travel agents in North America and elsewhere. Well positioned in the Northwest, Westours specializes in tour groups visiting Alaska and the Canadian Rockies.

The North Country is a hard one for the casual traveler. At some points of interest, hotels, meals and even the basic transportation are virtually nonexistent unless carefully arranged well in advance. With more than 28 years of experience, Westours is the leading tour operator in this remote part of the world.

A staff of about 275 employees operates the company's own network of transfer, sightseeing, and motorcoach services. The company owns its own hotel facilities at critical tour points.

In recent years, the company attempted to operate two wholly-owned cruise ships, which were financially unsuccessful. The ships have since been sold. Westours' President, H. J. Musiel, is very optimistic over the growth of North Country tourism and points to a 42% increase in 1974 tour sales, in spite of national recessionary trends. He projects Alaskan travel to grow at a higher rate than foreign and other domestic destinations in the near future.

Investors who have watched their assets "go to the dogs" in recent years would do well to study **Multnomah Kennel Club** of Portland. A venerable firm, Multnomah has been conducting greyhound racing meets annually in the Portland area since 1933.

Greyhound racing is licensed in 12 states presently and some 40 tracks are in operation. The track in Portland is the only U.S. track west of Denver and Phoenix. As an industry, greyhound tracks are the country's seventh leading spectator sport, with a total 1974 attendance of more than 16 million. Pari-mutuel tax receipts in the twelve states topped $84 million in 1974.

The Sport of Queens—"And they're off!"

Multnomah's revenues come from its share of the wagering pool (9.2%), concessions, program sales, and gate admissions. All expenses and winning purses to greyhound owners are paid from these receipts. The company has been operating a 65-day racing season, which will be increased to 75 days in 1976. In addition, Multnomah rents its facilities to the *Multnomah County Fair* and the *Pacific Livestock Exposition* each year, producing an additional ten days of revenue. Race dates for the 1976 season are scheduled for May 20 through August 26.

Multnomah's present track facilities, located at Fairview, Oregon (15 miles east of Portland) were built in 1957 and are upgraded annually. The property consists of 124 acres of land, a 3-story glass-enclosed grandstand, and a 495 yard track. Multnomah Kennel Club has no long-term debt.

Gross wagering receipts were a record $30.4 million in 1975. Earnings increased in each of the past three years, and exceeded $500,000 in 1974.

At the other extreme is a Seattle based company — **First Northwest Industries of America, Inc.** The company would have little to attract the average investor, except for one fact. First Northwest owns and operates the *Seattle Super Sonics,* a team in the *National Basketball Association.* The company also operates seven indoor tennis clubs and a small cable-TV system located in Tennessee. Also, in early 1975, the company acquired Universal Gym Equipment a company that sells exercise equipment. However, the one central fact concerning First Northwest is that it has operated at a loss in each of the past five years, and, in fact, larger losses in each of the last three years.

Convalescent Care Facilities

A number of investor-owned corporations serving the Northwest relate to the health field in one way or another. One such group of companies we have identified is operators of convalescent care centers. There are four such firms based in the Northwest, three in Washington State and one in Oregon. Patients in these facilities are of two kinds: (1) private patients, and (2) those receiving Medicare or other government assistance. In general, a somewhat greater portion of the patients are in the Medicare vs. private care classification, although the proportionate breakdown varies from company to company.

In terms of revenue, the smallest of the four is **American Care Centers, Inc.**, with headquarters in Portland. American Care owns and operates nine health care centers, seven in Oregon and two in Washington. Together these facilities have a total capacity of about 800 beds. Annual revenue has advanced in each of the company's last four years—from $2,097,677 in 1972 to $3,658,528 in fiscal 1975 (ending March 31).

Villa Care, Inc. operates wholly within the State of Washington. The company owns (or manages) eleven separate facilities with a total of approximately 1,500 beds. Net revenue for 1974 came to $6,550,848, up from $4,609,580 the previous year.

Centennial Villas, Inc. was founded in 1969 by the consolidation of various individual convalescent centers. As of mid-1975, Centennial Villas operated one convalescent center in California and eight in Washington State. Of these eight, the company owns four and operates four as lessee. Centennial has been profitable in each of the past three years, with 1974 revenue of $10.7 million.

The largest of the group of convalescent center chains is **Hillhaven, Inc.**, based in Tacoma. National in its scope, Hillhaven operates 95 convalescent care facilities with a capacity of approximately 10,000 beds. In addition, the company operates a national chain of retail pharmacies and retail optical stores. Revenue for fiscal 1975 (ending March 31 amounted to $78,122,954 with net income equal to $1,053,872.

Most of the convalescent care facilities operated by Hillhaven, Inc. are identified by the *Hillhaven or Healthcare* names. All of those belonging to Villa Care, Inc., use the *Villa Care* name. Others are identified as follows:

> **Centennial Villas:** *Bellevue Terrace; Emerald Terrace; Evergreen Terrace; Glen Terrace; Green River Terrace; Highland Terrace; Benton Terrace; Sherwood Terrace; Pinewood Terrace; and Torrey Pines.*

> **American Care Centers:** *Care Center East; Careousel Care Center; Crestview Care Center; Glenaire Care Center; Gold Leaf Convalescent Home; Royal Care Convalescent Center; Grandview Care Home; Seaside Care Center; and Silver Gardens Care Home.*

Medical Services

A new company in the Northwest is **HealthGarde Corporation.** The company was formed in November, 1974 as a consolidation of two other companies. These were *Med-Mark, Inc.* and *Bio-Logics Systems, Inc.*, both based in Salt Lake City.

Bio-Logics has developed minicomputer technology for automated data processing in the medical field. Some of the applications include Cardio-Pulmonary testing, automated Health-Profiling, and Hospital

At Villa Care, meals are planned to meet special dietary needs, and may be served in the patient's room or in dining areas convenient to living quarters.

HealthGarde's Bio-Logics Computerized Pulmonary Testing System is a fully-integrated minicomputer system designed for the modern cardiopulmonary lab.

Information/Communications. HealthGarde's other subsidiary, Med-Mark Services, offers services such as Respiratory Therapy, Physical Therapy, Cardio-Pulmonary Diagnostics, Medical Transcription and Hospital Administration.

HealthGarde has proposed to acquire *Ventilation Associates, Inc.* of Houston, Texas. Ventilation Associates performs services similar to Med-Mark Services. The acquisition, if completed, will give HealthGarde respiratory therapy contract services in some 75 hospitals throughout the United States.

An altogether different type of company is **Intermountain Laboratories, Inc.** of Salt Lake City, which specializes in veterinary medicine and supplies.

The main investor interest in Intermountain Laboratories is in the long-term potential of some of its research projects. For example, the company has developed a preparation for the treatment of cancer in the eyes of cattle. Preliminary tests showed the treatment to be more than 80% effective.

Intermountain also has a vaccine for the treatment of "pink eye" in cattle. Affecting about 20% of all cattle, the disease causes a pronounced weight loss in the cattle. Intermountain's vaccine has proved 95% effective in tests. Also interesting is a blood testing program for young cattle which can predict their potential for future weight gains. Thus, those with a low growth potential can be culled from the herd before expensive feedlot feeding begins.

Regional Stock Brokerage Firms

Paulson Investment Company is a broker-dealer firm designed to specialize in serving Northwest investors. Paulson set out in 1971 as a market-maker in over-the-counter issues working in the dealer-to-dealer wholesale market.

Rapidly changing economic and financial market conditions contributed to the firm's heavy trading losses in 1971 and 1972. Regrouping, management decided to seek retail commission business in addition to its dealer activities.

1973 and 1974 have shown small profits for the brokerage firm, and a core of trained, professional salesmen have joined the firm. Higher trading volumes in 1975, to date, would indicate the probability of better profits for the current year, as well. Paulson Investment Company recently purchased a seat on the *Pacific Stock Exchange*. Paulson executes orders for customers in NYSE and ASE listed stocks through a correspondent member firm.

Paulson continues to perform its original function as the largest market maker in Oregon based over-the-counter stocks. Thus, Paulson performs a valuable service for both Northwest companies and private investors. Many of the medium to smaller sized company stocks traded by Paulson Investment Company are primarily of interest to regional investors, and market quotations on some are difficult to obtain from other brokerage firms.

The list of regional stocks changes from time to time according to market conditions. Presently, Paulson's market making operations include these Northwest companies, among others: *Bohemia, Cascade Corp., Cascade Steel, Columbia Corp., Edwards Industries, Fabric Wholesalers, GranTree, Gregg's Food Products, Hayden Island, Kirkman Labs, Moore Clear, Oregon Portland Cement, Rem Metals, Smoke-Craft, Equitable Savings, Orbanco, U.S. Bancorp, American Guaranty, First Farwest Corp., Investors Insurance,* and *Telephone Utilities*.

Hinkle Northwest, Inc. is a regionally-oriented securities firm, with brokerage offices in Portland, Eugene, Salem, Medford, and Brookings, Oregon. The firm has been a market maker in a number of Northwest stocks including *Fred Meyer, Hyster, Willamette Industries, Oregon Freeze Dry Foods, Olympia Brewing, Rainbow Resources* and *First Farwest Corp.*

The Portland based brokerage firm recently became a member of the *Pacific Coast Clearing Corp.* This membership move is expected to simplify trading and delivery procedures in over-the-counter securities with broker-dealers in other parts of the country. Hinkle Northwest also executes orders for its customers in listed securities through a correspondent New York Stock Exchange member firm.

Computer Service Firms

We classify **Data Systems, Inc.,** of Portland as a service company because its primary business has been the operation of a computerized data service center.

However, in 1969 Data Systems acquired *Columbia Business Forms* which specializes in customized business forms and systems. Also in 1969 the company acquired *Diversified Industries, Inc.,* a distributor of hydraulic hose, fittings, and valves. Organized in 1966, Data

Systems has had rising sales in each of the past five years ($2,455,945 in 1974) and has been profitable each year.

Another small computer-based company is **Information Sciences, Inc.**, also headquartered in Portland. The company's principal business is providing computer and computer time-sharing services, utilizing a "PDP-10" computer. Historically the company's primary markets were in the fields of engineering and scientific time-sharing applications. Now the company reports that remote batch processing and business related commercial data processing uses are expanding company revenues.

Startup expenses for Information Sciences caused annual losses in the company's first three years of operation (1970-1972). Even so, revenue has increased each year, and 1973 and 1974 were profitable. Revenue for 1974 was $662,000 with net income of $194,000.

Miscellaneous Service Companies

Chem Nuclear Systems, Inc. specializes in the handling and disposal of nuclear waste materials, primarily for industrial and utility customers. The company operates the largest radioactive waste disposal site in the country—located near Barnwell, South Carolina. Other potential sites are under consideration.

As more nuclear reactor power plants are ordered by the utility industry, the need for safe waste disposal becomes essential. An estimate by Chem Nuclear's management (in 1973) stated that the number of nuclear reactor units necessary to service the United States by the year 2000 would be approximately 1,000 power plants. This contrasted to 27 plants actually in service at that time. Chem Nuclear's annual sales, $3 million in 1974, seem destined to go much higher in the future.

Design Arts, Inc. of Salt Lake City, is one of the types of companies that is difficult to categorize according to a single industry grouping. Formed to market metal-etched products to furniture and home decorating stores, the company soon switched its business. In November 1972 Design Arts acquired the *Utah Sign Corporation,* a 19-year-old company experienced in the manufacture and sale of all types of commercial signs.

Many of the installed signs are under lease and maintenance agreements which provide continuing income over a period of years. Typical customers include hospitals, airports, and government installations as well as commercial establishments. Sales for fiscal 1975 for Design Arts, Inc. amounted to $351,000. The company installs and maintains all of the highway signs in Utah for *Ford Motor Company, White Trucks,* and *General Motors.* It also does the sign work for all *Golden Villa* health spas nationwide.

Fifty-year-old **Loomis Corporation** is world-wide in the scope of its operations. Although few investors realize it, the company is headquartered in Seattle. Noted for its armored car and courier services, Loomis operates in eleven Western (including Hawaii and Alaska) and Midwest states plus five Canadian provinces.

Design Arts emphasizes quality and aesthetics in its sign, aiming for only the top part of the competitive market.

Chem Nuclear's motor carrier transports a mobile solidification system to a job site.

Walter F. Loomis and Armored Car No. 1 and Charles W. Loomis next to Armored Car No. 225 just off the assembly line in 1965.

In addition to the operation of its fleet of armored trucks, Loomis provides numerous other services. These include plant and area security guards (such as on Alaska's North Slope), airport security guards (Fairbanks and Anchorage airports), and roving patrols using dogs and radio communications.

Loomis also offers both national and international courier services for the delivery of securities, contracts, and other valuable papers. One example will show the value of such courier service to the Northwest.

Working with the *Federal Reserve Bank,* Loomis is achieving overnight check processing between banks on a regional basis. Loomis personnel are stationed at these locations: Coeur d'Alene, Idaho; Clarkston, Wenatchee, Walla Walla, and Pasco, Washington; and Medford, Pendleton and Coos Bay, Oregon. Each morning, Loomis air charters take Federal Reserve items from Seattle and Portland to airports in these cities where they meet the local agent and exchange material. Each local driver then makes daily deliveries within a 100-mile radius of his airport.

In 1974, Loomis acquired two trucking companies, *Lincoln Moving and Storage Company* and *Alaska-Orient Van Service* with a branch in Anchorage, Alaska. This is an historical echo since Lee B. Loomis, the company's founder, once transported gold dust and supplies across Alaska by dogsled! Revenue and income for Loomis have each doubled in the past five years, with 1974 gross receipts reaching $32.3 million.

Wayne's Photo Finishing, Inc., (Chehalis, Washington) is a wholesale photofinisher serving more than 1,300 chain stores and independent retail dealers in the Northwest and California. Wayne's operates photofinishing plants in Chehalis and Spokane, Washington and Burbank, California. Wayne's also engages in wholesale distribution of photographic products and supplies, and operates 27 retail drive-up kiosks in the Los Angeles area.

Although the company has been profitable in seven of the last ten years, it was a victim of the 1974-1975 inflation/recession, and posted losses totalling $1.3 million over the past two years on annual sales of $9 million. As we go to press, the company is seeking new long-term financing to place it on a sounder basis to pursue its basic business.

Dependable Building Maintainence Co., Inc. derives all of its revenue from building maintenance operations which serve businesses in Seattle and Portland. Its former subsidiaries involving interior design, masonry restoration, and mechanical maintenance were discontinued in recent years. The company contracts with a variety of professional, commercial, and industrial businesses for janitorial and related maintenance services.

GranTree Corporation (formerly *Granning and Treece Corporation),* headquartered in Portland, is a service company that is unusual and interesting in its orientation. After many years primarily in the consumer finance business, GranTree's basic business now is furniture rental. GranTree also offers an equipment leasing service to commercial accounts throughout the Northwest. At year-end 1974, over $10 million in lease receivables were outstanding for such items as store, restaurant, hospital, medical and office equipment. Early in 1975 GranTree sold most of its consumer loan operations.

GranTree is the largest furniture rental company in the western half of the United States, with 27 furniture rental showrooms in Washington, Oregon, Nevada, California, Arizona and British Columbia. GranTree entered the business by acquiring *Custom Furniture Rental* in 1971, and changed the name to *GranTree Furniture Rental* in 1973.

In today's highly mobile society, many families find it advantageous to rent, rather than own, their furniture. Most of the furniture is rented to apartment tenants. In case renters decide they do want to buy, there is an equity buildup in each rental payment which can be applied to an eventual purchase.

In addition to the direct rental to customers through the 27 showrooms, GranTree has also established a "Representative Lease Program" whereby furniture is rented to residents through apartment owners or managers as *agents* of GranTree.

After the furniture has been in rental use for a specified period of time (different for different items), it is sold through six "GranTree rental return sales outlets" located on the West Coast. Sales of new furniture (mainly furniture overruns and freight damaged furniture) was introduced through the rental return sales outlets in 1974, and now accounts for about 30% of the sales division's revenue.

GranTree Chairman Walker Treece is very optimistic about the future of the furniture rental business, feeling that its flexibility provides a service very compatible with the type of life style which many people these days wish to enjoy.

Furniture is being delivered by GranTree to new residents of the Portland Center.

18

Commercial Banking

The laws concerning banking practices vary somewhat from state to state, especially with regard to the extent to which banks are allowed to open branches. Statewide branch banking is practiced in Washington, Oregon, Idaho, and Alaska. Branch banking is not allowed, or is limited, in Montana, Wyoming, and Utah. However, bank holding companies get around this by opening new individual unit banks or acquiring others as subsidiaries, a more costly and less efficient means of developing statewide organizations. In Montana, bank holding companies not domiciled in the state are precluded from further bank acquisitions.

There are a number of reasons favoring statewide branch banking as a public benefit. The first is the collection of large pools of capital. Large banks can attract new industries and support business enterprises far beyond the scope of unit banks. This is especially true in areas of low population density such as the Northwest.

Another advantage of statewide banking is diversification of risks. A rural bank with predominantly agricultural loans may be pressed when crop failures occur. Likewise, a unit bank in Seattle could have a serious problem when a major manufacturer such as Boeing institutes a major cutback. In these cases, diversity of the bank's loans, deposits, and general economic base resulting from a statewide system is a welcome quality.

As with most things, there is a contrary opinion to that we have expressed on statewide banking. Those favoring unit banks state these points: (1) top management and decision making is far removed from the branch bank; (2) small independent banks are more interested in local trade than large commercial banks; (3) the number of banks decrease where branch banking is permitted; and (4) competition is reduced where large banks control most of the branches. The authors do not necessarily "buy" these and similar arguments but the reader can determine his own opinion.

Of the 18 commercial banking organizations discussed in this chapter, 10 are organized under holding companies. Each of the holding companies owns one or more banks, and may also own one or more non-banking subsidiaries. Most of the non-banking subsidiaries engage in related functions such as mortgage and lease financing. In all cases except Orbanco, the non-banking subsidiaries contribute less than 20% of the holding company's revenue and earnings, although the relative contribution of the non-banking subsidiaries is growing in most cases.

The reader can readily identify which are holding companies and which are not by the company name. Federal law prohibits the word "Bank" from appearing in the title of a holding company. The result is that the eight banking organizations discussed in the chapter **not** organized as holding companies have the word "Bank" in their titles, and the others do not.

We have not included any Alaska banks in this study, because, although most are publicly owned, a limited number of shares is available for public trading, and active trading markets in their stocks have not yet developed. There are also many other small banking organizations in the Northwest that are either privately owned or publicly owned but without an active trading market.

We also have not included Northwest banks that are subsidiaries of holding companies headquartered elsewhere. For example, **Western Bancorporation,** a holding company headquartered in Los Angeles, owns *Pacific National Bank of Washington, First National Bank of Oregon, the Bank of Idaho, Walker Bank & Trust Company* in Utah, and several unit banks in Montana and Wyoming. However, WBC's **United California Bank** is larger than all their Northwest/Intermountain operations put together. *The Bank of California,* with offices in Seattle and Portland, is headquartered in San Francisco, one of the very few banks operating across state lines under a "grandfather clause" allowing continuance of operations in existence prior to Federal prohibition of interstate banks. The holding company that owns Bank of California is called **BanCal Tri-State Corp.,** reflecting its three-state operation.

The following sections discuss the Northwest/Intermountain headquartered commercial banks and bank holding companies, starting with Washington, then moving to Oregon, and finishing up with the Intermountain states.

Washington Banks

The largest bank holding company in the Northwest is **Seafirst Corporation**, a one-bank holding company which owns the *Seattle-First National Bank*. The holding company was established in June, 1974.

Based upon total deposits as of year-end 1974, Seafirst was the 20th largest bank in the United States. Measured against the Keefe Bank Index (a composite record of the nation's 24 largest banks), Seafirst was above average both in growth of income and return on shareholder's equity.

Seafirst operates a statewide network of 149 branch banks. In addition, the bank operates automated "Firstbank Cash Machines". Introduced in 1971, there are now 95 such facilities operating 24 hours a

NORTHWEST BANKING ORGANIZATIONS
1974 Operating Summary

	Total Revenue (000)	Net Operating*** Income (000)	Return on Equity	Return on Total Assets
Bancorporation of Montana	$ 11,675	$ 1,138	11.9%	.75%
Bank of the West	9,959	288	5.0	.25
Citizens Bank of Oregon	6,534	737	15.3	.84
Citizens Valley Bank	5,196	649	12.9	.91
First Security Corporation	149,114	18,197	14.9	1.04
First State Bank of Oregon	11,309	1,277	13.6	.90
Idaho First National Bank	69,518	9,698	17.2	1.05
Orbanco, Inc.	48,751*	2,881*	11.1	.61
Peoples National Bank	59,652	3,325	8.3	.43
Puget Sound National Bank	26,827	2,633	15.3	.78
Rainier Bancorporation	214,233	13,932	11.4	.56
Seafirst Corp.	375,765	29,350**	14.8	.68
Seattle Trust & Savings Bank	23,223	1,339	10.9	.48
U.S. Bancorp	207,337	23,174	15.8	.82
Utah Bancorporation	13,748	1,311	16.3	.87
Washington Bancshares	43,725	4,192	10.3	.72
Wyoming Bancorporation	23,456	2,414	12.4	.91
Wyoming National Corporation	11,026	1,424	15.3	.94

*Includes non-bank subsidiaries
**Before extraordinary loss
***Net Operating income as shown is after securities gains and losses.
NOTE: Return on Equity and Return on Assets calculated on average of beginning and year-end figures.

Loan Portfolios—Year-End 1974

	Commercial Loans (000)	%	Consumer Loans (000)	%	Real Estate and Other (000)	%	Total (000)
Bancorporation of Montana	$ 20,640	24.6	$ 9,842	23.7	$ 43,290	51.7	$ 83,773
Citizens Valley Bank	22,007	61.7	7,363	20.6	6,316	17.7	35,686
First Security Corporation	387,544	36.0	269,958	25.0	414,302	39.0	1,071,804
Idaho First National Bank	217,253	38.0	189,447	33.2	164,234	28.8	570,934
The Oregon Bank	102,645	53.2	49,011	25.4	41,179	21.4	192,835
Puget Sound National Bank***	75,561	35.8	61,323	29.1	74,075	35.1	210,959
Rainier National Bank***	482,006	37.9	232,690	18.3	556,730	43.8	1,271,426
Seafirst Corp.	1,570,716	61.3	452,506*	17.6	541,410**	21.1	2,564,631
Seattle Trust & Savings Bank	82,484	54.0	32,359	21.1	38,023	24.9	152,867
U.S. Bancorp	971,778	58.6	292,417	17.6	395,049	23.8	1,659,244
Washington Bancshares	161,742	47.2	76,975	22.5	103,720	30.3	342,437
Wyoming Bancorporation	47,013	29.3	45,549	28.4	67,805	42.3	160,368

*And other loans
**Real Estate Only
***Average Daily Balances

Annual Reports of the following banks did not disclose the breakdown of their loan portfolios: Bank of the West, Citizens Bank of Oregon, First State Bank of Oregon, Peoples National Bank, Utah Bancorporation, Wyoming National Corporation.

day, seven days a week. Some 250,000 "Trans Action Cards" to operate the machines have been issued. Through the use of computers, this opens the era of paperless bank transactions.

SUMMARY OF 18 NORTHWEST BANKING ORGANIZATIONS
as of December 31, 1974

	Total Assets (000)	Deposits (000)	Loans (000)	Investment Portfolio (000)	Loan Deposit Ratio	Capital Equity Capital to Total Assets	Ratios Equity Capital to Loans
Seafirst Corp.	$4,624,900	$3,430,462	$2,564,631	$533,147	74.7%	.043	.078
U.S. Bancorp	2,902,990	2,156,134	1,659,244	504,155	76.9	.053	.093
Rainier Bancorporation	2,623,600	2,078,479	1,504,287	324,991	72.4	.049	.085
First Security Corporation	1,825,200	1,534,018	1,071,804	282,467	69.8	.070	.119
Idaho First National Bank	984,200	869,088	570,934	263,303	65.7	.062	.108
Peoples National Bank	815,800	615,431	396,842	120,914	64.5	.050	.102
Washington Bancshares	631,900	541,166	342,437	156,882	63.3	.066	.122
Orbanco, Inc.	520,000	273,063*	191,886*	93,089	70.3*	.053	.080
Puget Sound National Bank	358,600	301,764	220,092	59,001	72.9	.050	.082
Seattle Trust & Savings Bank	294,200	228,586	152,867	44,389	66.8	.043	.083
Wyoming Bancorporation	277,100	213,823	160,368	71,890	70.0	.072	.125
Wyoming National Corporation	165,400	138,826	74,340	61,685	53.5	.059	.131
Utah Bancorporation	162,400	133,415	95,044	31,759	71.2	.052	.089
Bancorporation of Montana	159,400	136,704	83,773	46,432	61.3	.061	.116
First State Bank of Oregon	147,000**	130,974	95,266	31,455	72.7	.068	.104
Bank of the West	117,000	98,324	70,149	15,254	71.3	.050	.083
Citizens Bank of Oregon	91,000	82,268	52,268	26,645	63.5	.055	.096
Citizens Valley Bank	73,600	66,222	35,461	24,701	53.5	.071	.148

*Includes Oregon Bank only
**Does not include 1975 merger

Bank Securities Portfolios—Year-end 1974
(at stated book value)

	U.S. Govt. Obligations (000)	%	State and Municipal Bonds (000)	%	Obligations of Federal Agencies (000)	%	Other Bonds and Securities (000)	%	Total (000)
Bancorporation of Montana	$ 23,407	50.4	$ 15,339	33.0	$ 7,686*	16.6	$ —	—	$ 46,432
Bank of the West	3,938	25.8	10,456	68.6	704	4.6	155	1.0	15,254
Citizens Bank of Oregon	5,639	21.2	15,583	58.5	—	—	5,423	20.3	26,645
Citizens Valley Bank	5,772	23.4	13,392	54.2	5,197	21.0	340	1.4	24,701
First Security Corporation	100,018	35.0	130,568	47.0	31,590	11.0	20,290	7.0	282,467
First State Bank of Oregon	4,559	14.5	22,187	70.5	4,585	14.6	123	.4	31,455
Idaho First National Bank	43,077	16.4	173,604	65.9	40,130	15.2	6,492	2.5	263,303
The Oregon Bank	12,463	13.4	67,878	72.9	—	—	12,748	13.7	93,089
Peoples National Bank	36,108	29.8	45,688	37.8	38,167	31.6	950	.8	120,914
Puget Sound National Bank	16,456	27.9	35,883	60.8	6,205	10.5	457	.8	59,001
Rainier Bancorporation	109,561**	33.7	204,685	63.0	—	—	10,745	3.3	324,991
Seafirst Corp	114,251	21.4	340,674	63.9	33,987	6.4	44,235	8.3	533,147
Seattle Trust & Savings Bank	8,184	18.4	19,791	44.6	16,072	36.2	342	.8	44,389
U.S. Bancorp	71,663	14.0	404,757	80.0	23,514	5.0	4,211	1.0	504,156
Utah Bancorporation	7,136	22.5	19,477	61.3	5,090	16.0	56	.2	31,759
Washington Bancshares	64,764	41.3	91,509	58.3	—	—	609	.4	156,882
Wyoming Bancorporation	10,716	14.9	53,950	75.0	6,806	9.5	418	.6	71,890
Wyoming National Corporation	6,325	10.3	28,034	45.4	18,718	30.3	8,608	14.0	61,685

* Plus Other
**And Agencies

SEAFIRST CORPORATION

SEATTLE·FIRST NATIONAL BANK

RAINIER
BANCORPORATION

RAINIERBANK

 PEOPLES NATIONAL BANK
OF WASHINGTON

Washington Bancshares, Inc.

OLD NATIONAL BANK OF WASHINGTON

FIRST NATIONAL BANK IN SPOKANE

 WBI

Puget Sound National Bank

Bank of the West

 **Seattle Trust**
SEATTLE TRUST & SAVINGS BANK EST. 1905

Seven publicly held Northwest commercial banking companies are headquartered in the State of Washington.

In 1974, Seafirst was the victim of a strange and highly unusual foreign transaction. On June 24, 1974, in a foreign currency exchange "spot" transaction, the bank's Swiss subsidiary sold 57,433,000 deutschemarks to *Bankhaus I.D. Herstatt* for 22.5 million U.S. dollars. In accordance with the well-established procedure for spot transactions, delivery was to occur on June 26, 1974. Delivery of the deutschemarks was to be made in Germany and delivery of the dollars to be made in New York City.

Heretofore, it had been assumed that a spot transaction, being virtually a simultaneous swap, entailed no risk. After delivery of the deutschemarks to Herstatt but before delivery of the dollars in New York, the banking license of Herstatt was revoked by the *Bundesaufsichtsamt*, the highest German banking agency. Upon learning that the license had been revoked, Herstatt's New York correspondent, *Chase Manhattan*, refused to make the required payment, even though sufficient funds were on hand for that purpose.

When it came time to close the books at the end of 1974, before all the dust surrounding the transaction had settled, Seafirst recorded an extraordinary loss of $11.7 million dollars on this item. This included the $22.5 million loss, plus related legal and court costs, less tax credits. Fortunately, the story has a happier ending. In the first half of 1975, after concerted legal actions, $19.4 million of the original sum was recovered.

It is important to emphasize that this widely publicized event was *not* a speculation in foreign currency, as many people, who do not understand, believe it to be. Furthermore, as a result of the incident, Seafirst and other banks conducting foreign exchange transactions have instituted new procedures to avoid any future recurrence of such an event.

Seafirst is the only Northwest bank holding company at this writing that has an investment management subsidiary, *Seafirst Investment Advisors*, separate from its trust department. Many of the functions that are carried on by other bank holding companies' non-bank subsidiaries are not separated at Seafirst, but undertaken directly by the Seattle-First National Bank.

Over the past five years, Seafirst has shown the following compound growth rates: 9.0% in income, 16.1% in total assets, 14.1% in total deposits, and 14.3% in loans.

Rainier Bancorporation, formerly *Marine Bancorporation,* was formed in 1927 as the first one-bank holding company in the Pacific Northwest. *Rainier National Bank, Rainier Mortgage Company,* and *Rainier Credit Company,* its three wholly-owned subsidiaries, offer a full spectrum of financial services to the people of Washington and neighboring states.

Prior to 1974, the holding company and its wholly-owned subsidiaries all had different names which was confusing to the general public because there was no common corporate identity. Late in 1974, Marine Bancorporation became Rainier Bancorporation, The National Bank of Commerce of Seattle became Rainier National Bank, Coast Mortgage Company became Rainier Mortgage Company and Commerce Credit Company became Rainier Credit Company in order to alleviate the identity problem.

Rainier National Bank, the principal subsidiary, was founded in 1889. During 1975 the Bank became the 41st largest bank in the United States in terms of deposits. With 119 offices in Washington, it is the second largest bank in the state and fourth largest in the Pacific Northwest.

The bank plays an important role in the region's trade with the nations of the Pacific Rim. International banking services to customers are provided through the International Division in Seattle, branch offices in Tokyo and London, a representative office in Singapore and Edge Act subsidiaries in New York and Los Angeles. In addition, the Los Angeles Edge Act subsidiary maintains six full service branches in

Hong Kong where the bank is one of only four American banks that can legally maintain branches in the Colony.

Rainier Mortgage Company is the largest locally-owned mortgage banking firm in the Pacific Northwest with 17 offices in Washington, Oregon, Hawaii, and Alaska. It operates in the latter state as Coast Mortgage Co.

Rainier Credit Company offers consumer and second-mortgage lending services through 19 offices located in northern California, Oregon, Idaho, and Washington. In contrast to finance company subsidiaries of many bank holding companies, Rainier Credit was formed de novo in 1972. During 1974 twelve new offices were opened.

Rainier Bancorporation also has a partially-owned (49.9%) subsidiary, Cascade Capital Corporation, which it owns jointly with U.S. Bancorp of Portland. Cascade Capital is a Small Business Investment Company which provides venture capital and management services for small businesses.

In August of 1973, G. Robert Truex, Jr. joined Rainier Bancorporation, from the *Bank of America*, as president and chief executive officer. Under his leadership, the management structure of the holding company and the subsidiaries has been substantially modified for the purposes of better communication, better accountability, and better profitability. Domestic and international operations have been regionalized; a Corporate Banking Division was formed to provide better services to the bank's corporate clients; and an automated general ledger system and other cost-saving systems have been installed.

In addition to reorganizing the corporate structure, Mr. Truex's arrival has also brought a greater management emphasis on profitability. Management's concentration on improving interest spreads, increasing fee income, and holding the line on costs has made for a dramatic improvement in consolidated return on assets and return on equity during the past two years. This has also resulted in consolidated equity being able to grow at a faster rate than consolidated assets in 1975.

Rainier Bancorporation is well positioned to meet the future financial needs of the Pacific Northwest. The good geographic coverage of the various subsidiaries' offices, the improved management system, the development of greater professional expertise, and the improved profitability all point towards Rainier Bancorporation becoming one of the best managed bank holding companies in the Pacific Northwest.

Peoples National Bank of Washington is based in Seattle and operates a total of 58 offices. The bank's modern 20-story main office building was opened in 1974.

In addition to its banking function, the bank owns the *Peoples Mortgage Company*. Peoples Mortgage produced $47.7 million in new mortgage loans in 1974, making it the second largest such lending institution in Seattle. The mortgage company has loan production offices in Denver and Phoenix in addition to those located in Western

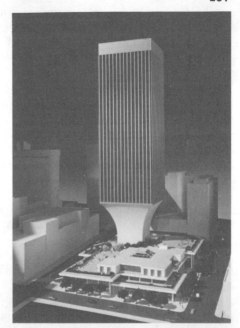

At right is a model of the 42-story Rainier Bank Tower under construction in downtown Seattle. The Tower at Rainier Square, which will be ready for occupancy in late 1976 or early 1977, symbolizes the dramatic growth of Rainier Bancorporation from its founding 86 years ago by the Spencer brothers pictured below.

Washington. The subsidiary is now servicing a total of $391 million in mortgage loans.

In 1972 another wholly-owned subsidiary, *Peoples Leasing Company*, was established to provide equipment and vehicle leasing in the Seattle area. Auto leases in 1974 more than doubled over the previous year. Peoples Leasing services about 75 auto dealers with more than $7 million in lease contracts outstanding. In the field of capital goods financing, Peoples Leasing has some $10.5 million outstanding in equipment receivables.

1975 marks the 70th year of operation of the **Seattle Trust and Savings Bank**. Seattle Trust is a full service commercial bank. Over one-half of its loans are commercial and a substantial portion of the bank's real estate loans also involve commercial property.

One new branch office, prepared in 1974, opened for business on January 2, 1975. The bank operates 25 offices in the Seattle-Tacoma area.

Over the past five years, annual revenue increased from $12.8 million to $23.2 million, while income grew from $1 million to $1.3 million.

Tacoma-based **Puget Sound National Bank** operates 33 branches and did not add any new ones in 1974. However, plans to open two new branches in 1975 were announced. The growing Port of Tacoma offers expanding export and international banking opportunities to the area. Puget Sound Bank's International department tripled its net income in 1973, and doubled it again in 1974. Puget Sound's total assets of $358.6 million at 1974 year-end represented a 14.3% increase over the previous year.

The largest banking system in Washington State not based in the Seattle area is **Washington Bancshares, Inc.,** headquartered in Spokane, a bank holding company dating back to 1929.

The corporation has five operating subsidiaries: the 60-branch *Old National Bank of Washington* headquartered in Spokane, the 6-branch *First National Bank of Spokane, Bancshares Mortgage Company, Union Securities Company* and *Old National Leasing Company.*

Union Securities and Old National Leasing are relatively new subsidiaries, organized in 1974. The leasing company is engaged in equipment leasing of all types and has offices in Spokane and Seattle. Union Securities sells a line of credit life, accident, health, and disability insurance to banking customers. The company contributed a modest profit in 1974.

Serving a primarily agricultural area, the Old National provided financing for 74 different agricultural crops in 1974. This ranked the Old National as the 20th largest commercial bank nationally in terms of agricultural lending.

Control of the original founders of Washington Bancshares passed to the present management group in 1968, and now less than 35% of the corporation's stock is closely held. Chairman and President David A. Clack explained to us that the system is working on a definitive five year program to raise WBI's return on capital to 12%, as well as to achieve a 12% annual earnings growth.

In 1974, Washington Bancshares purchased the *Guaranty National Bank,* adding three branches to the Old National Bank's system south of Seattle. Three new retail branches were also opened by the Old National. The banks, at year-end 1974, operated a total of 66 branches, predominantly in Eastern Washington.

The ultimate goal is to expand Westward, building a statewide banking system. At this writing, Bellevue-based **Bank of the West,** with 16 branches in the Puget Sound and Longview-Kelso areas of Washington, is in the process of being acquired by the Old National

Bank under an agreement approved by both companies' boards of directors, but still subject to the approval of shareholders at this writing. The addition of the Bank of the West operations, if completed, will give Old National 27 branches west of the Cascades.

Oregon Banks

U.S. Bancorp, a one bank holding company organized at year-end, 1968, has achieved a five-year compound annual growth rate in earnings per share of 13.3% which compares to that of the Keefe Bank Index of 8.6%

U.S. Bancorp is organized along function and product lines and has the following subsidiaries: *U.S. National Bank of Oregon,* the 54-year-old commercial bank with 140 offices throughout Oregon, provides a full spectrum of commercial banking and trust services. The bank also has two overseas offices. *Bancorp Leasing, Inc.* offers finance leasing on most types of business and industrial equipment; *Bancorp Management Advisers, Inc.* is the firm employed by *US BanTrust* to manage its affairs; *Cascade Capital Corporation* is a Small Business Investment Company owned 49.9% by U.S. Bancorp and 49.9% by *Rainier Bancorporation,* which provides venture capital to promising companies with an established "track record" of performance; *Commerce Mortgage Company* is a mortgage lending firm principally engaged in the orginization, sale and servicing of loans on residential, commercial and industrial properties; *U.S. Datacorp* provides commercial data processing services, including computer output microfilm, through 24 offices nationwide and, in a joint venture with *National Westminister Bank* in the United Kingdom, through offices in England, Germany and Sweden.

U.S. Bancorp's primary market objective is to increase its market share by offering quality services and products directed to the satisfaction of consumer wants and needs. Bancorp claims a number of firsts in Oregon. For example, U.S. National Bank was the first bank to install a statewide network of automated teller machines. It was the first to install a free standing teller machine. According to Chairman John A. Elorriaga, the bank also pioneered in establishing mini-branches open for limited hours to serve smaller communities. At year-end 1974, U.S. National Bank's Oregon deposit market share was approximately 34%.

For 1974, U.S. Bancorp's average total assets increased 8.8%, which approximates the rate of its five-year compound annual growth rate in average assets. Average assets per employee increased from $592,663 to $617,526 or 4.2% with about 4,700 employees.

U.S. Bancorp achieved a 15.8% return on average stockholders' equity in 1974 up from 14.7% in 1973. At year-end 1974, stockholders' equity totalled $153 million up 9.9% from $140 million at year-end 1973. The compound annual growth rate in book value per share for the last five years is 7.5%.

Average deposits at U.S. National Bank increased by 5.8% in 1974, compared with the bank's five year compound annual growth in deposits of 7%. Deposits per branch averaged about $15.3 million (134 offices) versus about $14.9 million in 1973 (130 offices). Loans outstanding in 1974 increased 9.6%.

The bank's net loan-to-deposit ratio at year-end 1974 was 68.8%, adjusted from a gross ratio of 74.2% to exclude money market assets and to relate domestic portfolio loans to domestic deposits.

On June 24, 1975, U.S. Bancorp issued $20,000,000 in 8% convertible subordinated debentures which mature on July 1, 1985. The purpose of the offering was to provide Bancorp with additional longer term funds so that its present and future fundings of subsidiaries and additional banking related activities would be supported by a more permanent capital base. The additional capital strength, brought to the balance sheet by the offering, soundly positioned Bancorp to participate fully in the Northwest's economy and to assist customers with their financial needs.

For the nine months ended September 30, 1975 net income was $18,039,000 up from $17,603,000 for the same period last year. Loans and discounts were $1,713,926,000 up 7.8%. Deposits were up 5.4% to $2,206,101,000.. Assets increased 10.3% to $2,900,420,000. Shareholders' equity was $165,937,000 as of September 30, 1975. Average assets for the nine months were $2,666,000. The ratio of equity to assets was 5.7% and to average assets, 6.0%. The ratio of equity to loans was 9.7%.

Orbanco, Inc., based in Portland, is a holding company with two primary subsidiaries. These are *The Oregon Bank* and *Northwest Acceptance Corporation.* Since formation of the holding company in 1969, each subsidiary has contributed roughly half of the parent's total earnings, although the relative contribution varies considerably from year to year.

Northwest Acceptance is a capital goods financing business. It finances heavy equipment such as construction, logging, oil drilling, and mining equipment, barges, truck trailers and helicopters. The company has been a major factor in financing logging equipment for the many smaller companies that are a very important part of the Northwest's forest products industry. Northwest Acceptance serves a broad area of fifteen states from Alaska to Texas, as well as Alberta, British Columbia, and the Yukon Territory in Canada. Northwest's ten offices have expanded loan volume from $44 million in 1969 to $145 million in 1974.

The Oregon Bank, with $273 million in deposits (year-end 1974) is the third largest banking system in Oregon. However, it is well behind *The First National Bank of Oregon* and *U.S. National Bank of Oregon,* both having deposits in excess of $2 billion each.

In 1974, Orbanco began acquiring the stock of *Security Bank of Oregon,* with eight branches in the Portland area. By early 1975, Orbanco owned 90% of Security's common shares. Following a bitter and acrimonious struggle, the two banks were merged on July 8, 1975.

The Oregon Bank now operates a total of 35 branches, of which 22

United States National Bank of Oregon

Five of the Northwest's major banking companies are headquartered in Oregon.

are in the Portland area. Over the past five years, Orbanco's total assets have increased from $218.6 million to $520 million. Meanwhile, net income grew from $1.9 million to $2.9 million.

Tracing its origin back to 1909, the **First State Bank of Oregon** was known as the *First State Bank of Milwaukie* until 1964. Following a series of mergers, First State is now the largest banking system in Oregon not headquartered in Portland. Its headquarters remain in Milwaukie, Oregon, and most of its branches are in the suburban areas surrounding Portland.

In August, 1975, First State Bank completed a merger with Portland's *Great Western National Bank,* bringing the combined organization to a total of 24 offices in the greater Portland area. Following this merger, First State has total assets of $209 million and total deposits of $185 million.

In the 10-year period from 1964 to 1974, First State's total assets increased from $40.8 million to $147.2 million. Total deposits grew from $37.5 million to $131 million. Net income in this same period advanced from $331,046 to $1,277,275.

Citizens Bank of Oregon is based in Eugene, Oregon. The bank operates ten offices. Seven are in Eugene and one each in Springfield, Veneta, and Harrisburg. A new 10 story headquarters and main office was opened in downtown Eugene in 1974.

Since 1965, deposits have increased from $22.2 million to $82.3

million. Total assets have climbed from $24.8 million to $91 million and capital funds have grown from $1.7 million to $5 million. As we go to press, the boards of directors of Citizens Bank of Oregon and **Western Bank** have agreed to merge the two banks, with the name of the combined operation to be **United Western Bank.** Western Bank, headquartered at Coos Bay, had 22 branches and $177.8 million in total assets at year-end 1974, which will make the combined operation the fourth largest bank in Oregon. The new headquarters will be at 975 Oak Street, Eugene.

Headquartered in Albany, Oregon, the **Citizens Valley Bank** serves a portion of the mid-Willamette River Valley with a population of approximately 75,000. Farming is one of the area's major economic activities.

Citizens Valley operates nine branch offices in eight communities, the largest being Albany. A new branch office in Albany (the bank's third) is scheduled to open in late 1975. The bank established its own trust department in 1973.

Citizens Valley has completed an application to form a bank holding company to be known as **Citizens Bancorp.** When approved, the bank and another corporation, *Citizens Development Company* will become subsidiaries. Citizens Development is a real estate enterprise with about $500,000 in net worth. Citizens Valley has total assets of $73.6 million. The holding company structure will allow the company to acquire other unit banks in Oregon.

Intermountain Banks

With 64 offices in the state, the **Idaho First National Bank** is the largest bank in Idaho and very much dependent upon its economy. Idaho's biggest industry is agriculture, but the general economy is well diversified.

Northern Idaho's Coeur d'Alene area is the nation's largest and one of the world's largest silver production areas. It is also noted for the production of copper, lead, zinc, molybdenum, antimony, and gold. Forest products and tourism are also important.

Southern Idaho is a busy commercial center. Boise, the capital, is headquarters for *Boise Cascade, Morrison-Knudsen,* and *Albertson's,* as well as many local and regional companies.

The Idaho First National is now 108 years old. Based on total deposits, it is the 107th largest bank in the United States. Idaho First is the fifth largest banking organization headquartered in the Northwest/Intermountain area, and the largest that has not adopted the holding company form of organization.

Over the past ten years, the Idaho First National Bank has set new highs each year in every important banking category. This includes total assets, total deposits, loans, capital funds, and net income. Since 1970 (year-end), operating revenue has increased from $36.3 million to $69.5 million. In the same five-year period, annual net income rose from

United States National Bank of Oregon has more than 140 branch offices throughout Oregon. Some are historic in nature. Many are spacious and modern in design using Northwest materials. Many even offer 24 hour banking with U-Bank teller facilities (top right). But U.S. Bank management emphasis is now on smaller offices, tailored to the individual community or neighborhood. Their Cannon Beach office (bottom right) on Oregon's North Coast is a prime example. It was the town's first bank, offering most of the firm's services with hours of operation tailored to local consumer needs. This "salt box" building seems nearly transplanted from the New England coast, but fits perfectly into Cannon Beach's tourist and artist colony setting.

$6.6 million to $9.7 million. Idaho First has done an outstanding job of aggressively achieving a high growth rate while maintaining a very conservative posture with a relatively low loan-to-deposit ratio, very few loan losses, and a very short maturity structure in its investment portfolio.

Idaho First also has a large trust department operation, and management estimates that Idaho First manages over two-thirds of all trust assets in the state.

UTAH BANKING FIRMS GROWTH-ORIENTED

Under decades-old Utah banking law, a bank cannot open a new branch in any city (except Salt Lake) which is already headquarters for another bank. However, there are no such restrictions against opening a new bank that is not a branch of any existing bank.

In the last ten years most Utah banks have organized themselves as bank holding companies, whereby a holding company can own one or

First Security Corporation

Idaho First National Bank

**WYOMING
BANCORPORATION**

Utah Bancorporation

**WYOMING
NATIONAL
CORPORATION**

**BANCORPORATION
OF
MONTANA**

**BANK OF MONTANA
SYSTEM**
BANCORPORATION OF MONTANA
AND ITS AFFILIATES

Six Intermountain banks are located in Utah, Idaho, Montana, and Wyoming.

more banks as well as other subsidiaries. Under this organization, if a bank wants to be in an area where it is prohibited from opening a branch, its holding company merely forms a totally new bank for that area, referred to in the trade as a "de novo" bank opening.

This is more costly to begin and less efficient to operate than a simple state-wide branch banking system, but it meets the requirements of an outdated law. Needless to say, we would hope the Utah legislature will eventually update the law to better serve current conditions.

In spite of this outmoded legal restriction, the rapidly-growing Utah economy is an excellent environment for growth-oriented banking organizations. This book contains background articles on two such organizations, Utah's largest, *First Security Corp.*, and an aggressive smaller group, *Utah Bancorporation.*

First Security Corp. is by far the largest banking organization in the Intermountain area, dominating the Utah market, second in size in Idaho, and owning one Wyoming bank in Rock Springs. It is the 66th largest bank holding company in the United States, with 129 banking offices in 103 communities spread over an area the size of California, but serving a population of only about 2 million. Approximately 8% of net operating earnings in the past two years were provided by non-banking subsidiaries.

Prominent domestic and international banker George S. Eccles, one of the original organizers and President and Chief Executive Officer since 1945, became Chairman and Chief Executive Officer in 1975, succeeding his older brother, Marriner S. Eccles. The post of president was filled by their nephew, Spencer F. Eccles, 40, Executive Vice President since 1973.

As a fairly mature banking organization, well represented in all major economic areas of its service region and holding over 30% of the total commercial bank deposits in Utah and Idaho, First Security has slowed down on opening new banking offices, and would be restricted by anti-trust laws in most cases from acquiring existing banking offices.

In addition to the banks' own $414 million real estate loan portfolio, the banks and other subsidiaries serviced $403 million of real estate loans for others at year-end. *Utah Mortgage Loan Corp.* was founded in 1898 and acquired by First Security in 1968, one of the first acquisitions of a mortgage company by a banking holding company. With offices in Logan, Salt Lake City, Boise, Idaho Falls, Denver, Albuquerque, and Phoenix, Utah Mortgage Loan Corp. handles real estate construction loans of all kinds and sells them in the secondary market, bringing new investment funds into the area.

First Security's most recent acquisition, in August 1975, Portland-based *Securities Intermountain,* can be described as a "correspondent-type lender." They originate and service mortgages for about 40 lenders, mostly eastern and midwestern institutions such as life insurance companies and pension funds. Offices are located in Portland, Seattle, Bellevue, Spokane, Palo Alto and San Diego. They presently service a mortgage loan portfolio of about $200 million, which will put First Security's total portfolio of loans serviced over $1 billion.

First Security Insurance, Inc. engages in a full-line general insurance agency business. *First Security Life Insurance Co.* of Texas has been in business for many years as a reinsurance company for credit life originating through the banks' consumer credit and mortgage loan departments. It has over $60 million insurance in force covering over 33,000 borrowers.

First Security Savings and Loan is headquartered in Pocatello, with assets of about $47 million. It has not yet been determined whether First Security will be allowed to retain the savings and loan under current bank holding company legislation. The company at present is in the process of making application to the *Federal Reserve Board* to retain the subsidiary.

First Security Leasing Company was started in 1972 and by spring of 1975 had leases covering equipment with an original cost of $179 million, including substantial amounts of railroad rolling stock, oil tankers and oil barges, trucks, and other miscellaneous types of leases.

Utah Bancorporation, a state-chartered multi-bank holding company, owns the 15-branch *Valley Bank and Trust Co.,* in Salt Lake, the *Weber Valley Bank* in Ogden, and the *Bountiful Valley Bank* in Bountiful. The bank was originally founded in 1948, and the holding company became operational in 1973. Weber Valley and Bountiful Valley were opened in 1975. Valley State Bank was the first new bank to be organized in Salt Lake City and Salt Lake County (1948) in more than fifty years where a previous bank or bank charter was not involved.

Valley Mortgage Corp., formed in 1973, originates and services residential and some commercial mortgages. They sell the mortgages to other financial institutions, with a few going into the bank's portfolio. Subsidiary *Intermountain Loan Corporation* has capital available for loans to Valley customers out of state. They also intend to get into lease financing when the availability and cost of money make it attractive. The bank has operated a trust department since 1966, and offers a full range of trust services.

Headquartered at Great Falls, **Bancorporation of Montana** is the largest multi-bank holding company domiciled in Montana, but not the largest banking organization operating there. Two much larger bank holding companies operate in Montana, *First Bank System* and *Northwest Bancorp,* but both are domiciled in Minnesota, and Montana revenue is a small part of their total operations.

Current Montana laws prevent out-of-state concerns from making new banking acquisitions. Thus, Bancorporation of Montana is unique in being able to negotiate acquisitions with limited competition. This is important, because Montana does not allow branch banking. Thus,

The demonstrator van above is used to show new automated teller facilities being installed in Bancorporation of Montana's affiliated banks. A Bank-Around-The-Clock instrument panel gives interested passersby a preview of the new 24-hour service.

growth can only come by acquisitions or opening new banks from scratch ("de novo").

Bancorporation's subsidiary banks are small and rural, primarily serving the agricultural industries. The corporation operates twelve banks in eleven Montana communities. The largest is the *Citizens Bank* in Havre, with total deposits of $27.6 million.

Bancorporation has announced an agreement to acquire the *First State Bank,* Thompson Falls, Montana although this may not be accomplished until 1976. A new charter application has been made for a bank in Lewistown, Montana. Management has also announced its intention to acquire the *Bank of Montana* in Helena, although the timing of this action has been deferred.

Wyoming Bancorporation, with headquarters in Cheyenne, is a five-year-old multi-bank holding company, the largest banking organization in Wyoming. Wybanco operates seventeen subsidiary banks throughout the state. This includes *The First National Bank of Kemmerer,* which was acquired in early 1975. The largest single bank in the system is the *Cheyenne National.* The Wyoming Bancorporation system is now positioned to offer service in more than 80% of the state's trade area.

Wybanco presently has a charter application pending for one additional bank in Gillette.

Wyoming National Corporation is based in Casper. Wyoming National's principal property is the *Wyoming National Bank of Casper,* which is the largest unit bank in the state. This was the corporation's only bank until October, 1974, when they established a new bank, the *Wyoming National Bank of Gillette.*

The Wyoming National organization places primary emphasis on retail customer-oriented services. The operating record for 1974 (almost entirely in the Casper bank) produced new highs in deposits, loans, assets, and earnings for the corporation.

The holding company was established as such in August 1970. In the 1971-1974 period, annual operating revenue increased from $5.2 million to $11 million. At the same time, net income grew from $765,566 to $1.4 million.

Both Wyoming bank firms are anticipating continued growth in the future. One reason is the state's strong position in national resources, vitally needed by the nation.

Home office of Equitable Savings & Loan Association

19

Non-Bank Financial Companies

Headquartered in Portland, **Equitable Savings & Loan Association** is the oldest and largest capital stock savings and loan association in the Northwest. Nationally, the *U.S. League of Savings Associations* ranks Equitable 41st in size of assets and savings among some 5,200 institutions.

Equitable is unique in the savings and loan industry and a unique institution in the Northwest in that it is allowed to operate branch offices in three Northwest states. A venerable firm, Equitable has been in business continuously since 1890, and precedes the restrictions which limit other savings and loan companies to operations in a single state. The association presently operates a total of 40 offices in Oregon, Idaho, and Washington. There are 27 branches in Oregon, 6 in Washington, and 7 in Idaho, as of mid-1975.

The accompanying tables emphasize the regional presence of Equitable Savings with respect to both savings deposits and loan disbursements. Also shown is the fact that Equitable's management has been more aggressive and more successful in attracting deposits in the last four years than the industry as a whole.

The geneology of Equitable Savings has a curious quirk. The company's shares were publicly traded in the over-the-counter market for many years until July of 1969. At that time about 98% of the shares were acquired by the *GAC Corporation,* and the stock's public market ceased to exist. However, on December 21, 1971, GAC disposed of all of its Equitable shares in a public offering (at a presently adjusted price of $13.50 per share).

Equitable's primary business is the making of residential mortgage loans, construction loans, and other loans on real property. A major wholly owned subsidiary is *Sherwood & Roberts, Inc.* which has been conducting business in the Northwest since 1932. Sherwood & Roberts

Equitable Savings and Loan Association

Business by location (000)

Location	Dec. 31 1974 % Savings	% of Total	1974 Net Gain Savings	% of Total
Oregon	$429,000	77.2%	$30,000	83.3%
Washington	74,000	13.3	1,000	2.8
Idaho	44,000	7.9	4,000	11.1
Other States	9,000	1.6	1,000	2.8
Total	$556,000	100.00%	$36,000	100.0%

	Dec. 31 1974 Real Estate Loans	% of Total	1974 New Real Estate Loans	% of Total
Oregon	$335,000	59.4%	$65,000	61.3%
Washington	154,000	27.4	18,000	17.0
Idaho	42,000	7.5	6,000	5.7
Other States	32,000	5.7	17,000	16.0
Total	$563,000*	100.0%	$106,000	100.00%

*Excluding $24.6 million in mortgage-backed securities.

Savings gains vs. total savings & loan industry gains
As % of January 1st balances each year

	Equitable	Industry		Equitable	industry
1967	9.3%	9.2%	1971	26.9%	19.0%
1968	6.8%	5.7%	1972	25.2%	18.7%
1969	3.6%	3.0%	1973	17.5%	.9%
1970	3.8%	8.0%	1974	.8%	.0%

Source: United States League Fact Book

(S & R) was acquired at the end of 1971. Primarily a mortgage banker, S & R originates and services all types of loans and engages in financing, real estate, and insurance brokerage. In addition, S & R owns *Washington Capital Corporation* — a Small Business Investment Company (SBIC) — chartered in 1961.

Headquartered in Seattle, Sherwood & Roberts has 250 regular employees plus some 170 real estate salesmen (commission basis). This force operates through 20 offices in a seven state area. These offices are located in Washington, Oregon, Idaho, Nevada, California, Utah, and Hawaii. Thus, they serve the same area as Equitable's branches, plus some additional territory in the surrounding states.

Since Sherwood and Roberts is not regulated to the extent that a savings and loan association is, funds can be raised by S & R on an intrastate basis on more favorable terms than Equitable could arrange on its own. S & R offerings of debentures, notes, and bonds are not subject to the same restrictions and controls that Equitable could face in raising capital through savings accounts and savings certificates. The net

EQUITABLE SAVINGS & LOAN ASSOCIATION
4-YEAR OPERATING SUMMARY—SELECTED YEAR-END STATISTICS

	1974	1973	1972	1971
Assets (000)	$698,673	$606,656	$523,485	$438,411
Real Estate Loans Receivable (Net) (000)	588,362	517,685	438,653	368,247
Savings Accounts (000)	555,560	519,982	442,491	353,543
Number of Real Estate Loans	23,344	22,879	21,311	19,956
Number of Savings Accounts	147,067	141,432	125,067	111,342
Number of Offices—Year-end	38	36	34	34
Number of Personnel—Year-end	379	394	391	340
Average Interest Rate				
New real estate loans	8.73%	8.06%	7.78%	8.12%
Weighted Average Yield,				
Mortgage portfolio	7.80%	7.63%	7.48%	7.40%
General & Administrative Ratio	18.22%	18.45%	19.09%	21.48%
Scheduled Items to specified assets	1.70%	1.61%	2.52%	2.83%

earnings contributed by Sherwood & Roberts to its parent company have exceeded $500,000 each year since its acquisition.

Since Equitable's release from GAC's control, a number of operating statistics have improved substantially, as can be seen from the accompanying table of year-end statistics. For example, the ratio of general and administrative expenses to revenue has gone down steadily for four years. Their "scheduled items" (what we might call "problem loans") have decreased significantly as a per cent of assets. At the same time, the growth in savings accounts and assets has been substantial.

Much smaller in it size and scope of operations, but aggressive in its growth plans, is the **Oregon Trail Savings and Loan Association.** Oregon Trail, as of June, 1975, had savings deposits of $51.5 million and loans outstanding of $47.6 million. Total assets amounted to $59.9 million. Headquartered in Gresham and operating totally within the greater Portland area, Oregon Trail has a total of eight branch offices serving the public.

A different type of financial enterprise is the real estate investment trust (REIT), which became a popular concept in the late 1960's and early 1970's. The purpose of REIT's was to invest in real properties in three ways: (1) Equities — involving the actual ownership of real properties — apartments, shopping centers, land, etc; (2) Short-term mortgages — loans generally limited to periods of seven or eight years and frequently for shorter periods of two to three years, usually construction loans or other interim financing; and, (3) Hybrid trusts — REIT's which invest in a combination of properties involving both loans and equity interests.

In the Northwest, there is just one real estate investment trust based in the region. **USBanTrust** is a hybrid type REIT which was organized in Oregon in 1972 and is managed in Portland. USBanTrust is managed by *Bancorp Management Advisers, Inc.*, a subsidiary of **U.S. Bancorp,** which is a $2.5 billion financial services holding company. U.S. Bancorp is the parent of the *United States National Bank of Oregon, Commerce Mortgage Company, U.S. Datacorp,* and *Bancorp Leasing, Inc.* (See chapter on commercial banks.)

Real estate investment trusts are, by their nature, dependent upon the economic climate and the level of short-term interest rates and construction activity. USBanTrust's first two years of operation saw a rapid expansion in total assets and produced satisfactory earnings. However, the chaotic fluctuation of interest rates and other economic factors such as rising unemployment caught up with the Trust in 1974 and 1975. The same was true for the entire REIT industry. Thus, USBanTrust reported a loss of $2.6 million in fiscal 1975 (ended May 31) and may show additional losses in fiscal 1976.

We should make the point that when a REIT holds a delinquent loan or a foreclosed property, in virtually all cases, they are adequately secured against the loss of principal. Therefore, the loss of current earnings does not also necessarily imply the eventual loss of investment capital as well.

A much smaller investor-owned financial services company is **Equities, Inc.** located in Salt Lake City, Utah. The company is primarily engaged in secondary real estate financing, purchase and resale of "special situation" real property receivables and real estate development.

Basically, Equities, Inc. invests in real estate notes and contracts which it purchases at substantial discounts from their face value. The company then receives the interest due on the full face amount of its contracts held plus the eventual repayment of the principal amounts. A small company, total revenue in 1974 was just $239,890. Even so, Equities, Inc. has been profitable and paid a cash dividend in each of the past five years.

Barnett Financial Corp. is actively engaged in the accounts receivable factoring business, particularly in the greater Seattle, Washington area. The company has a diverse clientele, from manufacturing to wholesale businesses, which it works with closely in the effective management of credit and control of accounts receivable.

20

Insurance

Although the Northwest is by no means a major insurance center by national standards, there are a number of strong and growing insurance companies headquartered in the region. As the tables accompanying this chapter show, ten Northwest insurance companies at the end of 1974 had over $15 billion insurance in force (nearly double the amount five years earlier), controlled over $2 billion assets (including stock and bond portfolios of nearly $900 million), and generated annual revenue over $850 million. Any way you look at it, the industry is a significant element in the economy and the investment scene.

All of the ten Northwest-based insurance companies discussed in this chapter are involved in issuing life insurance, and several of them also issue accident, health, property and casualty insurance. Four of the ten are organized under the holding company form, and three of those also have subsidiaries engaged in non-insurance activities.

Insurance companies are subject to jurisdiction by the insurance commissioners of each of the states in which they operate. The states have adopted a uniform procedure for the insurance companies to report their financial information to the various state commissioners. This is called *"statutory accounting,"* the accounting policies for which differ considerably from *"Generally Accepted Accounting Principles"* (GAAP). Almost all insurance companies reported to their stockholders on the "statutory" basis until 1973, when the Securities and Exchange Commission required all insurance companies under its jurisdiction to start reporting to stockholders on a "GAAP" basis. All the holding companies and two of the other insurance companies in this chapter now report on a GAAP basis, while four of the companies (not under SEC jurisdiction) still report on a statutory basis, designated by "G" or "S", respectively, next to the net income figure in the accompanying table. The major differences between statutory and GAAP accounting are summarized in a box elsewhere in the chapter.

Safeco Corporation (Seattle) is by far the largest insurance enterprise in the Northwest and, indeed one of the largest in the nation. A true Northwest success story, the company was founded by Hawthorne K. Dent on May 1, 1923. The company's original name was *The General Insurance Company of America.* An innovative company, Safeco's

NORTHWEST INSURANCE COMPANIES

	Total Assets	1974 Revenue	Net Income
Safeco Corporation	$1,241,162,000	$615,161,000	$16,515,000(G)
Farmers New World Life Insurance Co.	521,888,294	105,046,149	16,726,474(G)
First Farwest Corporation*	73,759,000	79,506,000	1,549,000(G)
American Guaranty Financial Corporation	61,846,379	16,740,048	1,032,890(G)
National Public Service Insurance Co.	56,732,806	9,098,405	881,533(S)
Continental Life and Accident Company	25,292,555	16,480,450	539,595(S)
Investors Insurance Corporation	17,699,723	9,375,928	(641,393)(G)
Western Resources Corporation	12,952,785	2,745,962	(230,370)(G)
Pacific Northwest Life Insurance Company	4,563,802	1,510,540	(234,878)(S)
Life Insurance Company of the Northwest	3,838,549	2,124,750	126,256(S)
Totals	$2,019,735,893	$857,789,232	$36,264,007

* Pro-forma, giving effect to the acquisition of Trans-Pacific Financial Corporation on April 29, 1975.
(G) GAAP reporting   (S) Statutory Reporting

LIFE INSURANCE IN FORCE (000)

	1974	1970	% Change
Safeco Corporation	$5,150,442	$2,342,193	+ 119.9
Farmers New World Life Insurance Co.	6,726,487	4,194,250	+ 60.4
First Farwest Corporation	1,672,000	74,000	+2159.4
American Guaranty Financial Corporation	673,000	525,000	+ 28.2
National Public Service Insurance Co.	266,879	224,862	+ 18.7
Continental Life and Accident Company	946,085	602,016	+ 57.1
Investors Insurance Corporation	203,164	142,622	+ 42.5
Western Resources Corporation	116,600	95,196	+ 12.2
Pacific Northwest Life Insurance Company	93,590	87,956	+ 6.4
Life Insurance Company of the Northwest	81,829	37,719	+ 116.9
Totals	$15,930,076	$8,325,814	+ 91.3

YEAR-END INVESTMENT PORTFOLIO—1974
(at book value)

	Stocks (Common and Preferred)	Bonds	Total
Safeco Corporation	$330,371,000	$313,099,000	$643,470,000
Farmers New World Life Insurance Co.	42,863,541	114,848,873	157,712,414
First Farwest Corporation	477,000	11,994,000	12,471,000
American Guaranty Financial Corporation	2,061,334	13,867,730	15,929,064
National Public Service Insurance Co.	323,999	35,955,240	36,279,239
Continental Life and Accident Company	2,111,538	13,398,464	15,510,002
Investors Insurance Corporation	586,497	4,835,223	5,421,720
Western Resources Corporation	243,359	6,062,399	6,305,758
Pacific Northwest Life Insurance Company	7,848	2,941,374	2,949,222
Life Insurance Company of the Northwest	2,937	3,421,480	3,424,417
Totals	$379,049,053	$520,423,783	$899,472,836

management has introduced new types of policies and operating procedures to the industry over the years.

In 1972, fifty years after its founding, the founders' original two million dollars in capital had grown to $1 billion dollars in assets, $500 million in annual revenue, and over $50 million in annual net income (1972).

Safeco is a multi-line insuror, doing business in 49 of the 50 states (all except Alaska), and its activities cover many areas: Property and Casualty Insurance, Life Insurance, Title Insurance, Credit Operations, and Computer Services.

In 1973 and 1974, the company was doubly damned. Rampant inflation caused property and casualty claims of unprecedented size. At the same time, a dismal stock market combined with skyrocketing interest rates did serious damage to Safeco's investment portfolio and reserves. So far in 1975, the stock market recovery has restored some of these values. The company is diligently upgrading the risks it will now insure and vigorously pursuing a number of rate increase proposals which they hope will return a measure of normalcy to the company's operations.

Some idea of the scope of Safeco's operations and their relative contributions to income can be gleaned from the following data from Safeco's 1974 Annual Report.

STATEMENT OF CONSOLIDATED INCOME

	Year Ended December 31	
	1974	1973
Net Operating Income (Loss)		
Property and Casualty Insurance Companies	$ 7,501,000	$ 28,071,000
Title Insurance Companies	1,258,000	2,762,000
SAFECO Life Insurance Company	3,971,000	4,221,000
Real Estate Companies	397,000	1,371,000
SAFECO Credit Company	497,000	379,000
SAFECOM, Inc.	230,000	118,000
Mutual Funds Sales and Management Companies	(149,000)	(86,000)
Miscellaneous	1,125,000	1,063,000
Total	14,830,000	37,899,000
Non-Operating Income:		
Realized Gain from Sale of Investments (Less applicable Federal income tax: 1974—$774,000; 1973—$1,230,000) (Excluding unrealized depreciation of investments—Note 2)	1,685,000	2,875,000
Net Income	$16,515,000	$40,774,000

The **Farmers New World Life Insurance Company** (Mercer Island, Washington) is the second largest insurance company based in the Northwest, in terms of assets. The company's total assets of $521.8 million are less than half that of Safeco Corporation . . . but substantially more than all of the other Northwest insurance companies. On the other hand, even with fewer assets, Farmers New World has more insurance in force, $6.7 billion, than has Safeco. The difference is that

Safeco's Seattle headquarters building offers employees a panoramic view of the city.

Farmers sells only life insurance whereas Safeco's insurance in force is mostly casualty insurance.

Farmers New World is a 52.4% owned subsidiary of *Farmers Group, Inc.* based in Los Angeles. Farmers New World has more than 7400 licensed agents selling the company's various life insurance policies, the same agents that sell Farmers' fire and casualty policies. Of these agents, 5800 are full time while the majority of the remainder are in rural areas or undergoing training to become full time agents. Fire and casualty and other types of insurance are underwritten by different subsidiaries of the Farmers Group.

In turn, Farmers New World itself has a wholly owned subsidiary, *The Ohio State Life Insurance Company* with more than 1400 licensed sales agents. Both companies have been successful in expanding life insurance sales at a rapid pace.

A smaller Seattle company is the **National Public Service Insurance Co.** This venerable company was founded in 1932 by the late Charles H. Leber, Sr., beginning under the name *Public Service Underwriters.* Mr. Leber also founded *Public Service Life, Health and Accident Company* in 1934. The National Public Service Insurance Company was organized in 1940, and all three companies were eventually merged and operate today under the present name. The company issued new life insurance policies in 1974 with a face value of $40.9 million and received total revenue of $9 million.

National Public Service is licensed in 12 states: Alaska, Arizona, California, Colorado, Idaho, Montana, Nevada, North Dakota, Oregon, Utah, Washington, and Wyoming.

Life Insurance Company of the Northwest, based in Spokane, in its ninth year of operation, is rapidly approaching the industry milestone of $100,000,000 of life insurance in force. About 90% of this amount is issued special permanent insurance plans featuring high cash values.

The company markets two special policies, the "Estate Builder" and the "Security Builder." The Estate Builder features a combination of permanent and term insurance with an annuity paying 8% interest, income tax deferred. The Security Builder was designed for the Individual Retirement Income market. Premiums for this policy are deductible from gross income of the owner for impressive savings on income taxes. The 8% interest on the annuity feature of this policy also accumulates on a tax deferred basis. It is anticipated that sales of these two policies will boost total income by year end 1975 to well over $2.25 million.

As a relative newcomer to the industry, the company has been able to take advantage of high current yields on investments for above industry-average results, and LNW has been unusually profitable for a young company.

American Guaranty Financial Corporation is a Portland-based holding company engaged in specialty insurance and related financial fields. The company operates through several subsidiary companies: *American Guaranty Life Insurance Company* (Portland), and its subsidiary *Sentinel Life Insurance Company* (San Francisco, Calif.), *American Planning Agency, Inc.,* (Portland), *Guaranty Acceptance Corporation,* (Portland), and *Nickerson Fleet Management Corporation,* (Portland).

The bulk of the parent corporation's revenue comes from funeral and other life insurance premiums (78%), with group and franchise contributing 16%. American Guaranty Life is the oldest legal reserve stock life insurance company based in Oregon. Equipment leasing and other financial services make up the remaining 6% of revenue.

Insurance sales are conducted by more than 1,000 agents in a 24-state area. The company has been very successful in writing specialty lines of insurance. These include the American Funeral Plan and creditor life (Sentinel Insurance) sold through banks and finance companies, and mortgage and disability insurance. American Guaranty also pursues Group and Franchise insurance for professional groups such as the Oregon Medical Association, Oregon and Washington Gas Dealers Associations, and the Washington Bar Association.

American Guaranty Life Insurance Company installed eight new video display units last year, enabling operators, such as Karen Overton, to instantly retrieve policy data. This service has greatly reduced time needed for policy-holder service.

During 1975, the company introduced its new tax-deferred investment annuity which is marketed through a number of savings and loan associations as well as several stock brokerage firms.

Investors Insurance Corporation (Portland) has made the management decision to change its sales direction; to build a sales force of career general agencies and to eliminate brokers primarily writing accident and health insurance. The company has offered a full range of insurance products — life, accident and health, and group credit. Investors Insurance has elected to concentrate its efforts on the most profitable line — ordinary life insurance and annuities. The number of company sales agents has been deliberately reduced from a peak of 1,325 (in 1972) to 325 at the end of 1974. Although the company was authorized to conduct business in twelve states in 1974, sales are presently being made in Oregon only.

Also based in Portland, **Pacific Northwest Life Insurance Company** sells a new form of cancer insurance as well as life insurance. According to President Ed Fulop, "Pacific Northwest Life is now the biggest writer of cancer insurance based in the West." Cancer insurance is a specialized form of major medical policy, and Fulop added that the cancer insurance business is much more profitable than life insurance. He said that cancer insurance tends to have a 95% persistency (renewal) rate, much higher than life insurance.

At this writing, Pacific Northwest Life is licensed in 14 states. Total premium income for 1974 was $1.5 million compared to $1.2 million in 1973. To give an idea of the difference between statutory and GAAP accounting, Fulop estimated that for 1974 the company would have shown an $11,000 profit had it been reporting on a GAAP basis vs. the $234,878 loss it actually reported on a statutory basis.

Continental Life and Accident Company, founded in Boise, Idaho in 1943, first operated under the name Security State Life Insurance Co. The present name was adopted in 1952. Continental Life is licensed to write ordinary and group life and health and accident insurance in 17 states, primarily in the West, and has a sales force of approximately 6,000 agents and brokers.

Continental Life and Accident has restored an historic structure to provide an attractive as well as functional new headquarters.

MAJOR DIFFERENCES BETWEEN STATUTORY AND GAAP ACCOUNTING POLICIES FOR INSURANCE COMPANIES

The following policies apply to *Statutory accounting policies as opposed to GAAP* accounting policies:

(1) Commissions and other acquisition costs relating to issuance of new policies are charged to current operations as incurred, rather than against the future related premium revenue.

(2) Policy reserves are based on factors established by statute and insurance regulatory authorities and not on actual company experience and current mortality tables.

(3) Capital stock dividends are charged to unassiend surplus at par value whereas under generally accepted accounting principles the difference between fair market value of the capital stock and its par value would also be charged to unassigned surplus.

(4) Realized gains or losses on investments are included or charged to unassigned surplus rather than to operations.

(5) The mandatory securities valuation reserve for fluctuations in the recorded value of investments, required to provide for possible future losses on such investments, has been provided by charges to unassigned surplus.

(6) Certain assets described as "nonadmitted assets" are excluded from the balance sheet and charged to unassigned surplus in accordance with regulatory requirements.

(7) The cumulative effect of the revaluation of policy reserves for prior periods is charged to unassigned surplus rather than to operations.

Source: National Public Service Insurance Company and Investors Insurance Corporation.

Two wholly-owned subsidiaries of Continental Life are *Cosmopolitan Life Insurance Co.* (Los Angeles, Calif.) and *Continental Financial, Inc.* of Boise. In 1974, Cosmopolitan reported a net gain of $182,910. Continental Financial performs trust work, leasing, and other financial services. Its second operating year just completed, this subsidiary reported a net gain of $52,379 in 1974.

Continental's staff moved into a newly compled headquarters building in downtown Boise in 1974, and a large new computer system became operative in 1975. For the year 1974, Continental's insurance in force rose 26.4% to $946 million, while investment income climbed 20.3% to $1,704,265.

One might think from the name that **Western Resources Corporation** would be some kind of a mining or natural resource company but such is not the case. Headquartered in Casper, it is a holding company whose sole subsidiary is *Western Resources Life Insurance Company,* Wyoming's largest life insurance company. It is licensed to sell insurance in 17 states, mostly in the West. In 1974, however, over 85% of all policies sold by the company were sold in Wyoming, Colorado, and New Mexico.

First Farwest Corporation is a true example of a successful Northwest company with diversified but related operations throughout the region. First Farwest traces its roots to the *National Hospital Association*, organized in 1906 to provide prepaid medical-hospital care for workers in the Pacific Northwest's logging industry. Later, in 1923, what is now *First Farwest Life Insurance Co.* was created to offer group hospital and medical coverage for workers in forest products, dam construction, and other industries, with life insurance being added in 1966.

First Farwest is one of the Northwest's faster-growing and more interesting companies, but still not well known to most investors. It adopted its present name in August, 1973, and on April 29, 1975 acquired *Trans Pacific Financial Corporation.* The total package puts First Farwest in broad lines of life and health insurance, equipment leasing, and the distribution, servicing and financing of heavy equipment and parts.

Two of First Farwest's greatest financial strengths are its high degree of liquidity and substantial tax shelters. The insurance business is highly tax sheltered, and the leasing business generates significant investment tax credits plus depreciation. With this liquidity and tax shelter, Board Chairman Forrest W. Simmons says the company is looking aggressively for acquisitions, especially in the transportation services area.

The company's wholly-owned insurance subsidiaries include *First*

Logotypes of a number of First Farwest insurance clients who helped make possible the firm's growth.

Farwest Life Insurance Co., National Health & Life Assurance Co., and *National Hospital Association.*

As of April 29, 1975 First Farwest, through an exchange offer, acquired over 98% of the common shares of *Trans Pacific Financial Corp.* (Each share of Trans Pac was exchanged for seven shares of First Farwest.) Trans Pac's wholly-owned subsidiaries consist of *Trans Pac Leasing, Inc., Trans Pac Equipment, Inc.,* and what is now *First Farwest Capital Fund.* Trans Pac also owns 29% of *Webster Industries,* a manufacturer of materials handling equipment and 50% of *Cascade Broadcasting Corp.,* owner and operator of four radio broadcasting stations.

First Farwest Corp. is now organizationally structured into two distinct areas of operation: the Insurance Group and the Financial Group. The Financial Group is made up of Trans Pacific operations which have been organized into the Financial Services Division and the Transportation Services Division. First Farwest's 1974 revenues and earnings according to this structure can be identified approximately as follows:

REVENUE	EARNINGS
Total	Total
$79.5 Million	$1,558,000
Financial—33.4%	Financial—37.0%
Insurance—66.6%	Insurance—63.0%

First Farwest's insurance business in 1974 resulted in a more than doubling of life premiums earned ($5,740,000 versus $2,157,000 in 1973), and a 13% increase in accident and health premiums earned ($45,342,000 versus $40,141,000 in 1973). Insurance in force jumped from $611,000,000 to $1,672,000,000 in 1974, largely a result of the addition of over $870 million due to the company's selection as insuror for the Oregon Veterans Loan Insurance Plan.

First Farwest insurance companies offer a wide variety of individual and group life, health, medical and disability, as well as specialty insurance programs in 16 western states. The company's major emphasis, however, is on group insurance, with over 80% of premium income derived from group policies. Of $1.672 billion life insurance in force, approximately 89% is in group and 11% in individual policies. Management says in its 1974 annual report that "although premium income from individual products is small when compared with premiums received from group products, individual programs hold excellent growth potential. This is one of the product areas which First Farwest intends to aggressively expand."

First Farwest's new Financial Group includes leasing operations in the western United States and Canada, various investment activities, and the finance and distribution of transportation equipment.

In its leasing operations, First Farwest enters into noncancellable, full pay-out financing leases, under which total rentals exceed the cost of the leased equipment plus anticipated financing and other costs.

The types of equipment leased by First Farwest are distributed approximately as follows:

Logging & Construction	26.2%	Electronic Equipment	5.6%
Heavy Trucks	13.4	Agricultural Equipment	4.0
Restaurant, Hotel & Hospital		Aircraft	3.9
Furniture & Fixtures	13.4	Automobiles & Light Trucks	3.8
Material Handling Equipment	11.4	Trailers	2.9
General Business Equipment			
& Furniture	5.6	All others	9.8

The Financial Services Division also generates substantial volume and income via conditional sales contracts principally through First Farwest equipment operations, but also through other vendors.

The Transportation Service Division has three operating divisions involved in the sale and service of heavy duty trucks and one in heavy duty parts distribution. Truck sales operations are located in Eugene and Albany, Oregon and Seattle, Washington, with franchises for the sale of White and Freightliner Truck products in most of Western Washington and Oregon. A new $1 million Farwest White facility, south of Seattle, opened for business in October 1975, and is expected to increase penetration in the western Washington market. The parts operation in Seattle operates in the Pacific Northwest and Alaska as a heavy duty equipment distribution house on both a wholesale and retail level. Parts sales and service operations at the truck franchises and parts sales at the parts house have been increasing their contribution to the Division's profits in recent years.

A recent development of significance is First Farwest's intent to acquire *Utility Trailer Sales Co. of Fresno, Inc.* and *Valley Kenworth Corporation*—both located in Fresno, California. Negotiations are still under way, but it is anticipated that the two companies will be acquired by the end of 1975 in exchange for new First Farwest convertible preferred stock.

On a combined basis, Utility Trailer Sales-Valley Kenworth had 1974 revenue of $19 million and assets of $19.1 million. If final negotiations are successful, and two companies will add both geographical and product diversity, and nearly double the division's revenue.

Pacific Insurance Investment Co., a private Portland company with fewer than 80 shareholders, controls approximately 52% of First Farwest's 7,117,000 shares outstanding.

21

Multi-Line Companies

Some of the Northwest's corporate enterprises are diversified in such a way that they defy any attempt to describe them in a single industry classification. We have chosen to call these "multi-line companies." By this we mean that the companies have a number of different operations which are not directly related to each other, but their development pattern is not so randomly diverse as the much-maligned "conglomerates."

Columbia Corporation (Portland, Oregon) is one such company. Columbia Corporation was formed in 1969 by the merger of four separate companies: *Great Western Malting, Columbia Plywood, Columbia Steamship Company,* and *Nye Systems.*

Several additions and diverstitures have occurred since that time. Since 1969, annual revenue for Columbia has increased from $54.7 million to $142 million in 1974. In the same period, net income grew from $1,570,000 to $4,577,000.

Present operations consist of three basic operating groups: (1) Building Materials; (2) Malting, and (3) Consumer and Industrial Products. The diversification of this multi-line company allows some degree of flexibility in meeting the different phases of the economic cycle.

Each of Columbia Corporation's operating groups was profitable in 1974, with the Malting and Building Materials groups contributing the bulk of net income.

The building materials group produces both hardwood and softwood products in a total of seven plants. Almost three and one-half million surface feet of veneer is produced per week by the company's two plants at Presque Isle, Maine and Newport, Vermont.

The plywood mill at Klamath Falls, Oregon utilizes hardwood veneers for the faces and backs of hardwood plywood. The inner plies are produced from softwood logs. The Klamath mill produces about 400,000 square feet of plywood per day on a ⅜" basis. The Cascade Locks (Oregon) operation has 100 million board feet annual capacity, primarily of dimension lumber.

All by-products are utilized. Wood chips go to hardboard and pulp mills, the cores to stud manufacturers, and bark is consumed as fuel.

Columbia Corporation's Great Western Malting Co. in Vancouver, Washington.

Great Western Malting is the largest malting operation located on the West Coast, where a large number of breweries are located. Most West Coast breweries use Great Western's malt, and Great Western enjoys an excellent reputation for quality in the brewing industry.

In the early 1960's Great Western initiated a program aimed at supplanting the use of Midwestern barleys by encouraging the breeding and growing of reasonable counterparts in the West. Successful, the company has been able in recent years to offer malts of high quality at sharply reduced prices as compared to competitive products.

With national beer consumption increasing annually, Great Western's plants operated at full capacity in 1974. In 1975, Columbia's management authorized preliminary engineering to increase the capacity of the Vancouver, Washington plant from seven million to

COLUMBIA CORPORATION AND SUBSIDIARIES
LINES OF BUSINESS REPORT

	1973	1972	1971	1970	1969
NET SALES (In thousands):					
Building Materials Group	$ 58,673	$ 36,049	$ 27,757	$ 20,522	$ 21,300
Malting Group	26,262	20,426	18,691	17,478	18,076
Consumer Division	7,740	—	—	—	—
Industrial Division	15,821	14,679	10,608	10,379	14,427
Less Intercompany Sales	(270)	(72)	—	—	—
TOTAL	$108,226	$ 71,082	$ 57,056	$ 48,379	$ 53,803
EARNINGS (LOSS) BEFORE EXTRAORDINARY ITEMS (In thousands):					
Building Materials Group	$ 3,933	$ 2,101	$ 1,125	$ (510)	$ 395
Malting Group	1,474	597	790	525	131
Consumer Division	73	—	—	—	—
Industrial Division	(276)	(81)	(527)	(1,037)	(392)
Discontinued Operations and Unallocated Corporate Expense	(339)	(3)	(1,291)	(1,409)	902
TOTAL	$ 4,865	$ 2,614	$ 97	$ (2,431)	$ 1,036

eleven million bushels annually. The Los Angeles plant has a four million bushel capacity.

Columbia's Consumer and Industrial Products division includes three subsidiaries: *Pierce-Pacific Manufacturing, Inc., T-Bird Home Centers, Inc.,* and *Republic Electric and Development Co.* Industrial products including crane carriers, log handling equipment, and custom fabricated metal equipment are manufactured by Pierce-Pacific. Republic Electric produces electrical controls at its Peoria, Illinois plant. Consumer sales come from T-Bird Home Centers,, a chain of 26 stores located mainly in the western United States and western Canada. The stores are retail home improvement centers. They offer a wide range of items including building materials, tools, plumbing and electrical supplies.

Another diverse company based in the Northwest is **Univar Corporation** (Seattle, Washington). A major national distribution and manufacturing company, sales for Univar in fiscal 1975 amounted to $522 million, with profits more than double those of the previous year.

In 1966 two prominent businesses, *Van Waters & Rogers, Inc.* and *United Pacific Corporation* merged to form *VWR United.* In March, 1974 shareholders approved a name change to Univar.

The company's wholly owned subsidiaries and divisions are *Centennial Mills, Pacific Resins & Chemicals, Inc., Penick & Ford, Ltd., Van Waters & Rogers, VWR Scientific,* and *Treck PhotoGraphic.*

Van Waters & Rogers is one of the nation's largest industrial chemical supply houses. It also handles laundry and dry cleaning supplies, agricultural chemical and supplies, upholstery supplies and fabrics. The company operates nationwide in Canada under its own name and also as *McArthur Chemical Co.*

VWR Scientific is a leading national distributor of laboratory supplies, scientific apparatus, diagnostics and pure chemicals. VWR

Working with wheat as its basic raw material, Centennial Mills manufactures an increasingly wide variety of food and industries products.

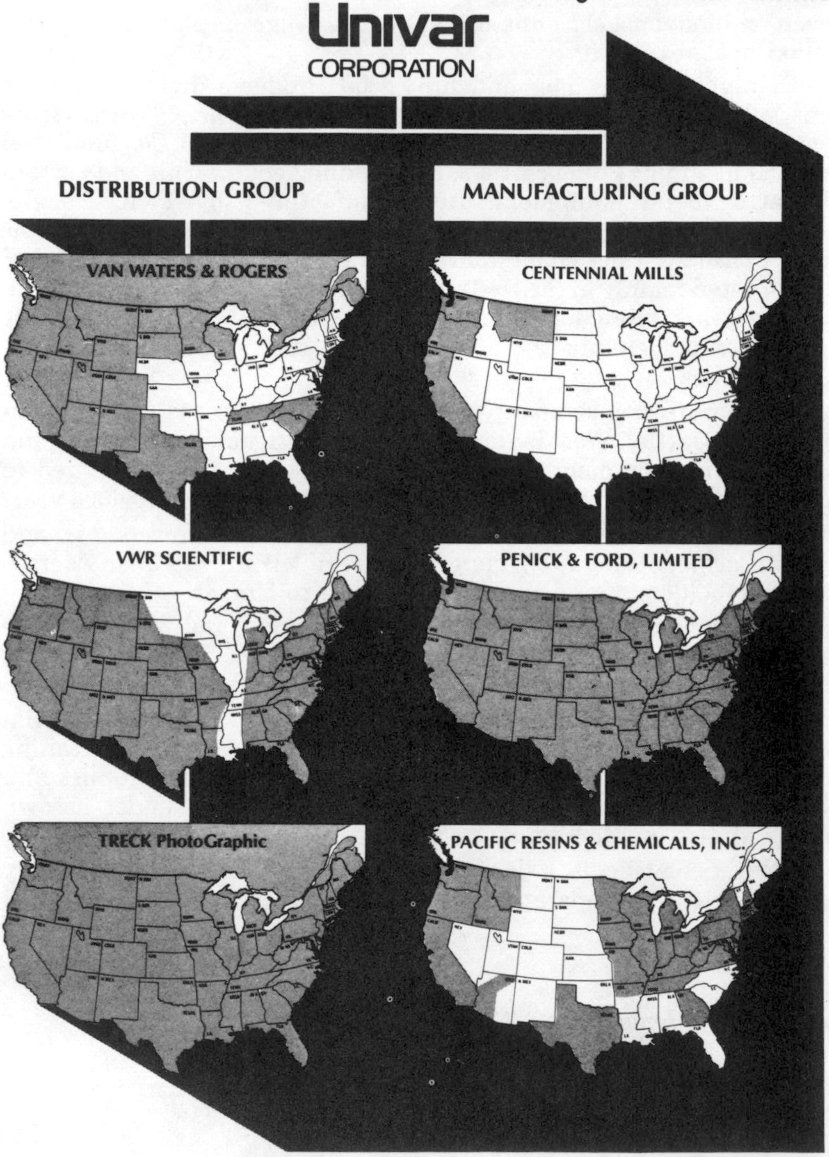

Univar
CORPORATION

DISTRIBUTION GROUP

MANUFACTURING GROUP

VAN WATERS & ROGERS

CENTENNIAL MILLS

VWR SCIENTIFIC

PENICK & FORD, LIMITED

TRECK PhotoGraphic

PACIFIC RESINS & CHEMICALS, INC.

Univar Corporation is a multi-divisional firm, having interests in chemicals, scientific apparatus and home furnishings distribution, and in chemical and food manufacturing. The corporation markets its wide range of products both nationally and internationally.

sells to schools, government, and hospitals as well as to industrial research and control laboratories. Through various predecessor companies, VWR Scientific's history goes back more than 100 years.

Univar's Centennial Mills division is the largest flour miller on the West Coast, with mills in Spokane, Portland, and Los Angeles. The three mills have a combined capacity of 19,000 cwt. per day. An expansion to double the capacity of the Los Angeles mill is scheduled for completion in 1976. Centennial is the only commercial producer of wheat starches and wheat gluten on the West Coast. Centennial also operates a number of grain elevators in Montana and Washington.

A 60-year old subsidiary, Pacific Resins & Chemicals, manufactures adhesives, binders, and finishing resins for use in plywood, hardboard, and paper. During World War II, the company developed needed phenolic resins and received the basic patents which were licensed to others well into the 1960's.

Penick & Ford, Ltd. is a venerable firm founded in 1898. Univar acquired the company from R. J. Reynolds Industries in 1971. Penick & Ford is a major producer of corn syrups for the food industry. They also

Sales and Income by Major Activities
For the Fiscal Years Ended February 28/29
(000's omitted)

	1975	1974	1973	1972[2]	1971[3]
Sales:					
Distribution Group					
Van Waters & Rogers	$234,969	$170,448	$129,864	$121,237 ⎱	$176,244
VWR Scientific	79,842	72,664	66,019	59,175 ⎰	
Manufactured Products Group					
Centennial Mills	74,446	59,832	39,797	31,119	31,184
Pacific Resins & Chemicals, Inc	32,902	20,783	16,825	15,563	15,153
Penick & Ford, Limited	100,274	75,412	52,330	40,382	—
	522,433	399,139	304,835	267,476	222,581
Interdivision sales	383	456	478	886	1,224
Total sales	$522,050	$398,683	$304,357	$266,590	$221,357
Income (Loss):[1]					
Distribution Group					
Van Waters & Rogers	$ 19,163	$ 10,191	$ 5,660	$ 4,630 ⎱	$ 5,800
VWR Scientific	2,453	1,138	112	(182) ⎰	
Manufactured Products Group					
Centennial Mills	3,017	2,404	1,470	973	1,488
Pacific Resins & Chemicals, Inc	3,811	1,149	785	696	405
Penick & Ford, Limited	9,602	5,165	1,254	(948)	—
	38,046	20,047	9,281	5,169	7,693
Less—Unallocated expenses:					
Interest	5,130	4,349	3,662	2,787	1,689
Other—net	3,093	1,090	509	882	532
	8,223	5,439	4,171	3,669	2,221
Income Before Provision for Taxes on Income	$ 29,823	$ 14,608	$ 5,110	$ 1,500	$ 5,472
Net Income	$ 15,544	$ 8,110	$ 2,825	$ 948	$ 2,792
Per Share—primary	$6.79	$3.31	$1.15	$ .39	$1.14

(1) In this schedule, income by major activities is reported on a pre-tax, pre-interest basis to provide operational trends and eliminate the effect of allocated interest charges.

(2) Penick & Ford, Limited was acquired on June 1, 1971. Results of its operations are included for the nine-month period to February 28, 1972.

(3) Data for the distribution divisions for the fiscal year ended in 1971 are shown as one figure due to the fact that this operation was not separated into the two divisions, Van Waters & Rogers and VWR Scientific, until the fiscal year ended in 1972.

make corn-derived starches for the food, paper, and textile industries. Penick & Ford is based in Cedar Rapids, Iowa.

Altogether, Univar's various divisions in the United States and Canada employ more than 3,700 persons.

Univar acquired Treck PhotoGraphic for $12.6 million in 1975. Treck distributes photographic supplies and equipment to some 27,000 professional and commercial customers, as well as industrial accounts, through 36 strategically located operations in the U.S. and Canada. Treck was unprofitable in recent years prior to acquisition, but Univar management is applying many management programs similar to those now in effect at VWR Scientific, and expects Treck to develop into an important earning asset during the years ahead.

HAWAIIAN COMPANIES WITH NORTHWEST INTERESTS

Alexander & Baldwin, although incorporated in 1900, is the youngest and most Hawaiian of Hawaii's so-called "big five" companies. Although all five have been diversifying from their base of land and sugar, A B's primary activities continue to be related to the general economic welfare of the State of Hawaii. Management's objective is "to build on the base of our solid operations in the islands with selected expansion efforts in other locations around the Pacific Basin," which includes the far reaches of the Orient as well as the Western U.S.

The doubling of A & B's 1974 revenue to $347.6 million and the approximate 350% rise in net income over 1973 was mostly a result of the unprecedented rise in the price of sugar. Alexander & Baldwin owns approximately 98,000 acres of land in Hawaii, of which about 46,000 acres are devoted to growing and processing sugar cane.

The company's plantations produced approximately 23% of total Hawaiian sugar production in 1974, or 242,415 tons. (Hawaii's total production of 1.2 million tons per year represents about 20% of total U.S. production and 11% of American consumption.) Most of A & B's sugar production is refined and marketed by *California and Hawaiian Sugar Co.* (C & H), a non-profit agricultural cooperative owned by all of the Hawaiian sugar companies. Alexander & Baldwin owns 22.12% of all the stock of C & H.

A & B purchased *Rogers Brothers Company*'s potato and dehydrated vegetable operations in Idaho, Washington and California in April of 1975. With roots dating back to 1876 in New York state, the company settled in Idaho Falls, Idaho in 1917. Rogers is a major processor of potato chips, flakes, French fries and other potato products. Approximately 10% of the State of Idaho's annual potato crop is utilized by Rogers Brothers. In fiscal 1974, sales from their operation came to $58.9 million.

Matson Navigation Co., another wholly-owned subsidiary of A & B carries on the company's ocean transportation operations with freight service between ports on the U.S. West Coast and ports in Hawaii and Guam, and container stevedoring and terminal services at Los Angeles,

ALEXANDER & BALDWIN, INC. AND CONSOLIDATED SUBSIDIARIES
FIVE-YEAR SUMMARY

OF FINANCIAL DATA(1)	1974	1973	1972	1971	1970
($000 omitted except in per share data, number of stockholders and shares outstanding)					
Revenues by Major Activities:					
Agriculture (2)	**$174,227**	$ 47,261	$ 41,650	$ 46,464	$ 42,877
Ocean transportation (3)	**152,985**	103,890	70,361	65,278	133,196
Property management (4)	**1,614**	2,595	4,757	5,692	2,397
Merchandising	**13,318**	11,285	10,322	12,202	13,390
Dividends and gain on sales of securities	**1,332**	3,771	4,079	1,953	1,621
Interest and other investment income (5)	**4,188**	1,445	1,335	748	1,189
Total revenues	**$347,664**	$170,247	$132,504	$132,337	$194,670
Income Contribution by Major Activities:					
Agriculture (2)	**$125,905**	$ 13,752	$ 8,821	$ 11,261	$ 10,042
Ocean transportation (3)	**11,836**	12,959	881	(4,758)	(3,869)
Property management (4)	**(915)**	543	3,407	2,517	1,580
Merchandising	**1,383**	874	1,033	402	172
Dividends and gain on sales of securities	**1,332**	3,771	4,079	1,953	1,621
Interest and other investment income (5)	**275**	906	485	444	555
Subtotal	**139,816**	32,805	18,706	11,819	10,101
Less unallocated corporate expenses	**4,336**	2,514	2,166	2,173	2,602
Income from continuing operations before income taxes	**135,480**	30,291	16,540	9,646	7,499
Income taxes (credit)	**64,579**	13,181	6,170	2,628	(1,273)
Income from continuing operations	**70,901**	17,110	10,370	7,018	8,772
Net loss of freight forwarding subsidiaries	**—**	(1,237)	(1,628)	(1,244)	(2,073)
Income before extraordinary items	**70,901**	15,873	8,742	5,774	6,699
Extraordinary items (6)	**—**	—	(996)	36	3,722
Net income	**$ 70,901**	$ 15,873	$ 7,746	$ 5,810	$ 10,421

Oakland, Portland, Seattle and Honolulu. The company estimates that it presently carries over 90% of the container cargo moved by ocean liner transportation between the West Coast of the U.S. and Hawaii.

Company property not utilized by A & B for agricultural purposes (approximately 20,000 acres) is managed by the company to produce income through leases and sales of property. Through a joint venture with *Northwestern Mutual Life Insurance Company* of Milwaukee, Wisconsin, the company is developing a community of condominiums and other residential units, resort hotels, shops and recreational facilities on 1,450 acres at Wailea on the island of Maui. Completion of the project is expected in 12-15 years.

Puna Sugar Co., a wholly-owned subsidiary of Amfac, Inc., is situated on the Big Island of Hawaii.

As the biggest of Hawaii's "big five" companies, **Amfac, Inc.** is one of the most diversified, with operations extending to 24 states and five foreign countries. Most of the company's expansion out of its Hawaii home base has come since 1968, through numerous acquisitions, reflected in the growth of company revenue from $205 million in 1968 to $1.1 billion in 1974. Total earnings from 1968 through 1973 grew at about a 20% compound annual rate, from $10.8 million to $27 million. Following is a five year summary which shows the contributions by the various divisions to both revenue and earnings:

	1974	1973	1972	1971	1970
			Revenues		
Food Processing	30%	20%	20%	21%	24%
Food	11	11	11	10	11
Agriculture	19	9	9	11	13
Merchandising	57	65	62	54	52
Retailing	25	31	35	34	38
Distribution	32	34	27	20	14
Hospitality	10	11	12	14	16
Asset Management[2]	3	4	3	5	4
			Income[1]		
Food Processing	85%	42%	23%	20%	20%
Food	4	21	15	16	14
Agriculture	81	21	8	4	6
Merchandising	11	15	43	41	38
Retailing	2	-	29	32	31
Distribution	9	15	14	9	7
Hospitality	5	10	13	12	9
Asset Management	1	31	28	27	30
Property	2	21	17	21	23
Financial[2]	(1)	10	11	6	7
Other	(2)	2	(7)	-	3
	100%	100%	100%	100%	100%

[1] Before unallocated corporate expenses, interest expense and income taxes.

[2] Financial services operations are conducted through non-consolidated subsidiaries.

1974's earnings jump to $55.9 million reflected the profits resulting from the unprecedented rise in sugar prices. The sugar segment of Amfac's business overshadowed the remaining businesses in 1974, providing over 80% of the company's income. Prior to 1973 it played a relatively minor role, contributing less than 10% of earnings. Amfac's five sugar companies on four Hawaiian Islands harvested 301,520 tons of sugar in 1974, representing about 29% of all Hawaiian sugar production.

The company's retailing operations, big in the Northwest, for many years provided the largest single percentage of company income. Amfac operates stores under the names of *Liberty House, Joseph Magnin, Rhodes, Gano-Downs* and *Kauai Stores* in Hawaii, California, Oregon, Washington, Arizona, New Mexico and Texas. Liberty House and Rhodes stores feature merchandise with a strong fashion approach in the medium to higher price ranges; Joseph Magnin stores feature high fashion women's apparel in the medium to higher price ranges, and Gano-Downs features men's apparel.

Amfac's *Lamb-Weston* subsidiary, a Northwest company acquired in 1971, processes frozen French fried potatoes for fast-food service, restaurant, and institutional markets in its five processing plants in Washington, Idaho and Oregon. It is one of the three largest U.S. processors of frozen French fried potatoes. It also produces frozen fruit turnovers and onion rings. New product line expansion is also being carried out in the fish processing subsidiary, *Pacific Pearl Seafoods* in Kodiak, Alaska. In 1974 a mushroom processing operation was added to the Food Group.

One of the three largest hotel operators in Hawaii, Amfac's Hospitality Group operates 10 *Island Holidays Hotels* with 3,471 rooms at year-end 1974. Late in 1975 a new 460-room *King Kamehameha Hotel* at Kailua, Kona will be opened. The *Fred Harvey* Division operates hotels, restaurants, and gift shops.

Amfac's Asset Management Group's revenues are derived from sales of land, property development rights, and residential units, rents, joint ventures, and interest income. Its projects include housing, shopping centers, a major office building complex, resorts, industrial properties, and mobile home parks. Real property interests include 65,645 acres in Hawaii, and 26,098 acres in California, Nevada, Oregon, Washington, Colorado, Idaho, and Alaska. In addition, 101,914 acres in Hawaii are held under long-term leases. Current major development projects of the Group include the *Kaanapali Beach Resort* on the Island of Maui, *Silverado Country Club and Resort* in California's Napa Valley, and a joint venture participation in the 1,400 acre *Crocker Hills* development near San Francisco.

Amfac Financial Corp. is involved in mortgage banking, commercial and construction lending, real estate development, real estate joint ventures, and equipment leasing in Hawaii. At year-end it was serving mortgage loans of about $78 million.

Portland-based *Amfac Mortgage Corp.* operates a mortgage banking business in 10 states, services loans totaling $860 million at year end 1974, develops real estate, participates in real estate joint ventures, and makes construction loans for its own account. Operations are financed by the sale of debentures in Oregon and advances from Amfac Financial, Inc.

Statistical Summary of 204 . . .

The following statistical summary of 204 publicly-traded Northwest companies was abstracted from the Fall 1975 issue of the *Northwest Stock Guide* (see Bibliography).

Number of shares outstanding and number of stockholders are based on latest available information from each company. Total assets are as of latest fiscal year end as stated by company in their annual report.

Where a trading symbol is shown for a stock traded in the over-the-counter (OTC) market, the stock was quoted on the *National Association of Security Dealers Automated Quotation* system *(NASDAQ)* at the time of publication.

Name	Mkt.	Number Shares (000)	Number Stock holders	Total Assets (000)	1974 Revenue (000)
Airborne Freight Corp.	NYS	2,719	2,519	28,233	108,934
Alaska Airlines	ASE	3,608	16,000	34,397	51,202
Alaska International Industries	OTC	2,022	1,300	36,245	45,120
Alaska Interstate Co.	NYS	3,324	5,188	196,952	147,236
Albertson's Inc.	NYS	6,657	6,660	172,797	1,046,105
Alexander & Baldwin	OTC	9,207	9,093	361,255	347,664
Alpine International Corp	OTC	2,440	1,100	6,295	74,395
Altex Oil Corp.	OTC	12,083	2,034	1,372	1,197
American Care Centers, Inc.	OTC	402	371	1,793	3,659
American Guaranty Financial Corp.	OTC	1,954	6,629	61,846	16,740
American Marine Industries	OTC	548	700	3,160	4,184
American Nuclear Corp	OTC	2,964	3,952	9,563	1,087
Amfac	NYS	11,557	12,954	749,824	1,145,362
Audiscan, Inc.	OTC	806	1,500	5,654	4,355
Bancorporation of Montana	OTC	488	1,086	159,451	11,676
Bank of the West	OTC	366	1,000	117,038	9,959
BANNAK	OTC	726	220	500	
Barnett Financial Corp.	OTC	256	280	757	1,898
Baza'r Inc.	OTC	760	3,299	35,190	188,214
Bingham Silver Lead	OTC	2,279	550	1,069	507
Boeing Company	NYS	21,297	81,800	1,683,059	3,750,000
Bohemia Inc.	OTC	1,828	3,600	92,000	93,810
Boise Cascade Corp.	NYS	29,487	78,686	1,575,697	1,453,550
Bronco Oil	OTC	5,000	7,000		
Brooks-Scanlon, Inc.	OTC	2,257	1,063	47,528	42,186

Publicly-Traded Northwest Companies

Each stock's price range and prior years' earnings per share have been adjusted for any significant stock splits and stock dividends. Earnings reported are "operating earnings," that is before extraordinary gains or losses. "Df." means deficit.

Much care has been taken in the compilation of the data from each company's published financial reports and other industry sources, but complete accuracy cannot be guaranteed. Extensive footnotes contained in the ***Northwest Stock Guide*** have been omitted.

We recommend that the company's annual and interim reports be consulted for further information.

Symbol	Latest Fiscal Year	Earnings Per Share 1970	1971	1972	1973	1974	1975	Price Range Jan. '74-Sept. '75 High	Low
ABF	Dec. 74	.72	.57	.52	.80	1.20		13⅜	4¼
ALK	Dec. 74	2.12Df	1.23Df	.91Df	.11	.71		6⅝	2⅜
ALKA	Dec. 74	5.10Df	2.72Df	.10	.41	2.98		24½	6¼
AKI	Dec. 74	1.49	1.29	1.50	.52Df	1.11		29⅜	5⅝
ABS	Jan. 75	.73	.83	.98	1.19	1.45	1.85	20⅜	10
ALEX	Dec. 74	.73	.63	.95	1.72	7.70		22½	11½
	Aug. 74	.01	.07	.18	.42.22Df			3¼	2¼
ALTX	Sep. 74	.005	.006	.004Df	.006Df	.007		.95	.45
	Mar. 75	.04	.15Df	.09Df	.20	.25	.26	2¼	1½
AMGR	Dec. 74	.23	.30	.30	.41	.53		4⅞	2⅛
AMRE	Dec. 74	.04	.53	.60	.54Df	.64Df		2⅝	⅜
ANUC	May 75	.18	.25	.06Df	.21Df	.09Df	.03Df	6¾	1½
AMA	Dec. 74	1.73	1.92	2.16	2.36	4.86		22	12⅝
ASCN	Jan. 75	.21	.21	.14	.36Df	.06	.25	1½	½
BMON	Dec. 74	1.88	1.67	1.75	2.20	2.30		17	13½
BKWT	Dec. 74		1.69	1.90	1.82	.79		17	9½
	June 74					Nil		1⅞	¾
	Dec. 74	.16	.08	.08	.07	.14		1½	¾
BAZR	July 74	.73	.79	1.92Df	2.72Df	1.78Df		4⅛	⅝
	Apr. 74			Nil	.01Df			5	½
BA	Dec. 74	1.02	1.04	1.40	2.38	3.42		31⅞	11⅝
BOHM	Apr. 75	2.39	.72	2.44	4.49	8.26	4.05	22½	8¾
BCC	Dec. 74	.74	.57	1.39	2.89	3.51		27¼	9⅞
BRKS	Dec. 74	.92	1.32	1.67	2.22	1.96		21	8¾

Name	Mkt.	Number Shares (000)	Number Stock holders	Total Assets (000)	1974 Revenue (000)
Burton/Hawks	OTC	7,256	1,380	1,119	956
California-Pacific Utilities Co.	NYS	1,381	6,454	95,629	40,312
Cascade Corp.	OTC	730	1,287	36,141	49,692
Cascade Natural Gas Corp.	NYS	1,931	7,220	107,248	65,331
Cascade Steel Rolling Mills	OTC	1,896	1,775	15,044	27,443
Centennial Villas, Inc.	OTC	2,906	1,047	7,078	10,764
Centralarm International	OTC	675	290	344	496
Chaparral Resources	OTC	8,093	3,112	1,361	817
Chem Nuclear Systems	OTC	1,699	1,820	3,543	3,167
Citizens Bank of Oregon	OTC	324	505	91,000	6,544
Citizens Valley Bank	OTC	300	1,488	73,645	5,196
Coeur d'Alene Mines Corp.	OTC	4,097	5,941	1,445	61
Columbia Corporation	OTC	3,160	1,700	76,197	141,493
Consolidated Freightways	NYS	11,938	13,000	346,403	798,579
Consumers Building Marts, Inc.	OTC	717	539	4,918	5,736
Continental Life & Accident Co.	OTC	2,053	2,308	25,293	16,480
Crown Zellerbach	NYS	24,550	32,980	1,526,875	1,766,190
Dant & Russell, Inc.	PSE	678	917	42,753	89,413
Data Systems, Inc.	OTC	625	890	1,502	2,456
Day Mines, Inc.	ASE	2,904	6,404	10,925	7,383
Dependable Building Maintenance Co.	OTC	357	250	422	1,704
Design Arts, Inc.	OTC	349	110		327
Discount Fabrics, Inc.	ASE	993	1,200	7,693	13,937
Discovery Oil, Ltd.	OTC	3,560	425	2,067	453
Double Eagle Petroleum & Mining	OTC	8,556	1,600	422	390
Eagle Exploration	OTC	12,700	1,600	519	98
Echo Oil Corp.	OTC	3,005	795	2,058	1,089
Edwards Industries	OTC	494	1,000	19,660	20,293
Ellensburg Telephone Co.	OTC	280	390	9,386	3,413
EMC Energies	OTC	9,726	1,680	1,467	749
Equitable Savings and Loan	OTC	1,828	2,500	698,673	52,729
Equities, Inc.	OTC	215	250	1,300	240
Equity Oil	OTC	1,473	2,345	14,806	7,647
Evans Products Company	NYS	16,617	7,120	709,105	1,132,892
Fabric Wholesalers, Inc.	OTC	609	1,100	3,636	5,431
Farmers New Word Life Insurance	OTC	6,600	6,000	521,888	105,046
Fentron Highway Products, Inc.	OTC	372	285	2,775	5,475
First Farwest Corp.	OTC	7,119	7,335	73,759	79,506
First Northwest Industries of America	OTC	512	1,346	6,608	5,050
First Security Corp.	OTC	5,349	5,825	1,825,265	149,114
First State Bank of Oregon	OTC	394	450	147,075	11,309
John Fluke Mfg. Co.	ASE	1,079	2,500	21,160	33,425
Gardner/Marlow/Maes Corp.	OTC	1,151	130	367	502
Gemini Venture Corp.	OTC	1,304	333	1,408	
Georgia-Pacific Corp.	NYS	56,196	93,683	2,230,670	2,432,350

Symbol	Latest Fiscal Year	Earnings Per Share						Price Range Jan. '74-Sept. '75	
		1970	1971	1972	1973	1974	1975	High	Low
BURH	Dec. 74		Nil	.02	.01Df	.04		1⅛	¼
CLP	Dec. 74	1.61	2.25	2.96	2.91	2.06		21	12⅝
CASC	Jan. 75	.52	.71	.73	1.06	3.95	4.05	13	6¼
CGC	Dec. 74	.82	.88	1.86	1.31	1.01		11	6
CSRL	Dec. 74	3.13Df	1.59Df	.23Df	.27	1.26		4¼	1½
	Dec. 74	.02	.04Df	.06	.04	.07		1	¼
	Apr. 74					.26Df		1⅜	¼
	Nov. 74			Nil	.01Df	.01		1¼	⅛
	July 74	.33Df	.18Df	.20Df	.09	.29	.14	1½	⅞
	Dec. 74	1.39	1.55	2.03	2.62	2.25		25	15
	Dec. 74	1.47	1.69	1.79	2.02	2.15		17	14
	Dec. 74	Nil	.01	.01Df	.01	Nil		7¾	3¼
CCOR	Dec. 74	.85Df	.03	1.03	1.51	1.43		5	2
CNF	Dec. 74	.70	1.78	1.98	.74	2.26		20⅛	8⅝
CBLD	Dec. 74	.21	.60	.65	.61	.48		3⅛	1⅜
	Dec. 74	.02	.08Df	.53	.27	.26		3½	2¼
ZB	Dec. 74	1.77	1.31	1.87	4.28	5.06		40⅝	19¾
DNT	Aug. 74	.38	.35	1.07	5.15	3.37		14	5⅝
	Oct. 74	.07	.12	.15	.15	.09		1⅜	½
DMI	Dec. 74	.03Df	.12	.15	.52	.49		19¼	3⅝
	Dec. 74	.02Df	.05	.07Df	.23Df	.07Df		1¼	⅛
	Feb. 74					.13Df		1¼	½
DFI	Sept. 74	.35	.49	.41	.55	.51		3⅞	1¼
DISV	Dec. 74		.04	.05	.03			1½	⅞
	Aug. 74					Nil		.40	.10
	Dec. 74			Nil	Nil	.01Df		.35	.11
	Sept. 74		.07Df	.15Df	.04Df	.13		4½	¾
EDWR	Mar. 75	.57	.33	.62	.49	.18Df	.31	3¼	1⅜
	Dec. 74	1.47	1.53	1.47	1.79	1.92		23	16
	June 75	Nil	.02	.02	Nil	.01	.02	.40	.08
EQTB	Dec. 74	.66	1.53	2.11	2.45	1.64		12⅛	4¾
	Dec. 74	.15	.25	.15	.13	.12		2	⅞
EQTY	Dec. 74	.30	.20	.35	1.01	2.27		24¾	9½
EVY	Dec. 74	.82	1.18	1.64	1.81	2.69Df		13¼	2
	Dec. 74	.66	.59	.11Df	.44Df	.03Df		3¼	½
FNEW	Dec. 74	1.36	1.51	1.96	2.32	2.53		62	23
	Mar. 75	.07	.37Df	.37Df	.91Df	.29	.58	2	¼
FFWS	Dec. 74	.08	.06	.18	.28	.22		1⅛	⅜
FNOR	May 74	.11Df	.07Df	.15Df	2.99Df	2.65Df		4	2¼
FSCO	Dec. 74	2.26	2.63	3.00	3.36	3.55		45½	23¼
	Dec. 74	1.72	2.26	2.62	2.92	3.21		23	10
FKM	Sept. 74	.53	.77	1.29	1.64	2.00		26¾	9¼
	Mar. 74				Nil	.02	.04	1⅜	⅜
	July 74							1⅛	⅜
GP	Dec. 74	1.26	1.13	1.74	2.90	2.91		48	21¾

Name	Mkt.	Number Shares (000)	Number Stock holders	Total Assets (000)	1974 Revenue (000)
Golconda Corp.	PSE	2,785	1.520	49,065	34,800
Grand Central, Inc.	ASE	1,587	1,300	30,738	128,604
GranTree Corp.	OTC	1,216	1,154	27,629	10,511
Gregg's Food Products	OTC	1,152	830	5,609	18,487
Hayden Island, Inc.	OTC	1,131	550	17,601	3,617
HealthGarde Corp.	OTC	4,189	1,700	1,568	2,074
Heath Tecna Corp.	OTC	649	8,741	23,360	39,372
Hecla Mining Co.	NYS	6,717	16,000	102,909	28,917
Heinicke Instruments Co.	ASE	2,820	2,849	4,286	5,980
Hillhaven Inc.	ASE	1,603	2,712	55,808	78,123
Edward Hines Lumber Co.	OTC	867	1,300	77,397	169,861
Hinkle Northwest	OTC	384	225	1,626	1,225
Hyster Company	OTC	5,956	4,675	303,895	342,273
Idaho First National Bank	OTC	2,414	3,071	984,180	69,518
Idaho Power Co.	NYS	7,350	18,761	708,401	100,428
Information Sciences	OTC	406	387	625	662
Interface Mechanisms	OTC	1,633	738	609	1,389
Intermountain Gas	OTC	1,122	5,110	83,112	41,986
Intermountain Laboratories	OTC	789	1,000	1,124	647
International King's Table	OTC	543	600	3,170	10,715
Investors Insurance Corp.	OTC	2,510	2,644	17,700	9,376
Jantzen Inc.	NYS	1,844	4,375	70,570	113,972
JB's Big Boy Family Restaurants	OTC	1,730	400	11,734	19,066
Kampgrounds of America	OTC	1,112	2,376	12,604	6,904
Kirkman Laboratories	OTC	296	320	508	693
Laser Link	OTC	2,944	1,300	6,509	10,180
Life Insurance Company of the N.W.	OTC	114	600	3,839	2,125
Lindal Cedar Homes	OTC	605	1,800	9,268	12,021
Longview Fibre Company	OTC	1,237	2,400	170,423	199,203
Loomis Corp.	OTC	1,229	957	14,721	32,311
Louisiana-Pacific Corp.	NYS	26,210	83,621	560,430	460,100
LRC, Inc.	OTC	1,240	702	376	263
Lynden Transport	OTC	532	500	9,302	16,441
Marco Dental Products	OTC	932	750	1,127	1,924
Medford Corp.	OTC	980	1,126	41,473	55,904
Fred Meyer	OTC	4,957	4,500	159,037	536,760
Midnite Mines	OTC	4,124	2,331	1,342	1,111
Millers International	OTC	262	450	6,265	2,776
Moduline International	OTC	1,400	768	14,971	41,406
Montana Power Co.	NYS	8,747	36,710	520,055	117,762
Moore Clear Co.	OTC	707	1,234	3,270	7,983
Morrison-Knudsen Company	NYS	2,644	6,313	324,299	677,947
Mountain States Resources	OTC	11,645		1,622	364
Multnomah Kennel Club	OTC	864	1,300	2,068	3,243
National Public Service Insurance	OTC	222	1,912	56,733	9,098

Symbol	Latest Fiscal Year	Earnings Per Share						Price Range Jan. '74-Sept. '75	
		1970	1971	1972	1973	1974	1975	High	Low
GOL	Dec. 74	.19Df	.17	.47	.95	1.66		8⅝	3
GC	July 75	.53	.83	.98	1.18	1.27	1.01	10	3¾
GTRE	Oct. 74	.20	.36	.48	.24	.13Df		3½	⅞
GRFP	Oct. 74	.31	.38	.62	.72	.29		5⅞	1⅛
	Dec. 74	.08	.08	.21	.32	.30		11	5½
	Dec. 74		.03Df	.03	.01	.01		1⅝	1¼
HTNA	Apr. 75	3.20Df	9.72Df	3.90Df	.19	1.22	1.87	16¼	6¼
HL	Dec. 74	.71	.54	.45	.63	1.25		36⅝	10⅝
HEI	Oct. 74	.23Df	.04	.13	.20	.05		2⅝	⅝
HIL	Mar. 75	.34	.07	.28	.47	.60	.60	5	2⅝
HINE	Dec. 74	1.30Df	4.27	5.32	14.39	3.11		43½	21
	May 75	.05Df	.07Df	.11Df	.10Df	.02	.06	1¼	⅜
HYST	Jan. 75	2.12	1.82	1.74	2.33	2.60	1.70	21¾	8¾
IDNB	Dec. 74	2.86	2.90	3.11	3.49	4.04		34	29
IDA	Dec. 74	2.41	2.81	2.95	2.95	3.37		30½	21
	Dec. 74	.96Df	.86Df	.25Df	.18	.25		1¾	½
	Mar. 75	.76Df	1.02Df	.14Df	.46Df	.09Df	.03	1¾	½
INMT	Sept. 74	1.25	1.91	2.02	2.24	1.80		15	9⅝
IMLB	Jan. 75			.02	.05Df	.06Df	.13Df	6¾	2
	June 75	.06	.14	.22	.32	.41	.56	4½	2¼
	Dec. 74			.30	.09	.26Df		1⅛	.20
JAN	Aug. 74	1.10	1.26	1.53	2.10	2.85		16¾	9⅛
JBBB	Sept. 74	.20	.23	.35	.37	.47		2⅝	1⅝
KAMP	Dec. 74	.35	.66	.95	1.00	.23		8¼	¾
	June 74	Nil	.18	.37Df	.75Df	.42Df		1½	¾
LASR	Dec. 74	.44Df	.52Df	.66Df	.31.Df	.16Df		3⅜	⅛
	Dec. 74	1.35	.52	.78	1.30	1.11		12	7½
LNDL	Dec. 74	.50	.80	.84	.72Df	4.08Df		3½	⅝
LFBR	Oct. 74	8.36	5.49	9.89	20.24	19.21		135	100
LOOM	Oct. 74	.36	.50	.48	.61	.77		8¾	2
LPX	Dec. 74	.34	.86	1.17	2.52	2.16		24¾	6¾
	Apr. 75					.08	.13Df	5	¼
LYND	Dec. 74	.79	1.38	.92	.47	1.69		23¾	7
	July 74			.11	.11	.16		2	¾
MFRD	Dec. 74	1.01	1.34	3.01	6.26	1.54		39	23½
MEYRA	Dec. 74	1.02	1.24	1.38	1.55	1.56		22½	11¼
	Apr. 75	.03Df.	.18	.24	.12	.15	.21	6¼	1.30
	Feb. 74	1.23	.52	.28	.67	1.14Df.		3	⅛
MDLN	Mar. 75	.34	.37	.64	.23	1.07	.60	6⅛	2½
MTP	Dec. 74	2.45	2.49	2.67	2.88	2.98		34⅝	20¼
	Dec. 74	.27Df	.06	.19	.23	.28		⅞	2
MRN	Dec. 74	1.63Df.	2.06	2.56	3.11	3.47		29½	11¼
	Mar. 75			Nil	Nil	Nil	.05Df.	.80	.15
	Dec. 74	.40	.33	.35	.46	.60		4⅜	3
	Dec. 74	2.56	3.37	3.08	3.38	3.97		33	18

Name	Mkt.	Number Shares (000)	Number Stock holders	Total Assets (000)	1974 Revenue (000)
New England Fish Company	OTC	593	162	80,620	92,709
Noble Metals	OTC	869	225	102	114
Nordstrom, Inc.	OTC	2,139	1,900	66,314	128,768
Normarc Inc.	OTC	1,159	140	3,905	15,609
Northwest Energy Company	NYS	3,491	111,000	405,569	276,402
Northwest Natural Gas Co.	OTC	6,114	18,020	211,972	109,125
Oil Resources, Inc.	OTC	4,726	7,100	5,402	1,803
Olympia Brewing Co.	OTC	2,090	6,562	55,406	182,016
Omark Industries, Inc.	NYS	4,529	6,928	128,951	129,335
Orbanco, Inc.	OTC	1,939	2,400	520,049	48,751
Oregon Freeze Dry Foods	OTC	899	3,108	4,768	10,196
Oregon Metallurgical	OTC	2,966	4,737	18,630	22,204
Oregon Portland Cement Co.	OTC	944	1,855	23,132	23,618
Oregon Trail Savings & Loan	OTC	388	895	37,638	2,483
Paccar, Inc.	OTC	8,250	4,000	338,454	907,987
Pacific Gamble Robinson	OTC	1,548	5,743	65,950	481,518
Pacific Northwest Bell	ASE	49,723	35,622	1,712,956	672,528
Pacific Northwest Development Corp. .	OTC	725	1,500	13,946	2,890
Pacific Northwest Life Insurance	OTC	1,001	2,045	4,564	1,511
Pacific Power & Light Co.	NYS	29,736	77,935	1,588,430	246,979
Pacific Western Industries	OTC	632	1,500	10,495	29,608
Paiute Oil & Mining Corp.	OTC	24,761	750	368	
Pak-Well Corp.	OTC	1,500	1,020	32,986	68,773
Palmer G. Lewis Co.	OTC	342	800	12,314	41,120
Paulson Investment Co.	OTC	178	300	691	465
Pay Less Drug Stores Northwest	NYS	2,653	4,000	52,663	172,888
Pay'N Pak Stores	OTC	1,519	1,256	26,003	61,471
Pay'n Save Corp.	OTC	4,242	5,451	69,379	223,566
Peoples National Bank of Wash.	OTC	636	1,292	815,825	59,652
Physio Control	OTC	1,110	350	7,356	10,014
Pope & Talbot, Inc.	NYS	3,089	1,788	73,630	88,415
Portland General Electric Co.	NYS	15,500	53,000	850,952	146,001
Potlatch Corp.	NYS	7,430	5,213	433,351	487,868
Power Resources Corp.	OTC	904	350	651	298
Precision Castparts Corp.	OTC	500	818	14,579	25,489
Process Systems	OTC	2,654		2,523	2,029
Puget Sound National Bank	OTC	720	1,685	358,601	26,827
Puget Sound Power & Light Co.	NYS	5,750	25,370	621,277	142,393
Rainbow Resources	OTC	2,092	1,270	12,458	6,024
Rainier Bancorporation	OTC	3,717	5,070	2,623,698	214,233
Rainier Companies, Inc.	OTC	2,121	3,000	32,383	43,650
Reinell Industries, Inc.	OTC	1,037	850	15,833	25,969
Rem Metals Corp.	OTC	734	1,343	7,223	8,587
Reser's Fine Foods	OTC	470	740	3,290	12,105

Symbol	Latest Fiscal Year	Earnings Per Share						Price Range Jan. '74-'75	
		1970	1971	1972	1973	1974	1975	High	Low
	Mar. 75	1.25	1.95	3.01	5.05	8.93	10.30 Df	44	15
	May 74				.05Df.	.02Df.		.37	.08
NOBE	Jan. 75	1.40	1.34	1.65	1.83	2.04	2.41	32	8¾
	May 75	.07	.12	.01Df.	.15	.08	.22	1⅜	¼
NwEn ot.	Dec. 74				2.60	4.23		31	11⅞
NWNG	Dec. 74	.73	1.11	1.23	1.13	1.05		9⅜	5¾
	Sept. 74	.17Df.	.13Df.	.05Df.	.13Df.	.15Df.		1¾	⅜
OLYB	Dec. 74	2.35	1.62	1.61	1.69	.79		23	7½
OMK	June 75	1.32	.83	1.17	1.44	2.17	2.59	13½	6⅞
ORBN	Dec. 74	1.00	1.38	1.63	1.77	1.50		15¾	5
OREG	June 75	.46Df.	.20Df.	.17	.21	.43	.54	5⅝	1⅜
OREM	Sept. 74	.15	.81Df.	.69Df.	.16	.81		3¼	⅞
OPRT	Dec. 74	.83	1.02	1.44	1.51	1.81		11¾	8½
	June 74	.42	.34	.49	.53	.29		4¾	3¼
PCAR	Dec. 74	1.78	2.95	3.61	5.20	2.83		37½	15¼
PGAM	Dec. 74	1.85	2.11	2.00	2.49	3.15		30¼	15½
PNB	Dec. 74	1.28	1.30	1.37	1.48	1.58		15	11¼
	Mar. 74	.57	.74	1.05	.23	.10Df.		1½	½
	Dec. 74	.41Df.	.12Df.	.01	.09	.23Df.		1⅛	⅝
PPW	Dec. 74	1.69	1.98	2.25	2.27	2.03		25½	13⅝
PWII	Dec. 74	.70Df	.54	.70	1.21	.36		3⅝	1½
	Dec. 74							.06	.02
PAKW	Dec. 74	1.01	1.15	1.05	1.16	1.44		14½	5½
LWIS	Jan. 75	.64	.59	.85	1.02	1.23	1.87	12	8
	Dec. 74		.31Df.	1.01Df.	.07	.14		1	¼
PAY	Jan. 75	.83	.86	1.09	1.30	1.51	1.75	16¾	5½
PAYP	Feb. 75	.45	.45	.77	.97	1.22	1.47	17½	5
PAYN	Jan. 75	.60	.64	.80	.92	1.18	1.70	22¾	8¾
	Dec. 74	5.29	3.62	4.87	4.29	5.14		38½	24
PHSO	Sept. 74	.05	.15	.34	.67	.95		15	9
POP	Dec. 74	.63	1.24	2.23	3.85	1.84		20⅞	7⅞
PGN	Dec. 74	1.63	2.00	2.11	2.04	2.17		19⅞	12¼
PCH	Dec. 74	.33	1.44	2.24	4.65	6.20		50¼	20¼
	Sept. 74				.06Df.	.17		3¾	1
PCST	Mar. 75	1.01	.27	.72	.88	1.90	2.31	13	4½
PSIC	Nov. 74		.01	.39Df.	.56Df.	Nil		2⅛	⅞
	Dec. 74	2.22	2.31	2.64	3.04	3.66		29	19
PSD	Dec. 74	2.70	2.80	3.15	2.94	4.03		28⅝	18⅛
RBOW	July 75	.09Df.	.07	.15	.43	.60	.42	11¾	4¼
RBAN	Dec. 74	2.76	2.76	2.53	3.14	3.73		28¼	13
RAIN	Mar. 75	.09	.22	.01	.28	.22	.03Df.	4⅛	1⅞
RNLL	July 74	.15	.14	.92	1.27	.04		6	1½
REMM	June 74	.04Df.	.22Df.	.39Df.	.05Df.	.55		2½	⅜
RSRS	Apr. 75	.14	.29	.50	.42	.06	.29	2⅝	1⅛

Name	Mkt.	Number Shares (000)	Number Stock holders	Total Assets (000)	1974 Revenue (000)
Rocket Research Corp.	OTC	1,512	6,108	10,988	16,450
Safeco Corp.	OTC	13,131	10,000	1,241,162	615,161
Seafirst Corp.	OTC	9,000	9,230	4,624,890	375,765
Seattle Trust and Savings Bank	OTC	266	850	294,242	23,223
Silver Dollar Mining Co.	PSE	1,692	4,000	3,340	1,708
Silver Metals, Inc.	OTC	21,987	850	364	408
Skaggs Companies, Inc.	NYS	4,952	5,732	125,597	500,696
Smoke-Craft	OTC	1,914	2,315	5,371	11,575
Sunshine Mining Co.	NYS	5,618	22,000	58,698	59,948
Systems Corp.	OTC	1,692	1,500	902	664
Tally Corp.	OTC	2,363	4,600	16,500	17,700
Tektronix, Inc.	NYS	8,772	8,359	306,616	336,645
Telephone Utilities, Inc.	OTC	4,728	3,280	101,160	25,628
Tollycraft Corp.	OTC	171	335	2,637	6,366
Trailer Equipment Distributors	OTC	541	550	10,148	15,487
Transportation Safety Systems	OTC	3,660	310	6,703	9,613
Trus Joist Corp.	OTC	1,740	450	17,662	41,641
U and I, Inc.	ASE	2,280	5,205	142,128	237,430
Uniflite, Inc.	OTC	511	1,410	8,768	15,838
U.S. Bancorp	OTC	8,101	9,783	2,902,990	207,338
US BanTrust	ASE	825	2,658	92,446	8,666
U.S. Energy	OTC	2,078	1,002	2,879	1,477
Univar Corp.	NYS	2,108	5,297	153,499	522,050
Utah Bancorporation	OTC	543	950	162,474	13,748
Utah Power & Light Co.	NYS	8,158	31,556	798,954	152,585
Valtek	OTC	1,705	900	2,823	4,655
Villa Care, Inc.	OTC	279	250	3,168	7,160
Washington Banchares	OTC	1,568	2,943	631,983	43,736
Washington Natural Gas Co.	OTC	3,276	10,446	177,350	98,957
Washington Water Power Co.	NYS	7,230	32,011	420,053	110,098
Wayne's Photo Finishing	OTC	725	540	6,902	9,004
Weisfield's, Inc.	OTC	631	1,500	33,597	81,945
Western Marine Electronics Co.	OTC	362	600	2,380	3,217
Western Resources Corp.	OTC	1,096	3,700	12,953	2,746
Western Standard Corp.	OTC	4,528	4,631	7,085	3,252
Western United Resources	OTC	8,750	751	2,226	9,813
Westours, Inc.	OTC	1,950	706	5,562	18,631
Weyerhaeuser Co.	NYS	128,200	29,751	2,878,510	2,529,013
Wien Air Alaska	OTC	3,743	3,015	45,134	38,434
Willamette Industries	OTC	11,928	5,800	362,090	388,712
WITS, Inc.	OTC	2,580	2,089	4,160	19,765
Wulf Oil	OTC	7,000	580	517	
Wyoming Bancorporation	ASE	2,029	3,000	277,087	23,456
Wyoming Coal Corp.	OTC	8,000	750	343	
Wyoming National Corp.	OTC	665	852	165,414	11,026

Symbol	Latest Fiscal Year	1970	1971	Earnings Per Share 1972	1973	1974	1975	Price Range Jan. '74-Sept. '75 High	Low
ROCK	Oct. 74	.27	.24	2.22Df.	.20	.22		9⅜	1
SAFC	Dec. 74	2.22	3.47	4.04	3.07	1.26		45¼	18
SEFT	Dec. 74	2.10	2.43	2.52	2.84	3.28		29	13
	Dec. 74	3.53	3.10	3.20	3.98	5.06		30½	21
SDM	Dec. 74	.24	.19Df.	.23Df.	.34	.62		10⅛	3
	Dec. 74		Nil	Nil	Nil			.035	.01
SKG	Dec. 74	1.44	1.03	.93	1.46	2.03		29¾	7¾
	July 74	.26	.20	.12	.14	.19	.05	1	⅜
SSC	Dec. 74	.55	.22Df.	.11Df.	.59	.90		24¾	7⅛
	Aug. 74				.32Df.	.33Df.		3¼	⅞
TALY	Dec. 74	.13	.97Df.	.77Df.	1.24Df.	.01		5	⅞
TEK	May 75	1.75	1.16	1.37	1.94	2.47	3.04	47¾	18⅛
TPHN	Dec. 74	.54	.60	.49	.73	.82		8½	3⅛
	Aug. 74	1.27Df.	1.14Df.	1.30	1.50	1.58		6½	2
TRLR	Sept. 74	.17	.50	.85	.61	.32		3½	⅞
	Dec. 74		.20	.55Df.	.04	.06Df.		⅞	.35
	Dec. 74	.28	.40	.61	.96	.65		15½	6
UIS	Feb. 75	1.45	1.20	1.26	.77	2.25	2.39	18⅞	11¾
UFLT	Oct. 74	.17	.51	.73	.84	.07Df.		6	1¼
USBC	Dec. 74	1.55	1.79	2.06	2.48	2.88		29	13¼
UBT	May 75				1.64	1.80	.62	25¼	5½
USEG	Sept. 74		.11Df.	.20	.12	.09		2¾	⅝
UVX	Feb. 75	1.13	1.14	.39	1.15	3.31	6.79	31	12⅝
UTBN	Dec. 74	1.26	1.25	1.86	1.89	2.31		17	12½
UTP	Dec. 74	3.22	3.44	3.77	3.95	3.40		36	22
	Apr. 75	.01	.03	.02	.07	.09	.16	2½	1
	Dec. 74	.25	.15	.33	.33Df.	.19Df.		1½	¼
WBAN	Dec. 74	2.02	1.74	1.67	2.05	2.63		19¾	13¾
WGAS	Dec. 74	1.16	1.27	1.58	1.48	1.51		12½	7¾
WWP	Dec. 74	1.80	1.88	1.96	2.04	2.11		21	15¾
	Mar. 75	.03	.05	.30	.30	.32Df.	1.47Df.	1⅝	⅛
WEIS	Jan. 75		.82	.42	.72	.44Df.	.11	5¾	1⅛
WMAR	Sept. 74	.12	.30	.50	.70	1.80		11½	4¾
	Dec. 74	.36Df.	.06	.09Df.	.33	.24Df.		1⅜	⅜
	Dec. 74							.55	.15
WURK	Feb. 75					.01	.03	.52	.14
	Dec. 74	2.42Df.	1.19Df.	.14Df.	.79Df.	.19		1¼	⅛
WY	Dec. 74	.94	.82	1.17	2.73	2.17		46	23⅞
WCON	Dec. 74	.04	.04	.02	.18	1.01		8⅝	3
WMTT	Dec. 74	.88	1.12	1.80	2.79	3.15		21¾	10⅜
WITS	Dec. 74	.01Df.	.03Df.	.05	.05	.10		1⅝	⅝
	Aug. 74					.02Df		.55	.10
WYB	Dec. 74	.60	.85	1.09	1.17	1.31		13	6½
	Feb. 75					Nil	.02Df.	.12	.02
WYNA	Dec. 74	.53	1.83	2.12	1.80	2.11		15½	9¾

Bibliography

The bibliography has been developed to help the reader find further information on topics discussed in this book. The first section covers items issued on a periodic basis, either free or by paid subscription. The second section covers relevant books, pamphlets, and individual articles.

Reference Sources Issued Periodically

Agri-Trends. Rainier Bancorporation, P.O. Box 3966, Seattle, WA 98124. Quarterly. No charge. "Agri-business industry of the State of Washington."

Alaska on Alaska. Newsletter on Alaska business published by Alaska Construction and Oil Magazine for Alaska Airlines, Seattle-Tacoma International Airport, Seattle, Washington 98158. Weekly. No charge.

Alaska's Economy in 1975, Mid-year Review and Outlook. Economics Department, National Bank of Alaska, Anchorage, Alaska, July, 1975. Economic summary usually published at year-end and mid-year. No charge.

Alaska News Review. Western Airlines, Studio 7, Pacific Building, Portland, Oregon 97204. Monthly. No charge. Brief economic news of each city in Alaska.

Argus. Magazine published by Argus Publishing Co., 6654 White Building, Seattle, Washington 98101. Weekly. $10 per year. "The Pacific Northwest's Independent Magazine of News, Comment and Opinion." Covers business, economic, political, social and cultural news and issues.

Barometer. Western Wood Products Association, 1500 Yeon Building, Portland, Oregon 97204. Weekly. $30 per year. Separate summary for Coast and Inland Regions on softwood lumber production. (WWPA has extensive list of periodical and one-time publications, some free and some available for sale, of which only a selected few are specifically referenced in this bibliography. Complete list available on request to WWPA.)

Boise Journal of Commerce. P.O. Box 7337, Boise, Idaho 83707. Weekly newspaper. $20 per year, $2.50 per month. "The newspaper for business and industry." Excellent financial news coverage on Idaho companies.

Boise Magazine, Greater Boise Chamber of Commerce, P.O. Box 8252, Boise, Idaho 83707. Quarterly. $3.50 per year. Articles and statistics on government, finances, education, recreation, manufacturing and transportation.

Bonneville Power Administration's 37th Annual Report on the Federal Columbia River Power System. December 31, 1974. BPA, P.O. Box 3621, Portland, Oregon 97208. No charge. *This is a superb job!* 64 pages, interesting, excellent pictures, maps, graphs and easy-to-read text, gives excellent picture of how the Northwest power system works. Highly recommended reading.

Brown's Business Reporter. P.O. Box 646, Eugene, Oregon. Weekly. $10 per year. "An every Monday business report for busy people," Eugene area business news.

Business Review. Business Research Division of Pacific Northwest Bell Telephone Co. Monthly. No charge. Statistics charts and articles on business activity in the Northwest and the nation.

California Business. Subscription Dept. 9420 Activity Road, Suite D, San Diego, California 92126. Weekly. $24 per year. "The West's Business and Investment Newspaper." Includes a fair amount of material on Northwest companies.

Crow's Forest Products Digest. Terminal Sales Building, Portland, Oregon 97205. Monthly. Marketing news of wood products and related building supplies.

Crow's Plywood Letter. Terminal Sales Building, Portland, Oregon 97205. Weekly. $76 per year. A report on plywood, particleboard, hardboard, and veneer, and financial news and market information.

Crow's Weekly Letter. Terminal Sales Building, Portland, Oregon 97205. Weekly. $76 per year. Features economic news and market summaries related to lumber and plywood and pinpoints prevailing mill prices.

Daily Journal of Commerce. 2014 N.W. 24th, Portland, Oregon 97222. Weekdays. $50 per year. "All the business news of each business day." Excellent financial news coverage on Oregon companies and many Washington companies. Also an annual industry edition.

Directory of the Forest Products Industry. Miller Freeman Publications, 733 S.W. Ash, Portland, Oregon 97204. Annually. $47.50. Forest industries in the U.S. and Canada by type of product, sawmill, plywood, logging, particleboard and specialty companies.

Directory of Mines. Western Mining News, P.O. Box 8237, Manito Station, Spokane, Washington 99203. Annually. $4.95. Information on mines in Idaho (Coeur d'Alene), Montana, Nevada and Washington.

Directory of Oregon Manufacturers. Oregon Department of Economic Development, 317 S.W. Alder, Portland, Oregon 97204. Biennially. $10. Arranged alphabetically and geographically and classified by products.

Economic Trends: Oregon and the Nation. Portland, Oregon: First National Bank of Oregon, Economic Research Department, 1300 S.W. 5th, Portland, Oregon 97208. Annually. No charge. Economic data comparing Oregon to that of U.S.—from 1950 to year completed.

First Security News Letter. First Security Corporation, 79 S. Main Street, Salt Lake City, Utah 84110. Quarterly. No charge. News of the area's general economy— industry, prices, employment, minerals, metals, electricity, construction and finance. Includes sections on business trends in Idaho and on business trends in Utah.

Forest Industry Affairs Letter. Dean Sherman, Inc., 213 S.W. Ash Street, Portland, Oregon 97204. Biweekly. $78 per year.

Idaho Economic Opportunities. Idaho Division of Tourism and Industrial Development, Room 108, Capitol Building, Boise, Idaho 83707. Biennially. No charge. Articles and statistics on exploring Idaho from an investor's point of view.

Idaho Image. Idaho Division of Tourism and Industrial Development. Bimonthly. No charge. Review of business and economic developments in the Idaho area.

International Trade Directory of Oregon and Southern Washington. Portland Chamber of Commerce, 824 S.W. Fifth Avenue, Portland, Oregon 97204. Updated at approximately five year intervals. $3. An alphabetical directory of firms listing products exported and imported.

Kellogg News Wardner. 401 Main Street, Kellogg, Idaho 83837. Weekly. $3 per year. Newspaper containing mining industry news of the Coeur d'Alene area.

Manufacturing Directory of Idaho. Idaho Division of Tourism and Industrial Development. Annually. $3 per copy. Idaho manufacturing industries in an alphabetical section, geographical section, and product section.

Marple's Business Newsletter. Marple's Business Roundup, Inc., Colman Building, Seattle, Washington 98104. Published alternate Wednesdays. $24 per year. Covers Pacific Northest business items. Very well done.

Mining Hi Lites. Brokerage Information Service, Spokane, Washington. Weekly. Available from Spokane Stock Exchange member firms. Most firms make nominal charge to cover mailing costs.

National Enterprise. Universal Investors Journal, Inc., P.O. Box 11778, Pioneer Station, Salt Lake City, Utah 84147. Weekly. $15 per year. Business news of local and national interest—news briefs, corporate profiles on O-T-C companies, oil, gas and mining news.

Northwest Investment Review. Willamette Management Associates, Inc., 220 S.W. Alder Street, Portland, Oregon 97204. Twice monthly. $135 per year. Provides profiles of individual corporations, company progress interviews, industry surveys, condensed company news, a summary of the latest transactions reported by insiders, schedule of forthcoming stockholder meetings and other investor meetings, earnings reports and earnings estimates on all major and many smaller listed and O-T-C companies headquartered in the Northwest/Intermountain area.

Northwest Stock Guide. Willamette Management Associates, Inc. Quarterly. $10 for 18 months. (Included free with subscription to *Northwest Investment Review*.) A directory of statistical information on publicly-held companies headquartered or with major operations in Washington, Oregon, Idaho, Alaska, Montana, Wyoming and Utah.

Oregon Blue Book. Office of Secretary of State, State Capitol Building, Salem, Oregon 97310. Biennially. $2 per copy. Information about government, education, finances, institutions, commerce, industry, and natural resources of the state.

Oregon Business Barometer. U.S. National Bank of Oregon, P.O. Box 4412, Portland, Oregon 97208. Quarterly. No charge. A summary of regional economic data.

Oregon Business Review. Bureau of Business Research, 140 Gilbert Hall, University of Oregon, Eugene, Oregon 97403. Triannually. No charge. Information and opinions by business leaders about topics of relevance to the Northwest business community.

Oregon Progress Newsletter. Department of Economic Development, State of Oregon, 317 S.W. Alder, Portland, Oregon 97204. Bi-monthly. No charge. News of Oregon development, information on individual companies and industries and economic indicators.

Oregon Voter Digest. 206 Graphic Arts Building, Portland, Oregon 97209. Semi-monthly. $8.50 per year. A "digest of legislation, finance, industry, taxation and public affairs in Oregon and the Pacific Northwest."

Pacific Banker & Business. One Yesler Way, Seattle, Washington 98104. Monthly. $7 per year. Banking journal serving the Far West.

A Performance Report of the Alaskan Economy. State of Alaska, Division of Economic Development, Pouch EE, Juneau, Alaska 99801. A review of the performance of the Alaskan Economy in 1974 and an analysis of the 1975 early trend.

Portland Magazine. Portland Chamber of Commerce, 824 S.W. Fifth Avenue, Portland, Oregon 97204. Monthly. $9 per year. Articles on recreation, travel, environment, industry and people. Directory included with April issue.

Post's Pulp and Paper Mill Directory. Miller Freeman Publications, 733 S.W. Ash, Portland, Oregon 97204. Annually. $35. Bulk paper and paperboard markets in USA and Canada, classified by mill grade and products list, alphabetical mill officials index, mill capacity and production statistics and information on mill machinery and equipment.

Pratt, Shannon P. **"Northwest Investing."** Syndicated weekly newspaper column. Carried in Portland *Oregonian* (Mondays), Spokane *Spokesman Review* (Sundays), Boise *Journal of Commerce,* and Seattle *Argus.*

Pratt, Shannon P. **"Northwest Utility Stocks 'Intriguing'."** September 8, 1975. and **" 'Wanted' Northwest Stocks 'Found'."** April 7, 1975, Media General *Financial Weekly.* These are part of an ongoing series of regional investment reports for which Shannon Pratt contributes the material on the Northwest.

Pratt, Shannon P. **"Pratt $ays—"** *Senior Profile* magazine. Monthly Investments column for senior citizens.

Production, Prices, Employment and Trade in Northwest Forest Industries. Pacific Northwest Forest and Range Experiment Station, Forest Service, U.S. Dept. of Agriculture, P.O. Box 3141, Portland, Oregon 97208. Quarterly. No charge.

Public Utilities Fortnightly. Public Utilities Reports, Inc., 1828 L Street, N.W., Suite 503, Washington, D.C. 20036. Biweekly. $37 per year. Covers all U.S. utilities; environment, risk factors, outlook, and regulation.

Pulp and Paper. Miller Freeman Publications, 733 S.W. Ash, Portland, Oregon 97204. Monthly. $12.50 per year. News analysis, feature articles and technical report on the industry in general. Includes a thirteenth issue which is an "American Profile and Review."

Random Lengths. Lester E. Anderson, publisher, 210 East 11th Avenue, Eugene Oregon 97401. $76.50 per year. "A weekly report on lumber and plywood prices and marketing."

Real Estate Trends in Portland, Oregon. Metropolitan Portland Real Estate Research Committee, 321 S.W. 4th Avenue, Portland, Oregon 97204. Semiannually. $7 per copy. Information on real estate activities, price trends, vacancy trends, unsold houses, building costs, Portland economy, new projects and Oregon economy.

Seattle Business. Magazine of Seattle Chamber of Commerce, 215 Columbia, Seattle, Washington 98104. Bimonthly. $4 per year. Subscription to also include weekly issue $15 per year. Articles on recreation travel, environment, industry and people.

The Silver Institute Letter. Silver Institute (a worldwide association of miners, refiners, fabricators and manufacturers), 1001 Connecticut Avenue, Washington, D.C. 20036. Monthly. No charge. Information on silver for industry.

State of Washington Pocket Data Book. Office of Program Planning & Fiscal Management, State of Washington. No charge. Information presented in statistical and chart form on population, economy, government, human resources, education, natural resources and transportation.

Statistical Yearbook. Western Wood Products Association, 1500 Yeon Building, Portland, Oregon 97204. Annually. $5 per year. Contains tables of statistics covering production in Coast and Inland Regions by state, county and species, summaries of industry production, new orders, etc. for each region by month; import and export data; forest products statistics for each western state; other data relevant to the lumber industry.

Summary of Pacific Northwest Industries. Economic Research Department Seattle-First National Bank, P.O. Box 3586, Seattle, Washington 98124. Quarterly, with Annual Review in May.

Utah Economic and Business Review. Bureau of Economic and Business Research, University of Utah, Salt Lake City, Utah 84112. Monthly. Up to 10 copies at no charge. News of interest to the business community and business statistics of Utah and statistics on local business activty.

Utah Facts. Utah Industrial Promotion Division, 165 South West Temple, Salt Lake City, Utah 84101. Updated annually. No charge. Designed to present accurately the state's characteristics to those making business location decisions.

Walker's Manual of Western Corporations and Securities. Walker's Manual, Inc. 5855 Naples Plaza, Suite 101, Long Beach, California 90803. Annually. $100. Descriptions of financial institutions and corporations which are publicly owned and headquartered in the thirteen Western states and Western Canada.

Wallace Miner. P.O. Box 140, Wallace, Idaho 83873. Weekly. $7.50 per year. Mining newspaper.

Western Bank Directory. Western Banker Publications, Inc., 111 Sutts, Suite 1330, San Francisco, California 94104. Annually. $9. Covers eleven states, all banks and branches and statement of condition.

Western Economic Indicators. Federal Reserve Bank of San Francisco, Public Information Section, P.O. Box 7702, San Francisco, California 94120. Bimonthly. No charge. Statistics and charts on income, trade, employment, production, construction, banking, and bond sales.

Western Lumber Facts. Western Wood Products Association, 1500 Yeon Building, Portland, Oregon 97204. Monthly. $15 per year. Charts and tables covering industry —production, orders, shipments, inventories, prices, employment and housing starts.

Western Mining News. Box 8237, Manito Station, Spokane, Washington 99203. Weekly newspaper. $7 per year. Devoted solely to the mining industry.

Wyoming Mineral Yearbook. Minerals Division, Department of Economic Planning and Development, 720 W. 18th Street, Cheyenne, Wyoming 82002. Annually. No charge. Information on minerals in the area with statistics on valuation and production by county.

Young's Forecasts of Softwood Lumber and Plywood Prices. P.O. Box 2891, Portland, Oregon 97208. Weekly. $100 per year. Get acquainted subscription $35 for 6 months. Week's highlights and recommendations regarding buying of lumber and plywood.

Books, Pamphlets, and Articles

Alaska. Division of Economic Enterprise. Articles on the Alaska economy including petroleum, construction, transportation, timber, Alaska's emerging industries, and key indicators.

Alaska Oil . . . Its Impact on the Puget Sound Region. Puget Sound Power & Light Company, Puget Power Building, Bellevue, Washington. October, 1972.

Basic Economic Data for Idaho. Research and Analysis Section of the State of Idaho, November, 1973. Contains statistics on labor force and employment by area and by county and information for cities on geography, industry, occupations, unions, housing, facilities, transportation and recreation.

Bryant, Dr. Ben S. **"The Pulp and Paper Industry of the Pacific Northwest."** Dr. Bryant is Professor of Wood Utilization Technology, College of Forest Resources, University of Washington, Seattle, Washington.

Business and Society in Change. New York: American Telephone and Telegraph Company, 1975. A series of talks on social issues given to managers in the Supplemental Training Program at AT&T. Worthwhile reading for both businessmen and students.

A Declaration of Policy, 1972/1973, American Mining Congress. San Francisco, California, September 17, 1972. "Sets forth the views of the mining industry of the United States on pertinent national issues and recommends courses of action."

"Don't Confuse Us With Facts." *Forbes,* September 1, 1975. An excellent review of the issues involved in nuclear power.

Dunham, Halstead F. **"The Consumers' Stake in Nuclear Power."** *Public Utilities Fortnightly,* April 24, 1975.

An Economic Profile of Seattle, USA. Seattle-King County Economic Development Council, 1218 3rd Avenue, Suite 1900, Seattle, Washington 98108, 1973. Sections on research and facilities, utilities and energy supply, markets, labor force, taxation, business and industrial sites, environmental control, and transportation.

Establishing a Business in Alaska. Division of Economic Enterprise Department of Economic Development, Pouch EE, Juneau, Alaska 99801, June 1974.

Forest Economy Council Report. Portland, Oregon: Northwest Chambers of Commerce/Forest Products Industry, 1975.

Frank, Helmut J. and Schanz, John J., Jr. **"The Economics of the Energy Problem,"** *Economic Topic.* New York: Joint Council on Economic Education.

Greenough, W. Earl. **First 100 Years Coeur d'Alene Mining District,** 1947.

Guthrie, John A. and Armstrong, George R. **Western Forest Industry An Economic Outlook,** Baltimore: The Johns Hopkins Press, 1961.

Horowitz, Eleanor C. J. **Clearcutting: A View From the Top.** Washington, D.C.: Acropolis Books, Ltd., 1974.

Innovations and Trees—Weyerhaeuser: 1900-1975. Weyerhaeuser Company, Tacoma, Washington, 1975. A history of Weyerhaeuser done in commemoration of their 75th year.

Keating, Bern, **Alaska.** Washington, D.C.: National Geographic Society, 1969.

Kursh, Harry. **This Is Alaska.** New Jersey: Prentice Hall, 1961.

Lapp, Ralph E. **"Nuclear Power Reactors: How Dangerous?"** *Reader's Digest,* April, 1975, pp. 169-172.

Magnuson, Richard G. **Coeur d'Alene Diary.** Portland, Oregon: Metropolitan Press, 1968. The first ten years of hardrock mining in north Idaho.

Mining: Wyoming's Future, published as a special supplement to the *Casper Star Tribune,* Casper, Wyoming, June 19, 1975.

Montana Data Book. Montana Department of Planning and Economic Development, Helena, Montana. 1970. Statistical information for state planning and development activities with chapters on labor; government; personal income; population; vital statistics and health; social welfare; education and research; forest industries; agriculture; mineral industries; construction and housing; transportation; communications; power; trade and services; and finance; insurance; and real estate.

Northwest Regional Profile. Seattle, Washington: Northwest Federal Regional Council, June, 1974.

Northwest/Alaska Corporate Guide. Seattle, Washington. Research Dept., Foster & Marshall, Inc. 1975. Economic outlook and information on individual companies.

"An Obscure Lab Does Big Jobs for Industry." *Business Week,* April 14, 1975. Article discusses the research for industry being carried on at the Oregon Graduate Center. P. 70-B & 70-F.

The Outlook for Timber in the United States. Forest Resource Report No. 20, Forest Service, U.S. Department of Agriculture, October, 1973.

The Pacific Northwest—A Study of Economic Growth in a Quality Environment. Columbus, Ohio: Battelle Memorial Institute, Columbus Laboratories. Basic Study, December, 1967—Review and Update March 1975. Copies also available from Pacific Power & Light Company, Portland.

Pacific Northwest Economic Base Study for Power Markets. Portland, Oregon: U.S. Department of Interior, Bonneville Power Administration, February 1973.

Pamplin, R. B. **"A Resource More Valuable Than Oil."** An address before the Zone Meeting, Garden Club of America in Augusta, Georgia, April 2, 1974. Reprinted July 1974 by Public Information Dept. of Georgia-Pacific Corp. 900 S.W. Fifth Avenue, Portland, Oregon 97204.

Pamplin, R. B. **"Isn't It Time for a Peaceful Uprising?"** An address before the Portland Chapter, Sales & Marketing Executives International May 21, 1975.

Peirce, Neal R. **The Pacific States of America.** New York. W. W. Norton, 1972.

Population, Employment & Housing Units Projected to 1990 for Western Montana, Idaho, Oregon and Washington and a Summary for the Northwest. Bonneville Power Administration, Public Information Office, P.O. Box 3621, Portland, Oregon 97208. No charge. (These are separate reports for each of the states and one for the Northwest.)

Pratt, Shannon P. **"Natural Resource Base Stimulates Economy of Pacific Northwest."** *Investment Dealers' Digest,* October 14, 1975, pp. 25-26.

Pratt, Shannon P. and Hoover, David C. **"Pacific Northwest Over the Counter Stock Market Performance Since 1960."** Portland, Oregon: Portland State University, 1968. Copies available from Willamette Management Associates, Inc., Portland, Oregon.

Proceedings of Conference on Magnitude and Deployment Schedule of Energy Resources. Oregon State University, July 21-23, 1975. Available from Oregon State University or from Omega Securities, Inc., 520 S.W. Sixth Avenue, Portland, Oregon 97204.

Progress in Matters of Public Concern. Portland, Oregon: Georgia-Pacific Corporation, Dept. FC, 900 S.W. 5th Avenue, Portland, Oregon 97204. An excellent exposition dealing with environment, recreation, wildlife, and recycling. Copies available at no charge.

Ray, Dixie Lee. Series of articles appearing in the Oregonian Forum Section, beginning October 26, 1975 (Page C-1) on nuclear energy. First article entitled, **"Irrational Fears of Runaway Nuclear Energy Don't Stand Up Against Scientific Evidence."**

Roberge, Earl. **Timber Country.** Caldwell, Idaho: The Caxton Printers, Ltd., 1973.

Rogers, George W. **The Future of Alaska—Economic Consequences of Statehood.** Baltimore: The Johns Hopkins Press, 1962.

Ross, Lawrence R. **Investing in Low-Risk Growth Companies.** Portland, Oregon: Willamette Management Associates, Inc., January, 1975.

"Rush to Nuclear Power: A Chain Reaction in the World." Article published in *U.S. News & World Report,* June 9, 1975.

Thompson, Wayne. **"Northwest Power Shortage Will Equal Four Bonnevilles— Delay is the Name of the Energy Game."** The *Oregonian,* August 24, 1975, Section F-1. A candid outside look at the realities of Northwest energy needs.

The Trojan Nuclear Plant. . .an Oregon First. Portland, Oregon: Portland General Electric Co. February, 1975. An easy-to-read and informative pamphlet on Trojan.

To Grow a Tree. Portland, Oregon: Georgia-Pacific Corporation, Dept. FC, 900 S.W. 5th Avenue, Portland, Oregon 97204. Copies available at no charge.

U.S. Industrial Outlook 1974 With Projections to 1980. U.S. Department of Commerce. For sale by Superintendent of Documents, U.S. Government Printing Office, Washington, D.C. 20402. Price $3.40. Stock No. 0325-00004. Special reports on general economic areas, the energy situation, pollution and control, a view of recent developments and a general summary of anticipated trends. Detailed analyses of industries such as building and forest products, materials, transportation, consumer goods, communications, machinery, power, and commercial banking.

Waterman, Storrs. **"Danger Ahead, Keep Our Environment Clean."** *Greater Portland Commerce,* Published by Chamber of Commerce, Portland, Oregon, March 3, 1967.

Western Sawlog Lumber Products. Portland, Oregon: Western Wood Products Association. No date.

What Mining Means to the United States. Pamphlet published and distributed by the American Mining Congress, 1100 Ring Building, Washington, D.C. 20036, 1972.

The Wilderness: Just How Wild Should It Be? Portland, Oregon: Western Wood Products Association. No date.

The Wilderness Resource. Portland, Oregon: Western Wood Products Association. No date.

Winther, Oscar O. **The Great Northwest, A History,** 2nd ed. New York: Alfred A. Knopf, 1950.

The Wyoming Economy, Wyoming Bancorporation, P.O. Box 1706, Cheyenne,- Wyoming 82001. April 1975. "A review of the 1974 Wyoming economy and certain judgmental forecasts for 1975 and beyond."

Young, Charles E. **"The Northwest Lumber Industry."** A paper by the publisher of *Young's Forecasts of Softwood Lumber & Plywood Prices.* No date.

Youngquist, Walter. **Investing in Natural Resources.** Homewood, Illinois: Dow Jones-Irwin, Inc., 1975. "Presents the basic facts of each resource along with projected demand and uses to the end of this century." Good reference work.

Index

Companies whose stocks were included in the Fall 1975 **Northwest Stock Guide** are shown in bold face type, other references in light face. Page numbers of primary references discussing company's activites are shown in bold face.

Data on the companies shown in bold face in the index are also included in the Statistical Summary, pages 296-305.

313

P

R

For Further Information . . .

We hope we have stimulated your interest in investing in Northwest stocks and bonds, and in pursuing additional information about them.

The authors and the publishers realize, of course, that the material covered in this book is subject to rapid change, especially the company statistics.

The basic statistics on the companies covered in this book are updated quarterly in the *Northwest Stock Guide*. Also, each issue of the *Northwest Stock Guide* contains a Reader Service Card enabling the reader to order over 100 different Northwest company annual reports, research reports, and other items of investment information at absolutely no cost whatever.

For those who want to follow the latest information on Northwest companies every two weeks, it is available in the *Northwest Investment Review*. (See Bibliography for descriptions of the two publications.)

To get a set of updated statistics and other recent information on the companies in this book, just send in this card, and it will entitle you to receive *absolutely free* (even postage prepaid) the latest issue of the *Northwest Stock Guide* and the latest *Northwest Investment Review*. Happy reading!

PLEASE SEND ME THE LATEST NORTHWEST STOCK GUIDE AND NORTHWEST INVESTMENT REVIEW

Name ....

Address ....

....

....

Zip